# COLLABORATIVE CAPITALISM IN AMERICAN CITIES

*Reforming Urban Market Regulations*

In many American cities, the urban cores still suffer. Poverty and unemployment remain endemic, despite policy initiatives aimed at systemic solutions. Rashmi Dyal-Chand's research has focused on how businesses in some urban cores are succeeding despite the challenges. Using three examples of urban collaborative capitalism, this book extrapolates a set of lessons about sharing. It argues that sharing can fuel business development and growth. Sharing among businesses can be critical for their economic survival. Sharing can also produce a particularly stable form of economic growth by giving economic stability to employees. As the examples in this book show, sharing can allow American businesses to remain competitive while returning more wealth to their workers, and this more collaborative approach can help solve the problems of urban underdevelopment and poverty.

Rashmi Dyal-Chand is Professor of Law in the School of Law at Northeastern University.

# Collaborative Capitalism in American Cities

## REFORMING URBAN MARKET REGULATIONS

**RASHMI DYAL-CHAND**
Northeastern University School of Law

CAMBRIDGE
UNIVERSITY PRESS

**CAMBRIDGE**
**UNIVERSITY PRESS**

University Printing House, Cambridge CB2 8BS, United Kingdom

One Liberty Plaza, 20th Floor, New York, NY 10006, USA

477 Williamstown Road, Port Melbourne, VIC 3207, Australia

314–321, 3rd Floor, Plot 3, Splendor Forum, Jasola District Centre, New Delhi – 110025, India

79 Anson Road, #06–04/06, Singapore 079906

Cambridge University Press is part of the University of Cambridge.

It furthers the University's mission by disseminating knowledge in the pursuit of education, learning, and research at the highest international levels of excellence.

www.cambridge.org
Information on this title: www.cambridge.org/9781107133532
DOI: 10.1017/9781316459836



First published 2018

Printed in the United States of America by Sheridan Books, Inc.

*A catalogue record for this publication is available from the British Library.*

*Library of Congress Cataloging-in-Publication Data*
NAMES: Dyal-Chand, Rashmi, 1970–
TITLE: Collaborative capitalism in American cities : reforming urban market regulations / Rashmi Dyal-Chand, Northeastern University School of Law.
Description: Cambridge, United Kingdom ; New York, NY : Cambridge University Press, 2018.
IDENTIFIERS: LCCN 2017048767 | ISBN 9781107133532 (hardback)
SUBJECTS: LCSH: Community development, Urban – United States. | Urban renewal – United States. | Urban policy – United States. | Public-private sector cooperation – United States.
CLASSIFICATION: LCC HN90.C6 D965 2018 | DDC 307.1/4068–dc23
LC record available at https://lccn.loc.gov/2017048767

ISBN 978-1-107-13353-2 Hardback

*For Ben, James, and Kieran*

# Contents


*Acknowledgments* — *page* viii

1 **Introduction** — 1

PART I COLLABORATIVE CAPITALISM DEFINED — 15

2 **Home Care in the Bronx and Philadelphia** — 17

3 **Capitalist Sharing and Economic Stability** — 50

PART II COLLABORATIVE CAPITALISM EXPLORED — 73

4 **Rehabilitating South Shore** — 75

5 **Regulating against Sharing** — 118

6 **More Than a Day's Work in Austin** — 132

7 **Understanding Collaborative Capitalism** — 159

PART III COLLABORATIVE CAPITALISM REINVIGORATED — 185

8 **Collaborative Capitalism Refined: The "Sharing Economy"** — 187

9 **Regulating for Sharing** — 207

10 **Reforming Laws to Support Collaborative Capitalism** — 225

Appendix — 266

*Index* — 277

# Acknowledgments

This book is a product of the rich conversations I had with the people who participated in the three networks I researched. They shared their time, knowledge, candor, and reflections with me about the work to which they have dedicated so much of their effort and passion. They invited me into their homes and offices, and gave me a window into their lives and work. Many of them took the time to follow up our formal interviews with informal conversations and reflections. They answered my additional, and sometimes repeated, queries with documents and references. I am deeply grateful to them.

Colleagues in the legal academy and well beyond it provided essential comments and suggestions at every stage of my research design, analysis, and writing. Libby Adler, Debbie Becher, Peter Enrich, Ron Grzywinski, Mary Houghton, Karen Kulp, John Lovett, Daniel Medwed, Jeremy Paul, Peggy Powell, and Rick Surpin read substantial portions of my manuscript, and I benefited so very much from their input and encouragement. Colleagues at the Progressive Property Conference, Northeastern University School of Law, and Loyola University New Orleans College of Law also read portions of the manuscript and gave valuable comments. For their wisdom, guidance, and astute feedback, I thank Michelle Wilde Anderson, Bernadette Atuahene, Jane Baron, John Bliss, Scott Cummings, Hanoch Dagan, David Dana, Dan Danielsen, John Infranca, Nestor Davidson, Stacey Dogan, Amy Ferrell, Julian Fray, Adam Friedman, Priya Gupta, Shelly Kreiczer-Levy, Jack McDevitt, Audrey McFarlane, Kristin Madison, Andrea Matwyshyn, Thomas Mitchell, Tim Mulvaney, David Phillips, Mark Rosen, Rachel Rosenbloom, Jessica Silbey, Ezra Rosser, Jim Rowan, Chris Serkin, Joseph William Singer, Jim Smith, Emily Spieler, Laura Underkuffler, and Margaret Woo.

I had the great benefit of spending part of my 2016 summer at the American Bar Foundation. For facilitating my visit there and for invaluable suggestions on my research design, I thank Ajay Mehrotra, Jothie Rajah, Stephen Daniels, Terry Halliday, Laura Beth Nielsen, Susan Shapiro, and Carole Silver.

I received essential financial support for the research underlying this book from the US Department of Commerce, Economic Development Administration (EDA), and also from Northeastern University. In addition to guiding me in the process of applying for the EDA grant, Steven Winter of the Metropolitan Area Planning Council shared with me his deep wisdom about local economic development.

This book would have taken me twice the time to write had it not been for the support of my dean, Jeremy Paul, and associate dean, Dan Danielsen. They provided extra funding, time, space, and encouragement at every step of the way.

My research assistants were intrepid in their support. Not only did they do essential research for the manuscript, but they also were sources of inspiration, humor, and wisdom. I thank Christopher Anderson, Anna Maria Annino, Seth Barron, Stephanie Knight, Daniel D'Lugoff, Russell Paul, Joel Quick, and Selena Poznak. Kimberly Elkin served as a postgraduate fellow, literally educating me on the entire "varieties of capitalism" canon. Keith Wise wielded his considerable technical and administrative skills to provide me with years of excellent administrative support. Finally, the librarians at Northeastern Law School continue to be a critical part of each of my research successes. I particularly thank Elliott Hibbler and Sharon Persons.

Notwithstanding these numerous and essential sources of support, the opinions, findings, and recommendations I make in this book are my own, and they do not necessarily reflect the views of these individuals and organizations.

My editor at Cambridge University Press, John Berger, has been my coach in this journey. I have benefited greatly from his involvement, from his initial interest in the project to his ongoing encouragement at each step of the writing and editing process.

My parents, Alda and Anand Dyal-Chand, in addition to giving me an education that taught me the value of writing, provided thoughtful editorial advice.

Finally, I thank my husband and sons. My husband, Benjamin Ericson, cheerfully took on extra household and family burdens – for years – as I worked on this project. He listened to me, reacted to half-baked ideas, and read drafts that I was not yet ready to share with anyone else. Not a day has gone by during this project without his encouragement, active love, and support. And my sons, James and Kieran, each in his own special ways, have inspired me, given me space and time to work, and kept me grounded in life. You have my deepest gratitude.

# 1

# Introduction

In the United States since the turn of the millennium, we have witnessed wild swings in the public's reaction to economic instability. In the wake of the Great Recession of 2008, the Occupy Wall Street movement ballooned into a national conversation about increasing income inequality. The jobless recovery that followed touched off a severe "populist" reaction that resulted in the election of Donald Trump. From Brexit, to Trump's wall, to elections in the Netherlands and elsewhere, anger and frustration about joblessness and income loss became associated with anti-immigrant campaigns. One thing has been clear in what may seem to be an irrational series of responses. Most of us – policymakers and members of the public alike – crave economic stability. And for most of us, economic stability starts with a stable income for ourselves and for our families.

This book provides three examples of enduring economic stability. They are examples that teach a set of lessons that originate in American cities. They are examples about things that have been happening in the shadows, but that have the potential to contribute to large-scale economic improvement in the city, and perhaps beyond. Indeed, some readers may have heard about these examples before. Yet what most of us have heard are fragmented pieces of the whole picture. No one has linked these examples together to define a larger pattern or to draw broader lessons.

The most basic lesson these examples teach is that sharing and collaboration can fuel business development and growth. Sharing among businesses can be critical for their economic survival. Sharing can also produce a particularly stable form of economic growth by virtue of the economic stability it can generate for those who work for those businesses. As these examples show, sharing can allow American businesses to remain competitive while returning more wealth to their employees. It can be the basis for a collaborative form of American capitalism.

On the basis of these three examples, this book offers a list of action items – areas for law reform – that have two key advantages. First, these action items advance core objectives that have long been the subject of interest and desire by politicians and policymakers across the political spectrum. Second, many of these action items can be enacted at the state and local levels even if, and to the extent that, there is too much division at the national level. Collaborative capitalism in American cities can be a source of economic stability, inclusion, and gain. This book explains how.

For decades, American cities have been the source of tremendous economic growth. It is distressing, then, that at the core of many of these cities lie areas of entrenched underdevelopment and poverty. Whatever the surrounding conditions of employment, development and mobility, these "inner cities" experience a distressingly constant level of unemployment, economic stagnation, inequality, and lack of mobility. In their embodiment of economic instability, American cities are a microcosm of the national economy. Current poverty and unemployment statistics may provide the best shorthand for this phenomenon. According to the well-respected Initiative for a Competitive Inner City, across the United States the average poverty rate for inner cities is 32 percent,[1] more than twice the poverty rate in the United States as a whole.[2] These statistics are constant across the nation, in the more well-known hot spots of urban distress as well as those that are largely invisible. Chicago's inner city neighborhoods have a poverty rate of 31 percent.[3] Inner-city Albany, New York, has a poverty rate of 42 percent.[4] Inner-city Peoria, Illinois, has a poverty rate of 41 percent.[5] Unemployment rates tell a similar story. Inner-city Detroit, Michigan, has an unemployment rate of 28 percent, more than four times the national average, which has hovered around 6 percent.[6] Inner-city Camden, New Jersey, has an unemployment rate of 23 percent.[7]

Moreover, these statistics defy trends in the broader metropolitan areas that surround the inner cities. Although the poverty rate across US inner cities is 32 percent, the average poverty rate in the surrounding central cities is 9.4 percent, even lower than the national average.[8] Indeed, since the 1980s, as the social safety net has been dismantled, urban cores seem to have borne the worst brunt of economic downturns and recessions. But they also have remained defiantly depressed during better economic times, contributing significantly to the nation's worsening scores on

[1] *Key Battlegrounds for the War on Poverty*, Initiative for a Competitive Inner City (2014), http://icic.org/key-battlegrounds-war-poverty; Lena Ferguson, *In America's War on Poverty, Inner Cities Remain the Front Lines*, Initiative for a Competitive Inner City (Feb. 3, 2014), www.icic.org/connection/blog-entry/blog-in-americas-war-on-poverty-inner-cities-remain-the-front-line.

[2] Carmen DeNavas-Walt & Bernadette D. Proctor, *Income and Poverty in the United States: 2013*, US Census Bureau, Current Population Reports 12 (2014), www.census.gov/content/dam/Census/library/publications/2014/demo/p60-249.pdf.

[3] *Chicagoland: Key Battleground for the War on Poverty*, Initiative for a Competitive Inner City (2014), www.icic.org/ee_uploads/pdf/ICIC_infographic_chicago.pdf.

[4] *Key Battlegrounds for the War on Poverty*, Initiative for a Competitive Inner City. [5] *Id.*

[6] *Labor Force Statistics from the Current Population Survey*, Bureau of Labor Statistics (2014), http://data.bls.gov/timeseries/LNS14000000.

[7] *Key Battlegrounds for the War on Poverty*, Initiative for a Competitive Inner City. [8] *Id.*

indexes measuring wealth inequality.[9] Hence the contemporary debates about the costs and benefits of gentrification in urban cores.[10] Gentrification is a phenomenon that revitalizes the infrastructure and wealth in urban neighborhoods, but often at the expense of its lower-income residents, who are marginalized or even displaced in the process.[11] As compelling as these statistics are, they tell only part of the story. The additional layers of segregation, educational disinvestment, and violence in many inner cities contribute to the sense of marginalization in the urban core.

Experts in a variety of fields have diagnosed the problem of urban economic instability more specifically. Leading historians and sociologists point to the enormous relevance of segregation, migration, and immigration in shaping contemporary inner cities. They describe the devastating effects of racism, ethnic strife, and violence, arguing that these are often determinative factors in the development of cities.[12] Whether in the course of outflow by more economically privileged whites to the suburbs during the early part of the twentieth century or in the gentrifying return of wealthier people to urban areas more recently, such movements have manifested distinctly racial and ethnic patterns.

The degradation of both labor markets and educational systems forms a vicious cycle with these segregationist patterns. Despite the programs for bussing, vouchers, common cores, and charter schools, educational opportunities follow wealth. Thus the overlay of housing segregation on educational opportunity yields a distressing picture of exclusion of those who are systemically unable to leave the inner city – even for educational opportunities that are in close proximity in wealthier parts of the city.[13]

Those who study labor markets and labor organization depict a similar pattern. Theirs is a story dominated by the increasing power of corporations and the decreasing power of labor unions. The corollary declines in the values of wages, pensions, and other labor and workplace protections lie at the heart of the devastating conditions in cities such as Detroit. It is also a story in which both suburbanization and globalization whisk away jobs from inner-city workers, leaving them with no easy path for retraining and reengagement in the work force.[14]

9 *See* Emmanuel Saez, *Striking It Richer: The Evolution of Top Incomes in the United States* (2013), http://eml.berkeley.edu/~saez/saez-UStopincomes-2012.pdf.

10 *Compare* Rolf Goetze, Understanding Neighborhood Change: The Role of Expectations in Urban Revitalization (1979); *and* Maureen Kennedy & Paul Leonard, Dealing With Neighborhood Change: A Primer on Gentrification and Policy Choices (2001).

11 Hannah Weinstein, *Fighting for a Place Called Home: Litigation Strategies for Challenging Gentrification* 62 UCLA L. Rev. 794, 801 (2015).

12 Prominent accounts of these phenomena can be found in William Julius Wilson, The Truly Disadvantaged: The Inner City, the Underclass, and Public Policy (2d ed. 2012) and Douglas S. Massey & Nancy A. Denton, American Apartheid: Segregation and the Making of the Underclass (1993).

13 For a historical account, see Kathryn M. Neckerman, Schools Betrayed: Roots of Failure in Inner-City Education (2007).

14 For a range of perspectives on these claims, see Paul Osterman, Securing Prosperity: The American Labor Market, How It has Changed and What to Do About It (1999); Michael L. Wachter, *Labor Unions: A Corporatist Institution in a Competitive World*, 155 U. Pa. L. Rev. 581 (2007).

Law has been central to these forces of urban underdevelopment. Urban segregation was a product of laws establishing racial zoning and protecting racial covenants. The legal production of educational inequality ranges from a clear refusal to recognize a right to education to the extraordinary influence of local tax and housing laws and policies.[15] And of course, from the recognition of corporations as persons, to the legal disinvestment in unions, to the regulatory support of corporate moves to the suburbs, and beyond, the legal construction of the current labor market is well known. As recent accounts by Elizabeth Warren, Edward Glaeser, and countless others have shown, the enormous investment by lawmakers and policymakers in suburban development has been accompanied by disinvestment in urban cores.[16]

Experts from a range of fields have also observed that the economies in many inner cities do not seem to work as well as the broader economies that surround them in the suburbs, in the larger metropolitan regions, and at the state and national levels. The combination of labor and employment laws, business laws, and the educational focus on transferable skills have created a highly mobile workforce that can move from region to region as businesses choose ideal locations. However, workers in urban cores have remained much less mobile, adaptable, and able to take advantage of new opportunities. Similarly, the industries that have thrived over the last several decades, such as the financial and high-technology industries, have built their successes on systems of investment, knowledge, education, and employment that rely on arm's-length relationships, public information, and globalized competition. These systems have been produced and shaped by a sophisticated legal infrastructure. The successes of these industries have rendered superfluous the possibilities of close ties, thick knowledge networks, and dense infrastructure that inhere in urban cores. Even worse, their successes seem somehow to exclude the inner cities from participation in the systems upon which they are built.[17]

It is as if the very institutions and structures that have led to what many Americans perceive as glittering success in the national and regional economies are somehow irrelevant in urban cores. This apparent truth is especially puzzling given the importance of location. For businesses that have the mobility to choose locations with a stable and well-developed infrastructure of housing, schools, public transportation, hospitals, and city services, urban cores ought to be a natural attraction. Instead, many businesses opt out of the infrastructure that is built and available,

[15] Myron Orfield, *Milliken, Meredith, and Metropolitan Segregation*, 62 UCLA L. Rev. 364, 372, 459 (2015).

[16] *See, e.g.*, Edward Glaeser, The Triumph of the City: How Our Greatest Invention Makes Us Richer, Smarter, Greener, Healthier, and Happier (2012); Elizabeth Warren & Amelia Warren Tyagi, The Two-Income Trap: Why Middle-Class Mothers and Fathers are Going Broke (2003).

[17] For a range of perspectives on these claims, building from Michael Porter's claims about the competitive advantage of the inner city, see The Inner City: Urban Poverty and Economic Development in the Next Century (Thomas D. Boston & Catherine L. Ross eds., 1997). *See also* Enrico Moretti, The New Geography of Jobs (2013); David Dante Troutt, *Ghettoes Revisited: Antimarkets, Consumption, and Empowerment*, 66 Brook. L. Rev. 1–69 (2000).

choosing locational blank slates and thereby often contributing to regional sprawl and other inefficiencies.[18]

Faced with these recurring examples of economic underdevelopment and instability, lawyers and policymakers often struggle. Their predominant response to what they perceive as inner-city failure has been to emulate models from outside the inner city as a means of fixing problems in the inner city. Despite their well-intentioned efforts to open up markets for participation by workers in urban cores, however, such participation still remains limited. Well-funded programs ranging from inner-city entrepreneurship projects to low-income housing tax credits are regularly criticized for helping a few relatively empowered inner-city residents at the expense of many others who are less empowered and less well off.

Rather than focusing on what has failed in the urban cores, this book begins by examining what has worked. It describes three ventures that have produced economic stability in the inner city for those involved over the course of decades. Private businesses and organizations undertook these ventures, at times with very little governmental involvement. One venture involves two of the largest worker-owned cooperatives in the country. The largest community development bank in the country catalyzed the second venture. A large nonprofit organization initiated the third. All three are pioneers. They succeeded not only in growing competitive businesses in supposedly failing markets, but also in providing a stable source of income for the workers involved in those businesses. All three have done this in quite different ways.

Yet there is a strong common pattern in their approach. The most important commonality is that the ventures involve networks of businesses that collaborate with each other. Their collaboration typically entails the sharing of key resources – such as training and vocational education, labor, financing, market data, suppliers and supplies, management expertise, and physical space – as a means of reducing costs for the network as a whole and for each business in the network. The sharing also typically makes use of local ties to instill a strong connection to a local community. Often this means that the businesses in the network have multiple "bottom lines." And the sharing within these networks consistently produces long-term, stable income for the workers.

Indeed, the business models developed by these three networks, while worth studying each in its own right, are in combination more than just models. They are a distinct form of capitalism. The *Oxford English Dictionary* defines "capitalism" as "an economic and political system in which a country's trade and industry are controlled by private owners for profit, rather than by the state."[19] A robust scholarship has recognized that capitalism can take a range of forms, at both the national

[18] Glaeser, Triumph of the City, 165–193; Peter Dreier, John Mollenkopf & Todd Swanstrom, Place Matters: Metropolitics for the Twenty-First Century 99–132 (2001).

[19] *Capitalism*, Oxford English Dictionary, https://en.oxforddictionaries.com/definition/capitalism.

and local levels.[20] This book describes the common pattern among these three examples as a distinct form of capitalism in recognition of this more generalized pattern of behavior. The networks described in this book exercise control within local industries and markets, but they do so qualitatively differently from businesses outside their networks. They share key resources rather than maintaining exclusive control over those resources. Thus in calling out this distinct business style as a distinct form of capitalism, I am using the term "capitalism" to describe an economic system rather than merely a cultural approach. I am acknowledging that a range of capitalist forms exists. I am arguing that the key variable distinguishing different forms on the capitalist spectrum is the extent to which property ownership and contract rights are used either to promote sharing or to maintain exclusive control over resources by individual businesses in a given industry. Most importantly, by defining this distinct pattern of capitalist behavior, I am calling for law reforms that support a broader range of capitalist behaviors than our current laws support.

The businesses described in this book demonstrate that business in America can be done differently. These are businesses that contribute to economic health in a way that some have been trying to achieve by means of benefit corporations and corporate social responsibility. Those ideas are important and well worth continuing to explore. But the businesses described here are already achieving many of the same goals as those kinds of nascent efforts. Moreover, while each of the networks described in this book is unique in important ways, they are three among many collaborative business networks that operate around the country. In the course of describing these three networks, I will give a range of examples of collaborative networks that are well worth studying and supporting.

This book argues that current responses to urban economic underdevelopment fall short partly because their proponents misunderstand the reasons for economic instability in the inner city. On the one hand, some experts have framed the problem too narrowly, thereby accepting the prevailing assumptions that the challenge is not macroeconomic in nature. Such assumptions are characterized by statements such as the following: the national economy is functioning well, and so the problem must be one of market failure in the inner city. In response, lawyers have worked hard to support inner-city market actors in deploying the tools of successful market actors. On the other hand, some experts define the problem so broadly that they are compelled to argue for unnecessarily extreme and somewhat idealistic prescriptions that focus on replacing certain market actors (such as corporations), legal structures (such as tax laws) and even the economic system (namely capitalism itself).

[20] *See* Varieties of Capitalism: The Institutional Foundations of Comparative Advantage (Peter A. Hall & David Soskice eds., 2001) (this book is the foundation of a vast literature on "varieties of capitalism"); William J. Baumol, Robert E. Litan & Carl J. Schramm, Good Capitalism, Bad Capitalism, and the Economics of Growth and Prosperity (2007).

This book argues instead that economic instability in American urban cores is a product of regulatory failure more than of market failure. The primary problem is the failure to recognize – *and support* – a range of business models and practices, some of which have produced tremendous economic stability and gain for their participants. This failure of recognition has inhibited the growth alternative forms of capitalist behavior. It has starkly narrowed the options for jobs and income available to inner-city residents. And it has made the options that are available more difficult for workers to navigate successfully. In exploring three successful examples of collaborative capitalism, this book calls for policymakers to make room for a broader range of market practices, and in doing so, to deploy law to meet the needs of urban America.

The book begins, in Part I, by defining collaborative capitalism. It does so first, in Chapter 2, by exploring a case study that exemplifies collaborative capitalism in action in the Bronx and in Philadelphia. In those two urban cores, an extraordinary network of businesses has taken root. Cooperative Home Care Associates (CHCA) in the Bronx is the largest worker-owned cooperative in the United States, with more than 2,000 employees, most of whom are owners. CHCA works in close collaboration with two affiliated organizations in New York City, including a nonprofit managed care provider (Independence Care System [ICS]) and a second nonprofit that focuses on training for direct care workers, consulting services, and research and policy development in the areas of eldercare and disability services (Paraprofessional Healthcare Institute [PHI]). These organizations have an affiliate, Home Care Associates in Philadelphia, which is also a worker-owned cooperative, with over 200 employees.

This network has the dual function of providing home care and other long-term health services (often to low-income individuals) while also providing long-term and livable jobs to local, low-income residents. The network has found a way to share (and thereby reduce) some of the costs of doing business that so burden many start-up businesses in the United States. For example, PHI serves as a research and development organization, developing curricula for training direct care workers and their supervisors and testing them in home care agencies and long-term care facilities in New York and beyond. CHCA serves as a learning laboratory for such curriculum development. Meanwhile, ICS is the major contractor or customer for CHCA's home care services. The Bronx network also works closely with the local chapter of the Service Employees International Union and city and state agencies to standardize wages and other employment terms for paraprofessional health care workers in New York.

Chapter 3 uses the example of this home care network to describe the features of collaborative capitalism that are also apparent in the other case studies discussed in this book. The chapter begins by discussing the two prevailing diagnoses of economic instability and underdevelopment in American urban cores, namely market failure and unequal distribution. Chapter 3 describes how these two different diagnoses have converged in their prescriptions by developing programs to encourage individuals in the inner cities to emulate market actors and institutions outside the inner cities. The goal of these programs is to learn from and copy the successes of businesses and industries outside of urban cores that have succeeded. However, as this chapter discusses, these programs have failed to systematically produce greater economic stability and development in urban cores.

Chapter 3 then sets forth the core theoretical framework for my claim that the home care network and the other case studies in this book exemplify a collaborative form of capitalism that is distinct from capitalism as most Americans understand it. These collaborative business networks use a markedly different approach from those seeking to make inner-city economies more like the economies outside the inner city. They operate using different rules, standards and norms of market behavior. The key characteristic of collaborative capitalism is the level of sharing of key resources among the businesses engaged within a given collaborative network. There are other characteristics as well. Collaborative business networks have institutions designed to promote the sharing that occurs within the network. They are highly local in mission, community, and even financing. They often have multiple bottom lines. And they typically operate within well-defined market niches.

The chapter concludes by comparing collaborative capitalism as a theoretical concept to other forms of capitalism that operate successfully in other parts of the world. The purpose of this comparison is to support my argument that collaborative capitalism is indeed a distinct form of capitalist behavior that can produce significant wealth and that is worthy of regulatory support. My analysis in this section of Chapter 3 is grounded in a rich literature that has developed around the theory of "varieties of capitalism." The theory, first propounded by Peter Hall and David Soskice in 2001, describes a range of capitalist forms that fall along a spectrum from the "liberal market economy" represented by the United States to the "coordinated market economies" of Germany, France, and Japan. In contrast to liberal market economies, businesses in coordinated economies engage in a high level of sharing of resources horizontally within any given industry. Critically, they do so with the help of what I term intermediary organizations and institutions that facilitate sharing. I adopt the same definition of "institution" as that used by Hall and Soskice and other institutional economists, namely "a set of rules, formal or informal, that actors generally follow, whether for normative, cognitive, or material reasons."[21] This sharing among businesses in a given industry is in sharp contrast to the more competitive, arm's-length relationships that we see between businesses in US markets, where such businesses privatize more information for their own market gains.[22]

[21] Peter Hall & David Soskice, *Introduction*, *in* VARIETIES OF CAPITALISM: THE INSTITUTIONAL FOUNDATIONS OF COMPARATIVE ADVANTAGE 9 (Peter A. Hall & David Soskice eds., 2001).

[22] *Id.*

Part II of the book provides empirical support for my claim that collaborative business networks in some American cities are a distinct form of collaborative capitalism by examining two additional examples of such networks. Developed through documentary evidence and interviews, these case studies provide a great deal of information about how collaborative capitalism works in local contexts. These examples also highlight the constraining effect of our regulatory framework on the development of these networks, a framework that I discuss in detail in Chapter 5. I provide more information about my methodology for data collection and analysis both at the end of this Introduction and in the Appendix. Part II concludes its exploration of collaborative capitalism by providing a cross-cutting analysis of all three of my case studies.

Part II opens, in Chapter 4, with my second case study in which I examine the famous example of ShoreBank in Chicago, Illinois, around which a network of mom-and-pop businesses developed to rehabilitate multifamily housing – and in the process to revitalize many of the neighborhoods on Chicago's South Side. For the decades during which the network flourished, it developed a particularly robust system of shared labor and financing that allowed each individual business not only to start up, but also to survive the ups and downs of the real estate market. ShoreBank played a central role, both in the development of the network and in its maintenance. Of course, financing was the most obvious form of support provided by the Bank, but it was by no means the only form. Through key personnel, larger strategic choices, and a sophisticated range of community relationships, the Bank acted as the glue that kept the network together. In addition – and critically – the businesses themselves developed a way to share labor with each other, supporting the myriad construction activities required for the completion of each building. The Bank also supported a network of Dunkin' Donuts franchisees that exhibited some of the same sharing characteristics as the rehabber network. In 2010, during the apex of the financial crisis, ShoreBank went out of business, and the rehabber network was deeply shaken. Numerous lessons can be learned both from the development of these extraordinary networks and from their current circumstances.

Chapter 5 is an interlude in my presentation of the case studies. This short chapter is about law. As I will demonstrate, laws at the local, state, and even national levels currently limit the efficacy of collaborative business networks. The chapter examines the dramatic extent to which property, contract, business, labor and employment, and financing laws are tailored to support particular capitalist institutions. For example, American corporations typically are not constrained by formal or informal rules or norms to hire local workers. This and other forms of corporate freedom limit opportunities for urban workers, for example by leaving them with few options other than to start their own businesses. More broadly, the regulatory framework limits the number of paths available to urban residents for earning income, and it makes those paths difficult to follow. As Chapter 5 discusses, because they are tailored to supporting a more "competitive" style of capitalism, American regulations largely fail to support the types of collaborative business networks described in this book.

In Chapter 6, I discuss my third case study. The collaborative business network that has developed in Austin, Texas, is a newer network of for-profit businesses that were started almost a decade ago by a large nonprofit organization, Southwest Key Programs. The central mission of the nonprofit Southwest Key is to serve immigrant youth and children by providing safe shelters, culturally relevant education, and other critical services. This organization used its own market needs to generate a small cluster of businesses to serve those needs. The network includes a café that provides catering for Southwest Key's charter school in Austin. It also includes a cleaning company that provides cleaning and landscaping services to the school and to Southwest Key's headquarters. And it includes a sizeable job placement company. As in my other examples, Southwest Key serves as an intermediary in the network that promotes the sharing of key resources. For example, it serves as a source of financing, shared management, and "back-office" support for the businesses. Its most important function may well be to have served as the initial source of stable demand for each of the businesses. In turn, the businesses contribute to Southwest Key's mission by employing a fair number of the parents of the children it serves. Like the other two case studies, Southwest Key is a pioneer. It developed a third model, distinct from my other two examples, for collaboration by a network of for-profit businesses. It is also useful as a basis for comparison with my other case studies because it is a newer network that includes a range of businesses in different industries rather than just in one or two market niches.

Chapter 7 closes Part II of the book by providing a cross-cutting analysis of the three case studies. My primary purpose in this chapter is to compare the three different forms of collaborative business networks described in this book. Each has intermediaries that serve different functions and that contribute differently to the networks' success. Each comes with its own advantages and challenges. Finally, as I elaborate more fully in Part III, each has benefited from, and been burdened by, a range of laws and regulations. Chapter 7 identifies critical needs that cut across all three sharing networks. It closes by articulating a number of core design principles that appear particularly efficacious (at least at this early stage of analysis) in the development of collaborative business networks, and in supporting urban workers more generally.

Finally, Part III addresses the question of how to deploy law and policy in support of collaborative capitalism in American cities. Chapter 8 begins by comparing and contrasting the collaborative business networks in this book with the so-called sharing economy, which has been the subject of much discussion in urban America. More recently, the sharing economy has been described as the "gig economy," and even the "taking economy." As Chapter 8 discusses, this is for good reason. The most critical factor that distinguishes the collaborative business networks in this book from the sharing economy is that the former return more wealth to their employees. More generally, it seems possible that each of the six features of collaborative capitalism operates to support a more equitable distribution within these networks than is apparent at least among sharing economy giants such as Uber. At the same time, it also appears possible that the platform technologies that serve as foundations for the sharing economy could be used to support collaborative business networks such as those described in this book. As Chapter 8 discusses, law may well play a major role in defining the line between gig economies and collaborative business networks.

The ultimate goal of this book is to provide guidance to lawmakers, policymakers and scholars interested in supporting collaborative capitalism in the United States. More broadly, the goal is to provide a range of practical measures that can be taken to increase economic stability for workers and businesses in the urban core. The book thus concludes, in Chapters 9 and 10, by offering specific suggestions for law reform measures that could be adopted at the local, state, and national levels to support collaborative business networks. Chapter 9 begins by considering regulatory approaches in other settings where more cooperative forms of capitalism are the norm. Chapter 10 then proposes specific measures designed to address each of the critical needs of collaborative business networks that I have identified in Chapter 7. Chapter 10 proposes state- and local-level measures to reform the law of business organization, zoning law, permitting rules, contract rules, laws governing crowdfunding and venture financing, wage laws, and rules and norms governing industry self-regulation and participation in regulatory development. At the federal level, the chapter discusses the importance of revising antitrust laws, amending banking laws for community development financial institutions, providing tax incentives for sharing, and supporting the development of adequate wages and benefits for sharing networks. By providing a menu of action items that policymakers at all levels of government can adopt, Chapter 10 demonstrates that it is important to reform laws to support collaborative capitalism – and that it is also entirely possible to do so.

## LEARNING FROM THREE CASES OF COLLABORATIVE CAPITALISM

This book relies largely on qualitative empirical methods to understand what collaborative capitalism is in American urban cores. The theoretical foundation for this research is the varieties of capitalism theory, as developed by Hall and Soskice. Hall and Soskice apply their theory to national economies, and the theoretical starting point of this book is to explore whether their theory is also relevant to local economies. Consistent with this theory, I define sharing as the range of collaborative behaviors exhibited by coordinated market economies in five critical spheres of business operations defined by Hall and Soskice, namely collaboration in the areas of interfirm relations, corporate governance, vocational education and training, industrial relations, and relations vis-à-vis their own employees.[23]

One of the central tenets of varieties of capitalism theory is that the institutions within a capitalist system work complementarily to maintain that system and maximize the benefits that flow from it. In keeping with this institutionalist focus and in order to test its relevance to the local context, the primary axis along which I have chosen my three case studies is institutional. Specifically, the central questions I set out to investigate are the following: How do intermediary institutions facilitate sharing in such a way as to allow some networks of businesses to survive and even thrive in impoverished urban areas in American cities? Relatedly, how, if at all, do these intermediary institutions inhibit sharing?

Because I hypothesize that intermediary institutions and organizations are critical to successful sharing within collaborative business networks and to the networks' success more generally, I have chosen cases with three different archetypes of intermediary institutions. My first case is a network of home care businesses that uses the institution of worker ownership as the foundation for both sharing and business success. My second case is a network of housing rehabilitation businesses that used a community bank – a financing source – as an intermediary organization. My third case is a social enterprise network that relies on a nonprofit organization as its main intermediary.

For two of my case studies, I chose examples that, by virtually any metric, stood out as the pioneers or ideal types of the particular institutional form. Specifically, CHCA in New York is by far the largest worker-owned cooperative in the United States, and its affiliate, Home Care Associates in Philadelphia, is one of the largest cooperatives in the country. Likewise, before it closed in 2010, ShoreBank in Chicago was the largest community development financial institution in the country, a model for 100 such community banks that President Clinton hoped to create.

My third case study, the Southwest Key network in Austin, Texas, is also a pioneer in many respects. It rivals most social enterprise clusters in the number of people employed and the length of its existence. But it is not the largest or oldest social enterprise cluster in the United States. I chose to study this particular network in large part because it serves as a critical case for purposes of my second major axis of analysis, namely the effect of the legal framework on a collaborative business network's development and success. As concerns the relevance of the regulatory framework, the Austin network provides a clear contrast with my other two case studies and thus has been a fertile subject for examination.

Along with the institutional and legal axes, I have chosen cases on the basis of four other significant variables: 1) type of industry in which the network of businesses operates, 2) geographical location of the city in the United States, 3) age of network, and 4) number of workers employed by businesses in the network. Finally, one very

[23] Hall & Soskice, *Introduction*, VARIETIES OF CAPITALISM at 6–7.

broad variable for my choice of cases is that I have focused just on urban cores, rather than on rural areas. Nevertheless, I have been expansive in defining "urban cores." These are not necessarily areas that are downtown, as my Austin example shows. In addition, smaller and midsized cities fit within my references to urban. My main point in limiting my research to urban cores is to focus in on metropolitan areas that have within them geographical locations with concentrated poverty. In addition, throughout this book, I use the term "urban core" interchangeably with "inner city," largely to provide continuity with the extensive, interdisciplinary literature on inner cities and urban development. While my claims may ultimately be generalizable beyond urban cores, my own research for this book does not support such a level of generalizability.

As I discuss more fully in the Appendix, my case selection changed and developed in significant ways as I began to collect data. Two are worth mentioning here. First, I discovered that the cases I chose are not clear-cut examples of just the one archetype for which I had chosen them. To the contrary, on the institutional axis alone, they exhibit more similarities than I anticipated. Second and at the same time, these cases are more unique than I had anticipated they would be as exemplars of the particular archetype that I had chosen. Consequently, I found myself unable at this early stage of exploring the concept of collaborative capitalism to select cases for the purpose of literal replication.

The primary data source for my exploration was a series of 55 semi-structured interviews of individuals who participate in the three collaborative business networks studied here. Within each collaborative business network, I interviewed individuals employed at different levels, including both management and workers. I interviewed individuals involved in both intermediary organizations that facilitate sharing within these networks as well as those who work in the for-profit businesses in the networks. In addition to the interviews, I relied on secondary sources, including books, newspaper and academic articles, and documents internal to the businesses in my study.

By studying these three collaborative business networks in depth, I hope to generate interest in the rich range of collaborative business networks that operate in many American cities and indeed in rural settings as well. If, as my research suggests, sharing is a critical component in the success of these networks, then we have much to explore about the value of sharing in supporting economic stability in American cities and beyond.

PART I

# Collaborative Capitalism Defined

# 2

# Home Care in the Bronx and Philadelphia

I'm the native New Yorker. I am in it, OK? I do not come from Queens. I do not come from Staten Island. This is me ... It means that there's ... a homebound health care center, or company, that services the people that I know. That I come in contact with ... daily ... So you've helped yourself as well as you've helped someone that didn't know how to even get involved with going for service, OK? They might have been in the hospital, social worker might have run across them, you know, but they don't really understand. Where you might be a neighbor to a neighbor's family member. And you're able to come and explain it to them, you know. So, yeah, it's a big connection for me.[1]

–Michelle Smith, Home Health Aide, Cooperative Home Care Associates

Cooperative Home Care Associates (CHCA) is the largest worker-owned cooperative in the United States. Michelle Smith is a long-time home health aide and an employee-owner at CHCA. As of the end of 2016, CHCA had more than 2,000 employees, approximately 70 percent of whom were employee-owners. Home Care Associates in Philadelphia (HCA) is an affiliate of CHCA. Like CHCA, it is a for-profit, worker-owned cooperative with more than 200 employees. These two companies are supported by the Paraprofessional Healthcare Institute (PHI), a nonprofit organization that provides training,[2] research and development, and consulting services to them and to many other businesses involved in the home health care industry. CHCA also works closely with Independence Care System (ICS), a nonprofit managed care organization that accounts for 70 percent of CHCA's revenue.

The purpose of this chapter is to explore how CHCA and HCA became what they are today, namely two of the largest and most successful worker-

[1] Interview with Michelle Smith, Home Health Aide, Cooperative Home Care Associates (May 5, 2016). I have used a pseudonym for this interviewee.

[2] While I refer to training and vocational education interchangeably throughout the rest of this book, in this chapter I use the term "training" in deference to the terminology used by the participants in the home care network, who view vocational education as associated with high schools and community colleges.

owned cooperatives in the country. More broadly, the purpose is to understand how this whole network of businesses has succeeded for so long in remaining competitive while providing a stable source of income to their employees. Theirs is a story about being in the right place at the right time. It is a story about a visionary set of leaders. It is, as their leaders have described in their own writings, a story about worker ownership and about a "sectoral approach" to changing work conditions in an entire industry. It is also a story about collaboration.

## CONTEXT

The story begins in the South Bronx, which, as Jill Jonnes describes in her wonderful book, *South Bronx Rising*, was a term originally used to define a one-square-mile area in the southeast corner of Mott Haven. Over time, the term became "attached to each new neighborhood stricken by the vicious cycle of poverty, drugs, crime and then arson."[3] By the mid-1980s, the South Bronx covered 20 square miles in the southwestern neighborhoods of the Bronx, which itself is the only borough of New York City situated on the mainland – directly across the river from Manhattan.[4] In 1995, a *New York Times* article commented, "everyone agrees that pinpointing the South Bronx's northern boundary has little to do with geography ... but has everything to do with money, race, ethnicity and image."[5]

Over the course of the twentieth century, the South Bronx experienced enormous changes in demographics. In the first few decades of the century, as public transportation extended to the Bronx, Irish, Italian, and Jewish immigrants began to settle in the area. From the 1940s onward, the South Bronx saw significant demographic changes due to immigration into the area of Puerto Ricans and African Americans. In these decades, the area experienced massive white flight and increasing levels of poverty.[6]

By the late 1960s, as Jonnes describes,

> [T]he rental apartment building ... suffered a dramatic demise as an economic entity, becoming in short order a worthless investment. Costs had soared, rents remained controlled, while rent delinquency and vandalism were rampant. Some landlords just abandoned their buildings, others milked them – paying no taxes, providing no services, but collecting what rents they could. The most venal turned to arson to recoup their losses ... Arson emerged as a sordid solution, a fact

3 Jill Jonnes, South Bronx Rising 8 (2d ed. 2002). 4 *Id.*

5 Norimitsu Onishi, *Neighborhood Report: South Bronx; Mapping the Lower Bronx: It's South, But South of What?*, N.Y. Times, Feb. 19, 1995.

6 Jonnes, South Bronx Rising at 91–182. *See also South Bronx Environmental Health and Policy Study: Population Characteristics and Trends in the South Bronx*, Institute for Civil Infrastructure Systems (June 20, 2017), www.icisnyu.org/south_bronx/Demographics_001.html.

> New York City stolidly denied for years . . . In truth, it would be hard to exaggerate the dimensions of this unnatural disaster.[7]

In the mid-1980s, the area was ravaged by a second unnatural disaster, namely the crack epidemic. By then, the South Bronx neighborhoods were the poorest in the country. Jobs were scarce. The majority of the residents were below the poverty line and on welfare. Even by the mid-1990s, half of the residents of the area were on welfare.[8]

However, the mid-1980s also saw significant opportunities in the South Bronx. According to Jonnes, a combination of a vast financial investment (ultimately almost 1.9 billion dollars) by the city for housing development in the Bronx as well as deep involvement and participation by local grassroots organizations began to substantially revitalize the area.[9] Over the course of the next decade, more than 100,000 new housing units were built, and there were enough home buyers and renters to fill them. Jonnes describes the interesting cast of characters that participated in this effort, including local community groups like the Mid-Bronx Desperadoes, a range of local and sophisticated community development corporations, and a number of Catholic priests. These local members of the community were supported by large and sophisticated nonprofits in achieving, as Jonnes describes, a "phenomenal resurrection of the South Bronx."[10]

## ORIGINS

This, then, was the setting in which the founders and original leaders of CHCA began their work in the early 1980s: in a neighborhood that had been beset by poverty, drugs, and arson, but also one that was just beginning to receive an enormous influx of resources for revitalization. As the former and present leaders of CHCA articulated in different ways, the purpose of founding CHCA in 1985 was to create quality jobs for low-income individuals in the Bronx.[11] According to CHCA's cofounder Peggy Powell,

> [W]e didn't come in as industry people. We came in as community economic development individuals, who were really looking at, on the economic development side, creating good jobs – and creating more access to jobs, and jobs that would be quality jobs from the perspective of the people who were doing that work.[12]

[7] Jonnes, South Bronx Rising at 7. [8] *Id.* at 404. [9] *Id.* at 393–394. [10] *Id.* at 397.

[11] Several of the employees I interviewed discussed the value to them of working for a business that was in their own neighborhood. Smith Interview; Interview with Margarita Pillot, Home Care Worker, Cooperative Home Care Associates (June 22, 2017); Interview with Denise Clark, Service Delivery Supervisor, Cooperative Home Care Associates (June 23, 2017).

[12] Interview with Peggy Powell, National Director, Workforce and Curriculum Development, PHI (May 12, 2016).

In fact, cofounders Rick Surpin and Peggy Powell had no experience in the home health care industry. Both individuals were employed by the Community Service Society, a nonprofit organization with a unit dedicated to developing innovative approaches to employment and empowerment for low-income individuals in New York.[13] Surpin, leading a small team of like-minded individuals, began searching for opportunities to create cooperative businesses in markets with several characteristics. Specifically, the team sought markets that could be served by large numbers of unskilled and semiskilled workers such that the business could grow substantially over time. Moreover, they sought to intervene in markets in which relatively poor-quality jobs could be significantly improved. As Surpin described,

> I know construction was the biggest thing we saw as an opportunity, and we started a small company that had serious management problems and ultimately failed. It was certainly a market opportunity, but we didn't have the ability to run a construction company or to support the running of a construction company, and we learned a lot about what not to do. Health care was the next biggest, and home care was the biggest in health care. The home care one took off relatively quickly. It . . . didn't take off in the first six months . . . but . . . it was clear there was an opportunity there if we could learn how to run it right . . . The market was growing . . . Medicare and Medicaid were in place . . .
>
> Basically the market, when we entered it, was dominated by temporary personnel agencies that were hiring people from central Brooklyn . . . and sent them on assignments all over the place. And going from the middle of Brooklyn, central Brooklyn, to the Bronx takes a long time. And, so . . . the chances of being late for your home care visit were good. But in our feasibility research we found a home care agency that was part of a community hospital that was looking for something other than a temporary personnel agency, and they didn't know what they were looking for, but they knew that this notion of worker ownership, and paying a dollar more an hour . . . sounded good to them. And so we knew that we had an open door.[14]

One of my interviewees, someone with a great deal of experience in the home care industry whom Surpin had consulted many years ago when he was considering starting CHCA, described the market opportunity from his perspective:

> Rick [and his team] were trying to figure out what kind of a business to go into, and they thought home care, and they got my name as somebody to go talk to about it, because I was involved in it. I did talk to them about it [and] told them what a horrible deal [home care] was for the workers. [They] weren't respected, they weren't paid properly, they weren't trained properly . . . and I told them all about this. [And Rick] said, "Sounds perfect."[15]

[13] Steven L. Dawson & Sherman L. Kreiner, Cooperative Home Care Associates: History and Lessons 6 (1993).

[14] Interview with Rick Surpin, President, Independence Care System (May 5, 2016).

[15] Interview with Eric Jensen (May 4, 2016). I have used a pseudonym for this interviewee.

## DEVELOPMENT OF A MARKET

But as Surpin also described, the goal of job creation could not drive the development of a sustainable business over the long term:

> There's no question that the beginning of Cooperative Home Care was about creating jobs for poor people. They were intended to be good jobs, and therefore have good income and the other characteristics that we talk about a good job [having]. And we quickly came to learn that when you do that in an enterprise, the enterprise isn't getting paid to create quality jobs. It's getting paid to provide a service or a product – in this case, to provide quality health care. And if it's not able to provide quality health care, no one will buy the services, and there won't be any jobs. So we quickly learned that we were in business for providing quality home care, and creating quality jobs was a strategy for adding value to the service.[16]

This recognition led to a business strategy that propelled CHCA into a national spotlight as a model business, *both* for its ability to create quality jobs and also for its impact on the entire home health care industry.[17] The strategy was captured by the catchphrase "quality care through quality jobs."[18] The idea was for CHCA to develop a niche in the market by providing high-quality care through home care service agencies that valued long-term relationships between elderly and disabled clients and their caregivers, higher levels of training, and ultimately also the creation of higher quality jobs.[19] Indeed, especially in its early existence, CHCA was able to find a few major home care providers that really valued these things and entered into contracts with CHCA, thereby allowing the company to survive and begin to grow.

But even this entree into the market did not alone provide the stability that its leaders sought in order to continue to grow and create long-term, high-quality jobs. Many of the managers I interviewed discussed the razor-thin profit margins forced by

16 Surpin Interview.

17 Anne Inserra, Maureen Conway & John Rodat, *The Cooperative Home Care Associates: A Case Study of a Sectoral Employment Development Approach*, The Aspen Institute, Sectoral Employment Development Learning Project 2 (2002), www.aspenwsi.org/wordpress/wp-content/uploads/02–018.pdf (describing CHCA as a "yardstick" for the industry). This model has been the subject of numerous publications. *See, e.g.*, Stephen Greenhouse, The Big Squeeze: Tough Times for the American Worker (2008); James DeFilippis, Unmasking Goliath: Community Control in the Face of Global Capital (2004); Christopher Eaton Gunn, Third-Sector Development: Making up for the Market (2004); Ruth Glasser et al., We Are the Roots : The Organizational Culture of a Home Care Cooperative (2002).

18 *Who We Are*, Cooperative Home Care Associates (May 10, 2017), www.chcany.org (CHCA's mission statement lists the following three goals: "To provide reliable, high quality home health care services for those who are elderly, chronically ill, or living with disabilities; To offer the highest possible salaries and benefits while building a profitable worker-owned company; To give workers opportunities to learn and grow as members of a health care team").

19 Daphne Perkins-Berry & Stu Schneider, *Improving the Quality of Home Health Aide Jobs: A Collaboration Between Organized Labor and a Worker Cooperative*, *in* Employee Ownership and Shared Capitalism: New Directions in Research 59 (Edward J. Carberry ed., 2011); Inserra et al., *The Cooperative Home Care Associates*; Carmen Huertas-Noble, *Worker-Owned and Unionized Worker-Owned Cooperatives: Two Tools to Address Income Inequality*, 22 Clinical L. Rev. 325 (2016).

the system of Medicaid and Medicare reimbursements in the home care industry. It was, and continues to be, excruciatingly difficult to increase wages to a livable level when reimbursement rates are so low, something that the industry can do little to control. And reimbursement rates are the same, regardless of the quality of care provided. The market niche was important, but it did not alone suffice as a strategy for long-term survival.

The cap on reimbursement rates also created another problem for CHCA, which it confronted in the first few years of its existence. It was very difficult for CHCA, as a for-profit, worker-owned company, to finance the level of training for direct care workers necessary to make good on its promise of quality care from fees for services alone. This, then, was the impetus for the creation of PHI,[20] the second organization in the network to come on line in 1991. According to Powell,

> [I]n order to be able to have sufficient revenue to ... have the type of training program we really wanted to put in place – and over time that vision got bigger and bigger in terms of where the needs were – but in order to be able to afford the investment in the worker on the training side ... we needed to be able to raise money from foundations or from public sources to cover the cost of doing training in a different way. And doing training at all, because there's very little money in the system itself to then support what we would call quality training ... CHCA is a for-profit agency ... So to raise that type of money as a for-profit, we were more limited. We made a decision to establish an affiliated 501(c)(3) organization as a nonprofit educational organization that would allow us to further develop the training model internal to Cooperative, but would support our broadening work that began to include planning for replication of the CHCA model with foundation support.[21]

As Powell and others have described, Powell and Surpin believed that a high-quality training program would enable CHCA's aides to provide a higher-quality service and would be a major distinguishing feature for CHCA in the market for home care services. This required more money than the cooperative could afford. Consequently, the cooperative's leaders turned to foundation and public funding for further developing and implementing the training model.

This was a critical moment for the development of CHCA and for the network that ultimately grew around it. CHCA's leaders decided that the new nonprofit should be formed "outside" of CHCA, with a separate identity and mission. It would certainly provide support for CHCA's training program. But the nonprofit would also have a broader mission. Again, from Powell:

> Both from an R&D sort of model for best caregiving and job quality practices and as a business model, it's enormously beneficial for PHI to be independent of Cooperative. And the way that our relationship with Cooperative and/or with ICS

[20] This organization was originally named Home Care Associates Training Institute.
[21] Powell Interview.

is . . . here in New York, we continue to see each other as both business developers in the sense of leading again as models . . . They're important if you want to move beyond one great-looking boutique company . . . You have to be able . . . to have more of an impact and influence on the field, to be recognized more broadly. We'd have to be able to be seen as not simply promoting Cooperative.[22]

Thus, the creation of the nonprofit eventually named PHI achieved more than just utilitarian efficiencies for CHCA by allowing it to externalize the costs of research, development, and training. It also led to a refinement of the goal of creating quality jobs.[23] As Powell described, the mission became more broadly "to change long-term care."[24] And PHI sought initially to fulfill that mission by, in Powell's words, "replicating core elements of our model in other markets."[25] The extent and focus of replication is a subject of some difference of opinion among the leaders in the network.[26] As I will describe later, the attempt to replicate CHCA's cooperative business model in other markets failed. However, what survived and was refined over time was the replication of the training model developed by PHI and used by CHCA and HCA, and ultimately also the development of best practices in training direct care workers and their supervisors that could be disseminated to the entire industry.[27]

As the home health care industry grew and became more complex, CHCA continued to cope with the limitations imposed by the Medicaid and Medicare systems. Despite growing in size, the business struggled with providing sufficient hours and wages to fulfill its vision of ensuring livable wages and full-time work to its home health aides. The struggle was intensified as a result of several changes in the market. For example CHCA's major contractor, the Visiting Nurse Service of New York (VNS), moved toward trying to consolidate its providers, called partner agencies. CHCA was designated one of those agencies, but this was accompanied by both significant staffing changes at VNS and jockeying among the partners for even more business.

The realization that VNS or any contractor might change its strategy for providing home care services led to a bold decision by CHCA, and in particular, Rick Surpin. As Powell put it,

No matter how great our training is with Cooperative, no matter how great . . . the models for career and other development internally . . . while that's something we are respected for and known for here . . . in the New York market, what's really driving the growth and survival of the licensed agencies in the New York market,

22 *Id.* 23 Perkins-Berry & Schneider, *Improving the Quality of Home Health Aide Jobs*.

24 Powell Interview. 25 *Id.*

26 *See* Inserra et al., *The Cooperative Home Care Associates* at 21–23 (describing the replication program); Dawson & Kreiner, Cooperative Home Case Associates at 23 (describing the replication plan as of early 1993, when the report was written).

27 Perkins-Berry & Schneider, *Improving the Quality of Home Health Aide Jobs*; Inserra et al., *The Cooperative Home Care Associates*.

> and ... nationally, is managed care. And managed care historically has not done a lot of home care services.[28]

Surpin decided to develop – and ultimately, to lead – a managed care company, one that was a nonprofit and focused specifically on home care services:

> ICS enabled Cooperative to grow, and Cooperative has doubled in size as a result of ICS. That wouldn't have happened if it wasn't for us, because ... I believed that at some point our major customer ... was going to change its view of the world, and it had developed its own managed care operation, and that it would put its marbles with ... its own managed care organization, which is what happened ... And so Cooperative is much more reliant on ICS than ever before.[29]

This, then, was how the third organization in the cluster, Independence Care System, founded in the year 2000, came to be.[30] And as they had done with PHI, Surpin and the other leaders involved in creating ICS decided to give the organization its own identity and mission, distinct from those of CHCA and PHI, but also mutually beneficial to both organizations. According to Surpin,

> We decided that it was important for Cooperative to maintain its identity. And then because it was worker-owned, it could not be a subsidiary of anybody ... We could have changed the structure, but we did not want to do that then. And then we wanted the new organization, ICS, to be seen as consumer-driven, and consumer-friendly, and to serve people who were physically disabled and on Medicaid – a population that was historically marginalized in the health care system. It could not be a cooperative, because people on Medicaid can't own anything.[31]

But the decision to create a separate business platform for ICS also meant that this distinct business had to pay attention to market concerns. Again, from Surpin:

> What I've come to learn as a business-person is that market share means something ... So we have a funny business strategy. We want to be in the middle of a market, and we don't want to be too big, and we want to be distinct enough that in the consolidation that takes place in the market, we can survive any consolidation ... We don't want to be bought, and we want to stand out enough that we can get away without being bought ... But ... in a Medicaid market, you can't be a boutique, either. So the traditional strategy of a small player would be to be the boutique that sells high-end products, ... and usually at a high-end price. We can't do that. So what else makes us distinct? So this niche of serving people with physical disabilities, it wasn't originally thought of as the thing that will make us so different. It ... was as much a personal interest as well as a clear place where home care didn't put its energy. It was mostly around people who were elderly that it put its energy. But it served both purposes. It really is a very distinct niche. We're the

28 Powell Interview. 29 Surpin Interview.

30 Harris Meyer, *A New Care Paradigm Slashes Hospital Use and Nursing Home Stays For the Elderly and the Physically and Mentally Disabled*, 30 HEALTH AFFAIRS 412, 412–16 (2011).

31 Surpin Interview.

only managed care organization in New York that focuses on people with physical disabilities.[32]

## A SECOND MARKET IN PHILADELPHIA

Given the extraordinary success of this group in starting and growing the largest worker-owned cooperative in the country, it is not surprising that they thought about replicating their model elsewhere. Nor is it surprising that foundations and others encouraged them to do so. Indeed, the pressure to replicate is a common experience among all three of the networks described in this book, especially the home care and South Shore networks. Thus, in 1993, the leadership of CHCA and PHI worked together to support the opening of Home Care Associates in Philadelphia (HCA). Like CHCA, HCA was founded as (and still is) a for-profit, worker-owned cooperative. Within two years, HCA had obtained enough business to reach a break-even point financially.[33] Although it has had its ups and downs, the business not only survived, but has for years now been thriving. HCA has always shared CHCA's mission of providing quality jobs through quality care. As HCA's president, Karen Kulp, stated, "every decision that I make, everything I think about really is around that . . . focus . . . [W]ithout a quality job, is [there] going to be quality care? . . . It just has a lot of clarity."[34]

But the market challenges and opportunities in upholding this mission have been qualitatively different in Philadelphia than they have been in the Bronx. HCA's chief operating officer, Tatia Jones-Cooper, captured much of this in her description of the market HCA initially entered and the adaptations HCA had to make to the model developed by CHCA in (and for) the Bronx:

> Pennsylvania has a population that was underserved, that did not have quality providers, and I think there was desperation on behalf of the legislators to move people from nursing homes into home. And it was great timing. And I think great timing along with the model, and the mission is what contributed to our success, because we could have done the same thing somewhere else and not been successful.[35]

Jones-Cooper continued, by describing HCA's adaptations to the original model:

> In New York, many of . . . the consumers that they serve get long hours, meaning . . . four to eight, sometimes more hours a day. So providing employees with a full-time job was not as much of a challenge as it was for us. When we first started, many of the cases that we were providing service to were two hours, one hour. If we had a three- or four-hour case, that was like gold. So it was difficult, you know, we couldn't ask [CHCA's] schedulers how they did it because we couldn't do it that way. So finding a full-time job for someone who may have to go four and five

[32] *Id.* [33] Inserra et al., *The Cooperative Home Care Associates* at 22.

[34] Interview with Karen Kulp, President/CEO, Home Care Associates (March 23, 2017).

[35] Interview with Tatia Jones-Cooper, Chief Operating Officer, Home Care Associates (March 23, 2017).

> different places on public transportation creates additional challenges for retention of workers .... We had to work that much harder to schedule people in areas that were close and consistent. ... So for us, the scheduling piece was a big deal. Pennsylvania did not reimburse as much, and the idea of long-hour cases then was unheard of. Now it's changed. But then it was completely unheard of. So that was one example of how we had to adapt. Of course the reimbursement being lower was another one ... So you know, we had less to work with. And I know in New York, there's cost of living, and it's far more expensive, but we didn't have the same cushion that they did in terms of wages and benefits, and so we had to be creative about how to do that, and still get people the benefits that they needed.[36]

HCA also responded to new market challenges as they arose using at times a markedly different strategy than that used by its New York affiliates. Perhaps most notably, while the New York organizations expanded by creating their own market demand within the network (through the formation of ICS), HCA began to diversify its customer base. These different strategies were adopted in response to the same general problem in both locations of having two or three large customers who began to bring home care "in-house" within their own businesses or vertically integrated networks. As it had done in its start-up phase, HCA relied on a combination of support from especially PHI in New York in creating systems that were appropriate for HCA *and* developing its own network to address the unique challenges in the Philadelphia health care market.

HCA responded first by helping its largest customer start up its own home care company. This collaboration may seem surprising, because the result was that HCA lost many of the home care clients that this customer had provided. But in the meantime, HCA began to develop a new line of business for itself: The new program allowed people to be trained as home health attendants who can provide in-home health care to family members or friends below a certain income and be paid through their loved one's health insurer. It appears that, because of HCA's support of its customer in starting its own home care company, HCA received referrals from that customer for individual clients who wanted to choose their own home health attendants.[37] HCA's second move was to grow its work with LIFE programs in the area, which Kulp described as "programs ... for seniors who are nursing-home eligible, who want to stay in their own homes."[38]

Finally, and most recently, as Kulp described, HCA has entered into a partnership with a local nursing home (Inglis House) to participate in an innovative "virtual LIFE program":

> [T]he head of Inglis came to me and said, "Look, we want to start to close some of our nursing home beds, and we want to do a LIFE program for people who are younger." ... [W]e know about the work you do, and ... we know that you're a really good provider, and we'd like to work with you." So we've been working with them

[36] *Id.* [37] Kulp Interview. [38] *Id.*

> for a very long time to try and figure out how this model would work . . . [T]hey built an apartment building, which they've done all over the city, but this one is close to Inglis, with 80 apartments, and 20 of those were reserved for people moving out of Inglis House. So last July, we got 20 consumers, who basically moved from this nursing home to this building, and we started to take care of them, which was a real boost in our business.[39]

On the training side of the business, there are some noteworthy parallels with CHCA's approach, but also some key differences. According to Kulp, when she first arrived at HCA in early 2002, HCA "probably had two million dollars of revenue, and one million dollars of training funding" that came from federal and local sources.[40] The federal grants were related to the Temporary Assistance for Needy Families program and administered by the state Department of Public Welfare. The local grants came through the City of Philadelphia pursuant to the Workforce Investment Act. But what distinguishes HCA from its New York affiliates' provision of training, as Jerilyn Dressler described, is "that training program, which still exists today, does not receive any more grant funding. It's therefore self-funded: so that rate per hour has to cover training costs as well as operating costs."[41] Dressler is HCA's part-time controller, who, interestingly, is a consultant to HCA and an employee of an agency that provides part-time controllers mostly to nonprofit organizations in the area. The hourly rate to which Dressler referred is the reimbursement rate from Medicare and Medicaid, which, as Dressler described, currently covers virtually all of HCA's costs (including at this point, training for home care aides). As it does for CHCA, PHI continues to provide deep consultation on the training curriculum to HCA. But it does not provide funding, and it is also clear that HCA has extensively developed and shaped its training for its own distinctive needs.

## THE NETWORK IN MATURE FORM

Today, CHCA is the largest worker-owned cooperative in the United States, probably by a long shot. It currently has over 2,000 employees, approximately 70 percent of whom are owners and the vast majority of whom are women of color living in the Bronx.[42] Every year, it trains over 600 people to become home care aides.[43] Thanks to the New York state wage parity law and the higher minimum wage, and before that thanks to its own prioritization of higher wages, it provides livable wages to its employees. It is also typically able to provide at least 30 hours of work per week for all employees who have attained senior aide status. As Michelle Smith described,

39 *Id.* 40 *Id.*

41 Interview with Jerilyn Dressler, Controller, Your Part-Time Controller LLC (March 23, 2017).

42 Jensen Interview.

43 *Who We Are*, Cooperative Home Care Associates (May 10, 2017), www.chcany.org; Interview with Lamont Spence, Director of Workforce Development, Cooperative Home Care Associates (July 3, 2017).

> Many have given up hours, possibly due to the economy and different things within the company, so that others would be able to have some type of work. So that someone else will be able to have maybe even 15 as opposed to me having 44. So maybe X amount of hours have to be taken from me, and two hours from you, and two hours from that case, and that's the goal, so that at least everyone can have some type of employment.[44]

The company also has retention rates of between 70 and 80 percent, meaningfully higher than the industry average of 40 to 60 percent.[45]

Employees of the company emphasize that despite its size, CHCA still feels like a family that cares about the individual workers. In the words of home health aide Clara Calvo,

> They gave me support. They gave me the hours that I can work, and I can pick up my kids from the school ... They support me, and they help me. Now my daughter is 22 years old. And she finished college, and my younger son is in college too. And ... I still feel the support, because the agency gave me the opportunity to grow in the inside there ... The agency opened the door, like this is your house, this is your family.[46]

Meanwhile, ICS is a nonprofit managed care organization with 6,700 members, the majority of whom are Latino or African American. In the managed care field in New York, it is a midsized business, with a distinctive focus on providing long-term home-based care for people with physical disabilities and chronic illnesses or conditions.[47] It has approximately 5 percent of the market share for the managed long-term care market. It also serves many elderly people. ICS is regulated as an insurance company. It coordinates care for its members, most of which is paid for by Medicaid or Medicare either to ICS or directly to the providers with whom ICS contracts. ICS provides 70 percent of CHCA's contracts, while approximately 15 percent of ICS's business goes to CHCA.[48]

PHI serves more of a dual function. As Surpin described, "about half of what PHI has done over the years is connected to the two systems [CHCA and ICS]."[49] But the other half of PHI's work is nationally facing research, practice, and advocacy intended to contribute to the broader agenda of transforming both the quality of long-term health care and the lives of people who do this type of work. PHI carries out this work in two departments, one focused on practice and the other on policy. On the practice side, PHI's areas of focus are on workforce and curriculum development as well as coaching and consulting services. PHI's efforts are to propagate the kind of quality training described by Peggy Powell throughout the long-term care industry. The organization's coaching and consulting services are intended to complement

44 Smith Interview. 45 Interview with Jodi Sturgeon, President, PHI (May 12, 2016).

46 Interview with Clara Calvo, Home Care Worker, Cooperative Home Care Associates (June 23, 2017).

47 Rick Surpin, *Independence Care System: A Disability Care Coordination Organization in New York City*, 30 Journal of Ambulatory Care Management 52, 52–53 (2007).

48 Surpin Interview. *See also* Surpin, *Independence Care System*. 49 Surpin Interview.

this training by developing systems by which nurse managers and other managers of home health aides can provide appropriate levels of support and infrastructure for those who provide quality care to homebound clients.[50] As Jodi Sturgeon, PHI's president, described:

> [W]e use ... the home-care workers at Cooperative to field test curriculum that we're developing, and we then refine it, bring it back to them ... For PHI, it's an unbelievable resource for us to be able to have our folks develop training, ... and then be able to test it out and see how it works in an environment that's right here with us. [W]e [also] provide executive coaching and leadership training for middle managers to Cooperative.[51]

PHI then takes these materials and services out to a broad range of providers, workforce agencies, unions, and governmental agencies.

On the policy side, PHI provides research and analysis to support policy changes at what it describes as the "intersection of Aging/Disability Services and Workforce Development." This has also been described as a sectoral strategy, in which the policy aim is to transform work conditions in an entire industry.[52] In the recent past, PHI's policy efforts resulted in an enormous victory for home health aides in New York: PHI and Local 1199 of the Service Employees International Union (SEIU) convinced the state to pass the New York State Home Care Worker Parity Act, which sets a minimum "total compensation" requirement for home care aides,[53] as part of a major transition to Medicaid-managed care. Currently, PHI's policy focus in New York is largely on reimbursement rates, which continue to put significant financial pressure on CHCA and many other providers.[54]

For me as a lawyer, some of the most interesting moments in my interviews with the leaders of these three organizations were on the subject of the legal and personal relationships among these organizations. Legal considerations were certainly fundamental to the choices of business forms that were made when each of these businesses was founded. But law arguably plays a small role in ensuring the extremely high level of cohesion that persists between these three businesses. Let us start by examining the formal choices about business form. CHCA was originally organized as a for-profit, worker-owned cooperative. To accomplish this form, CHCA's leadership had to work

50 Sturgeon Interview. *See also* PHI, The PHI Quality Care Through Quality Jobs Approach: Designing Training and Support Programs for Direct-Care Workers and the People They Assist (brochure on file with author); PHI, The PHI Coaching Approach: Building Skills. Strengthening Teams. Managing Change (brochure on file with author).

51 Sturgeon Interview.

52 *See* Peter Pitegoff, *Worker Ownership in Enron's Wake – Revisiting a Community Development Tactic*, 8 J. Small & Emerging Bus. L. 239, 252 (2004); Peggy Clark & Steven L. Dawson, *Jobs & Urban Poor: Privately Initiated Sectoral Strategies*, Aspen Institute (2001), https://assets.aspeninstitute.org/content/uploads/files/content/docs/pubs/jobsurbanpoor.pdf; Inserra et al., *The Cooperative Home Care Associates*.

53 PHI describes these changes on its website. *Wage & Labor Protections*, PHI (May 10, 2017), https://phinational.org/policy/state-activities/phi-new-york/wage-labor-protections.

54 Sturgeon Interview.

with a team of lawyers to push for the enactment of a state statute governing the formation of worker-owned cooperatives. As Surpin described, the lawyers also had to convince the attorney general that they should not be subject to securities laws:

> [W]e didn't fit into securities law, because we were so small, and yet we were essentially selling stock, even though we didn't think of it that way. We never in a million years would have thought of it that way. So we had to get special approval from the state attorney general's office to issue stock in the way that we did. [S]o we didn't fit in anything. They never heard of a worker-owned cooperative. We had to get fairly high up in the attorney general's office to have this discussion.[55]

In 2012, CHCA also obtained certification as a B corporation, a status that denotes a high level of corporate social responsibility.[56]

Several years later, when the decision was made to form PHI, as Powell and others have described, the decision was driven initially by the desire to develop an even higher-quality training program that could serve as an industry model. And this in turn required foundation funding. This desire was what necessitated both the creation of a new business, and the designation of that business as a nonprofit organization. Meanwhile, it was important for all involved to maintain CHCA as a worker-owned business, and thus a for-profit.

The same set of considerations was largely present when Surpin and others decided to create ICS. In Surpin's words,

> ICS was designed to be bigger, broader, and typically, you would either set up a holding company, or you would set up a larger organization, and Cooperative would be a subsidiary ... We decided that it was important for Cooperative to maintain its identity. And then because it was worker-owned, it could not be a subsidiary of anybody ... We could have changed the structure, but we did not want to do that then.[57]

Surpin and his team also chose nonprofit status for ICS, in part to emphasize its consumer-facing mission.

Formally, then, neither a holding company structure, nor any other legal form of organization has bound the three businesses together. Instead, the leaders have maintained intense legal cohesion by means of cross-board relationships. In Steven Dawson's words,

> Each of these have cross-board relationships, and cross chairmanship relationships. So Rick is chair of the other two organizations, I was chair of ICS for many years. A few other of Rick's leaders were on the other boards ... But there's no command and control among any of them ... [T]hey call it in management school, a loose-tight kind of structure, where what was tight is a shared mission, clarity of roles, each of the organizations playing a very, very distinct role. And a set of personal relationships among leaders

55 Surpin Interview.

56 B corporations are certified by B lab, a nonprofit organization, after undergoing a "B impact assessment," according to B lab's website, www.bcorporation.net.

57 Surpin Interview.

> that was mutually supportive. What was loose is that we didn't have to necessarily check with each other to do anything. So it allowed this kind of cluster of organizations that were, outward-facing in different roles, and had a fair amount of entrepreneurial freedom, in each case. So PHI took on a more national role that only secondarily benefited the system, I would say. But nevertheless did. CHCA has pursued both the training as well as the service delivery. ICS is engaged in this incredible managed care world. So that . . . balance of really clear purpose and mission and relationships. But having that kind of flexibility really allowed a degree of creativity and innovation that probably wouldn't have happened if one of those organizations was controlling the others.[58]

Thus, throughout the 30-year existence of this network, its leaders have also sought to maintain a deeply personal connection. Indeed, Sturgeon stated that "it's all about relationship":

> [I]t's a pretty unique situation in terms of just the depth of personal relationship, in addition to work relationship, and just the synergy of, you know, mission-driven, we [a]re all completely on the same page.[59]

As the original group of founders has begun to transfer leadership to a new generation, they have sought various means of ensuring this personal and cultural set of connections. In Surpin's words,

> Something that I think was done really well is there's a successor to Michael [Elsas] at Cooperative Home Care who's chief operating officer. She actually grew up in the company, Adria Powell. Her mother is Peggy [Powell]. And she started out working in the company at 17 years old. And she told me when she was someplace around 17 to 20, she said to me, "When I grow up, I want to be president of the company someday." . . . So that's pretty amazing. And, at ICS, Regina Estela, has been here for 15 years, she's chief operating officer, and . . . when I retire, or something like that, she hopefully will become CEO.[60]

These kinds of long-term connections with the network's culture and history are also apparent among the top management at CHCA and PHI, each of whom has worked with these organizations in various capacities for decades. Jodi Sturgeon also pointed out that these relationships are matched by extensive contractual relationships between the three organizations:

> There [are] contractual relationships between the organizations. So obviously ICS contracts with Cooperative for home-care services . . . PHI contracts with both ICS and Cooperative Home Care to do . . . innovations, provide technical assistance.[61]

It thus appears that deep intergenerational personal, professional, and contractual relations supplement the organizational forms chosen for this network of organizations.

While the leaders of these three organizations all described the advantages of having three separate organizations, it is also important to recognize the

58 Dawson Interview. 59 Sturgeon Interview.
60 Surpin Interview. Adria Powell did indeed become the president of CHCA in January 2017.
61 Sturgeon Interview.

disadvantages. It is, of course, more complex to have to manage three different organizations with three different sets of practices and cultures. As Surpin described,

> Ideally, these three organizations would have one governing board, and the executives would have responsibilities as executives, and profit or loss responsibilities, but more like subsidiaries do. And I don't know that they would have separate boards so much as – you would connect them in a different way legally. But I don't know how to do that and address the concern of mixing for-profit and nonprofit.[62]

CHCA, ICS, and PHI are at the center of this extraordinary network, but it is fair to say that their network in New York is much broader than just these three organizations. Indeed, several members of these organizations mentioned that one advantage of having three organizations with distinct identities and missions is that each is part of a distinct network. For CHCA, one of the key players in its network is the local chapter, Chapter 1199, of the SEIU. Jensen described the unionization of CHCA's employees in 2004:

> [H]ere we were, sort of leading the industry for so many years when it came to salaries and benefits. But then after a while, we weren't leading the industry, because we didn't have the same entree into government funding as the union did . . . And so when the union did come, the workers at first were reluctant, saying, "We don't really need a union. We decide on what the benefits are, so what do we need a union for?" . . . [I]n this company, management has the same interests as the union has, and that takes a little bit [of] getting used to . . . [W]e sit down to have a negotiation about a new contract, it's more [a] discussion about what resources are available. And what benefits can we provide for the workers.[63]

As Michelle Smith described, the union provides a range of important services to CHCA's employees:

> Every Friday, 1199 is here. Any questions you want to ask. The education fund, they let you know about that. Your dues paying . . . They have lawyers, immigration, a lot of things are offered to the members . . . I was a part of the union in my old agency, but it wasn't that ongoing intimacy of every Friday you had a table with an organizer . . . We had information fairs, where you could come up to the thirteenth floor on a Friday . . . where banks would come up and have tables. They would tell you things that you could take advantage of. Not just direct deposit . . . We had a partnership with the farmer's market on 49th Street.[64]

Several of those I interviewed emphasized the importance of the union's educational funding as a starting point for a career in the health care industry.[65]

62 Surpin Interview. 63 Jensen Interview. 64 Smith Interview.

65 Pillot Interview; Smith Interview; Calvo Interview; Clark Interview; Spence Interview. As Margarita Pillot described, the union is another avenue for democratic participation in the workplace, alongside being a worker-owner.

In addition to the union, local government agencies (for example, the city's Human Resources Administration, which refers many workers to CHCA), the network of B corporations, and the cooperative movement all are important parts of CHCA's network.[66]

Given ICS's role as a managed care company, it has relationships with a broad range of providers. As Surpin stated,

> [W]e are now in relationship with primary care physicians, and neighborhood health centers. And we're much more of a player in the health care system than we were at Cooperative, because of the role of home care in the health care system, versus we're now paying for and providing a broader range of services.[67]

ICS also is deeply involved in a network of consumer advocacy organizations, including the Center for Medicare Rights, which recently honored Surpin for his work in making ICS such a consumer-focused managed care organization. Surpin was also very active in the Home Care Association of New York, including as an officer and chairperson. This organization was an advocate in promoting policies to support both quality care and quality jobs in the home health care industry.[68]

Although it is one-tenth the size of CHCA, HCA in Philadelphia is still one of the largest worker-owned cooperatives in the country. In Philadelphia, it has the distinction of being the third-largest woman-owned business.[69] HCA currently has over 200 employees, the majority of whom are women of color. Approximately 30 percent of its employees are owners.[70] Pennsylvania and Philadelphia do not yet have laws requiring a higher minimum wage than that required by federal law, but HCA does manage to pay its employees a higher wage than the federal minimum. As Jerilyn Dressler has described, HCA's wage rate is much higher than the federal minimum if one calculates in the value of the range of benefits (unemployment, health, monthly pass for public transportation) that HCA provides. Most of HCA's employees have full-time work.[71]

As with CHCA, many of my interviewees from HCA emphasized the value of working as part of HCA's family: "[T]hey really make you feel like family, you know . . . They make you feel good, they make you feel like you're part of something. And that's what I like about it . . . [T]hey really pay you some attention, and they really show you a lot of love, and it's kind of needed."[72] "[T]his is home, this is how Home Care Associates is. You come in . . . nobody is on your back . . . Other companies I worked for, they stop you at the door. You couldn't even get a glass of

66 Spence Interview. 67 Surpin Interview. 68 Surpin Interview.

69 Sharon Oliver, *The Largest Women-Owned Businesses, Ranked by Total Local Employment*, Philadelphia Bus. J., July 19, 2013.

70 Dressler Interview.

71 Interview with Janie Dixon, Training Coordinator, Home Care Associates (March 23, 2017).

72 Interview with Recanell Carroll, Home Care Aide, Home Care Associates (March 23, 2017).

water. Here we got water, food, and we [are] like a family."[73] "[When a relative] passed away, they called, they were asking me, "How you doing? How you pulling through?" That's . . . love."[74] "[I]t's like a family here. . . . When the aides come in, it's like they're coming home, you know. They're embraced, we love to see them. Our whole temperament here is different."[75] Moreover, the feeling of family extends to the New York organizations. Tatia Jones-Cooper said about the New York group: "They are truly like family, so I can't say enough about the relationship with them. We wouldn't be here if it were not for them, I'm sure."[76]

Finally, given its dual mission, PHI has a network that includes both a range of players in the New York state long-term health care industry and a more national network of policy and advocacy organizations. In New York, one key example within PHI's network is the group of community colleges and workforce development organizations with which PHI has partnered to provide training for direct care workers.[77] The local union is also involved in this effort because it is a major source of funding, both by obtaining grants that it can use to support training through PHI and CHCA, and by providing education financing to its members.[78]

The resulting network, if one were to attempt to present it in a diagram, might look something like this:

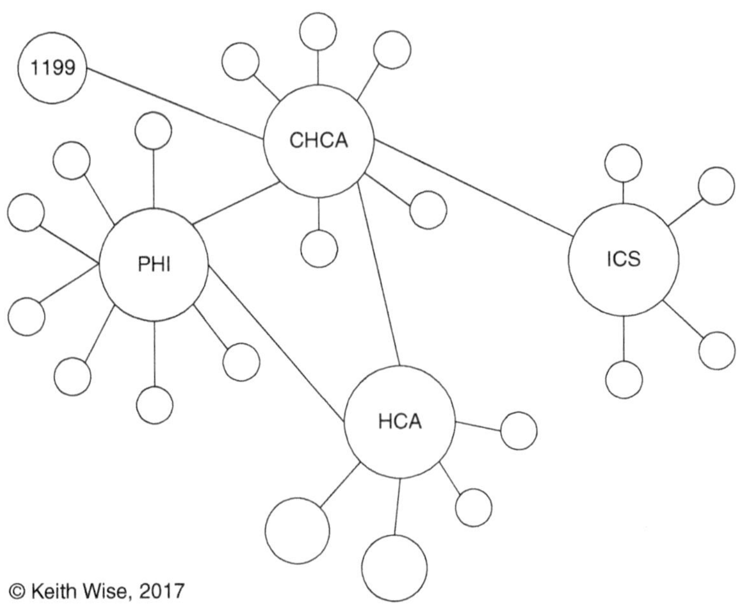


[73] Dixon Interview.
[74] Interview with Nana Nemeiar, Home Care Aide, Home Care Associates (March 23, 2017).
[75] Interview with Ronnette Perkins, Human Resources Director, Home Care Associates (March 23, 2017).
[76] Jones-Cooper Interview. [77] Powell Interview. [78] *Id.*; Smith Interview.

## INTERMEDIARIES IN THE NETWORK

It is no doubt evident by now that the four main organizations in this network have a complex structure built on sharing of resources that serves ultimately to support the dual mission of providing quality long-term home health care to individuals who are elderly and/or have disabilities *and* providing quality jobs to low-income people. This network works with and is supported by a range of additional institutions. The purpose of this section is to explore the contributions made by intermediaries in this network, and thereby also to explore in greater depth the sharing that occurs.

PHI's major contributions to the network, and especially to CHCA and HCA, take the form of support for training of direct care workers and their supervisors. Both Sturgeon and Powell have described the rich range of services that PHI provides in this regard. Both also have described this work as "research and development" to support the dissemination of best practices in the provision of quality training and ultimately quality health care, work that would likely be too costly for CHCA to internalize. As Sturgeon said, "You're doing really time-intensive, costly work, right? How do you take that into market at a design and a cost that the market can bear? So that's our constant challenge."[79] On the policy side, Surpin described the relevance of PHI's policy work to the *business* of home health care:

> What we learned very quickly at Cooperative was that home care policy and reimbursement policy [had] a ceiling ... It wasn't a free, private market. And there probably is no such thing as a really totally free, and totally private market, because of government law and regulation. But in this case, it was also law, regulation, and *financing* that was coming from the government ... We got into writing ... policy things that led to realizing, well we needed our own policy capacity, as well as the nonprofit vehicle.[80]

But it is also critical that PHI's voice in the policy discussions is augmented by its relationship with CHCA and ICS. As Surpin stated, in describing his policy paper on Medicaid redesign that ultimately influenced the Cuomo administration to support wage parity,

> I wrote it under PHI's name ... But I had a platform because of CHCA's, PHI's, and ICS's combined experience and reputation ... If I was just a policy analyst someplace, I wouldn't have known enough, and I wouldn't have had the leverage to do it. So it's really because I was an executive and a practitioner in these places.[81]

Sturgeon provided a detailed example demonstrating exactly this point on the "practice" side of PHI's work:

> One of the things that we're doing ... is an example of how all three of us work together, and I think is a huge plus and a benefit of the transition to managed care. We have worked over the last 18 months or so at creating an advanced role for aides

79 Sturgeon Interview. 80 Surpin Interview. 81 *Id.*

> focused on the care transition space with Cooperative. So for aides at Cooperative, but then also two other licensed agencies within ICS's network, what they call their preferred-provider network ... [W]e have trained experienced home care workers, they've transitioned to full-time salaried-with-benefits roles, and they are supporting home care workers in the field. And so there's a total of eight of them, and they're impacting about 1,400 of ICS's members that are being served by the three agencies ... [W]e got funding from the state actually, a fairly large amount, to test this model, with a focus on reducing hospitalizations with emergency room visits and improving family caregiver satisfaction ... [W]hat we discovered was ... that we could improve communication ... and outcomes from the home to the clinical care team with these aides, with a dedicated clinical manager, and with technology. We absolutely proved that. But what we also learned was the connection between the clinical manager and the care coordination team at ICS improved, and had a positive effect. So PHI is right now working with ICS on a way to colocate their care management staff right at these three licensed agencies.[82]

PHI also provides efficiencies connected to basic business maintenance. For example, all three organizations are colocated in a building in the Bronx for which PHI holds the lease.[83] The businesses also share cleaning services.

ICS's primary contribution has been to serve as the main source of CHCA's business, in effect its main customer. Many of the leaders in the network attribute CHCA's enormous growth over the past 15 years to the creation of ICS. It is a stable source of demand for exactly the kind of niche services that CHCA has carved out for itself. The relationship between ICS and CHCA could be viewed as a move toward vertical integration in a service delivery chain. But the leaders of both organizations have emphasized the independence of each organization.

Because ICS is higher up on the "value chain" in such a highly regulated industry, ICS is also effectively responsible for managing many of the regulatory issues faced by the network. As Surpin, among others, has stated,

> Cooperative has very little financial regulation. ICS has [a] tremendous amount of financial regulation, so we could be insolvent as an insurance entity, but solvent by generally accepted accounting principles. It's just a whole different regulatory framework.[84]

Powell added,

> [I]t is ICS who is recognized as struggling, within its limitations, [with] the biggest payer, i.e. Medicaid, and the state ... It is ICS who is trying to look at the model of determining what would be ... a quality rate for its preferred providers ... And if we didn't have an ICS, ... Cooperative would be in even greater harm's way. And I think all the licensed agencies are in harm's way right now, until things shake out with the Medicaid rates, and all of the issues that are going on in the external environment.[85]

[82] Sturgeon Interview. [83] Dawson Interview. [84] Surpin Interview. [85] Powell Interview.

In New York, CHCA is the employer of thousands of low-income individuals in the Bronx. It is thus the primary source of skilled labor of the type that ICS requires in order to provide the quality care that it pledges to provide its consumers. It is also, as Sturgeon put it, a "learning lab" where PHI can test its innovations in training and organizational support in a rich, well-established, and trustworthy setting. In Philadelphia, HCA plays an analogous role to CHCA.

Finally, and perhaps most importantly, this network shares the ethos of worker ownership, which in itself is a core institution that binds these businesses together and fulfills many of the functions of a sharing intermediary as I use that term in this book. Indeed, the mission of worker ownership seems to have been the basis for originating the network and for the sharing of resources within the network. For example, the ICA Group, which is one of the major organizations supporting worker-owned cooperatives in the country, was a key source of financing and consultation during CHCA's start-up phase.[86] And the imperative of remaining a for-profit, worker-owned business was the catalyst for forming PHI as an organization that could receive grant funding to support the development of the training program.

While these four organizations are at the core of the network, it is also appropriate to note the role of Chapter 1199 of the SEIU in supporting the network. As described, the union provides support for additional vocational education for health care workers employed at CHCA, for example for those who wish to pursue nursing degrees. The union also provides support for labor in a variety of forms.

## WORKING WITHIN THE NETWORK

The leaders of this network of organizations all emphasize that part of their core mission is to provide quality jobs for home health aides working in their system. To these claims, I would add that the collaboration among these organizations is integral to fulfilling this mission. The purpose of this section is to explore what exactly a quality job means and further, how the network relies on sharing institutions to create quality jobs.

Perhaps the most distinguishing feature of a "quality job" within the network, and specifically at CHCA and HCA, is that of worker-ownership. Again, 70 percent of the 2,000 employees at CHCA, including management, are owners. HCA also has a high level of worker-ownership. Employees commented extensively on the benefits of worker-ownership. Many emphasized the value of the financial investment: "I really think it's a good investment . . . At the end of the year they get incentives. So that might be just at the time when you need that money . . . [H]ow many of us out here nowadays can actually say, 'My job did this?'"[87] Many also commented on the value of participating in decision-making for the company: "You get to make the different decisions . . . to better the company . . . I think it's cool because a lot of women work

[86] Dawson & Kreiner, Cooperative Home Care Associates at 6–9.

[87] Interview with Stephanie Whitehead, Home Care Attendant, Home Care Associates (March 23, 2017).

here ... and [typically] people don't listen to us too much."[88] "You get a voice in the agency ... That's the best part ... I can raise my hand, and they listen, and they respect my idea."[89] Deborah O'Bryant commented, "I'm a board member and I'm on the finance committee also. Lot of things I didn't know about the finances I know. I know when we're making money, when we're not making money, and everything."[90] HCA's Human Resources Director Ronnette Perkins stated,

> That was one of the selling factors, the fact that you could own part of this company while you were here, and had a say in the way that the company was developed and shaped. I thought that was just totally awesome ... If the company makes money ... you know, we did well this year, and then we have an excess of x amount of dollars, we actually vote on how we're going to use that money. If it's to have better health insurance, if we take it out in a dividend, ... so I just really love it about the company.[91]

While CHCA and HCA have what is described in the cooperatives world as "professional management," worker-ownership certainly translates into a deep level of democratic control over both companies. Specifically, as a member of CHCA's management described, there is a very clear breakdown of decision-making control between management, labor, and the board, which includes representatives from labor:

> [Before CHCA became unionized,] the main component within CHCA that was involved in this thing was something called the Worker Council. And that worked fine up until, you know, say, 500 staff. After that, it just doesn't work, because the Worker Council would meet and discuss things. And they represented most of the full-time staff, and so that was fine if you had a couple of hundred workers, but when you have 2,000, it doesn't. And also, when you have a union, the union ... believes, and rightly so, that they're supposed to represent the best interest and come up with the best benefits.
>
> So we created the first and still only labor–management committee in home care, with the union ... In our case, we set up subgroups. So if, for example, we thought that there was a problem with morale, there was a morale committee ... If at one point we thought that lots of our workers were faced with issues about child care, ... we set up a child care subcommittee that did work on that. Those committees, if they found issues, and found problems, and wanted to make recommendations, on a quarterly basis, ... executive management attends those meetings ...
>
> The board hires the president, the CEO, to run the company, and it's very clear what those responsibilities are. If it has to do with bigger-picture issues, like should we go into a new business, should we move the office, ... then the board [makes] those decisions. An example is ... last year, we had to change our policy on overtime. That's not a decision that the president can make. That's something that the board has to make. So it's very clear, the board's responsibilities in terms of a strategic decision, those kinds of things; but anything that has to do with running the company is the responsibility of the management ...

[88] *Id.* [89] Calvo Interview. [90] O'Bryant Interview. [91] Perkins Interview.

> The other thing, . . . and I think it's probably one of the most effective mechanisms that we have in terms of involvement, is what we call our open door policy. Any worker can come at any time during the day to see anybody that they want, about anything that they want. They don't need an appointment, and they'll be able, maybe not 10 minutes after they walk in, it may take 20 minutes. But they'll have the opportunity to voice their concern. Does everybody do that? Absolutely not. Do 10 people every week do it? Yeah.[92]

Smith described her experience with the labor–management committee as follows:

> So being at CHCA, I got involved in some groups. One of them was LMC [labor–management committee], which I didn't go venturing for them. Someone just contacted me from CHCA and said, "We want to put you on a committee, because we've heard you've been in home care for 20-some odd years, and we think this would be a good thing." Me, on the other hand, I was not as into this as they were. I was real questionable about it. "Who told you all about me? What would I have to say?" Things of that nature. But I found it to be very rewarding . . . So I became more and more intrigued with this, because I always wanted to know the inside of the company. It could have been just curiosity of being around so long, but that's what I wanted to do. And I found each year, it opened more and more to me. And I no longer wanted to get out of it. I was in awe that I really did have something to say, and might make a difference.[93]

Regarding the open-door policy at CHCA, Margarita Pillot commented, "That's one of the best things CHCA has."[94] And Deborah O'Bryant stated,

> One thing about Cooperative Home Care, the president, you could see anytime. You . . . go to the desk and ask if the president's there, she's there, she'll see you . . . They have a big kitchen, you can sit down and have lunch. I go down to the main floor where everybody's at. You got your coordinators, you got your president.[95]

A similar level of transparency and participation exists at HCA. As Dressler described,

> About half of the board members are worker-owners. Many of them have had a good deal of longevity with the company, so they've seen ups and downs, and they understand decisions that are being made. I think that the board meetings are very productive, because they're honest, transparent, and the worker-owners ask great questions. Part of my job in talking about the finances is making it understandable to the worker-owners. I use data visualizations such as charts and graphs to present the results. I can then explain to them why the results happened, what we propose to do, and obtain their input regarding the plan of action.[96]

[92] Jensen Interview. [93] Smith Interview. [94] Pillot Interview. [95] O'Bryant Interview.
[96] Dressler Interview.

Joining CHCA and HCA as an employee creates a career opportunity that is completely distinct from the job choices otherwise available to most of those employees. Home health workers at CHCA and HCA listed the following jobs they had held prior to joining these companies: Burger King, TJ Maxx, "working at a nursing home doing housekeeping," security work,[97] retail, Wal-Mart,[98] cashier, waitress.[99] The vast majority of the workers I interviewed had previously held jobs that required little or no skill, and they held them typically for short periods of time. There were, however, clear exceptions such as Mark Peterson, who had extensive experience in home health care and a range of related fields before joining HCA as a home care attendant.[100] A few had held home care positions with other companies. Many of the employees commented that prior experiences in their personal lives had led them to consider home care for their professions. They talked about the "heart" and the sense of caring that is required for this work.[101]

One of the greatest differences that employees within this network experience, in contrast to prior work settings, is the feeling of family, and even of being visible and loved.[102] Employees connect this to their ability to share in the ownership of the businesses. They also connect it to the high levels of communication among coworkers. Another difference is job stability and longevity. Angelique Montgomery, who has been with HCA for 16 years, said,

> [B]efore, my other jobs, I worked maybe eight months, not for a long period of time. And then I didn't like the job, and then I would leave.... [B]ut I don't think I would ever leave Home Care Associates completely. I somehow would still find a spot at Home Care, whether it would be dropping down to part time, working on a weekend.[103]

In addition, it is remarkable how many members of the management in both HCA and CHCA began as home care workers and then moved on to other positions in the company.

A third feature that sets these jobs apart is the level of benefits employees receive. In addition to the standard unemployment and other benefits, employees receive health benefits and retirement plans, which appears to be exceptional in this

97 Interview with Angelique Montgomery, Home Care Aide, Home Care Associates (March 23, 2017).

98 Whitehead Interview. 99 Carroll Interview.

100 Interview with Mark Peterson, Home Care Attendant, Home Care Associates (March 23, 2017).

101 Pillot Interview; O'Bryant Interview; Calvo Interview; Dixon Interview; Whitehead Interview; Peterson Interview.

102 Pillot Interview; Nemeiar Interview; Carroll Interview; Dixon Interview.

103 Montgomery Interview. Denise Clark, who began as a home health aide at CHCA and now holds a supervisory role, commented, "It's the environment that encourages the growth, that opens the door to the opportunities. I think that makes us different from other organizations. I've known people who have left Cooperative seeking other opportunities. But when they went to those other organizations, it was nothing like here. They didn't get the support. They didn't get the additional training. So ultimately they're back at Cooperative."

industry.[104] At HCA, they also receive monthly passes for public transportation and paid time off, although one employee did express concern that the flexibility of HCA's paid-time-off policy can be a constraint as well as a benefit. HCA also has an association with a local credit union, where employees can have their wages directly deposited and can open savings accounts with no required minimums. To supplement these benefits, HCA has provided classes on personal financial management. Finally, HCA has a monthly "bill raffle," where employees can put a bill in a raffle box and every month HCA picks out and pays one bill.[105]

The relationship between these aspects of a "quality" job and higher wages is a complex and interesting one. Almost universally, workers that I interviewed in the home care network expressed a desire for higher wages. This was an especially acute wish in Philadelphia, which does not have a higher minimum wage floor than the national minimum wage: "Granted, technically, we don't have a lot of titles behind our name, but we have a lot of job responsibilities, and I feel like the pay should be a little more for what we do."[106] By contrast in New York, the entry of ICS as a major contractor for CHCA has resulted in higher wages and longer hours. The union's involvement has also helped. Especially in Philadelphia, some workers described the low wages as grounds for seeking employment elsewhere, and for seeking more education that would lead to higher wages. But most of the workers articulated worker-ownership, job stability and longevity, access to full-time work, and the feeling of being part of a family as off-setting – at least to some extent – the low wages they receive. As Jerilyn Dressler described,

> There are people here who have had opportunities to take a higher wage from other organizations, and then they've come back to HCA because they said it's not worth it. They're miserable. They don't feel supported, and they don't like the work that they're getting. They recognize that a job is not just a dollar amount. It's the quality of work, and by extension the quality of life, that needs to be taken into account. People talk about how it feels like a family here. And it really does.[107]

Finally, employees commented extensively on the value of the vocational education they receive.[108] Recanell Carroll, for example, stated:

> The training was really good. I think everybody should go through that. It kind of helped you just to let you know what you're getting yourself into . . . The instructors was good . . . They explained things. And . . . they're hands-on. It was really acting like [this] was somebody's home that we was in. They was acting like they was sick, like they was really letting us know how people will be . . . The instructors was what

104 Pillot Interview; Smith Interview; Dressler Interview. 105 Dressler Interview.

106 Montgomery Interview. 107 Dressler Interview.

108 Pillot Interview; Calvo Interview; O'Bryant Interview; Carroll Interview; Whitehead Interview. Margarita Pillot commented that the other home care agency she had worked for had provided a week-long training for which she had had to pay, as distinguished from the month-long training provided by CHCA for which CHCA paid "everything," including a metro card.

> makes the training good. . . . [T]he stuff that they said, is the things that I see when I go to work.[109]

In addition to the quality of teaching, Stephanie Whitehead commented, "you meet different people in this field. And that's a beautiful thing. Of all nationalities and everything. That's the best part about it."[110] Training coordinator, Janie Dixon, stated, "[W]e want to give people the real deal. What's out there. We don't sugarcoat nothing . . . So we do have a day where once they complete training, we have a mock visit, where we give them a case situation . . . It's just like giving them their first case."[111] Deborah O'Bryant said, "Whatever you learn that day, before you leave that class that day, you're going to get a test."[112] Clara Calvo noted, "You feel like you are a professional."[113] In my own visit to HCA, I sat in on a portion of a training session. The instructor, Terrell Cannon, lived up to the reputation described by my interviewees: She was engaging, direct, deeply responsive, thoughtful, and (as one interviewee noted) "hilarious." Meanwhile, the ten or so trainees, a highly diverse group, were completely engaged. Each of them asked questions, raised new scenarios, shared concerns and doubts and demonstrated a high level of understanding. As a teacher myself, I felt that I would have achieved complete success to have a class session such as the one I witnessed.[114]

## REGULATORY CONTEXT

The development of this extraordinary network is certainly attributable to the leadership involved, and to timing, luck and hard work. But the purpose of this section is to show that the legal framework also played a significant role, especially in New York. In this particular case, for example, it is not an exaggeration to say that the survival or failure of the network – and the industry as a whole – depends on Medicaid and Medicare reimbursements. As Surpin described,

> As a managed care entity, [ICS is] paid by the state, we're regulated highly by the state . . . Medicaid is 50/50 state-federal money, but it's controlled by the state, in every state. Medicare is national and controlled by the federal government.[115]

All of the managers and many of the home care workers that I interviewed stated in one way or another that it is impossible to imagine participating in the long-term health care industry successfully without relying in large part on governmental funding. Again, from Surpin,

109 Carroll Interview. 110 Whitehead Interview. 111 Dixon Interview.
112 O'Bryant Interview. 113 Calvo Interview.
114 It is noteworthy too that CHCA spends several hours screening each applicant before even accepting her or him into the training program, and that something like 90 percent of applicants are referred by current CHCA employees. Spence Interview.
115 Surpin Interview.

> Any major health care provider would say, without Medicare and Medicaid, there's nothing. That's what's funny, I mean, health care and the defense industry. This is the funny thing about American capitalism, is we think of everything as privately held. Well, [the] two biggest industrial sectors in the country, which are huge, would not be around were it not for direct public financing and expenditure ... So there's a very different mix of public and private capital that makes the economy work ... We're never willing to talk about it that way.[116]

The reimbursement structure means that prices are effectively capped in the market in which ICS and CHCA operate. The market demand for quality care cannot be fully reflected in prices. As Surpin observed, the government's role as an ultimate buyer in this industry displaces the so-called invisible hand of the market.

As a result, these organizations have had to rely – perhaps unusually greatly – on law to ensure a pricing structure that will allow them to survive. In this regard, New York state has provided meaningful support, passing legislation that has set a wage floor that is livable (though by no means extravagant) for home health aides and also stabilizing Medicaid reimbursement rates at a level that rewards providers for quality care. The New York State Home Care Worker Parity Act sets a floor for base salary and overall wages and benefits that prevents home care service providers from cutting wages below a certain level as a way of competing in the market.[117]

New York is also in the vanguard of states that have passed minimum wage legislation at the state level that exceeds the federal minimum wage level. This law will further protect the salaries of home health aides as it is phased in over the next several years.[118] It is noteworthy, of course, that the broad network in which CHCA, ICS, and PHI operate has recognized the importance of these protections for home health workers' wages and benefits. All three organizations have worked alongside the SEIU and many others to push for the enactment of these laws. They have then leveraged the value of these laws by negotiating further standards for livable wages with managed care organizations and other major players in the industry.

Even before this very recent set of victories in protecting wages in New York, CHCA had long had in place a worker-ownership model, a structure for channeling more of its income to workers. As Sturgeon stated,

> [W]hen I first came on staff at PHI, and was on the board of Cooperative, ... it was 80 cents of every dollar that came in at Cooperative went directly to the workers. And we prided ourselves on that. This was before wage parity, right? It did much above what other providers in the city did. Today, because of the different mandates, that's more like 93 cents. And everyone is paying 93 cents, you see.[119]

116 *Id.* 117 N.Y. Public Health Law § 3614-c (Consol. 2012).

118 N.Y. Labor Law § 650 et seq. (Consol. 2015). The New York State Department of Labor website provides useful details about the yearly increases in the minimum wage until it reaches the $15 minimum under that law. *See* www.labor.ny.gov/workerprotection/laborstandards/workprot/minwage.shtm.

119 Sturgeon Interview.

Law was relevant in that earlier effort to provide livable wages as well: CHCA pushed for the passage of a worker-ownership law as a way of ensuring that patronage distributions and other aspects of the worker-owned cooperative structure would be recognized and not subject to inappropriate taxation or inapplicable regulations. For example, Surpin and others had discussions with the New York attorney general's office to ensure that they fell within an exception to the securities laws. They reprised some of the same kinds of questions when, in organizing ICS as a nonprofit corporation, they engaged in discussions with the Internal Revenue Service about the logic of allowing an organization such as this, which was regulated as an insurance company, to have 501(c)(3) status.

This suite of laws regulating wage setting and business organization has allowed CHCA, ICS, and PHI to establish a business model that is uniquely protective of workers' wages, benefits, management, and control of the business. Although it would have been possible to do virtually all these things without the benefit of this legal framework, the framework has helped by reducing costs along the way. It has also contributed to the robust nature of the business model. Surpin has noted, for example, that they could have structured a worker-owned cooperative by writing the bylaws to create such a business. But the New York law on worker cooperatives allowed them to register with the state as a cooperative, which protected the business from an unfriendly board of directors' decision to amend the bylaws.[120]

Finally, these laws have protected the network from price competition by providers who might be tempted to cut wages as a way of providing lower-cost services to managed care companies and other customers:

> [I]t really does help to level the playing field within our industry . . . as far as salaries and benefits. We're all pretty much working with the same set of regulations, and I think there's a certain advantage to that. We can focus on other aspects of the job, like training, like being more supportive, like figuring out how can we change the role of the home care worker and make that role more advanced? So that home care workers can do more. I think it really does afford us the opportunity to focus more on that, than simply fighting for better wages and better benefits.[121]

Aside from passing legislation to support its workers, New York has also invested in health care workers, and other low-income workers, by infusing large amounts of funding into workforce development. Several leaders within the network have commented that New York is uniquely progressive in this regard. By working with PHI and the local union, CHCA has received millions of dollars in grant funding to support the training of its employees. Indeed, New York's particular forms of investment have also given organizations like CHCA and ICS a seat at the table in determining appropriate standards for this area of training as well as the certificates necessary to work in this realm.

120 Surpin Interview. 121 Jensen Interview.

It is important to note, however, that there is still a great deal of room for improving even New York's approach to businesses such as CHCA. By far the greatest need for supportive regulation lies in the realm of financing. This is a problem wistfully articulated by Sturgeon:

> How do we think about having . . . access to a base of funding, you know, that allows someone like PHI to be thinking differently about innovation, because three-quarters of my time is thinking about how I'm covering the budget.[122]

Sturgeon continued:

> Is there a way in which we could look at equity financing, or capital, for these types of enterprises that are not within publicly funded systems like cities, or states, that are not . . . traditional banking relationships, but facilitate investment into these types of enterprises? One of the interesting things that we have going on right now [is that] there's a huge influx of for-profit, often private-pay focused platform economy home care agencies.[123]

Sturgeon's point is that this kind of equity capital does not seem available for a more traditional enterprise dedicated to quality care in this field. And it certainly does not seem available for one organized as a worker-owned cooperative, where the *workers* own the equity in the business.

Crowdsourcing, a new form of equity investment whereby members of the public use online platforms to invest in various enterprises, also seems only remotely available for businesses such as CHCA. In this regard, it is interesting to note that California has a new law that opens the door for this form of financing for worker-owned cooperatives.[124] New York does not. As Dawson noted, "the absence of equity capitalization has been a huge barrier for the cooperative movement." And it also takes "huge amounts of time" to assemble debt packages for cooperatives, because, like equity investors, traditional banks question the risk of investing in worker-owned businesses.[125]

A similar problem arises in the ability of CHCA and other worker-owned businesses to obtain public contracts. In its own public bidding process for contracts, New York City does not recognize CHCA as minority-owned, even though the vast majority of its workers are women of color. As Dawson stated,

> You literally have to have all the owners in person show up at the registration office where you register, so that they actually see the person . . . So we have 1,100 people . . . So physically it's impossible to meet the standard. So we've never been able to claim that status.[126]

Until now, this cluster of businesses has dealt with the problem of lack of access to traditional capital by externalizing some of CHCA's financing needs to PHI, which

122 Sturgeon Interview. 123 *Id.* 124 AB-816, California Assembly (2015).
125 Dawson Interview. 126 *Id.*

serves those needs by obtaining funding through foundation and government grants. While this form of collaboration has resulted in tremendous success for both organizations, it is also important to recognize that it is a result of legal and structural constraints. Most notably, the leadership of these businesses has not found a way legally to structure these businesses using a holding company model. Surpin ruminated that he might have chosen to structure CHCA as a subsidiary of PHI, but neither he nor their lawyers could find a way for a nonprofit to serve as a parent holding company for a for-profit, worker-owned cooperative. Among other consequences, Surpin noted the additional costs. Ultimately, Surpin and all the other leaders observed that there are many advantages to having completely separate organizations. But the point remains that they had no real options under the law but to organize in this fashion.

CHCA has recently attained certification as a B corporation, which should give it additional opportunities to receive foundation funding even though it is organized as a for-profit business. HCA in Philadelphia is also a B corporation. However, as I will discuss in more detail in Chapter 10, these possibilities are arguably quite narrow, and they are also anticipated more than they are currently available.

More broadly, these legal constraints on financing converge for a business such as CHCA because they are a very real limitation on the business's ability to grow. It is important to consider exactly which aspects of CHCA are financed through grants and what would happen to its business model if those grants became unavailable. The leadership of these organizations is having just this conversation.

HCA's experiences in Philadelphia have been shaped by some of the same considerations, such as the level of Medicare and Medicaid reimbursements. HCA would also likely benefit from state-level laws supporting crowdsourcing and other means of financing worker-owned cooperatives. Additionally, Pennsylvania has made important progress in recognizing the valuable work that home care workers do, as Tatia Jones-Cooper described:

> When I started here, the idea of home health aide from a legal perspective, or the state legislative perspective was not a respectable job . . .. And not only was the language in various regulations offensive, but the reimbursement spoke to that, and the lack of training spoke to that, and even not paying overtime in the beginning spoke to that . . . And then aides were very limited in terms of what they can do, and they were doing so much more. And so since then, the regulations have changed . . . to allow aides . . . to do more, like clean a wound, or assist with someone who needs to do a finger-stick to check their diabetes. [T]hose regulations have changed to allow aides more room to do those kinds of things, and of course get paid overtime . . . [A]nd to me that contributes to again the idea that this is a job. This is a profession.[127]

But HCA does not have the benefit of the New York laws that require a higher minimum wage and also wage parity for health care workers. As I have described,

[127] Jones-Cooper Interview.

this important difference in the legal framework within which HCA operates may have compelled HCA to develop a different business model than CHCA's. As a market competitor, partly as a result of the low threshold for licensure of home care agencies in Pennsylvania, HCA has had to deal with price competition from other home care agencies. This may well have forced HCA to keep its wages lower. It seems that HCA has reacted in part by successfully distinguishing itself as a quality care provider and diversifying its customer base to include a range of clients interested in quality care. On the employment side of the equation, this also may be one reason why HCA provides such excellent benefits as a means of offsetting low wages. Meanwhile, HCA has been an active participant in the network of home care providers, the Pennsylvania Home Care Association, which negotiates reimbursement rates statewide. Thus it appears that key differences in legal context may have contributed to different paths for the growth and development of HCA and CHCA.

## COOPERATIVE HOME CARE OF BOSTON

As I have described, for their first decade or more of existence, CHCA and PHI explored the possibility of replicating their model in cities across the United States. Thus, in 1994, shortly after supporting the start-up of HCA in Philadelphia, these organizations helped Cooperative Home Care of Boston (CHCB) to open.[128] In many respects, CHCB shared the mission, market approach, and strengths of both CHCA and HCA. It, too, was a worker-owned cooperative with a mission of providing quality jobs through quality care. It used the same innovative approach to training. It provided health and other employment benefits that, as the CEO of CHCB has said, were exceptional in the industry: "No organization gave benefits to their aides."[129] And as a workplace, it appears to have had the same warm, family atmosphere as its sister organizations. For the first five years of its existence, CHCB operated successfully, providing stable work to mostly low-income women of color.

By the late 1990s, however, CHCB was struggling with a number of difficulties, which PHI's leadership described in a report on CHCB's closure as both external and internal. Perhaps the most critical internal factor, as described in that report as well as by Maryann Colaizzi (CHCB's CEO in its final year), was the insufficiency of staffing at the management level which management at CHCB and in New York did not identify in time. This was partly a result of a change in chief executive officers in the final year or so, which no doubt contributed to difficulties in diagnosing needs and prescribing solutions.[130]

128 Inserra et al., *The Cooperative Home Care Associates* at 31–33; Steven L. Dawson, Peggy Powell & Rick Surpin, Closure: Cooperative Home Care of Boston (2000) (on file with author).

129 Interview with Maryann Colaizzi, Former President, Cooperative Home Care of Boston (May 11, 2017).

130 Colaizzi Interview; Dawson et al., Closure at 12–13.

Some of the factors identified by both Colaizzi and the report as contributing to CHCB's closing were factors that existed in Philadelphia and that HCA had successfully overcome. Two factors in particular stand out. First, Massachusetts experienced the same market challenge as Pennsylvania whereby state-level Medicare and Medicaid cuts forced home care agencies to provide home care in shorter visits, of 1.5 to 2.5 hours rather than the four- to eight-hour visits that were typical in New York. This required CHCB to string together several visits per day to make full-time jobs for its aides. Second, like HCA, CHCB had the challenge of needing to diversify its customer base as a result of its one or two major customers reducing their level of demand.[131]

However, CHCB also faced several additional challenges, which appeared to contribute to its inability ultimately to address these two issues successfully. One challenge was that CHCB could not find a way to manage the problem of finding efficient transportation for its aides to use in going to several different visits each day. In addition, even though Colaizzi had started to develop highly innovative means of diversifying CHCB's customer base, the company was unable to find enough workers to meet that new demand. The report on CHCB's closure describes this problem as follows: "Boston's full employment economy, the shrinkage of the 'post baby-boom' workforce, and changes in welfare policies combined to make recruitment of new aides exceptionally difficult."[132]

Thus, despite the help of PHI, and despite the network of customers and partners that CHCB had begun to develop, it simply was not able to survive the multiple and difficult changes in the home care market that occurred around the end of the millennium. As the report notes, CHCB was one of 26 home care agencies that closed in 1998 and 1999.[133] It appears that some combination of timing, unsupportive state-level regulations, unique infrastructural challenges (such as inefficiencies in public transportation), and a network that was not extensive enough in efficiently finding and training aides contributed to CHCB's ultimate closure. Colaizzi also noted the difference in support from state agencies, which in New York were more closely invested in the success of agencies such as CHCA than they appear to have been in Massachusetts.[134]

While CHCB's closure teaches important and difficult lessons about these market factors, it may be fitting to end with a more positive lesson from the efforts of Colaizzi and others after the decision to close CHCB had been made. Colaizzi recalled,

> I was like an obsessed mother trying to make it better for everybody. And I remember how emotionally exhausting it was, trying to find every aide a job. And . . . because home health aide work was getting less, but the CNA world still needed [people], we did a CNA training, all in the midst of everything going on.[135]

[131] Colaizzi Interview; DAWSON ET AL., CLOSURE at 14. [132] DAWSON ET AL., CLOSURE at 8. [133] *Id.*
[134] Colaizzi Interview. [135] *Id.*

In fact, it appears that seven of CHCB's approximately 50 aides at the time of closure were able to obtain certified nursing assistant certification as a result of that training, thereby building a career ladder for themselves even as the company was in crisis. Moreover, thanks to the support of partners in its network, CHCB arranged for home health aide jobs for all employees who wished to remain in such positions.[136] Finally, Colaizzi herself went on in her career to support a workforce development effort that became formalized as the Extended Care Career Ladder Initiative.[137] While the company itself did not survive, it contributed meaningfully to creating long-term work opportunities for low-income women in Boston.

[136] DAWSON ET AL., CLOSURE at 9. [137] Colaizzi Interview.

# 3

# Capitalist Sharing and Economic Stability

What explains the extraordinary success of this network of home care businesses? The answer is no doubt complex. It is not reducible to a single factor, nor is it the purpose of this book to provide a causal explanation.

But one important ingredient for its success appears to be the network's sharing of critical resources, including training, financing, and management expertise. For example, CHCA must provide a sufficiently high level of training for its home health aides to be able to make good on its business mission of providing quality care. But as Peggy Powell and others described, if CHCA had had to internalize the cost of research and development of a high-quality training program, the company would not have been able to provide it. Instead, CHCA has relied on PHI to provide this kind of research and development and to obtain the financing for it. It externalized this cost to the network. This sharing of costs and resources in turn allowed CHCA to continue to fulfill its dual mission of providing quality care to its clients and quality jobs to its employee-owners.

The sharing within this home care network appears to have produced businesses that are resilient and competitive – and that are able to provide stable, long-term income for their employees. Sharing seems to provide a foundation for survival, success, and economic stability in markets where many others have failed. This chapter continues the exploration of sharing as a basis for capitalist success by building on my description of the home care network in the Bronx and Philadelphia. First, this chapter analyzes the standard diagnoses for urban underdevelopment and the programmatic solutions that have been attempted in light of those diagnoses. Despite heavy investment, those solutions have not produced significant economic development and stability in the urban cores. Second, this chapter offers a theory of sharing that may well be a powerful alternative to those programs. My theory of sharing also helps to explain the home care network's success where others have failed. The chapter develops this theory on the basis of a pattern observable both in the home care network and in the other two case studies described in this book.

## DIAGNOSTIC CONVERGENCE

Depending on the observer's perspective, the story of inner-city underdevelopment boils down to one of two conclusions. For many economists and legal scholars who view the problem through a neoclassical economic lens, the story is one of market failure. According to this view, markets in the inner city are so highly imperfect that they are essentially failing. The reasons vary, but they do share some commonalities. For example, many observers have argued that the poverty and sheer "difference" – of race, national origin, and culture – of inner-city populations compared to those in the greater metropolitan region result in informational vacuums. Businesses and investors do not "know enough" about how things work in the inner city to feel comfortable doing business there. The complement to this argument about information asymmetry is that people living in the inner city can also be exploited because of their lack of knowledge about how markets outside their very local contexts function and prosper.[1]

Another claimed inner-city market failure is the sheer paucity in numbers of businesses willing to participate in inner-city markets. Big chains do not expect to do enough business to make it worth their while to site stores in inner cities. Banks do not expect enough investment to justify siting branches there. The disinvestment spirals from the effect of abandoned properties and violence. In short, these locations lack the large numbers of sellers and buyers that produce robust market competition, a problem that Harvard Business School professor Michael Porter has famously worked to counteract.[2] A complement to this argument is that the costs of entering and exiting such markets are prohibitively high.[3]

Meanwhile, thanks to the Occupy movement and Thomas Piketty, among others,[4] for a growing number of policymakers, the story of inner-city underdevelopment is a story about basic inequality of distribution. These observers focus on some of the same indicia of failure identified by neoclassical economists, such as the much higher costs of doing business in inner cities and the lack of access to capital. But they attribute these problems to an inequality in distribution of wealth and resources that is more basic than (and unexplained simply by) market failure. They also expand the picture by pointing to unequal educational opportunities, lower levels of income and inherited wealth, and lower skill levels as contributors to economic failure in the inner cities. The more forceful version of this argument is

[1] For discussions and critiques of these views, see WILLIAM H. SIMON, THE COMMUNITY ECONOMIC DEVELOPMENT MOVEMENT 42–48 (2001); David Dante Troutt, *Ghettoes Revisited: Antimarkets, Consumption, and Empowerment*, 66 BROOK. L. REV. 1–69 (2000).

[2] Michael E. Porter, *The Competitive Advantage of the Inner City*, HARV. BUS. REV., May-June 1995, 55–71, at 55.

[3] Michael S. Barr, *Credit Where It Counts: The Community Reinvestment Act and Its Critics*, 80 N.Y.U. L. REV. 513 (2005); Keith N. Hylton, *Banks and Inner Cities: Market and Regulatory Obstacles to Development Lending*, 17 YALE J. REG. 197 (2000).

[4] THOMAS PIKETTY, CAPITAL IN THE TWENTY-FIRST CENTURY (2014).

that the successes of the suburbs have been won at the expense of the inner cities, and indeed that the inequality between them serves the larger economic structure.[5]

Although these perspectives on inner-city underdevelopment are not explicit about it, one conclusion to take especially from the story about market failure is that the individuals located in the inner city are a big part of the problem. They lack information or they are exploitable. They are not worth the investment. They are too hard to understand and thus do not justify market entry. They desire products and services that are too unique to be worth providing. Often, this set of unspoken assumptions is backed by qualitative comparisons focusing on individual successes and failures. Samuel Walton, Oprah Winfrey, George Soros, and Steve Jobs all embody the ideal of individual achievement harnessed to our system of capitalism. Such achievement is possible whatever one's origins, and it is only a matter of trying enough. And as an economic matter, this set of assumptions in turn leads to models that focus on a relatively narrow subset of solutions for inner-city failures. Even for policymakers concerned about unequal distribution, the rhetoric of individual achievement is hard to overcome in attempts to redirect resources to the urban core.

This more limited focus on individual, or at least localized, failure dictates the proposed solutions. Two prominent examples of this diagnostic call and response are particularly relevant to this book. The first is Michael Porter's famous claim, first made in 1995, that the key to solving the problem of inner-city economic distress is to create incentives for profit-making companies to do business in the inner city. Porter's diagnosis was about market failure. Not surprisingly, therefore, his proposed solution has been to fix the problems that produce market failure, namely the disincentives for market entry, participation, and flourishing by established private businesses. Once businesses invest in the inner cities, Porter claims, they will create the jobs, innovation, and competition required to produce healthy and flourishing inner cities.[6]

A second example is the enormous attention and hope placed in entrepreneurship and small business development programs in the inner city. This is a solution propounded by policymakers and scholars across the political spectrum, whether they attribute the problem to one of market failure or structural inequality. If businesses outside the inner city are not willing to participate in these highly localized markets, the standard argument goes, then individuals living in the inner city can succeed by developing their own small businesses. By doing so, these individuals can create their own markets, and ultimately, their own wealth.[7]

5 Timothy Bates, *Political Economy of Urban Poverty in the 21st Century: How Progress and Public Policy Generate Rising Poverty*, *in* THE INNER CITY: URBAN POVERTY AND ECONOMIC DEVELOPMENT IN THE NEXT CENTURY 111 (Thomas D. Boston & Catherine L. Ross eds., 1997); ENRICO MORETTI, THE NEW GEOGRAPHY OF JOBS (2013).

6 Porter, *The Competitive Advantage of the Inner City* at 55–71.

7 For nuanced discussions of this argument, see Susan R. Jones & Roger A. Clay Jr., *What is Community Economic Development?*, *in* BUILDING HEALTHY COMMUNITIES: A GUIDE TO COMMUNITY ECONOMIC DEVELOPMENT FOR ADVOCATES, LAWYERS, AND POLICY MAKERS 3–5 (Susan R. Jones & Roger A. Clay, Jr.

Together, these two solutions have garnered vast public and private investments. Michael Porter's insights have produced a highly successful and respected nonprofit organization, the Initiative for a Competitive Inner City (ICIC), that has amassed significant resources from foundations in operationalizing his claims. Aside from conducting critical research on the conditions of urban underdevelopment, ICIC has for 15 years run the Inner City 100 program. The purpose of this program is to identify and support (including by means of financial investments) the 100 "fastest growing businesses in America's inner cities."[8] As influential as Porter's call to action has been, the investment in inner-city entrepreneurship has been even more massive. It is fair to say that since President Clinton's dismantling of the welfare system, small business development is the single most highly supported project for inner-city development.[9]

Thus, even though the two prevailing diagnoses of inner-city underdevelopment differ significantly, the prevailing responses to both diagnoses have largely converged. In their attempts to fix the problem, they have created programs and incentives for individuals living in inner cities to emulate those who are succeeding outside the inner cities.

Unfortunately, however, these programs have failed to systematically reduce poverty and achieve development in the urban cores. Take Michael Porter's proposed solution of increasing investment by large, established businesses in the inner city as a means of rapidly generating jobs, wealth, and development. It is clear that a meaningful number of businesses, encouraged by funders and policymakers, have taken his idea seriously enough to invest substantially in certain inner cities. This is worth lauding because, far from failing, these businesses have grown and flourished as a result of doing brisk business in places they thought could not support business. But taking the next step and considering the systemic effects of these investments, the story is more mixed. In some places, neighborhoods remain dilapidated, and the benefits from the increased business activity really do seem to flow straight out to the surrounding central city and beyond.[10]

But even in inner cities where Porter's ideas have produced the greatest successes, those successes by and large have accrued to the newer, middle class members of the communities rather than to the original residents who were the intended beneficiaries. The new jobs, wealth, and community development have largely flowed to

eds., 2009); Susan R. Jones, *Small Business and Community Economic Development: Transactional Lawyering for Social Change and Economic Justice*, 4 CLINICAL L. REV. 195 (1997).

8 *Inner City 100: Celebrating Urban Entrepreneurship at Its Best*, INITIATIVE FOR A COMPETITIVE INNER CITY (2014), www.icic.org/resources-for-inner-city-ceos/inner-city-100-programs.

9 *See* Scott L. Cummings, *Community Economic Development as Progressive Politics: Toward a Grassroots Movement for Economic Justice*, 54 STAN. L. REV. 399, 426–429 (2001).

10 *See* Richard C. Schragger, *Mobile Capital, Local Economic Regulation, and the Democratic City*, 123 HARV. L. REV. 482, 510 (2009). This issue is discussed extensively throughout a 1997 volume of essays responding to Porter's thesis. THE INNER CITY: URBAN POVERTY AND ECONOMIC DEVELOPMENT IN THE NEXT CENTURY (Thomas D. Boston & Catherine L. Ross eds., 1997).

those who were not previously impoverished or unemployed.[11] This, then, is the story of gentrification that has accompanied reports of some of Porter's successes. It is a story in which an anchor institution or a small group of powerful private businesses reap the benefits of new markets (for such things as health services and new technology) without meaningful incentives to share this surplus wealth with the original residents. Without the imperative that jobs first go to low-income local residents, neighborhoods revitalize for the benefit of new residents who can afford the higher rents that push out the original residents. In these contexts, markets are "fixed" by continuing to exclude those participants who were originally excluded.[12] After two decades, it is right to question the original claim that this method of lifting inner cities on a more competitive tide will eventually raise all boats.

When it comes to describing the successes of the many programs that support inner-city entrepreneurship and small business development, the results are equally thorny. Over the last two decades, vast amounts of public and private investments have been poured into small business development. One among many examples is the 2014 federal budget, which allocated $16 billion in Small Business Administration loan guarantees to small businesses and $200 million in matching funds for investment in "innovative" small businesses, along with various tax cuts and credits for small businesses.[13] Meanwhile, a wide range of private foundations provides funding for entrepreneurship.[14]

Despite important examples of social entrepreneurship within the inner city and sometimes by individuals below the poverty line, however, these programs have not succeeded in systematically transitioning failing markets into successful ones. The survival rates, profit levels, and other measures of success of these small businesses are distressingly low. As Scott Shane has described in detail, the success rates of small businesses in general are much lower than larger, more established businesses.[15] But for lower-income and minority-owned enterprises, the numbers are

11 Consider, for example, the businesses included in the Inner City 100. While they have grown and benefited from their inner-city locations, only some of these businesses employ inner-city residents and even these typically do so at low rates of pay. *Inner City 100: Celebrating Urban Entrepreneurship at Its Best*, Initiative for a Competitive Inner City (2014), www.icic.org/resources-for-inner-city-ceos/inner-city-100-programs; *Inner City 100: 15 Years of Urban Entrepreneurship at Its Best*, Initiative for a Competitive Inner City (2014), www.icic.org/ee_uploads/pdf/Inner_City_100_Flyer.pdf.

12 *See* Scott L. Cummings, *Between Markets and Politics: A Response to Porter's Competitive Advantage Thesis*, 82 Or. L. Rev. 901 (2003); Schragger, *Mobile Capital*.

13 *Supporting Small Business and Creating Jobs*, Office of Mgmt. & Budget (2014), https://web.archive.org/web/20140419024558/www.whitehouse.gov/omb/factsheet/supporting-small-businesses-and-creating-jobs.

14 *See, e.g.*, *About the Pearson Foundation*, Pearson Found. (2014), https://web.archive.org/web/20140208064454/www.pearsonfoundation.org/about-us.html; *Entrepreneurship*, Ewing Marion Kauffman Found., www.kauffman.org/Section.aspx?id=Entrepreneurship; *Entrepreneurship Education*, Coleman Found., www.colemanfoundation.org/what_we_fund/entrepreneurship.

15 Scott A. Shane, The Illusions of Entrepreneurship: The Costly Myths That Entrepreneurs, Investors, and Policy Makers Live By 147 (2008).

even starker. Using a broad dataset, James Barth, Glenn Yago, and Betsy Zeidman found "a striking imbalance in distribution" of "firms, receipts, employees, and payroll" among small businesses depending on the gender, race, ethnicity, and income level of those businesses' owners.[16] In short, small businesses organized to take advantage of the current legal infrastructure produce few jobs, lower quality jobs, and limited economic growth.[17]

Overall, it simply has not been the case that governmental and private investments have lifted marginalized entrepreneurs to the point where they have produced large numbers of jobs and contributed meaningfully to economic development. Viewed as a story about individual poverty alleviation, the statistics are even more striking. They depict a system in which governmental and private agencies assist low-income individuals in investing vast amounts of time, money, credit, and other resources to develop small businesses with no guarantees of success for the business or a stable source of income at the end of the process. In fact, the vast majority of the time, the resulting businesses do fail, and their proprietors are left with fewer resources than they had when they began their start-up activities.[18]

Meanwhile, as is the case with Porter's programs, regularly, the best innovations of social entrepreneurs are captured by individuals and groups above the poverty line and often outside the urban core. This effect is evident in places like Boston, where the "innovation economy" reaps the advantages of programs supporting entrepreneurs by producing a market that privileges highly educated workers with limited space for workers attempting to transition from low-skilled or manufacturing jobs.[19]

## DIAGNOSTIC DIVERGENCE

In this book, I diverge in large measure from that subset of diagnoses that focuses on market failure in the urban core. More importantly, I diverge from the belief that the two solutions described above can solve the problem of inner-city underdevelopment. It is true that the puzzle of inner-city underdevelopment is an *economic* puzzle – one that cannot be solved without a better understanding of how markets in the urban core can best succeed. The problem in some urban cores, however, is not that these markets are failing but rather that the laws and programs intended to support such markets are failing them. To explain more fully the basis for my

[16] James R. Barth et al., *Stumbling Blocks to Entrepreneurship in Low- and Moderate-Income Communities*, *in* ENTREPRENEURSHIP IN EMERGING DOMESTIC MARKETS 69, 73 (Glenn Yago et al. eds., 2008).

[17] SHANE, ILLUSIONS OF ENTREPRENEURSHIP at 148–158.

[18] Rashmi Dyal-Chand & James V. Rowan, *Developing Capabilities, Not Entrepreneurs: A New Theory for Community Economic Development*, 42 HOFSTRA L. REV. 839, 866 (2014).

[19] Porter acknowledges the reality that such an economy provides only low-wage jobs and opportunities for such workers. Porter, *The Competitive Advantage of the Inner City*. *See also* Cummings, *Between Markets and Politics: A Response to Porter's Competitive Advantage Thesis* at 901–926.

diagnostic divergence, I will begin by defining programmatic success (and more broadly, successful urban-core development). As will become apparent, my definition of success is both more specific and more focused on economic stability than most current approaches. Then, in light of this more specific definition of success, I will identify a different approach to business and market development that appears better able to achieve economic development and stability in the urban core.

## *What Is Success in Urban-Core Development?*

My beginning point in describing successful urban-core development is much the same as the starting point of many others involved in local development. Successful urban-core development should prioritize two goals: poverty alleviation and robust development of – and participation in – local markets for especially housing, credit, and locally desirable products and services. Indeed, these are the twin goals of the community economic development movement, which has sought over the last several decades to correct and improve inner-city markets.[20] These are also the articulated goals of Michael Porter, the Small Business Administration (SBA), and other governmental and nongovernmental agencies and actors that are deeply involved in American urban development.[21]

Of these two goals, however, I prioritize poverty alleviation. This may well be the most significant point of divergence between my definition of successful economic development and the prevailing views. To make this point, let me return to the predominant solutions developed for inner-city workers. As I have discussed, many programs focus on entrepreneurship, either by successful businesses moving into the urban core (Porter's focus) or by low-income residents starting their own businesses (as emphasized by the SBA and many others).

Turning first to the assumptions underlying small business development programs, the expectation seems to be that some number of businesses founded by inner-city entrepreneurs will be high-growth engines of innovation that will link into the regional and even national economies by producing products or services in high demand. Though there may be very few such successful innovation enterprises, they will nevertheless reduce poverty by providing jobs for low-income people living in the neighborhoods where the businesses are located. Moreover, according to this reasoning, the infusion of jobs from high-growth enterprises will produce a virtuous cycle of investment in the community, including better infrastructure, such as schools and public transportation,

[20] Dyal-Chand & Rowan, *Developing Capabilities, Not Entrepreneurs* at 851, 894; SIMON, THE COMMUNITY ECONOMIC DEVELOPMENT MOVEMENT; Cummings, *Community Economic Development as Progressive Politics* at 400–402.

[21] Dyal-Chand & Rowan, *Developing Capabilities, Not Entrepreneurs* at 848, 849; Kenneth L. Karst, *Equal Citizenship at Ground Level: The Consequences of Nonstate Action*, 54 DUKE L.J. 1591, 1617 (2005); Cummings, *Community Economic Development as Progressive Politics* at 409–421.

and better housing.[22] The hope even appears to be that the jobs produced by these businesses will be stable enough to provide the accessories, such as health care, that middle-class employees typically take for granted.[23] In short, the focus of these programs is in discovering and supporting innovative outliers that can serve as engines of growth. Meanwhile, Porter's project of inner-city investment seeks to bring innovation in from the outside by finding successful companies willing to do business in the urban core.[24]

While these programmatic efforts clearly are committed to poverty alleviation, their methods prioritize the correction and growth of local markets by supporting entrepreneurship on the inside and from the outside. By contrast, I prioritize poverty alleviation over market growth and arguably even over market development. I measure programmatic success by the extent to which a given approach directly alleviates, or indirectly prioritizes the alleviation of, the poverty of low-income residents in the urban core.

Moreover, in adopting outcomes or metrics for measuring poverty alleviation, I adopt a broader framework than one focused just on increasing individual income. While this book examines programs that seek to develop income-generating opportunities in the urban core, my measures for success include a broad range of outcomes of the kind that are typically associated with theoretical frameworks for poverty alleviation such as human flourishing and human capabilities.[25] In addition to increased income, the following outcomes most interest me: longevity of employment; increased access to better shelter, education, and credit; and reduction in racial and gender disparities. Again, these are all important to programs associated with community economic development, but it is not clear that they are a programmatic priority.

To be clear, my focus is still on poverty alleviation *through* market development. Although welfare and other parts of the social safety net are not only important, but also related, to market development, my focus is on *capitalist* programs, those that use the market to produce wealth. But because I prioritize poverty alleviation, my interest is not in entrepreneurship for the sake of entrepreneurship. Nor am I interested in pure innovation or in the proliferation of businesses for the sake of more businesses. Rather, my focus is on business development that leads more

[22] *See* Tim Lohrentz, *Inclusive Business Practices, in* BUILDING HEALTHY COMMUNITIES: A GUIDE TO COMMUNITY ECONOMIC DEVELOPMENT FOR ADVOCATES, LAWYERS, AND POLICYMAKERS 357, 373 (Roger A. Clay, Jr. & Susan R. Jones eds., 2009) (discussing the impact of small businesses beyond their economic importance, extending to their importance in cultural, political, and social realms).

[23] *But see* SHANE, ILLUSIONS OF ENTREPRENEURSHIP at 156. Currently, as Scott Shane and others point out, health insurance is less available for employees of small businesses than of larger ones. *Id.* at 65; Richard J. Pierce, Jr., *Small Is Not Beautiful: The Case against Special Regulatory Treatment of Small Firms*, 50 ADMIN. L. REV. 537, 560–561 (1998).

[24] Porter, *The Competitive Advantage of the Inner City* at 55, 56, 61.

[25] *See* AMARTYA SEN, THE IDEA OF JUSTICE 253 (2009); Martha Nussbaum, *Human Rights and Human Capabilities*, 20 HARV. HUM. RTS. J. 21 app. A at 23–24 (2007); Amartya Sen, *Conceptualizing and Measuring Poverty, in* POVERTY AND INEQUALITY 30, 32–33 (David B. Grusky & Ravi Kanbur eds., 2006).

directly to poverty alleviation. This difference in focus can be described as an emphasis on economic stability. In the markets and business networks I describe, longevity of employment is as important as increased income. Similarly, increased access to housing, education, and credit is an indicator of greater economic stability. So too are reductions in racial and gender disparities. These are all well-known measures of poverty alleviation that are embraced by the United Nations and other international bodies.[26] They are also measures indicative of individual and, I argue, *market* stability.

While individual indicia of economic stability are important outcomes for my purposes, I am also interested in outcomes that indicate the economic stability of businesses that employ inner-city residents. Thus, the business-related outcomes that interest me include business viability, productivity, and profitability. In addition, and perhaps most importantly, I am interested in tracking the mechanisms used by such businesses to ensure that business income is used to prioritize stable employment for employees.

One way to describe my divergent perspective on successful urban-core development is that I begin with a foundational assumption that success is not possible without poverty alleviation in the urban core. If goals such as innovation, entrepreneurship, and market growth are prioritized over poverty alleviation, it becomes all too easy for low-income residents in such areas to remain marginalized and to sink into greater poverty. As programmatic efforts over the last few decades have shown, the de-prioritization of these individuals leads to greater economic instability and inequality in the urban core. Thus, my definition of successful development and the outcomes I use to measure it prioritize poverty alleviation and economic stability.

## *A Diagnostic Reassessment*

Inner-city markets are clearly different in important ways. I fully acknowledge the historical, sociological, educational, and other contributors to urban distress and underdevelopment. Indeed, these factors are critical to developing the right design principles to move inner cities beyond their current state of stagnation. In detailing the extent of difference and the relevance of inequality, I align myself more with those who attribute the problem of underdevelopment to structural inequality.

However, neither of the prevailing diagnoses of inner-city underdevelopment adequately considers the possibility that these differences could be the basis of economic strength and success. Rather than asking why inner-city economies are failing, I ask why a system of laws, institutions, and relationships that appears to work so well in the surrounding state and local economy fails to work in these inner-city microcosms. Could the problem be with the way current policies address inner-city

26 For examples of their uptake by international bodies, see *Human Dev. Rep., Composite Indices – HDI and Beyond*, U.N. Dev. Programme, http://hdr.undp.org/en/2016-report; *Int'l Human Dev. Indicators, United States*, U.N. Dev. Programme, http://hdr.undp.org/en/countries/profiles/USA.html.

difference rather than with inner-city difference itself? That is the central puzzle that this book examines. My diagnostic conclusion – that the problem is indeed with current policies as much as or more than with inner-city economies – leads me to urge policymakers to move beyond asking inner-city businesses to be more like their successful counterparts.

In brief, this book argues that a critical mass of capitalist initiatives in American urban cores points toward a markedly different diagnosis for inner-city underdevelopment. These examples demonstrate that the problem is not with the individuals living and working in the inner cities. These individuals are not merely exploited or clueless. Rather, in the examples I present, they are using their own systems of information gathering and sharing to develop robust markets that provide desirable products and services to their residents.

But what is so noteworthy about these markets is that they are succeeding for different reasons than what Michael Porter, the SBA, and others claim – and they are making use of different institutions and support than what the SBA, ICIC, and others are providing. CHCA and its affiliates have been described as extraordinary in their success. ShoreBank, which is the subject of my second case study, has also been lauded as being the most successful community bank to have existed. But these two examples are not stories about market failure overcome by the traditional tools of American capitalism. Though they may have started from lack of information or access, these are not examples in which markets and market actors overcame market imperfections by taking advantage of the same legal and institutional structures that serve the surrounding cities and suburbs so well. Instead, in the Bronx and in my other examples, these actors developed a very different set of market practices that led to their success.

Unfortunately, however, there is a dearth of information about those market practices, and in particular about the common features of these two networks and others like them that are developing and even thriving in urban cores across the country. Partly because these networks have not followed many of the usual rules of capitalist behavior in the United States, it appears difficult to understand quite why they have done so well. For example, although CHCA and HCA are organized as for-profit businesses, they are worker-owned. They have not obtained ample financing from sources that usually value the traditional corporate form of organization or the associated corporate practices. Most surprisingly, they are deeply committed to hiring a particular – local – population of inner-city residents rather than hiring cheap labor wherever it can be found. This is not a form of capitalism with which many contemporary Americans are familiar.

Yet if we closely examine poverty and employment indicia within networks such as the home care networks in the Bronx and Philadelphia, it becomes evident that capitalist "outliers" such as CHCA and HCA are succeeding far more in improving the lives, well-beings, communities, and markets where they operate than the average entrepreneurship or business development program designed to mimic larger American businesses. Meanwhile, the workers within these networks have access to stable income and employment, and to a range of accompanying benefits. In short, the approach of the Bronx and Philadelphia networks appears to be fulfilling the very goals identified and shared by Porter, the SBA, the community economic development movement, and many others.

## A DIFFERENT KIND OF CAPITALISM

The investment in American urban cores to date has failed to recognize that a markedly different kind of capitalism is developing in some urban cores. Because policymakers have not noticed this, they have failed to provide a legal and institutional infrastructure to support it. In this section, I will describe the attributes of this different form of capitalism.

If we return to the example of the home care workers using a lens that is sensitive to a broader range of market practices, we can see the market quite differently from the way Michael Porter views it. From his perspective, viewing such an example through a lens primed on the problem of market failure, Porter places great value on the industry "clusters" that draw strength from an environment in which multiple businesses are racing to develop the same types of products or services. Porter acknowledges the advantages to such businesses in finding skilled employees and developing specialized knowledge by participating in industry clusters. But his interest is in creating the proper incentives and support for each of the individual businesses involved in this market to compete in such a way as to maximize its own use of the information, research, development, and labor skills that spin out of that cluster of activity.[27] Thus, looking at the home care market in the Bronx, Porter might emphasize the positive synergy that flows from the competition among CHCA and its competitors. He might argue that the race to provide higher-quality services should benefit consumers while also increasing demand and further improving the ultimate services and products sold. Porter's approach is also consistent with the approach of "business incubators," which are premised on the idea that simply locating industry clusters in one place creates a synergy of competitive activity.

But if we keep in mind a broader range of possible or acceptable market practices, what leaps out about the home care example is its ability to maximize the value of that industry cluster for the benefit of the long-term (often poor) residents of the area. The success of this particular industry cluster flows not from intense competition among the individual businesses involved, but rather from their *collaboration*. The success of the individual businesses is analogous not so much to the race among professional baseball teams for the best players, but rather to the sharing of

[27] Michael E. Porter, *Clusters and the New Economics of Competition*, Harv. Bus. Rev., Nov. 1998, at 77, 77–90.

resources among professional football teams to ensure that each franchise can field a viable team. The businesses in the network cut the costs of doing business by sharing resources such as training, financing, and strategic planning so that each can have a better chance of success. The fact that they do so alongside a commitment to hiring local and low-income residents allows these successes to accrue to those in the urban core most in need of the public and private investment in that network. This approach has been especially efficacious in a market where competition has traditionally involved cutting wages in order to remain competitive in pricing of services.

The market behavior of the home care network is nothing less than a different form of capitalism. As I will discuss, this different form is more similar to the form of "coordinated" capitalism practiced in countries like Germany, France, and Japan than the "liberal" form of capitalism practiced for the most part in the United States.[28] Let me turn now to the task of describing the attributes of this different form of capitalism. Briefly outlined, it has several features that are qualitatively different from the "liberal" or "competitive" market form that predominates in the United States:

1) Businesses involved in a discrete market, often defined geographically, operate in a coordinated or collective manner.
2) One or more institutions serves as an intermediary among those businesses to coordinate their activities or to act on their collective behalf. These institutions also serve as facilitators of democratic participation by workers in the network.
3) The coordination of business activities lowers the costs of doing business, the risks associated with market participation, or both.
4) The reasons for collaboration among the market participants include objectives other than the so-called bottom line. These may include priorities such as local hiring, neighborhood revitalization, or some other form of community investment.
5) The stakeholders involved in the individual businesses are predominantly insiders, defined as a matter of geographic location, and often also social or ethnic community. The financing for the individual businesses is dominated by local sources of financing.
6) The businesses in these collaborative networks typically operate within a niche market or industry that is conducive to collaborative behavior.

## *Coordinated Activities of Businesses*

One of the most critical features of this different form of capitalism concerns the interaction of individual businesses within the system. Rather than competing with each other in a race for employees, market information, and product development,

[28] Peter Hall & David Soskice, *Introduction*, *in* VARIETIES OF CAPITALISM: THE INSTITUTIONAL FOUNDATIONS OF COMPARATIVE ADVANTAGE (Peter A. Hall & David Soskice eds., 2001).

these businesses collaborate to acquire at least some of these resources and achieve business goals. Thus, in the Bronx network, the businesses collaborate to provide training to home health workers. PHI is the driver of the collaboration on education. It has developed a highly sophisticated "learning lab" to create, pilot, and disseminate a curriculum that is both efficient and effective. PHI has also worked with the state of New York, the local union, and local community colleges to set standards for the necessary levels of training and to disseminate parts of the curriculum. HCA in Philadelphia also relies meaningfully on PHI's research and development of best practices in education.

In addition, the Bronx businesses participate in a more extensive network for the coordination of wage setting, wage parity, and even work conditions. This network includes, most prominently, the local chapter of the Service Employees Educational Union. It has also included a range of advocacy groups pushing for a higher minimum wage and also wage parity for health care workers in New York. This level of coordination on issues of wages and workers' rights is astonishing in contemporary America. The leaders of these organizations have described their work on behalf of health care workers as a sectoral approach intended to change work conditions in an entire industry. For my purposes, what stands out about this approach is the level of coordination required among a broad range of actors in order to successfully implement it. Of course, both CHCA and HCA have focused extensively on developing the worker-owned cooperative as a significant piece of their overall model. This approach, too, has resulted in participation in a broad network of organizations dedicated to supporting worker-owned companies in the United States.

The network also coordinates extensively on financing, particularly of its training. By obtaining grants from foundations and governmental agencies, PHI has been able to develop a sophisticated educational curriculum, buttressed by a consulting operation and learning lab. In doing so, it has provided extensive support to both CHCA and HCA, and to many others in the home health care industry. Here, a more specific innovation has occurred that is also evident in the Austin case study described in Chapter 6. The network has found a way to use funding that is typically available for nonprofit organizations for the purpose of financing its training program.

Finally, the Bronx and Philadelphia networks have benefited from the shared expertise of their extremely thoughtful and committed leaders. This expertise has been shared formally through cross-board relationships, and informally through personal relationships. CHCA and HCA have added to their networks in the area of management by joining and participating robustly in the growing network of B corporations.

We will see evidence of coordination among businesses in the other case studies as well. In the case of the South Shore networks discussed in Chapter 4, the individual businesses shared labor as well as information about the real estate market and available financing. And in the Austin example discussed in Chapter 6, they share financing, back-office support, and cross-business leadership. This level of coordination far exceeds what we might see among competitors in a market outside of these enclaves. In contrast to the collaboration over financing, training or market data in these networks, a firm operating in the liberal market economy would internalize the cost of obtaining such services. It would do so by researching appropriate providers of financing or other services and then entering into arm's-length contracts with those providers.[29]

Although this means of doing business is markedly different from the norm that we see in the United States, a neoclassical economist might argue that such networks are really just giant firms or franchise operations. Such an argument would attempt to slot sharing networks into Ronald Coase's famous theory of the firm, in which he discussed the conditions under which individuals organize themselves into firms (or corporations) and take orders from managers higher up in the hierarchical structure within firms.[30] Coase argued that firms are formed when they are the most efficient means of achieving economic gain, namely when the costs of doing business by means of a firm are lower than the costs to individuals of going it alone in the marketplace in reliance on pricing signals. By sharing critical business functions, a Coasian economist might argue, businesses in sharing networks are essentially joining together as a larger firm. Or even if they are not united as a firm or as a franchise operation, they function as an extension of Coase's theory by means of a wide-ranging network of contracting relationships that achieve vertical integration.[31]

Such an economic analysis, however, would have to ignore several truths about the sharing networks described here. For example, some of these networks rely very little on formal contracting arrangements. In contrast to large corporations or franchises, the businesses within the networks also retain their own independent ownership of physical and intangible assets. Moreover, in some cases they manage to balance sharing of certain resources with robust competition within the network for market opportunities. Sometimes they do this by developing subniches within the market. At other times, they compete actively for the same customers, but still manage to share resources particularly that channel benefits to their workers. These are situations in which individual businesses share resources outside a firm structure. Indeed, they could be described as horizontal rather than hierarchical networks of resource management.

For this book's purposes, however, it matters very little whether such networks could fit within a Coasian framework. Indeed, I acknowledge that these sharing

29 Hall & Soskice, *Introduction*, VARIETIES OF CAPITALISM.

30 Ronald H. Coase, *The Nature of the Firm*, 4 ECONOMICA 386 (1937). Harold Demsetz's justifications for the institution of private property ownership are often used alongside Coase's theory of the firm to explain the behavior of businesses. Harold Demsetz, *Toward a Theory of Property Rights*, 57 AM. ECON. REV. 347 (1967).

31 *See* Benjamin Klein et al., *Vertical Integration, Appropriable Rents, and the Competitive Contracting Process*, 21 J.L. & ECON. 297 (1978).

networks and the many others that are out there fall on a spectrum, and that some networks look very much like franchises and other vertically integrated business models. Others may well fit patterns of "interfirm collaboration" observed by Gilson, Sabel, and Scott in their discussion of "rapidly innovating industries."[32] What matters for my purposes is that the networks I describe are coordinating their activities to achieve efficiency and also, as the remaining factors of collaborative capitalism will demonstrate, to achieve other important goals. The most important commonality tying my examples together is the sharing of resources for the ultimate purpose of economic stability and poverty alleviation.

### *Institutional Intermediaries That a Serve Coordinating Function*

Another key feature that leaps out across the diverse examples of coordinated capitalism in US urban cores is that the individual businesses in these coordinated networks make use of one or more intermediary organizations and institutions to accomplish key coordinating functions. In the case of the home care network, PHI is a key intermediary. It has been the source of training, research and development, consulting, and financing for the two worker-owned cooperatives in the network. It has also provided extensive consulting, coaching, and training for managers at ICS. It is worth noting in this regard that even PHI's "outward-facing" work has contributed meaningfully to the development of this particular business network. By contributing its lobbying expertise and its work on policy development in New York and well beyond that state, PHI has worked to develop, legitimize, and strengthen the role of direct care workers in the market for home health care services.

In addition, the Bronx network has benefited from several other prominent intermediaries. The first is Independence Care System, which has provided a critical customer base supporting CHCA's considerable expansion in the last decade. By developing a business within the network that created a demand for *quality* care, rather than for home care that was less expensive, the leaders in the Bronx network found a way to increase market demand for just the niche in which they are operating. Another important intermediary in this network is the local chapter of the Service Employees International Union. The union has been a critical partner on issues relating to health care workers' wages and benefits. The union's role as an intermediary has been particularly interesting because it has been outward-facing, helping to disseminate the best practices developed by CHCA throughout the home health care industry.

Consistent with the much broader literature on institutional economics, I also use the term "institutions" to refer to "rules, formal or informal, that actors generally

[32] Ronald J. Gilson, Charles F. Sabel & Robert E. Scott, *Contracting for Innovation: Vertical Disintegration and Interfirm Collaboration*, 109 Colum. L. Rev. 431 (2009).

follow, whether for normative, cognitive, or material reasons." Thus in some of my examples, the institutional "glue" keeping these networks together includes commonly shared rules or values in addition to, and indeed propounded and enforced by, the organizations "whose rules ... contribute to the institutions" of a particular economy.[33] Most prominently, in the home care network, the ethic of worker-ownership is an important network-wide institution. It is a core principle guiding the mission and focus of the entire network. It is a basis for a great deal of strategic – and even day-to-day – decision-making. Thus both CHCA and HCA function in meaningful ways as part of the organizational glue for this network, because they are the embodiments of the worker ownership philosophy.

We will see examples of institutional intermediaries at work in the other case studies as well. In the case of the Austin network, a large nonprofit organization serves as the parent holding company, providing essential services such as strategic planning, management, and new business development services to the network as a whole. In the Austin example, the social entrepreneurship mission also serves as a form of institutional glue. In the South Shore networks, a community bank acted as the institutional glue for a large network of real estate rehabbing businesses and also for a smaller network of Dunkin' Donuts franchisees.

These intermediaries serve different functions in the different networks. One of the subtheories in this book is that the institutional intermediaries may well be the most critical component of collaborative capitalist success in the American context. This is one of the reasons that I have chosen case studies that feature several different types of institutional intermediaries.

It is important to note in these examples how vital the services provided by these intermediaries are to the success and even survival of the individual businesses in the network. These are not the average trade associations, which in the US provide important services, but often services that increase the success or efficiency of individual members at the margins. Rather, in these microcosms of collaborative capitalism, the intermediary organizations perform key functions that outside of these systems are performed *within* individual businesses. Said another way, the costs of these functions are shared among the network of businesses rather than borne by each individual business.

Finally, one commonality among the intermediary organizations and institutions in these three case studies is that the intermediaries all facilitate a greater and more democratic level of participation by the workers in the businesses that employ them and in the networks more broadly. As I will discuss, this is one critical distinction between the intermediaries in my case studies and the intermediaries in sharing economy giants such as Airbnb and Uber. The most obvious manifestation of this role is the ethic of worker ownership in the Bronx and Philadelphia network. So too is the focus on quality training and worker wage increases and parity. The South

[33] Hall & Soskice, *Introduction*, VARIETIES OF CAPITALISM at 9.

Shore example revolves around small business ownership by the rehabbers in that network. But here too, we see the Bank facilitating relationships of mutual support and community investment by those businesses. And in the Austin network, the ethic of social entrepreneurship encompasses support for the children of the workers and for the workers themselves.

### *Coordination Lowers Costs and/or Risks*

As is evident from my description of the functions served by intermediaries, one critical feature of the coordination in these markets is that it occurs with respect to business needs and functions that are critical to the success of the individual member-businesses. The business activities that are externalized to the network as a whole are often critical to the very survival of those businesses.

Think again of the role of training in the home care network. Without effective training for workers and their supervisors, this network could not have developed its market brand of high quality care. As Peggy Powell remarked, it is questionable whether the Bronx network could have survived without being able to externalize the research and development of its training curriculum to PHI. Reflecting on my conversations with members of that network in both New York and Philadelphia, no message was clearer than the importance of high quality training.

The same can be said for the other case studies. In the case of the South Shore network, there is no better evidence of the importance of financing from the ShoreBank than the fallout that occurred from its 2010 closing. In the case of the Austin network, the nonprofit intermediary in the network has provided multiple and critical supports, including serving as an initial and stable customer base, providing back-office support, and maintaining long-term and deeply committed management.

### *Multiple (and Localized) Bottom Lines*

Strikingly, businesses involved in these examples of coordinated capitalism have priorities in addition to – and seemingly coequal with – the so-called bottom line of profit-making. In the case of the home care network, there is a clear imperative to hire from within the urban core and to ensure a living wage and healthy working conditions. Moreover, as the mission "quality care through quality jobs" makes evident, there is also a broader commitment within the network to serve disabled and elderly low-income individuals in urban-core neighborhoods who are in need of home care. Numerous interviewees emphasized that they are providing a level of service that is exceptional and would otherwise be unavailable to those whom they serve. Both parts of the network's mission are clearly important.

This feature of collaborative capitalism is also strongly apparent in the other case studies. ShoreBank is famously described as having a triple bottom line of being a profitable bank, revitalizing the neighborhoods where it located its branches, and promoting environmental sustainability. In addition, some of the rehabbing businesses that borrowed from the Bank appeared to share the mission of investing in those neighborhoods. And of course, the Austin network's self-description as a "social enterprise" cluster speaks to its commitment to multiple bottom lines. As will be evident in my analysis, these additional bottom lines are typically local in their focus, and they are regularly enforced and enhanced by the intermediary organizations that serve the coordinating function for business networks.

These additional priorities also spawn a set of values that appears quite distinct from those that are associated with businesses such as Wal-Mart or General Motors. For example, there is an explicit emphasis on the sharing of resources and wealth that *replaces* the valorization of private and individualized ownership. The very business plans of some of these networks deprioritize individualized ownership, competition, or productivity at the expense of protecting labor interests. Indeed, it is ironic to note that these values are sometimes derided as not "American" because they do not support the competitive drive for success that is associated with our understanding of capitalism, even though such values were everywhere evident in pre-industrial, pre-corporate America when businesses did not have the option to be organized in such a way as to limit individual risk and liability.

## *Local Stakeholders, Local Financing*

Regularly, the multiple bottom lines of the networks discussed in this book are expressed in the form of business organization. The most obvious example is that of the two worker-owned cooperatives in the home care network. Instead of having shareholders in the business comprised of far-flung investors who have no connection to the business other than profit making, these two businesses are employee owned. As is unmistakably clear, the value of owning the company is far greater than financial. It is about having a voice in the company's future.

As the other case studies show, even where the businesses are not organized as worker-owned cooperatives, they seem more often to be locally owned or largely so. Often, in their start-up phase, the businesses develop products and services that are targeted to a more localized population, though the target customers regularly expand over time. In addition, both by means of their intermediary organizations and localized priorities and more broadly by a generally higher level of community engagement among the managers and employees of the businesses, they involve more stakeholders from the community. In short, these collaborative microcosms include a range of local stakeholders.

Moreover, the degree of local stakeholding extends even – and necessarily – to sources of financing. Regularly, the start-up capital for the businesses involved in these microcosms is from local sources, including venture capitalists and angel funders that are more oriented toward "social entrepreneurialism."[34] Worker-owned cooperatives also achieve equity investment from their own employees. ShoreBank is of course a dramatic example of this phenomenon. It is a case in which a community development bank, itself founded as a result of a federal law encouraging community development, took on the mission of generating and funding local business and community development.[35]

### *Niche Markets*

One final feature of the collaborative network that developed in the home care network turned out to be of such importance, in all of the case studies, that it seems appropriate to claim it as one of the core features of collaborative capitalism in the United States. The feature could best be described as the existence of a niche or special industry that has one or more characteristics that make it particularly susceptible to collaborative practices. In the United States, one of the special characteristics of the niche industry appears to be that it protects the network from being subsumed by the more competitive market behavior in the surrounding regional and national economies.

In the case of the home care network, the niche involves the particular industry for home health care services, and it also involves specialization within that industry. As Rick Surpin described, when CHCA first started out, it was able to grow very quickly because of market demand and a clear source of payment (namely Medicare and Medicaid reimbursement). These features distinguished the home care industry from other markets, such as construction, that CHCA's founders also tried to enter. It was also a relatively low-cost proposition to think about entering the market. No large equipment was required. The necessary skills were relatively teachable. The market was neither unionized, nor did it impose other barriers to entry.

Moreover, as Surpin also described, even within the home care industry, CHCA in collaboration with ICS developed a niche of serving individuals with disabilities. Of course, it has also been a clearly definable niche in both New York and Philadelphia for the network to focus on providing quality care rather than low-cost care. This has involved developing a market demand for home health aides that stay with a customer over a longer term, thereby contributing to the quality and consistency of care provided.

In the South Shore example, the clearly definable market niche was the local residential rehab market. Over time, other niches developed, most notably the

[34] The Evergreen story is an excellent example, with its seed financing from local hospitals and educational institutions. Another well-known example is Zipcar, which received venture capital financing from Boston Community Capital. *Support for "Double Bottom Line" Investments in Mission-Driven Companies*, Boston Community Capital, www.bostoncommunitycapital.org /impact/impact-story-zipcar.

[35] Fiona S. Wilson & James E. Post, *ShoreBank Corporation: Let's Change the World, in* Banking With Integrity: The Winners of the Financial Crisis? 141–157 (Heiko Spitzeck et al. eds., 2012).

network of Dunkin' Donuts franchisees. The Austin example is interesting in this regard because the development of a niche appears to have been essential to the most successful businesses, such as the café and the workforce development business, in that network. At the same time, the Austin network has businesses operating in a number of different industries and the absence of a niche market for the network as a whole may teach important lessons about collaborative capitalism in the American context.

By means of a close examination of these six attributes in context, this book will provide two overarching reasons for promoting collaborative capitalism in US urban cores. The first is that the sharing networks discussed here have developed an efficient way of doing business that is a *legitimate* alternative to so-called liberal market capitalism. With the help of examples from mature coordinated economies such as Germany, policymakers can nurture this potential by creating a supportive infrastructure. The second reason is that collaborative capitalism is a *better* choice for urban-core contexts than the more competitive capitalist structure imposed by current policy because of the multiple bottom lines that inhere in the collaborative capitalist framework. Stated bluntly, a legal structure that supports pure profit maximization has not proven successful in urban cores across the United States. Mature coordinated economies exhibit multiple goals beyond profit maximization, including worker welfare and inclusion, democratic participation, and poverty alleviation.[36] By supporting a form of capitalism that has succeeded in promoting a fuller range of goals, policymakers can respond more accurately to the needs of inner cities. Beyond fixing market failures, they can more directly address the structural inequalities that exist in urban cores. Indeed, many of the practical reforms proposed in this book have the potential to support not just collaborative networks of the type described in this book, but also workers engaged in a broad range of traditional and less traditional income generating activities.

## SHARING IN MATURE CAPITALIST ECONOMIES

I have argued that the sharing apparent in the home care network, especially when viewed as part of a more basic pattern evident in my other case studies, is more than just a distinctive business model. It is also a distinctive style of capitalist behavior. I make this claim both to stimulate more research about this basic pattern as well as to advocate for regulatory support for business networks that engage in this capitalist form. In this final section, I bolster my argument that this collaborative pattern of business behavior is indeed a capitalist form. I do so by comparing collaborative

[36] Hall & Soskice, *Introduction*, VARIETIES OF CAPITALISM at 39–40, 50–51. As is the case with much of the literature building on the original "varieties of capitalism" thesis, there is a range of opinions on this point. For one quite different view, see KATHLEEN THELEN, VARIETIES OF LIBERALIZATION AND THE NEW POLITICS OF SOCIAL SOLIDARITY (2014).

capitalism in American cities to a startlingly similar form of capitalism that operates in a range of markets in other parts of the world.

Unless we came of age before 1950, most Americans assume that capitalism is capitalism, just as a rose is a rose, and that our experience of markets defines capitalism writ large. This is especially so since the fall of the Soviet Union, which many Americans take to be an absolute vindication both that capitalism is the only viable form of national economy and that the highest or most developed form of capitalism is what is practiced in the United States.[37]

The rise of the European Union, the economic dominance of countries such as Germany and Japan, and the many analyses of these phenomena in the 1990s all demonstrated that capitalism can be practiced successfully in many different ways. But it was not perhaps until the early part of this millennium that these intuitions and analyses gelled into a highly influential claim, first definitively made by Peter Hall and David Soskice, that there is no one ideal *kind* of capitalism. Hall and Soskice point to Germany and the United States to describe two polar archetypes.[38] Later chapters detail the two archetypal forms, as well as the literature that built on their insights, in part by identifying more of a range of forms than only two polar archetypes. My purpose here is simply to note that a well-defined field of study has developed to examine the so-called varieties of capitalism and to outline very briefly what this field of study has found.

In short, what Hall and Soskice have shown us is that American capitalism is only one form of capitalism. Hall and Soskice label this form a "liberal market economy." The practices of businesses engaged in this form of capitalism are marked by competitive and arm's-length market transactions making use of information that is privately acquired and used by individual businesses, and only a small subset of which is publicly accessible. This liberal form of capitalism is in sharp contrast to its archetypal polar opposite, a coordinated system that makes much more extensive use of noncompetitive relationships and institutions, such as trade associations, unions and other organizations, that serve to network individual businesses. Contracting in such a capitalist system is often more informal and there are different systems for monitoring and sanctioning errant behavior within the network. Businesses in such a system coordinate their activities much more extensively and explicitly than in a liberal market system.[39]

This critical insight from the literature on varieties of capitalism is wholly relevant to law reform and institutional design in the urban core. The solutions proposed by Porter, the SBA, and others are a response to the *specific form* of capitalism that prevails in the United States. But what if the capitalism being

[37] Such assumptions have been fueled by commentators such as Hernando de Soto, who has written a hearty endorsement of American capitalism and a call for exporting it to developing countries. HERNANDO DE SOTO, THE MYSTERY OF CAPITAL: WHY CAPITALISM TRIUMPHS IN THE WEST AND FAILS EVERYWHERE ELSE (2000).

[38] Hall & Soskice, *Introduction*, VARIETIES OF CAPITALISM.

[39] *Id.*

practiced in some inner cities is a different form? In that case, it may simply be wrong to try to fix it by imposing on it an institutional and legal infrastructure designed for the liberal or competitive market form of capitalism that prevails outside of the inner city.

That indeed is my diagnosis of the problem, though I should note that my focus is on law reform rather than on the theory concerning varieties of capitalism. Nor am I taking aim at liberalism writ large. Instead, my focus is on adding choices for participants in capitalist markets who have been excluded by the traditional American rules of market behavior.

Indeed, my claim is that the behavior of market participants in these particular inner-city locations is so qualitatively different that it literally breaks or defies the rules of capitalism as most Americans understand it. The most critical difference is the collective behavior of businesses in achieving success in certain inner-city markets. These businesses collaborate to such an extent that they risk breaking some of the legal rules of market participation and cannot make use of many other rules. For example, zoning laws sometimes prevent, and often limit, the ability of sharing networks to develop in optimal locations, including in places where they can avoid competition from well-established competitors. Additionally, even with some states' recognition of worker-owned cooperatives and "benefit corporations," state laws on entity formation have hindered the innovations underway in such networks.[40] Very often, such networks struggle with permitting and licensing requirements that impose burdensome costs. And financing arrangements ranging from crowdfunding to equity financing from local investors run the risk of violating securities rules. Meanwhile, examples from other places in the world show us that this qualitatively different kind of capitalist behavior can lead to tremendous success and wealth *if the market participants have the right legal and institutional infrastructure to support them.*

In this regard, the following chapter, about the network that developed around ShoreBank in Chicago, presents a compelling counterpoint to especially the Bronx home health care network. In the Bronx example, the network worked closely with state and local officials to develop a legal infrastructure that supported its efforts to provide "quality care through quality jobs." In the South Shore example, as we shall see, the legal infrastructure was only supportive up to a point. Ultimately, that infrastructure did not allow the Bank to survive the financial crisis, even though laws *were* passed to support bigger banks that provided capital to businesses involved in more national markets.

40 For a discussion of worker-owned cooperatives, see Scott L. Cummings, *Developing Cooperatives as a Job Creation Strategy for Low-Income Workers*, 25 N.Y.U. Rev. L. & Soc. Change 181 (1999). For a discussion of the new "benefit corporation" laws, see Alicia E. Plerhoples, *Delaware Public Benefit Corporations 90 Days Out: Who's Opting In?*, 14 U.C. Davis Bus. L. J. 247 (2014); Joseph Karl Grant, *When Making Money and Making a Sustainable and Societal Difference Collide: Will Benefit Corporations Succeed or Fail?* 46 Ind. L. Rev. 581 (2013).

# PART II

# Collaborative Capitalism Explored

# 4

# Rehabilitating South Shore

[O]n one day, they were the owner of the building, and they contracted with another guy to do the work of a particular trade. And then maybe the next year, they flipped, and the guy who had been the owner was the subcontractor and the guy who had been the subcontractor was the owner. So they changed roles with each other, which would have been a way of smoothing out income and also of having a proven labor force. And ... every time that the next person bought a building at a market price, that reinforced the value of the other network members' buildings, so that repeated sales strengthened everybody. [1]

–Mary Houghton, Cofounder, ShoreBank Corporation

It is widely believed that the famous ShoreBank of Chicago, Illinois, is the most successful community development financial institution (CDFI) to have existed in the United States.[2] From 1973 onward, when its cofounders Ronald Grzywinski, Mary Houghton, Milton Davis, and Jim Fletcher began operating it as a community development bank, the Bank transformed itself into a generator of local economic development. In the process, over the course of 40 years, it transformed many of the neighborhoods on the South Side of Chicago and beyond.

Thanks in part to the approachability of its founders, a considerable literature exists about the Bank.[3] This body of work focuses especially on the

[1] Interview with Mary Houghton, ShoreBank Corporation (April 10, 2015). For interviews with former employees of ShoreBank and its affiliates, I reference their institutional affiliation at the time they were employees of the Bank or its affiliates rather than their current affiliation or employment.

[2] In its very early years of operating as a community development bank, the Bank retained the name South Shore National Bank. In 1978, after the Bank became chartered as a state bank, it operated under the name South Shore Bank, and this is still the name used by many of my interviewees. In the 1980s, the Bank adopted the name ShoreBank, which it retained until its closing in 2010. In this book, I will consistently refer to the Bank as ShoreBank. I will also refer to its parent holding company and the other subsidiaries and affiliates of the holding company by the last names under which they operated.

[3] For a sampling of the discussion in law journals, see Mehrsa Baradaran, *How the Poor Got Cut Out of Banking*, 62 Emory L. J. 483 (2013); Bob Solomon, *The Fall (And Rise?) of Community Banking:*

question of how to replicate the Bank's work in other parts of the United States and beyond. Indeed, shortly after becoming president, Bill Clinton pursued the goal of replication in pushing for passage of the Community Development Banking and Financial Institutions Act, which he hoped would create "one hundred South Shore Banks" across the United States.[4] Thus, much of the analysis of ShoreBank rightly discusses the law, policy, and design principles contributing to the development of financial institutions that can successfully anchor local economic development. The principal question addressed is how to create more *banks* like ShoreBank.

But during the decades when it fueled economic growth in the South Shore neighborhood of Chicago, the Bank stood at the center of a vibrant network of small, local rehabbing businesses. Though frequently referenced in the literature, that network has been the subject of relatively little study. The purpose of this chapter is to describe the network and, further, to analyze it as a set of capitalist practices. In doing so, I will discuss ShoreBank's participation in the network as an intermediary serving some of the functions that we see intermediaries serving in mature coordinated economies.[5]

*The Continued Importance of Local Institutions*, 2 UC IRVINE L. REV. 945 (2012); Keith N. Hylton, *Banks and Inner Cities: Market and Regulatory Obstacles to Development Lending*, 17 YALE J. ON REG. 197 (2000); Senator Nellie R. Santiago et al., *Turning David and Goliath Into the Odd Couple: How the New Community Reinvestment Act Promotes Community Development Financial Institutions*, 6 J.L. & POL'Y 571 (1998); Cassandra Jones Havard, *Synergy and Friction-The CRA, BHCS, the SBA, and Community Development Lending*, 86 KY. L. J. 617 (1997–1998); Jeffrey S. Lesk & Richard M. Price, *An Introduction to the Community Development Bank Network*, 4-SUM J. AFFORDABLE HOUSING & COMMUNITY DEV. L. 267 (1995); Michael Klausner, *Market Failure and Community Investment: A Market-Oriented Alternative to the Community Reinvestment Act*, 143 U. PA. L. REV. 1561 (1995); Anthony D. Taibi, *Banking, Finance, and Community Economic Empowerment: Structural Economic Theory, Procedural Civil Rights, and Substantive Racial Justice*, 107 HARV. L. REV. 1463 (1994); Rochelle E. Lento, *Community Development Banking Strategy for Revitalizing our Communities*, 27 U. MICH. J. L. REF. 773 (1994); Peter R. Pitegoff, *Urban Revitalization and Community Finance: An Introduction*, 27 U. MICH. J. L. REF. 613 (1994). The Bank has also been discussed in numerous books on topics ranging from social entrepreneurship, to socially responsible lending, to self-employment and much more. *See, e.g.*, JAMES L. GREER & OSCAR GONZALES, COMMUNITY ECONOMIC DEVELOPMENT IN THE UNITED STATES: THE CDFI INDUSTRY AND AMERICA'S DISTRESSED COMMUNITIES 93–108 (2017); ARCHIE B. CARROLL ET AL., CORPORATE RESPONSIBILITY: THE AMERICAN EXPERIENCE 295–299 (2012); DAVID BORNSTEIN & SUSAN DAVIS, SOCIAL ENTREPRENEURSHIP: WHAT EVERYONE NEEDS TO KNOW (2010); BEN COHEN & MAL WARWICK, VALUES-DRIVEN BUSINESS: HOW TO CHANGE THE WORLD, MAKE MONEY, AND HAVE FUN 3–5 (2006); HOWARD ROTHMAN & MARY SCOTT, COMPANIES WITH A CONSCIENCE: INTIMATE PORTRAITS OF TWELVE FIRMS THAT MAKE A DIFFERENCE (2003); PATRICIA WATKINS MURPHY & JAMES V. CUNNINGHAM, ORGANIZING FOR COMMUNITY CONTROLLED DEVELOPMENT 250–251 (2003); TIMOTHY MASON BATES, RACE, SELF-EMPLOYMENT, AND UPWARD MOBILITY: AN ILLUSIVE AMERICAN DREAM 172–173 (1997).

4 EDWARD J. BLAKELY & NANCEY GREEN LEIGH, PLANNING LOCAL ECONOMIC DEVELOPMENT: THEORY AND PRACTICE 286 (4th ed. 2010).

5 *See* James Head & Kelly Mogle, *Race, Poverty, and Lending*, 27 CLEARINGHOUSE REV. (Special Issue) 353, 361–362 (1993) (enumerating the myriad ways in which ShoreBank functioned as anchor and partner in local economic revitalization).

## A NETWORK OF MOM-AND-POP REHABBERS

### *Context*

Chicago's South Shore is located at the southern edge of what is known as Chicago's South Side. Its eastern boundary abuts Lake Michigan, while its western and southern edges are major commercial streets. Its northern boundary is defined by a golf course that lies between South Shore and the planned Obama presidential library. As Ron Grzywinski described,

> [T]he South Shore neighborhood, which was our base, but then later expanded to most of the South Side and some of the West Side, was an almost ideal neighborhood ... It is a 20-minute drive along the shore of Lake Michigan ... from downtown Chicago, with one 18-hole golf course on one side, ... another 9-hole public golf course on the other side, ... lagoons where large boats could park, I mean it would be a realtor's dream.[6]

The neighborhood has been the site of significant shifts in migration and immigration in the twentieth century. Over the course of the first half of the twentieth century, South Shore was populated by an increasingly diverse mix of white residents, giving the area "an ethnic heterogeneity ... which was perhaps unusual among high-status residential areas of large cities."[7] As African Americans began to be crowded out of the northern parts of the South Side in the 1970s, they moved further south into the South Shore neighborhood. In the ensuing decades, the neighborhood was a locus of white flight, redlining, and segregation.[8] By 1970, the neighborhood was 69 percent African American. By 1980, it was 95 percent African American.[9] As Irving Cutler noted in 2006, "Chicago is still rated as one of the most segregated cities in the country."[10]

Sociologist Harvey Molotch describes a building boom in South Shore in the decade between 1920 and 1930 that produced a neighborhood in which approximately 75 percent of the housing stock was apartment buildings. While these buildings were solidly constructed and architecturally pleasing, as Molotch describes, by the 1960s "the increasingly sooty air of Chicago's South Side had given much of the area's brick and concrete exterior a dingy cast appropriate to what is frequently called a grey area."[11]

6 Interview with Ronald Grzywinski, Cofounder, ShoreBank Corporation (April 10, 2015). Locals refer to this particular geographic area as "South Shore" rather than "*the* South Shore," and thus I will do the same in this book.

7 Harvey Luskin Molotch, Managed Integration: Dilemmas of Doing Good in the City 42 (1972).

8 *See* Patricia H. Werhane, *Moral Imagination and the Search for Ethical Decision-Making in Management*, Bus. Ethics Q., The Ruffin Series, Special Issue No. 1, 75, 92 (1998) (describing racial and socioeconomic demographic changes in South Shore during the 1960s).

9 Wallace Best, *South Shore*, The Electronic Encyclopedia of Chicago, www.encyclopedia.chicagohistory.org/pages/1176.html.

10 Irving Cutler, Chicago: Metropolis of the Mid-Continent 172 (4th ed. 2006).

11 Molotch, Managed Integration at 43.

Richard Taub, a sociologist who studied ShoreBank extensively in its first decade or two of existence as a community bank, commented about the area in 1988:

> At present, the variety of buildings is illustrative of the range of life-styles and classes in the community. The Highlands is the home of University of Chicago doctors and professors, important black professionals as well as such celebrities as Jesse Jackson and Ramsey Lewis. Some of the old walk-up buildings house welfare mothers, single men who have no visible means of support, and other members of the poverty class. In between, there are some professional singles and couples along the lakefront, the solid two-earner families – he a bus driver, a postman; she a teacher or a nurse – and other members of the middle class. The population is almost all black.[12]

While there were a variety of socioeconomic classes, occupations, and housing on the South Side, the real estate market, and the economy more generally, were more distressed in the South Shore neighborhoods where the Bank first began working. As Sara Lindholm, who was the head of an affiliate of the Bank that focused on real estate development, described,

> [W]hen the neighborhood changed racially, [the large real estate companies that owned big apartment buildings in the area] were finding it hard to manage. And then they were trying to unload these buildings, and of course nobody was lending on them . . . So the buildings were not being upgraded, and it was a long-term recipe for failure.[13]

As for the commercial areas of the neighborhood, according to Lindholm, "71st Street became essentially just full of currency exchanges and little five-and-dime stores, and liquor stores."[14]

As this brief history suggests, by the early 1970s, South Shore had suffered intensely from the disinvestment associated not just with white flight, but also with active governmental support of redlining and other segregationist practices.[15] The availability of consumer financial services has long been recognized as one of the indicia of a healthy local economy,[16] and on this metric, too, South Shore was suffering. Indeed, by the early 1970s, the South Shore National Bank was one of only three banks still open in South Shore. Thus, it was a harbinger of worse ills when in

[12] Richard P. Taub, Community Capitalism 30 (1988).

[13] Interview with Sara Lindholm, ShoreBank Development Corporation (March 21, 2017). [14] *Id.*

[15] *See* Daniel T. Friedson, *Greenlining Toward a Community of Local Entrepreneurship, Home Ownership, and Quality of Life*, 9 WTR J. Affordable Housing & Community Dev. L. 183, 190 (2000); Phillip Fellin, *Development of Capital in Poor, Inner-City Neighborhoods*, 5 Journal of Community Practice 87, 89 (2008) (highlighting the disastrous economic effects of "white flight," redlining, and capital drain in South Shore).

[16] *See* Fellin, *Development of Capital* at 89 (discussing ShoreBank's local focus and ability to reduce capital flight from the neighborhood); Kenneth Temkin, *The U.S. Housing Finance System for Low-Income Families: A Review of Recent Innovations and Changes*, 15 Housing Finance Int'l 17, 27 (2001) (highlighting the critical importance of community development banks as the only source of consumer financial services in many inner-city neighborhoods).

1972 its management sought approval from the Comptroller of the Currency to move the bank to downtown Chicago.[17] The response by neighborhood residents was vociferous. They argued that the bank had an obligation to remain open, because without it, South Shore residents would effectively have no local access to consumer banking services.[18]

## *Origins*

It was at this point that four bankers, who had worked together at a local bank in the nearby neighborhood of Hyde Park, joined the conversation about banking services in South Shore. In their work, Ronald Grzywinski, Mary Houghton, Milton Davis, and Jim Fletcher had been looking for opportunities to use their bank's services and their own banking knowledge to increase investment in areas like South Shore. They had already begun raising funds and working with consultants to identify an opportunity to purchase a bank that could be converted to a community development bank.

Their vision was substantially reinforced by Congress's adoption in 1970 of amendments to the Bank Holding Company Act, which authorized the Federal Reserve Board to define permissible activities for bank holding companies. The resulting federal regulations authorized bank holding companies to create subsidiaries for the purpose of "promot[ing] community welfare, such as the economic rehabilitation and development of low-income areas by providing housing, services, or jobs for residents."[19] When, one year later, the Federal Reserve Board included investment in community development corporations in the list of permissible activities,[20] the four actively began to explore the idea of a bank holding company *being* a community development corporation. Thus, when the South Shore National Bank threatened to pull out of South Shore, the four individuals saw an opportunity to put these pieces together by purchasing the bank and converting it to a community development bank that was a subsidiary of a bank holding company.[21] As Grzywinski described, the founders' vision in 1973 was to "take a much more comprehensive approach to the needs of urban neighborhoods."

> [W]e weren't going to be just a bank. We were going to be a bank holding company, and that bank holding company would be able to initiate large-scale redevelopment through a wholly-owned real-estate development company. It was going to be able

[17] Ronald Grzywinski, *The New Old-Fashioned Banking*, HARV. BUS. REV., May-June 1991, at 87, 88–89.

[18] *Id.*

[19] This rule is known as Regulation Y, 12 C.F.R. § 225.25(b)(6) (2012). The 1972 Federal Reserve Bulletin provides a compelling description of the intended role of bank holding companies: "Bank holding companies possess a unique combination of financial and managerial resources making them particularly suited for a meaningful and substantial role in remedying our social ills." *Investment in Corporations or Projects Designed Primarily to Promote Community Welfare*, 58 FEDERAL RESERVE BULLETIN 572 (June 1972).

[20] 12 C.F.R. § 225.25 (2012). [21] *Id.*; Grzywinski Interview.

> to make equity investments in businesses that were otherwise well-managed but did not have enough capital to qualify for bank credit. And thirdly, we were going to have a not-for-profit affiliate that would raise money from foundations and government so that it could do more of the soft things that neighborhoods need, like job training, job placement, remedial education, the list is endless.[22]

For several decades, the Bank did that and more. The new owners of the Bank hired employees who embraced their mission of comprehensive community development.[23] They rearranged furniture to make the Bank more inviting to potential customers. They experimented with different lending terms for consumer and small business loans.[24] With its new drive-in facility and parking lot, welcoming interior, and accessible consumer lending and other financial services, the Bank functioned as a physical, institutional and financial anchor for the neighborhood.[25] As Grzywinski described, prior to their conversion of the Bank into a community development bank,

> the people who ran the bank . . . were fearful of doing almost any kind of lending in the neighborhood, because they had all the biases and prejudices. They saw the hole in the doughnut rather than the doughnut, and so would do a couple of single-family loans per year, would do no multifamily loans, and the single-family loans were generally FHA-insured or VA-guaranteed.[26]

The new owners reversed that course completely: "What we knew we would do is that we would make real estate mortgage loans only in South Shore."[27] In doing so, they made use of a model that had once been familiar across the country: they became a neighborhood bank, which underwrote loans on the basis of its knowledge of the community.[28]

In this regard, the deep community connections that each of the founders either had already, or built in the early years, were critical. Although both Milton Davis and Jim Fletcher passed away sometime ago, many of those I interviewed described their exceptional imprint on the Bank as it developed into a community institution. Indeed, many commented that each of the four founders was an irreplaceable part of the whole. Michael Bennett, who was on staff at the Bank's holding company in its very early years and who is now a professor at DePaul University, described Jim

22 Grzywinski Interview. 23 *Id.*

24 Friedson, *Greenlining* at 195 (discussing the difficulty of small business lending in South Shore due to the lack of a retail sector as well as the requirement that real estate loans contained a rehab component).

25 *See* Head & Mogle, *Race, Poverty, and Lending* at 361–362 (discussing ShoreBank's unique approach of combining ancillary services with banking to bolster and improve multiple facets of the South Shore neighborhood). *See also* Friedson, *Greenlining* at 194–195; Werhane, *Moral Imagination* at 92–93.

26 Grzywinski Interview.

27 *Id.* The Bank later relaxed this geographic preference, and ultimately made mortgage loans in the South Side and beyond.

28 *Id.*

Fletcher as having "deep relationships . . . with community action and community development groups . . . [A]nd he leveraged all that to get people to respect the Bank."[29] About Milton Davis, Bennett remarked,

> Milton Davis, who had been the actual director of the Urban Development Division at the Hyde Park Bank, had been the regional director of the Congress on Racial Equality here in Chicago. He was one of the ones that helped get Dr. Martin Luther King here in 1966. And he . . . had a number of ties with particularly the black community, but city-wide with community activists.[30]

## *Development of a Market*

As is true of the other examples in this book, neither ShoreBank's founders nor the network of mom-and-pop rehabbers that the Bank supported set out to create a different kind of market with different capitalist practices. Indeed, it is noteworthy that among the examples in this book, the participants describe a broad variety of goals at origination. In the case of ShoreBank, the original goals of the founders did not even include rehabilitating the real estate market in South Shore. Instead, as Grzywinski described, the background of the four founders was in "more typical small business lending and not real estate":

> We did all kinds of small business lending [to] minority-owned businesses throughout the Chicago metropolitan area, and it was quite successful . . . So when we came to South Shore, in August of '73, I think we pretty much thought . . . that what we were going to do was to expand what we already knew, that we were going to do what we had done.[31]

True, ShoreBank was going to become part of a bank holding company structure. But the expectation was to implement the broader community development mission by working with the holding company's nonbank subsidiaries to invest in large-scale real estate developments and provide other financial development services, not by using the Bank's "bread and butter" banking services to create a whole *new* market in real estate.

However, the physical condition of the neighborhood in which the founders sought to invest changed their understanding of how to meet their goal of community investment. The founders quickly came to realize that the South Shore neighborhood was undergoing the same pattern of disinvestment that had shattered adjacent neighborhoods. Unless some meaningful intervention occurred, the next step in that pattern would be demolition of the many buildings in the neighborhood that were approaching a level of deterioration that would be illogical to fix. As Grzywinski recalled,

[29] Interview with Michael Bennett, Professor, DePaul University (July 19, 2017). [30] *Id.*

[31] Grzywinski Interview.

> We didn't realize until we got there what the building ... stock was like, and I remember clearly my own sense that we had inherited, I always had this image of ... a ticking time bomb – and it would all go down even, and just after, we had invested.[32]

At this point in the cycle, it was clear to the founders that investing in small businesses would not alone reverse the decline. They needed a strategy to directly address the physical deterioration.

Approximately 75 percent of the building stock that the founders encountered in South Shore consisted of multifamily, three- or four-story, walk-up apartment buildings.[33] From the experience of other banks that had attempted to make multifamily loans in surrounding neighborhoods, the founders concluded that they could not generate enough of a reversal just by making individual loans to rehabilitate the neighborhood building by building. Instead, they sought a more forceful stimulus by convincing RESCORP, a nonprofit consortium of savings-and-loan associations, to invest in an 11-building, 302-apartment renovation project spanning a four-block area of a subneighborhood that was threatened with imminent decline.[34] The redevelopment was a major success, achieving immediate high occupancy and producing the kind of community energy and investment that the founders had sought.[35]

Many of the rehabilitated units were rented at market rates, and the influx of middle-class renters signaled to the Bank that there was considerable market demand for good, safe housing in South Shore.[36] The arrival of suitable renters also caught the attention of local residents who were interested in the possibility of buying and rehabilitating more such housing. A number of my interviewees described the size and diversity of the rental market in South Shore. Many of the renters were local residents who were able to use working-class salaries to rent in these new buildings. Others came from nearby neighborhoods.[37] According to rehabber Andy Schcolnik, "We were able to have mixed races, and mixed incomes."[38] Margie Smigel, who worked closely with some of the rehabbers as a real estate broker for about a decade in the 1990s, stated,

32 *Id.* 33 *Id. See also* Grzywinski, *The New Old-Fashioned Banking* at 93–95.

34 RESCORP had already made investments in South Shore, and would go on to make more.

35 Grzywinski Interview. *See also* Grzywinski, *The New Old-Fashioned Banking* at 93–95.

36 Grzywinski Interview.

37 Interview with Eiran Feldman, First InSite Realty LLC (May 4, 2017); Interview with Len Hoyles, Archer Investments, LLC (May 4, 2017); Interview with Ocie Windham, O&S Management (May 3, 2017); Interview with Andy Schcolnik, Ansco Real Estate Investments (April 5, 2017); Interview Margie Smigel, The Margie Smigel Group, LLC (May 23, 2017).

38 Schcolnik Interview. Rehabber Michael Silver stated, "We got a very mixed group of buyers, both racially and ethnically and by income distribution. Obviously you have to qualify for a mortgage to get one, but we were building condos that sold in the low ones, to start-up houses, detached single-family houses, that sold in the mid to high fives. None of it was 'capital A' Affordable Housing, but it was market rate in a neighborhood where if you wanted to sell something it was going to be 'small A' affordable." Interview with Michael Silver, In/Site Investment Group, LLC (May 4, 2017).

> [W]hat was exciting about it is that in some ways we were reintegrating the neighborhood. So people were coming from everywhere. People living downtown, people living on the North Side. People living in the South Side. And the other thing that was lovely was that we were also selling to people who were coming back to the neighborhood from which they had fled. And African Americans who grew up in the neighborhood and had to leave because the buildings were falling apart and they perceived it as being too dangerous and scary to live there. They were coming back.[39]

More broadly Gordon Hellwig, a long-time employee of the Bank, compared the market to that in other cities:

> [T]he commercial real estate was successful ... partly because the demand was there. There [were] lots of buildings that needed to be fixed up, there was lots of demand for affordable housing, either subsidized, or market rate ... But people need a roof over their heads, so there's lots of opportunities to rent apartments. And there were a lot of dilapidated or abandoned buildings that needed to be gutted, but could be put back together. And our experience in Chicago certainly was better than either Cleveland or Detroit, because there was much more multifamily housing in Chicago that, although it might be blighted, might have been vacant for a long time, the bones were still pretty good.[40]

Once the founders had a hint of the size of the market demand, they concluded that they had found a way to exponentially increase the impact of RESCORP's investment. Indeed, RESCORP followed that initial investment with a second, even larger development in the Parkside neighborhood, thereby multiplying its effect. As the founders described, by making conventional loans to local rehabbers, they could finance the development of several market-rate units for each subsidized unit.[41] Thus, the catalyst provided by RESCORP's investments produced an explicit reprioritization of the Bank's goals. While maintaining its dedication to small business lending, particularly to minority-owned businesses, the Bank expressly began to direct much of its lending attention to rehabilitating multifamily housing. In Grzywinski's words,

> We knew that we would make loans only if we could build into them a rehab component. We would not finance anybody ... just for the sake of changing ownership. We consciously used the bank's power of the purse strings to force rehabilitation.[42]

One of the most striking aspects of this particular story of local market success is that the existence of the market was so invisible until it blossomed, even to community insiders such as the founders of ShoreBank. As Grzywinski has described on multiple occasions, "[T]he small housing entrepreneurs ... appeared from

39 Smigel Interview. 40 Interview with Gordon Hellwig, ShoreBank (May 3, 2017).

41 Grzywinski, *The New Old-Fashioned Banking* at 95. 42 Grzywinski Interview.

nowhere."[43] "They make up a body of small-business people that no market survey could possibly have identified."[44] "They were invisible, and now they're an industry."[45]

Yet once there was evidence of market demand, individual residents in the neighborhood began to see the potential for using their own skills and experience to connect to that market. Many of these early entrants into the market were African American residents of the area. As Grzywinski described,

> When I said that you would never have found an industry in South Shore, it means that there was no industry, but there were many people whom homeowners … could hire to do electricity or to do carpentry. They were nonunion.[46]

It was not a big leap for such individuals to imagine using these same skills to rehabilitate their own buildings in order to turn them into market-rate rental properties. Likewise, it was possible for the subgroup of individuals who did building maintenance work for their day jobs to imagine maintaining their own buildings once the buildings were purchased, rehabilitated, and rented out. This was a (largely Croatian) group that Grzywinski described as having found its way to ShoreBank through cultural connections with one another.[47] While several steps were necessary for these individuals to be able to go into business for themselves as owners and rehabilitators of multifamily buildings, it became clear to them – and to the Bank – that they either had the basic skills necessary to rehab the properties or that they could acquire those skills through their own social networks.[48]

Of course, one of the steps required for those individuals to go into business for themselves was to obtain the capital to purchase the buildings. Lack of start-up capital is perhaps the most common denominator in stories of failed business endeavors. Its availability in the form of large volumes of accessible business loans from ShoreBank bespeaks the extraordinary efficacy of a financial institution as a generator of local economic development.

But that was not all. It appears critical to this story that there was a large enough volume of individual rehabbers obtaining a large enough volume of loans to create a centripetal force. Each of the inputs to market participation had to contribute to the same push for market development in order to create a sustainable market. Considering each of the inputs in turn, the individual participants needed enough market demand to be able to use their initial investment in one building to revolve into a second investment in a larger building, and then a third, and fourth, until they were able to quit their day jobs and earn a livelihood just from their rehabbing businesses.[49] If they had not been able to do so, they would not have been able to satisfy the market demand quickly enough, thereby risking its dissipation.

[43] Grzywinski, *The New Old-Fashioned Banking* at 95. [44] *Id.* at 96. [45] *Id.*
[46] Grzywinski Interview. [47] *Id. See also* Grzywinski, *The New Old-Fashioned Banking* at 96.
[48] Grzywinski Interview. *See also* Grzywinski, *The New Old-Fashioned Banking* at 96.
[49] Windham Interview; Hoyles Interview; Interview with Alice Lamos (May 19, 2017).

The same can be said for the Bank's participation. First, the Bank had to be able to make lending in such high volume to a single industry workable from the perspective of basic banking safety and soundness. To do this, the Bank quickly had to develop specialized knowledge of the local real estate market. As Mary Houghton described,

> [T]he bank had the opportunity of specializing just in rehabbing, whereas the commercial loan department had to know about shoe stores one day, and apparel shops the next day, and day care centers the day after that. . . . The opportunity to specialize was only because there was a big enough market that was profitable enough for a growing number of entrepreneurs, and that's in the end what created the network . . . [A] network could form because there was an evolving market that was worth everybody's time and energy, and the fact that that network could evolve allowed the Bank to get better and better and better at what it was doing because it was specializing . . . [W]e didn't really have that opportunity to specialize very often. I think in very large banks, they can run commercial loan departments that have a group that specializes in oil and gas, or a group that specializes in something else, but in a community bank that's pretty rare.[50]

Second, the Bank had to develop lending criteria specially designed to support that unique market while also protecting the Bank. I have already described the Bank's requirements in the early years that real estate mortgage loans be made only in South Shore and only to people committed to rehabilitating their properties. To this, we can add the Bank's requirement in the first few years that borrowers who purchased three-flat and six-flat buildings live in one of the units in the building.[51] Although the Bank relaxed this requirement during its first decade of lending for multifamily rehab, its early imposition, combined with the Bank's attention to the income-earning plans of its borrowers, developed a market in which, in Houghton's words, the owners "were long-term holders. And they had to be good at property management as well as rehab, so they weren't buying and flipping."[52] For safety and soundness reasons, the Bank also required personal guaranties, regardless of how large a business the borrower had become.[53]

At the same time, the Bank developed a lending protocol that was, in Houghton's words, "unorthodox because [it] was so simple and unbureaucratic."[54] Through a process of experimentation, the Bank settled on a practice of making its multifamily loans on 20-year repayment terms, but with a rate review and adjustment every two years. This structure allowed the Bank to adjust loans as interest rates fluctuated, while inducing borrowers to invest in their properties without concern that their loan would be called in five to seven years. The two-year rate review also allowed the borrowers to raise rents as necessary in order to adjust to the new monthly

[50] Houghton Interview.

[51] Grzywinski Interview. See also Friedson, *Greenlining* at 195 (noting the owner occupancy requirement was a lending "preference" that strongly benefited the bank and South Shore residents).

[52] Houghton Interview. [53] *Id.*; Silver Interview. [54] Houghton Interview.

payments.[55] One of the most noteworthy features of this protocol concerned its loans for rehab, as distinguished from acquisition, of properties. As rehabber Alice Lamos described,

> [W]hat South Shore did was that they gave you the rehab money in stages. Let's say you asked for a $300,000 rehab [loan]. They would dole it out in stages. You'd do x amount, they'd come by and look at it. You'd do x amount, they [would] come by and look. They were overseeing.[56]

This last piece was, in the founders' view, crucial to successful development of a previously invisible market. But it also set the Bank completely apart from even the other banks operating in nearby neighborhoods, which continued to impose very standardized lending criteria on prospective buyers, regardless of their size, experience level, and business prospects.[57]

Finally, there appear to have been several features of the South Shore real estate market that aided the development of such a powerful local market. For example, as Houghton has described, repeated sales produced higher market values across the neighborhood. It is one of the special features of real estate markets that the value of one property is determined by comparable values in the neighborhood. In contrast to other cities where the Bank later tried to develop a similar market, South Shore had an enormous inventory of multifamily housing.[58] As I discovered during my own walks in the area, the housing was also beautifully and solidly built, often with well-crafted stonework and brickwork, elegant facades, and attractive courtyards. In addition, Houghton hypothesized that running a real estate rehab business "on some level … was a simpler set of management tasks than running a retail business. Simpler both for the borrower, and simpler for the bank to get their arms around."[59] It also appears crucial that, at its inception and in its early stages, the network of mom-and-pop rehabbers had so little competition from larger and more established real estate development businesses. As Houghton described,

> Compared to the retail and service sectors, … the competition for those businesses was local shopping malls or mass market businesses who could out-compete the little retailers every day of the week on selection and price. And so on some level, a bank can't do anything unless there is a market for what it's peddling. And in this case, the rehab market, there really was a big market, and the market just kept growing.[60]

55 *Id.*

56 Lamos Interview. Many others commented on this protocol. O'Connor Interview; Payne Interview; Hoyles Interview.

57 Interview with George Frazier, Retired Owner/Manager (May 19, 2017); Lamos Interview; Hoyles Interview; Interview with Mark Sutherland, President, Wicker Park Apartments, Inc. (May 8, 2017). Michael O'Connor, who was chief appraiser in that department for many years, described the lending process from the Bank's perspective: "[W]e saw a lot of deals that we rejected where either they were paying too much up front, or their renovation budget was out of line, and we'd determine that this just doesn't make sense. … And we'd never charge an application fee … or even an appraisal fee." Interview with Michael O'Connor, ShoreBank (June 23, 2017).

58 Hellwig Interview. 59 Houghton Interview. 60 *Id.*

### *The Network in Mature Form*

This first guy: his uncle knew the trowel trades, and his uncle agreed I think to be a co-borrower. And they bought a building that we financed. And that was the beginning. Because out of that, he came back, and he did that building successfully. He came back. So the first building was probably a three-flat, which is all that Jim [Bringley, the head of the real estate lending department] would allow people to do. As Jim used to say, "Rookie building owners get rookie buildings." … [And then he did a] six-flat, and Jim took the first building as cross-collateral. He probably came back and then did a 12-flat. And so then, you know, this guy knew enough other people who knew some other businesses. So I think it all developed organically.

Ron Grzywinski[61]

The formation of the mom-and-pop rehabbing network in South Shore is an extraordinary story with its own important lessons. But it is equally critical to understand what sustained that network for decades, allowing generation after generation of rehabbing businesses to develop, grow, and become sustainable. As Houghton described, "there was such a big market opportunity for successive waves of entrepreneurs to actually make very substantial cash flow."[62] Of course, the Bank's steadfastness as a source of financing cannot be understated. Borrowers could return again and again for more financing. But the stability of financing was only one piece of the longevity puzzle. The question that remains to be answered is this: how did the individual entrepreneurs sustain their participation in the market for so long?

At the most basic level, the answer is that each of these entrepreneurs found a low-cost way to accomplish tasks that absolutely had to be accomplished but that they could not do themselves. Mary Houghton has described the exchange of labor that occurred in the early years among owners, and her account is supported by that of other Bank employees. In addition, as I will describe, the rehabbers shared, in one rehabber's words, "a small industry" of local contractors who worked with them over the course of decades to redevelop and improve buildings. Just as they had found a large enough market to allow them to become full-time rehabbing business owners, the rehabbers in turn provided a large enough volume of work to these contractors to allow them to specialize just in rehabbing buildings in South Shore.[63] This led over time to their ability to take on larger and more complex projects. As Sara Lindholm described, "Bringley's borrowers got so good … with more and more practice. They actually started taking on the larger buildings. And they could do the rehab so much more cheaply than [the Bank's real estate development affiliate] could."[64]

61 Grzywinski Interview. 62 Houghton Interview.

63 Frazier Interview; Lamos Interview; Hoyles Interview; O'Connor Interview.

64 Lindholm Interview.

In part, the thickness of the network was due to the racial, cultural, and, more broadly, social connections among the subgroups involved in the rehab market. I have already mentioned the example of the Croatian rehabbers. These individuals found their way to the Bank through cultural connections: a local soccer club, a dormitory that they used upon arrival from Croatia run by a member of the soccer club, referrals from other soccer-club members for janitorial jobs, and ultimately referrals from the dormitory owner to Jim Bringley in the Bank's real estate lending department.[65] The same is true for a community of African American rehabbers, who were the first to take advantage of the Bank's real estate lending and who invested significant resources in rehabilitating properties with the expectation of longer term neighborhood improvement.[66]

But the ethnic, social, and cultural ties also received significant help from Jim Bringley, whom Grzywinski, Houghton, and many others described as the "glue" that kept the network together for so long. According to Grzywinski, "He knew all the players, the players all trusted him. And Jim was at risk through the bank, was at risk on all those deals."[67] Specifically, Bringley was the source through whom all real estate loan applications flowed. As he assessed each application, and the ability of each applicant to successfully redevelop a property, he made explicit connections. Again, from Grzywinski:

> Jim Bringley, looking for as many ways to succeed as he could, probably began to put people together. If he saw somebody was doing something well, he would say to Omar, "Why don't you go over there and talk to Michael, or take a look at that?" Or he would suggest that Michael, the concrete guy, could do the work on this building that Charlie the carpenter had bought.[68]

In this respect, Bringley, using the Bank's resources, was able to extend the informal, social networks beyond their original limitations. As he expanded the networks, he made the knowledge within the networks thicker. And he facilitated the exchange of critical resources.[69]

Bringley also served a more formal organizing function. Once a stable network of rehabbers had developed, Bringley began to invite small groups of them to participate in a home-grown vocational education program of sorts. According to Grzywinski,

> Jim . . . began . . . to invite 20 of the best performers one Saturday a month to come to the bank for a Saturday morning, in which they would discuss a single element of building rehab and maintenance. One Saturday, discuss heating systems, the next,

65 Grzywinski Interview. 66 *Id.*; Frazier Interview; Lamos Interview. 67 Grzywinski Interview.

68 *Id.*

69 Jim Bringley's role was the subject of virtually universal commentary, all of which involved expressions of gratitude, praise, or both. Frazier Interview; Hoyles Interview; Lamos Interview; Windham Interview; Schcolnik Interview; O'Connor Interview; Grzywinski Interview; Houghton Interview; Lindholm Interview; Interview with Dan Broughton, ShoreBank (March 29 and May 3, 2017); Hellwig Interview; Interview with Cliff Kellogg, ShoreBank Corporation (May 10 and May 11, 2017).

> discuss building insurance, and the next time they would talk about roofs . . .. I think Jim did that for . . . 18 to 24 months, but then after that . . . I understand that they . . . on their own used to get together at a local McDonald's.[70]

Rehabber Len Hoyles described the formalization of this educational function:

> Bringley called me one day, and he asked me to give a talk at the Bank . . . And that opened the floodgates, and I probably made 20, 25 speeches. One time I went to the . . . branch on the West Side . . . and [so many came that] they had to turn people away.[71]

These formal and informal means of strengthening the network over time proved to be enormously powerful, especially combined with the unwavering support of the Bank and the natural capacity of the real estate market to gather strength through participation. Twenty years after its conversion to a community development bank, ShoreBank had supported the development of thousands of housing units, essentially underwriting a previously nonexistent market for residential rental real estate in South Shore.[72]

Although the home care network described in Chapter 2 and the South Shore network described here are very different, one interesting commonality between them is that the connections between the businesses involved were more personal than legal. Specifically, there was no formal legal connection between the Bank and the rehabber businesses other than through the contractual form of loan agreements. The Bank did not have any ownership stake in these businesses. Nor did the businesses have any ownership stake in the Bank. Moreover, unlike the home care network, there were no cross-board relationships between the Bank and the rehabbing businesses.

Instead, as I have described, Jim Bringley and the other members of his lending department maintained steadfastly personal connections with the rehabbers. Almost every one of the business owners I interviewed (and many of the Bank employees) commented that Bringley met with the owners personally when they came in for loans or at other critical points in their borrowing relationships with the Bank. Bringley encouraged a number of these owners to build their portfolios. When borrowers had financial or business troubles, he managed workouts that sometimes involved buyouts by more successful rehabber-borrowers of the Bank. Within his own department, he organized the space as a "bullpen" where everyone sat and worked close to each other and with a team culture.[73] This structure paralleled the close personal and cultural connections among the subnetworks of borrowers themselves, which involved close mentoring relationships, meetings at McDonald's, soccer clubs, and eventually more formal associations.

[70] Grzywinski Interview. As rehabber Peter Payne described, "Bringley and Mike O'Connor and some others would ask questions about how we were doing certain things. Because they were learning at that time too." Payne Interview.

[71] Hoyles Interview. [72] Lento, *Community Development Banking Strategy* at 786.

[73] Broughton Interview.

Of course, the Bank itself was nested within a legal structure that was at the center of this network of personal connections. What I have been referring to as the Bank was actually a subsidiary of the ShoreBank Corporation, which was a bank holding company formed pursuant to the federal Bank Holding Company Act. The Bank operated, and was regulated, as a full-service commercial bank, providing both a full range of consumer and business depository and lending services. In addition to the Bank, ShoreBank Corporation had several other major Chicago-based subsidiaries and affiliates. One subsidiary was the ShoreBank Development Corporation, formerly City Lands Corporation, which was a real estate development company that focused primarily on the development of affordable housing and commercial properties in low- and moderate-income neighborhoods in Chicago. A second affiliated entity was the Neighborhood Institute,[74] which was a nonprofit organization that focused primarily on workforce development and other services for low-income residents of South Shore. A third entity, ShoreBank Capital Corporation, was a special small business investment corporation that was licensed by the US Small Business Administration. Its function appears to have been primarily to provide subordinate debt and equity financing to local minority-owned businesses. Finally, a fourth entity, ShoreBank Advisory Services, was a consulting business that provided consulting on community development issues nationally and around the world.[75]

Although some of the literature on the Bank suggests otherwise, my own research on these other subsidiaries and affiliates of the holding company indicates that they had very little direct connection with the network of rehabbers.[76] As I will describe in the following section, this network involved a number of intermediaries, including both the Bank and informal and formal trade associations. However, even though the ShoreBank Development Corporation was a real estate developer, it did not directly provide services to the rehabbers. Nor, in its role as a workforce development agency, did the Neighborhood Institute.[77] Instead, it was Bringley and the members of his department who worked directly with rehabbers on questions involving choices of properties to acquire, location, and development costs. Moreover, the rehabbers themselves developed access to affordable providers of the trades necessary to develop properties.

On the other hand, the nature of real estate development also makes clear that the work of especially ShoreBank Development Corporation, and also probably ShoreBank Capital and the other subsidiaries, complemented the work within the rehabber network. While this is an indirect effect, it is a powerful one, as described by George Surgeon, who was with the Bank from 1976 onward, ultimately as the CEO of the holding company:

74 This organization was formerly named the South Shore Neighborhood Institute and the Chicago Neighborhood Institute.

75 Karl F. Seidman, Economic Development Finance 205–206 (2005). The bank holding company had a number of other nonprofit affiliates, many of which operated in other cities.

76 Interview with Jennifer Tescher, ShoreBank Corporation (April 25, 2017); Interview with Jack Crane, Senior Vice President and Director of Lending, Community Investment Corporation (July 6, 2017).

77 Tescher Interview.

> [W]hen South Shore was developed after World War I, . . . developers built a lot of big buildings on the corners, and then they would fill in the block with mostly six flats and three flats and twelve-unit buildings. And by the time [the Bank] became involved in South Shore, many of those corner buildings were in deep trouble. Many were vacant and needed really serious amounts of money for renovation to be brought back. . . . So City Lands could take on these large problem buildings on the corner that needed gut rehab that the Bank at that time didn't think the ma-and-pa rehabbers could address. And then the ma-and-pa rehabbers could go in and take on the six flats, the twelve flats, the three flats in between that were maybe a little run down, but were still operating, and instead of needing 50,000 dollars in rehab per unit, a ma-and-pa rehabber might spend $5,000 or maybe maximum $10,000 dollars a unit to renovate a building . . . [A]nd the work of City Lands also indirectly facilitated their attracting good tenants, because all of a sudden you didn't have this terrible derelict building on the corner. You had this really attractive, recently renovated structure on the corner, and people could say, "Well, hey that's really great. I live on a great block."[78]

Thus, the broader network in which the Bank operated might look something like this:

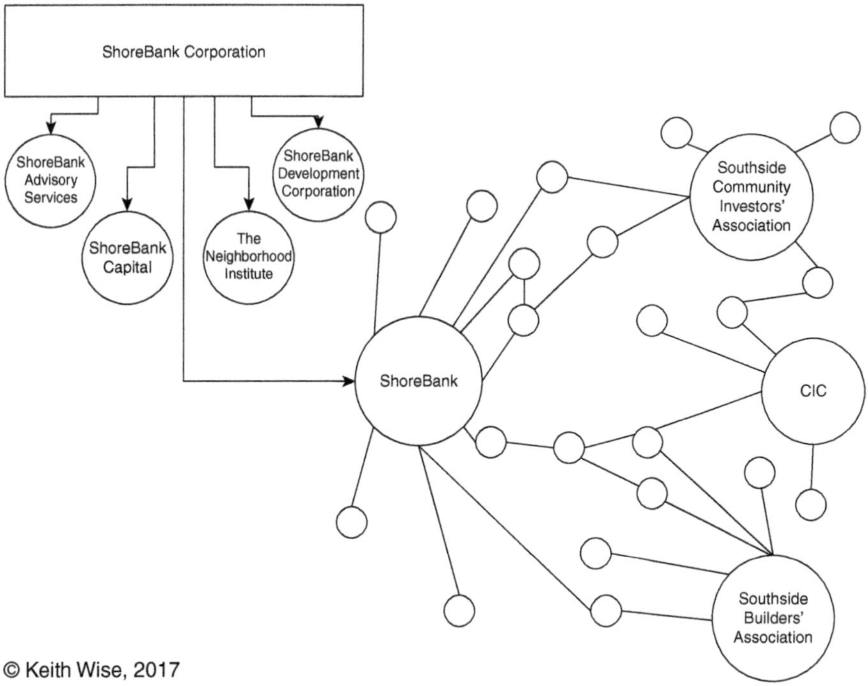


[78] Interview with George Surgeon, ShoreBank Corporation (March 14, 2017).

## *Intermediaries in the Network*

While the Bank did many things to facilitate sharing within the rehabber network, its largest contribution was as a financing source. Indeed, it is hard to overstate this contribution and the myriad reasons for the Bank's usefulness as a source of capital. First, the Bank provided financing that was consistently available. Both the Bank's founders and many of the rehabbers I interviewed commented that the Bank was, for quite a long time, the only game in town. And, although its criteria were strict, once a borrower met them, the Bank was committed to lending to that borrower repeatedly.[79] Second, many borrowers also commented that the Bank's lending criteria were fair and understandable.[80] Third, the criteria were based on deep personal knowledge, of both the market and the individual borrowers.[81] This led to good lending decisions, and it also reduced costs for borrowers. Fourth, this meant that the Bank loaned very comprehensively in the neighborhood. It was a remarkably significant source of capital.[82] Fifth, the comprehensiveness of its financing also applied at a project level, because borrowers received financing for acquisition and for rehabilitation, thereby eliminating the inefficiencies of having to seek additional sources of financing. A number of the rehabbers I interviewed, especially those who started rehabbing in the first decade of the Bank's work in South Shore, commented that the Bank was their major, and sometimes sole, source of financing.[83] Sixth, the Bank was able to build borrowers' businesses by virtue of its repeat lending. This contributed to their ability to stabilize their income over time, thereby turning avocations into vocations and developing a stable market both for the Bank and for its borrowers.[84] In sum, the Bank was an exceptionally efficient and patient source of capital.

Looking at the market more broadly, the Bank's decisions to make loans in a coordinated manner within subneighborhoods allowed it to develop, and then take advantage of, its knowledge of the local real estate market. This, in turn, benefited both the Bank and the borrowers by contributing to a virtuous cycle of lending and development.

79 Grzywinski Interview; Houghton Interview; Lindholm Interview; Broughton Interview; Schcolnik Interview; Hoyles Interview; Windham Interview; Interview with Peter Payne, Tocal Management (May 19, 2017); Lamos Interview; Frazier Interview; O'Connor Interview; Crane Interview.

80 Payne Interview; Sutherland Interview; Hoyles Interview; Windham Interview; Frazier Interview.

81 Feldman Interview; Frazier Interview; Hoyles Interview; Windham Interview; Lamos Interview; O'Connor Interview. Jack Crane stated, "We assessed the individuals very thoroughly, we got to know them, we got to know their families, we got to know their strengths and their weaknesses. We spent a lot of time with the individuals. We spent a lot of time in the buildings themselves to a point where we knew value very well. We knew every building, every block ... So we could make fast decisions." Crane Interview.

82 Sutherland Interview; Schcolnik Interview; Grzywinski Interview.

83 Lamos Interview; Frazier Interview; Hoyles Interview; Payne Interview; Schcolnik Interview; Sutherland Interview.

84 Lamos Interview; Frazier Interview; Hoyles Interview; Payne Interview; Windham Interview.

The Bank also facilitated sharing in other ways. Jim Bringley's work in actively extending the social networks of his borrowers was an organic form of what has been described in mature economies as institutional monitoring. In the Bank's own interest, he connected people, as Mary Houghton described, like "connecting dots."[85] Although the founders have not articulated it in this manner, it appears that this form of knowledge thickening was a critical component for the Bank in transforming itself into a source of long-term capital. To be clear, formally, the Bank's financing was traditional debt financing, although the loan terms were tailored to the particular market. However, thinking more abstractly about the Bank's knowledge and support of its borrowers over such a long term, the *effect* of the Bank's financing looked remarkably similar to that produced by sources of "patient capital" in mature coordinated economies.

These financial and nonfinancial investments by the Bank acted to strengthen the connections *among* businesses in the network. The relationship did not flow in one direction, namely financing from the Bank in return for repeat and reliable customers. The network was much thicker than that, involving a range of formal and informal cross-network relationships. The builders' associations that developed among the Bank's borrowers, some of which continue to operate to this day, are excellent evidence of these enduring relationships and of the democratic participation that they embody.

These associations began informally, as described by several of the rehabbers. According to George Frazier,

> See at one time [Keith] Banks started a kind of like a club of rehabbers. And one purpose of the club was that people who were starting out rehabbing, they could meet with us and we could give them advice and guidance and stuff like that. And also ... Banks used to have us go to the Bank as a group and discuss what was happening ... [McDonald's] – that was our office ... [A]nytime you go in there, there was somebody there that was part of the group. You know, and Banks was the head one. And people would come there to see Banks and talk to him and ask him questions and stuff. Oh yeah, McDonald's.[86]

Keith Banks was one of the Bank's first rehabber-borrowers. His name will appear again in the following section.

In the last decade, these associations have begun to formalize. For one thing, Keith Banks and some of his contemporaries passed away, and the McDonald's store at which they used to meet moved to a different location.[87] For another, it appears that the networks began to diversify in attendance. And finally, it appears that the Bank's closing in 2010 motivated some of the rehabbers to meet more regularly and formally with each other, both to share information about financing resources and simply to "share stories."[88] Currently, there are at least two formal associations of

85 Houghton Interview. 86 Frazier Interview. 87 *Id.*
88 Sutherland Interview; Feldman Interview; Hoyles Interview; Silver Interview; Payne Interview.

builders who do much of their property investment in South Shore. Andy Schcolnik, the president of the South Side Builders' Association described the origin of one:

> [W]e got together with some guys that had had some success, and said, "You know, I bet there's guys out there that are all by themselves, like we are, and they'd like to sit together and have lunch and share stories, . . . and say which bank is doing what for whom." And . . . and so we started with a small group, and became 16 really quickly, 20, 25 really quickly.[89]

Mark Sutherland, who is the vice president of the same association, added,

> I guess a group of us just decided, hey, we're all building stuff down here. Why don't we get together and talk? And we were careful about not violating any antitrust laws, and not doing anything . . . in terms of unfair competition. But we all got together, and we talked, and we shared subcontractors' names and phone numbers. And we talked about what was working for us, what we were doing. We also do some joint marketing of our homes together . . . I would say my involvement in that organization allowed me to get involved with others in the business. It enabled me to meet people that are either home builders themselves, or other people that do things like sell title insurance, or bankers, and kind of create a network with others in the industry.[90]

Eiran Feldman is the president of the other formal trade association of South Shore rehabbers, the South Side Community Investors' Association. As he described,

> [T]hat's how you help also elevate the quality of a certain profession . . . in an area . . . So I felt that it was really critical for the area to have a good, solid property owners' association, . . . and that it wasn't just important for the property owners. It was important for the communities . . . And because a lot of the old timers and their kids got wiped out in the crash, there was an issue. There [were] a lot of vacant properties, there were a lot of boarded-up properties, and there was a question of who's picking them up, and what they're going to do with them. And I think seeing that kind of an organization, seeing that kind of interaction, was very important.[91]

Feldman also described the connection between the original group that met in McDonald's and this formal trade group: "That core group was very important in the . . . launching of this new group. And they came in, they attended the meetings, and they participated very passionately."[92]

89 Schcolnik Interview. 90 Sutherland Interview.

91 Feldman Interview. When I asked Jack Crane of CIC to reflect on why the rehabber network has been so successful, he emphasized the importance of these trade associations. He also commented, however, that the market continues to change dramatically in South Shore, and one of the most dramatic changes is that large-scale developers with tremendous liquidity are able to buy up and rehabilitate hundreds of units at a time, thereby amassing a much larger market share than the "mom-and-pop" businesses have. Crane Interview.

92 Feldman Interview. Several members of that "core group" commented on the importance of this association, for which Peter Payne served as the first president. Payne Interview; Lamos Interview; Hoyles Interview.

Finally, although it was central to this network of rehabbers, the Bank was not the only financing source that served some of the key functions of an intermediary as I have described them here. Most prominently, the Community Investment Corporation (CIC) in Chicago also has played a critical role. CIC has been providing loans for rehabilitation of apartment buildings since 1984, and especially after the Bank closed in 2010, CIC has become a major source of financing for rehabbers in South Shore.[93] In addition, CIC works with its own affiliates, Community Initiatives, Inc. and the Preservation Compact, to return hundreds of units of distressed and abandoned housing back to the market.[94]

### *Working within the Network*

Over the course of decades, the rehabbers of South Shore had a profound effect on the local economy. Through their businesses, they revitalized block after block, virtually eliminating the area of abandoned properties and contributing to a healthy local market in real estate. The purpose of this section is to examine this story from the perspectives of the owners and workers involved in the rehabbing businesses. I focus especially on how this work affected their own economic circumstances, their personal and economic stability, and their professional trajectories. Of course, there were hundreds of diverse individuals involved in these businesses, and many of them participated over the years in one or more smaller networks, which revolved around ShoreBank. But looking broadly at the rehabber network as a whole, a distinct set of themes emerges. Not surprisingly, this is partly due to the Bank's deep connection with so many of these businesses.

The Bank's founders have described both to me, and in the literature, two distinct networks of rehabbers that sprang up in the very early days of the Bank's work in South Shore, and that arguably originated the larger rehabber network that took shape over decades. One was a group of African American individuals, who lived in or near South Shore and started investing in properties from the late 1970s onward. The other, smaller, network is what Ron Grzywinski has described as the "Croatian janitors," who worked in maintenance jobs not far from the area and, thanks to cultural connections, began to buy and rehabilitate properties in South Shore.[95] By the late 1980s, a third group had developed, namely individuals from especially the North Side of Chicago who began investing in the relatively inexpensive real estate in South Shore. In this section, I describe the individual stories of some of the

93 Crane Interview.

94 *Id.* In this work, there is a much closer working relationship between CIC and its affiliates than there was between ShoreBank's real estate lending department and ShoreBank's nonbank affliates.

95 Grzywinski Interview. Michael O'Connor, the chief appraiser in the real estate lending department, related a number of examples of these two early networks, each of which had its own strong mentoring system, collaborating with each other both to develop certain streets and blocks and in sharing contractors and suppliers. O'Connor Interview.

African American rehabbers who were among the Bank's earliest rehabber-borrowers. I also describe the stories of some of the North Siders.

Although the Bank's very earliest African American rehabber-borrowers have now generally passed away, I spoke with several of their protégés, and they described a fairly common starting point. This is Alice Lamos's description:

> I came to Chicago with my company in 1979. I worked for Sears Roebuck. We transferred from New York City to the Sears tower . . . [When] I moved from New York to Chicago, I purchased a house. And . . . like in any other house, you have things in there [that] need to be done. There was a woman in New York City, it was a friend of the family, told me she knew somebody in Chicago that [was a] handyman . . . So he told me the person who could really help in real estate was Keith Banks, and you can meet him at McDonald's. And I went to McDonald's several times, until I was able to find him. And I introduced myself to him, and I told him what I wanted to do. And he said that's fine, and he said he would help me. So what he did was that he took me around to the areas, . . . and he introduced me to real estate brokers. And he had one real estate broker [who] . . . told him about this 31-unit apartment building that the Bank had, and they wanted to liquidate it.[96]

Another rehabber, Len Hoyles, provided further details about how both Keith Banks and ShoreBank supported businesses like his:

> So here I am, I got this building . . . But I needed some repairs. So I said, "Now where am I going to get this money to do this?" . . . So then Keith Banks literally said, "Come with me. Let's go." We went to the Bank. He had no appointment, no nothing, because he knew Jim Bringley very well . . . And I filled out the papers, and they gave me a $43,750 loan. Still didn't know what the heck I'm doing. So Keith said, "Tell you what. Tell you what." And he had about five guys working for him. "When my guys get off at four o'clock, let them go home and get something to eat, and then you pay them, you get the material, they know what to do." And they did it, . . . they did the apartments . . . [T]he place looked really good. I have to say so myself.[97]

Keith Banks and Jim Bringley are common threads that tie together the stories of most of the rehabbers from this early network whom I interviewed. Rehabber Ocie Windham told of a similar starting point in the business, and he continued the story in a fashion that, again, is common to many of those I interviewed:

> I rehabbed the building. It was one of the prettiest buildings in South Shore. I kept the building for like 17 years . . . It took me about probably eight months to get it fully running . . . And I didn't have a vacant apartment once I fixed it up . . . for maybe four or five years. But it was three or four people within that block that did other properties in that area, because it was really gang-infested in that area. Anyway, what I did, and what three or four other operators with large buildings did, it changed the area . . . No problem renting then, all of us . . . And I did well with that . . . I bought another one. Then when I bought that building, Jim

[96] Lamos Interview. [97] Hoyles Interview.

> [Bringley], he called me to the side to say, "Ocie, you have too much to have a job. Now you need to quit your job and do this full time." So I said, "OK." But he said, "How many units you think that you need in order to feel comfortable?" I sa[id], "I'd probably need about another 75 to a hundred." He said, "Find them." So I went out and looked, got good deals. He financed them for me ... [A]ll of my properties, I can get to them in five or ten minutes ... I kept all of my stuff close, so I can keep a close eye.[98]

These three businesspeople and others whom I interviewed also provided many details about the workers they hired over the years, both as employees and as contractors.[99] While their workforces are typically quite lean, they are also quite stable, as Windham's example shows:

> I have one guy right now, he [has] been working for me 28 years. One 24 years. And one 18 years ... A lot of guys [say], "You pay 'em too much." ... I don't worry about paying 'em too much. I worry about what they [are] doing for me, how they [are] making my business thrive.[100]

My interview with an employee who worked for seven years for one of the rehabbers, shortly after the employee had been released from prison on a drug conviction, suggests a range of informal investments by these employers in their employees:

> [H]e was one guy that took a chance on me, and then also he ... had enough patience to sit there and let me learn as I worked. So I would go to apartments, lady's toilet is leaking. So I called ... I said, "What am I doing here, man? This toilet leaks." So he had to tell me what I had to do. So I borrowed the instructions, and I would do it. So the next time, something else would come up. You know, the lady got a pipe up under her sink is leaking ... [A]nd I would listen, and I'd go do it. But at the same time, I was building up skills. So I worked up under [him] for ... seven years, and then, you know, I just took some of my hustling trade skills I learned from the streets, and just incorporated with working with [him]. So when he would have a vacant apartment, he would give me the first chance to get it done. [I]t worked out good for me for seven years, and then, I ended up getting a better offer from my company, established company. And they were willing to give me much more than what [he] could afford to pay me at the time ... and benefits ... I'm living in one of his properties now, and he reduced my rent, because he said, you know, I've done so much for him. He gives me below-market rent.[101]

Similarly, rehabber Eiran Feldman said about his business,

> [I]t's a point of pride for us that we hire within the community. Some positions lend themselves as an opportunity for people who need a, not second chance or third

98 Windham Interview.

99 Lamos Interview; Hoyles Interview; Windham Interview; Payne Interview.

100 Windham Interview. Peter Payne had a very similar staff with similar longevity. Payne Interview.

101 Interview with Matthew Dale (May 10, 2017). I have used a pseudonym for this interviewee.

> chance, but maybe their tenth chance. And so we feel good about being able to also fill those kinds of positions, and allow people to have success later in their life ... And I think it puts a lot of people at comfort that this company is about the community and understands the needs of the residents.[102]

In addition, all of the rehabbers I interviewed described using the same general network of contractors to do some of the specialty work, such as plumbing and electrical. All of these contractors were nonunion, most appear to have lived in or near South Shore, and it appears many were members of racial minorities. As George Frazier commented, "That kind of started a small industry in itself of contractors."[103] Alice Lamos concluded, "So we did two things. We had the ability to keep them working all the time. And they made sure that the quality of the work was there."[104]

It appears over time that this network of rehabbers involved several hundred rehab owners, regularly including both spouses; hence Ron Grzywinski's reference to "mom-and-pop rehabbers." And each of these owners employed anywhere from one to 15 or more permanent employees and also relied on multiple skilled and unskilled tradespeople to do their rehabbing work. The result was the creation of long-term, generally full-time, jobs for local workers in South Shore. As their descriptions suggest, the owners chose this career path for a range of reasons, including the availability of mentorship and financing, but also as Hoyles described, "to do something for [themselves]."[105] Windham commented, "I had a dear friend [who] kept telling me, 'Go into real estate. You can make it in real estate,' you know. They were ... moving jobs out of the country."[106]

The stories of the North Siders, who began building in South Shore in the late 1980s onward, are more varied in how their businesses began, the networks upon which they relied, and their patterns of growth. However, they share important commonalities with the stories told by the rehabbers who were mentored by Keith Banks, and also with the Eastern European rehabbers described by Grzywinski and others. Most notably, the connection with ShoreBank, and particularly with the individuals in the commercial real estate department, were very similarly described. This description from Mark Sutherland could well have been made by any of the rehabbers I interviewed, although the details of financing would of course vary depending on whether the borrower was rehabbing or doing new construction:

> It was easy and painless. And, you know, when you're building houses, there's so much time and energy required, and you have to focus on the details, like pouring the concrete the right way, ordering the right materials, getting it built so it doesn't leak or fall apart. It's so many little details that it's just like financing, ... having as little red tape as possible was important to me ... It was just nice to find ... a lender that made it all easy. And after we had done, you know, a, a few deals, it seemed like

[102] Feldman Interview. [103] Frazier Interview. [104] Lamos Interview. [105] Hoyles Interview.
[106] Windham Interview.

> it just got easier and easier and easier. Typically we would buy the land for cash, and then get a construction loan for 100 percent of the cost of the construction ... And we always sold the houses for enough to pay back the construction loan first of course, and our equity, and then be left with a profit as well.[107]

Of course, for African American borrowers, it was also about financial access. As George Frazier noted,

> South Shore Bank, they would work with the people in the community, you see. And the other banks – no, they would not. They would not. Now, we are talking 40 years ago. Thirty years ago. Now, the fact [is] that things have improved a little since then because those other banks when they saw this and how successful South Shore Bank was, then they started being a little more liberal.[108]

Jack Crane, who worked in that department for seven years, and now leads the lending department at Community Investment Corporation in Chicago, commented,

> It was a wonderful place, because ... it was a place where people with talent, chutzpah, and a little bit of capital ... could come to 71st and Jeffery on the South Side, at ShoreBank, and they were welcomed.[109]

As with the two original networks of rehabbers, it appears the North Siders relied heavily on financing from the Bank.[110] And as with these other networks, this third wave of rehabbers who invested in South Shore from the late 1980s onward received enough support from the Bank to make a career out of their development work, though it does not appear that Bringley was so deeply involved in helping them make the transition from rehabbing on the side to quitting their "day jobs" and doing it full time.[111]

Another theme that cuts across most of my interviews with rehabbers is the extraordinary importance and resource intensiveness of property management in their work. All but one of the rehabbers I interviewed manage their own rental buildings, and they described this as the norm in South Shore. They all emphasized that it is absolutely critical to screen and manage tenants well, and that this is a learned skill.[112] As Windham described,

> [T]hat's the key to renting in an area like this, with large buildings. Who you put in there ... Don't put drug dealers ... If I took young men, I wanted to know what high

107 Sutherland Interview. 108 Frazier Interview. 109 Crane Interview.

110 Silver Interview; Sutherland Interview.

111 Crane Interview. Jack Crane also commented that it appears to have been harder for some of the North Siders to develop a network of contractors, because they did not have the consistently strong mentoring relationships through which the network of contractors was built in the first decade of the Bank's multifamily lending.

112 Feldman Interview; Payne Interview; Hoyles Interview; Windham Interview; Frazier Interview; Lamos Interview; O'Connor Interview.

> school they went to, . . . what kind of student. I'm going to sit down and have a heart-to-heart talk to you about what are you expecting in living [here].[113]

Even when he owned several hundred rental units, Windham personally interviewed every prospective tenant.[114] Lamos commented, "I think one of the reasons why South Shore area has been successful is most of us are our own managers. And that makes a big difference."[115] As Hoyles described, this can be difficult and indeed heartbreaking to do, but it can also create opportunities:

> [W]e did a credit check, and it came back that he had been [evicted]. I said, "Well, give me three months security." And then, you know, "you pay your rent on time, and I'll give you back a month." He did that, and then I gave him another month, because he was on time. He eventually got his college degree. He's a coach; he went to coaching football.[116]

### *The Bank's Closing and Its Aftermath*

In 2010, ShoreBank closed, becoming the fifteenth Illinois bank to fail that year.[117] Not surprisingly, the Bank was unable to ride out the waves of job losses, leading to rent reductions and defaults, and ultimately mortgage defaults by its own borrowers. Although the Bank was reopened as the Urban Partnership Bank by a consortium of major banks and philanthropic groups, that effort at continuing the community development mission of the original bank in South Shore also faltered when, in December 2013, the Urban Partnership Bank closed the South Shore branch in which the original ShoreBank had remade itself.[118]

At first blush, the Bank's failure in the midst of the financial crisis might appear to be a unique story of unprecedented risk that could not be anticipated or avoided in the future. It might appear that the Bank failed because of the terrible bad luck of businesses caught up in the "perfect storm" of the financial crisis of 2008. In addition, it might seem that the Bank made the awful mistake of diversifying its portfolio too little. It might seem that it never broke out of a thin, local market. Or it might seem that it was too limited in its range of investments, too focused on the needs of insiders, and too weighed down with too many priorities. This could appear to be a story about a Bank operating on too thin a margin of risk.

Irrefutably, if we take into consideration the failures in the national market for residential mortgages, this was partially a story about market failure. The

[113] Windham Interview. [114] *Id.* [115] Lamos Interview. [116] Hoyles Interview.

[117] Becky Yerak, *Chicago's ShoreBank Fails, Is Bought by Investors*, CHICAGO TRIBUNE, Aug. 20, 2010, http://articles.chicagotribune.com/2010-08-20/business/ct-biz-0821-shorebank-20100820_1_fdic-assets-david-vitale.

[118] Steve Daniels, *Why Urban Partnership Bank is Downscaling*, CRAIN'S CHICAGO BUSINESS, Dec. 16, 2013, www.chicagobusiness.com/article/20131214/ISSUE01/312149985/why-urban-partnership-bank-is-downscaling.

informational asymmetries that confounded the secondary market had a devastating domino effect on banks like ShoreBank. As Grzywinski described,

> [T]here were more delinquencies as the economy got worse, but there were still a lot of people repaying loans. We had gotten up to ... 30 percent unemployment rates in most of our markets. And so people were having a more difficult time paying rents, and our building owners had a more difficult time making their loan payments. But what the regulators did was write everything down based on current values, and that was what took the Bank's capital down from ... 6 percent or so ... to 1 percent, which was then undercapitalized. If they would have done what they had done in the past, and when loans remained current, they were not written down, ... we probably would have skated by and would have had enough capital to survive.[119]

Even at that point, the Bank put together a plan for survival, which involved raising 153 million dollars of capital in order to obtain 72 million dollars of money allocated for CDFIs under the Troubled Asset Relief Program (TARP). Despite the Bank having raised the required amount, however, an inter-governmental body of federal regulators refused to release the TARP money to save the Bank.[120]

Today, almost a decade after ShoreBank closed, and several years after its successor closed its South Shore branch, there is talk of a sale by the building owners to a developer who plans to demolish the main bank building and install a McDonald's drive-through-only restaurant in the location of the former Bank parking lot.[121] One local resident described the pullout by Urban Partnership Bank, combined with the closing of a local supermarket, as having created a "food desert" overnight and as contributing to "redlining and corporate disinvestment" in the neighborhood.[122] While the neighborhood remains the site of local activism, residents appear to fear a falling back from the levels of local investment and community spirit that it achieved over the previous four decades.

The focus of my research was on the experiences of those involved in the rehabber network while the Bank was still operating as their main source of financing. Thus, I have no statistics about the number of rehabbers who survived the Bank's closing. On the basis of my interviews, it is at least fair to say that many rehabbing businesses failed around the time that the Bank closed. But many also survived.[123] Not

119 Grzywinski Interview.

120 Sheila Bair, Bull by the Horns: Fighting to Save Main Street from Wall Street and Wall Street from Itself 286–289 (2012).

121 Sam Cholke, *McDonald's to Replace Urban Partnership Bank? Some Neighbors Not Thrilled*, DNA Info (Feb. 27, 2014), www.dnainfo.com/chicago/20140227/south-shore-above-79th/mcdonalds-replace-urban-partnership-bank-some-neighbors-not-thrilled.

122 Steven Vance, *South Shore Residents Resist Demolition of Walkable Retail Block*, Streets Blog Chicago (Mar. 20, 2014), http://chi.streetsblog.org/2014/03/20/south-shore-residents-resist-demolition-of-walkable-retail-block. Business owner Alice Lamos also discussed the difficulty of operating rental properties in neighborhoods that lacked local stores selling groceries and other essentials. Lamos Interview.

123 Schcolnik Interview; Feldman Interview; Hoyles Interview; Windham Interview.

surprisingly, one of the most significant factors impacting their survival was the ability of these businesses to find other sources of financing. For some of the rehabbers, ShoreBank was still the only game in town. Thus, when the Bank failed, those businesses had no other meaningful source of financing to which to turn. Others were stabilized enough that they could turn to private equity and to other banks, though many of my interviewees commented that the market for real estate loans in South Shore has tightened considerably.[124]

As for the current level of demand for rentals in South Shore, the rehabbers I interviewed made a range of comments. George Frazier commented,

> [W]hen I first started, there were blighted buildings, abandoned buildings ... on almost every block ... There was our little group of rehabbers, but there were other people too that we didn't know ... rehabbing apartments in South Shore. And it got to a point where there were hardly any abandoned buildings in South Shore ... [T]hen it started looking like it was going down. You started seeing abandoned buildings again.[125]

Len Hoyles noted the changes in the rental market:

> Certain things were easier back then than they are now. And one of them is getting tenants. Back in the day, if you had a vacancy and you talked to five people, you're going to get at least one or two out of that five that [were] decent. You know, they had a 600, 625 credit score ... It just seems now, I gotta go through 10, 12 people, to get a decent tenant.[126]

A few of the rehabbers with whom I spoke reacted to these changes by moving their businesses to other parts of the city. Others are in the process of retiring. But despite the acknowledged difficulties with the rental market, most of the rehabbers I interviewed remain explicitly invested – both financially and psychologically – in South Shore.[127]

### *Regulatory Context*

As I have described, the legal opportunity on which the Bank built its remarkable model came in the form of the 1970 amendments to the Bank Holding Company Act, pursuant to which the Federal Reserve Board explicitly authorized investment in community development corporations and the formation of subsidiaries to engage in community development activities. The passage of the federal

124 Feldman Interview; Silver Interview; Hoyles Interview; Payne Interview; Windham Interview.

125 Frazier Interview. 126 Hoyles Interview.

127 Hoyles Interview; Schcolnik Interview; Lamos Interview; Windham Interview. Eiran Feldman commented, about his business's approach, "We're very passionate about what we're doing. We care about the communities that we operate in. We believe in being involved in the communities. We help organize different events and different initiatives. And we enjoy what we're doing." Feldman Interview.

Community Development Banking and Financial Institutions Act of 1994 added another layer of regulatory support for institutions like the Bank,[128] although the Bank was already so large and well established by 1994 that it did not have to rely on that statute to support its growth and operations. Both the language of the 1994 statute and my interviews with Bank employees suggest that the real value of the statute is in supporting the chartering of new community banks. But as I will discuss in Chapter 10, it also appears that other constraints have severely limited the statute's utility even for this purpose.

A third federal statute, passed in 1977, that some Bank employees did describe as very helpful to the Bank is the Community Reinvestment Act (CRA).[129] The purpose of the CRA is to encourage banks to meet the credit needs of individuals and businesses in low-income neighborhoods.[130] The CRA requires banks to keep a record of their efforts in this regard. Federal regulatory agencies review this record when banks apply to them for approval of applications to merge with or acquire other banks. Banks are evaluated under the CRA for their levels and forms of lending to, investment in, and service to underserved communities. According to Cliff Kellogg, who was employed by the Bank for a number of years, there were enough banks merging and opening new branches in the area that they were looking for low-risk ways to meet CRA requirements. And investing in ShoreBank was a great way to do it:

> I think we at ShoreBank benefited most . . . from the Community Reinvestment Act, because that motivated other banks to look for banking opportunities in these communities, and to look at ShoreBank as an example of how to lend profitably in them . . . [The] CRA . . . also was very helpful in raising shareholder capital from banks as investors . . . The investment test was an area where many banks did not have a strong performance. The purchase of equity shares in the ShoreBank holding company could count that towards their investment tests under CRA. There's no question that was a big motivator for banks to become ShoreBank shareholders.[131]

For banks such as ShoreBank, however, these federal laws have several important limitations. First, even under more recent federal rules, they do not really provide alternative benchmarks for community development financial institutions or other banks investing in urban cores to meet. For example, safety and soundness requirements are keyed to markedly different banking contexts, and they provide no clear consideration for the special role of community banks, nor for the special risks they take on. One observation to make about this lacking, as the Bank's long-time general counsel so nicely articulated, is that "[i]f every one of your loans pays off, you should be taking more risk."[132] Some risk may well be appropriate for banks such as

128 Community Development Banking and Financial Institutions Act of 1994, Pub. L. No. 103–325 §§ 101–185, 108 Stat. 2161 (codified at 12 U.S.C. § 4701 et seq. (2016)).

129 12 U.S.C. § 2901 et seq. (2016).

130 Indeed Ron Grzywinski testified before the Senate Banking Committee in favor of enacting the CRA.

131 Kellogg Interview.

132 Interview with Chris Horsch, ShoreBank Corporation (October 29, 2015).

ShoreBank to take on. It may be "healthy risk," but it is not recognized as such by banking laws and regulations. Second, these laws provide very few financial incentives or support for the healthy *maintenance* of community development financial institutions.

Finally, and more broadly, these laws appear to focus more on creating incentives for community investment by large, national banks in urban cores rather than for smaller, neighborhood banks. This insufficiently motivates banks to develop local specializations, making ShoreBank's achievements in this respect all the more exceptional. As Dan Broughton so eloquently put it, "A community development bank's mission is to invest in the location. It should ask what is healthy for the community and engage in mission-driven activities. But this is a harder way to make money."[133] I would add to Broughton's point, that the current banking framework does not recognize this basic fact.

Thus, after initially offering a regulatory means for banks to support community development and multiple bottom lines, policymakers provided very little ongoing support either for that structure or for the banks that relied on it. During the financial crisis, for example, Congress provided a federal guaranty of the obligations of large banks, effectively raising the cost of borrowing for small, community banks.[134] Meanwhile, credit unions, which are key players in lower-income communities, received less than one-ten-thousandth of the monies disbursed through TARP.[135] Even in the face of popular pressure to "move your money" to local banks, a limited structure still exists for certifying, capitalizing, and supporting such banks.[136] Viewed through a lens sensitive to a range of capitalist forms, the response by banking regulators and other federal authorities to the financial crisis was a dramatic and instinctual falling back: regulators "socialized loss" in order to protect the portfolios and wealth of the banking institutions that had most benefited from the period of banking deregulation that iconically served the national liberal market economy. But for those community development banks, credit unions, and neighborhood banks that served a more limited function within the liberal economy, there was very little legal and institutional support in bad times.[137]

Thanks to Houghton's and Grzywinski's extraordinary reflexivity, however, there are more regulatory lessons to be learned from the details of the Bank's untimely demise. The Bank's lending portfolio as a percentage of total assets was large in

[133] Broughton Interview.

[134] *See* Ronald J. Mann, *After the Great Recession: Regulating Financial Services for Low- and Middle-Income Communities*, 69 Wash. & Lee L. Rev. 729, 731 (2012).

[135] Clifford Rosenthal, *Credit Unions, Community Development Finance, and the Great Recession*, 43 (Fed. Reserve Bank of S. F., Community Development Investment Center Working Paper No. 2012–01, 2012).

[136] *Id.* at 46–47.

[137] For a compelling discussion of the efforts to save the Bank during the Great Recession, see Bair, Bull by the Horns at 285–291. *See also* James E. Post & Fiona S. Wilson, *Too Good to Fail*, Stanford Social Innovation Review, Fall 2011, at 66.

comparison to similarly sized banks. The Bank also had a high CAMELS rating (which rates safety and soundness) and passed all applicable tests for capitalization. But as both founders described, even in the best of times, the Bank was capitalized at a lower level than they would have liked. It was less well capitalized than its counterpart institutions in Canada and Europe.[138] As the Bank's general counsel Chris Horsch has described, however, the Bank was, for the most part, limited to the same options for raising equity capital and deposits that were available to other financial institutions. Some of these were very useful, such as the ability to solicit FDIC-insured "development deposits" – social investments before their time – from individuals around the country. In addition, the "program related investments" from major national foundations were a clear exception in this regard.[139] These were possible because the foundations that made them could easily demonstrate both that their investments were "below market" and that they supported the foundations' charitable goals. But the Bank's status as a CDFI did not open many special pathways for funding. Indeed, it seems fair to say that the equity shares that the Bank's holding company sold in private placements, which were already illiquid by virtue of not being publicly traded, were especially illiquid because the Bank prioritized its community development mission at least equally with making a profit.

Moreover, much of the Bank's risk was indeed concentrated in the real estate market on the south and west sides of Chicago. As Houghton described, "The rehab loans were high-quality assets and profitable, so nobody wanted to sell them. But with hindsight, we had too much concentrated risk within that market."[140] For a financial institution, the standard solution to this problem would be to diversify one's lending portfolio. But, perhaps assuming that such a move would have substantially diluted the power of their lending strategy, Houghton and Grzywinski always had another solution in mind, one which they articulated still when reflecting on the Bank's collapse five years later. Their solution would have been to create a secondary market in the multifamily loans they were making, one that "was more tolerant and more open to local practices and to local underwriting."[141] Such a market exists for single-family loans; indeed, that is the market that spiraled out of control in 2008 as a result of subprime lending. Moreover, the Federal Housing Finance Agency has recently issued a new regulation requiring Fannie Mae and Freddie Mac (the government-sponsored entities that catalyzed such a market for single-family loans) to facilitate just such a market for loans for small multifamily rental developments.[142] But Houghton and Grzywinski concluded that their loans were so unorthodox that no institutional investor would seriously consider investing in them on the secondary market.[143]

138 Houghton Interview. 139 Horsch Interview.

140 Houghton Interview. The Bank's former borrowers were sympathetic to this fact, recognizing that it put the Bank in a difficult position. For example, Michael Silver aptly stated, "[T]hey suffered by proximity to all of the riskiest loans. Even if they didn't make the riskiest loans, their loans were in the same location as the riskiest loans." Silver Interview.

141 Grzywinski Interview. 142 12 C.F.R. § 1282 (2016).

143 Houghton Interview; Grzywinski Interview.

If in the last few decades of deregulating banks in the name of increasing competition, federal regulators had carved out some regulatory space for protecting financial institutions that were interested in community investment rather than national competition, perhaps the Bank could have survived the storm. Such a space could have been created by making even broader exceptions for community banks from the conflict-of-interest rules that prevent banks from engaging in non-banking activities. In turn, those rules could have allowed for cross-subsidization of banking activities that might be perceived as riskier because they were targeted to a previously unbanked population. Or regulators could have created greater benefits for banks engaged in "community reinvestment."[144] Or they could have created a structure in which community banks could be supported more expansively by public-private partnerships. This was something Chris Horsch devised but was never allowed to implement because of banking regulations.[145] Or, of course, they could have chosen to bail out banks that were more deeply invested in developing low-income communities.

As both founders described, a broader range of options for raising capital combined with a secondary market for spreading risk would have allowed the Bank to invest in South Shore as a business strategy, while acknowledging that the strategy was, as Houghton described, "inherently more risky."[146] Thinking in terms of the "bottom line," regulators ultimately told the Bank that this strategy was too risky. But thinking in terms of their "double bottom line," Houghton and Grzywinski could imagine several strategies for spreading the risk *in order* to accomplish the important goal of neighborhood (and local market) development.[147]

While the federal banking regulatory framework played a significant role in shaping the work of the Bank within the rehabber network, local law also was a significant factor. The most obvious impact of local laws was, and still is, in the area of building codes. Like many other cities, Chicago imposes complex regulations on rehabilitation, as distinguished here from new construction.[148] While my

144 *See* Barr, *Credit Where It Counts*.

145 The idea of public/private investments in community banks was also raised sometime ago by economist Hyman Minsky. *See* L. Randall Wray, *Minsky's Money Manager Capitalism: Assessment and Reform*, *in* AFTER THE GREAT RECESSION: THE STRUGGLE FOR ECONOMIC RECOVERY AND GROWTH 61, 81 (Barry Z. Cynamon et al. eds., 2013).

146 Houghton Interview.

147 *See* Werhane, *Moral Imagination* at 93 (admiring the "moral imagination [of the founders] to engage in a project that no other Chicago bank at that time would engage in, in a neighborhood that leading sociologists had written off, and to see the low-risk element in this kind of venture, particularly when the project is neither a government project nor a charity but is a for-profit and a profitable enterprise. The bank worked within given social conditions and banking regulations, and then reconfigured the framework of traditional 'banking logic' to test the hypothesis that they could do banking under challenging circumstances and under redefined conditions.").

148 *See* CHICAGO, ILLINOIS, MUNICIPAL CODE §§ 13–200-010 – 13–200-480 (2017). The complexity of the codes has been the subject of activism and discussion. The codes have also been revised to lower the costs of rehabilitating multifamily housing. *See* Fassil Demissie, *Globalization and the Remaking of Chicago*, *in* THE NEW CHICAGO: A SOCIAL AND CULTURAL ANALYSIS 19, 28 (John P. Koval ed., 2006);

interviewees clearly found ways to comply with such regulations, it was also apparent that their compliance with (and their time spent learning about) these codes added costs to their work. One obvious impact of these costs was that they had to offset them with lower costs for labor. This raises the question whether the City could have found ways to streamline and lower the regulatory burden of its building code for a network such as this, partly in order to create incentives to hire locally and pay higher wages to local residents. In situations where rehabbers were engaged in conversions of buildings from rental to condominium and in new construction, they also had to navigate local zoning codes, boards and authorities at additional costs.

Many of the rehabbers I interviewed also raised the issue of landlord-tenant regulations. While none complained about the protections for tenants, many commented on the lack of certainty for landlords in some of these regulations. Their message was that they were more than willing to comply, but that they regularly wished for guidance on how exactly to comply. Several rehabbers also raised the difficult bind they found themselves in when tenants used or sold illegal drugs in their buildings. Their particular concern was that the length of time required to evict such tenants sometimes caused the buildings to "turn," meaning that good tenants moved out because of the danger and nuisance caused by their neighbors.[149] While there is no easy answer to these concerns, it is important for local authorities to take them seriously, given the important balance of protecting tenants while also preserving space for market activity and economic development.

Finally, it is noteworthy in this context that the network has not been subject to higher minimum wage and similar employment laws. This provides an interesting counterpoint to the home care network, which I will take up in Chapter 7. For now, it should suffice to note that the rehabbers hired locally and created work conditions that resulted in relatively long-term employment opportunities for those whom they hired. In contrast to the home care network, however, they did this in the absence of a regulatory framework that required some of these things.

## *Other Networks, Other Markets*

While the rehabber network was the largest, most successful, and most well-known business network to grow up around the Bank, it was not the only one. In this section, I describe two other networks that the Bank supported, one of which was more successful than the other. These networks received support from a different department than the one that supported the rehabbers. The rehabbers received loans

Community Investment Corporation, *City of Chicago Announces Building Code Relief to Encourage Redevelopment of Affordable Housing Across the City*, The Preservation Compact (Feb. 24, 2017), www.preservationcompact.org/wp-content/uploads/TPC-Building-Code-Announcement-2.24.17.pdf.

149 This is the subject of some discussion within the trade associations operating in the South Side and beyond. Feldman Interview; Sutherland Interview; Hellwig Interview.

through the commercial real estate department headed by Jim Bringley, while the networks described in this section received loans through the business banking department. In important respects, the Bank applied the same lending approach to these networks as it did to the rehabbers, but it could only do so up to a point. This was partly because of the important differences in market context experienced by these other networks. The focus of my analysis will be on these differences in market context, and the ways in which they impacted both the Bank's lending and the networks' ability to grow and succeed.

**Franchises**

All of the Bank employees that I interviewed who had experience with the business banking department commented that one of its lending challenges was the great variety of businesses to which it made loans. As Mary Houghton, who headed the department for some time, described, it was hard for the department to specialize and thereby create the kinds of efficiencies that Jim Bringley's commercial real estate department was able to achieve. One important exception to this claim was the lending that this department did to franchise owners, in particular owners of Dunkin' Donuts franchises in the Chicago area. Although the Dunkin' Donuts network of ShoreBank borrowers never got close in size to the rehabber network, it was nevertheless a stable network that shared some significant similarities with the rehabber network.

It appears that the Bank made loans to franchise owners from its earliest years as a community development bank. Among its first franchisee-borrowers were African American owners of McDonald's stores.[150] In the early 1990s, the Bank also began to lend to Dunkin' Donuts store owners. The first such borrower was a South Asian man who already owned one Dunkin' Donuts store and came to the Bank for financing to buy several more. As Dan Broughton, who was involved in making the loan decision, recalled,

> [W]e looked at it, and we really liked [the borrower]. He's a very good business person and just sort of low key, but works real hard, . . . a good customer. So we went out on a limb; we were fairly aggressive as a bank in financing this acquisition for him, and we really looked at it as a cash flow deal. A cash flow and a character deal, which for a bank is hard to do. You know, normally you're underwriting cash flow and collateral. With a Dunkin Donuts location, if it doesn't work, you have used equipment which is worth ten cents on the dollar.
>
> But when we looked at it, there are some things about that group of borrowers which give you some confidence, and also about the particular franchise. What we found over the years, and is still true today, is that people's addiction to coffee and to doughnuts is a pretty powerful thing . . . So the cash flow was pretty stable, and then the Dunkin Donuts in Chicago, it's primarily Indians and Pakistanis . . . And [they] approach their business more as families than as individuals. It's really sort of

[150] Broughton Interview.

> interesting, you know, over the years, having conversations where families were buying another location, or starting another location, and you talk with them ... You know, you got a father and two sons at ... the table. "Who's gonna own this?" And they sort of look at each other like, "Well, you wanna own it?" or "You wanna own it?" And so they don't think about, "This is mine," whereas in the American culture, you want to own things personally ... And that really allowed us to underwrite the cash flow. And then as we got more involved, we got a little bit more sophisticated, and developed some additional ways of thinking about it, but that's really how we got involved in the first place.[151]

As with the original group of rehabbers, this original Dunkin' Donuts borrower spread the word to others, and the network evolved from there. Broughton continued:

> [W]e started getting referrals from our existing franchisees. There was a time where we were one of the few games in town ... And so people heard about us, and we really had wonderful opportunities to meet people ... [W]ell then you really had a source of information about who was doing well, and how their locations were doing.[152]

Thus, these borrowers developed not only a network of referrals for financing from the Bank, but also a network of information for the Bank to use in making loan-related decisions. Also like the original rehabbers, the network was bound together by ethnic, social, and cultural ties. Indeed, Broughton's colleague in that department, Kaushik Shah, noted that many of the Dunkin' Donuts borrowers were also members of the Ismaili Muslim community.[153]

As the network of Dunkin' Donuts borrowers grew, they began to share more than just information about financing. According to Broughton,

> Then what they started doing was they would have one larger location with a kitchen, and two or three or four smaller locations, and they would just bake at one location, and then deliver to the other locations. And then two or three or four of the franchisees would get together, and figure out how to do a central kitchen, and I think that model continued to develop.[154]

Shah described the end result:

> [T]hen they individually also became part of this program, ... almost a co-op after they had initially opened [the doughnut manufacturing facility]. [A]nd then bought the building, put the lines in, and hired somebody to run the manufacturing side of selling doughnuts. ... You have people working from 4 p.m. to say 3 a.m. And then 3 a.m., your doughnuts are ready, and they're being supplied to 150, I believe now, stores.[155]

Indeed, this seems to be a relatively common pattern among Dunkin' Donuts franchisees outside of Chicago as well.

[151] *Id.* [152] *Id.* [153] Interview with Kaushik Shah, ShoreBank (March 31, 2017).
[154] Broughton Interview. [155] Shah Interview.

Ultimately, as Shah described, the network was able to grow quite aggressively thanks in part to the Bank's financing:

> [T]here was an aggressive growth plan by a lot of these Dunkin' franchisees. We felt secure enough with our existing portfolio, our referral base, our existing customers, and their locations were strong, throwing off excess cash flow. Dunkin' was making a push to grow in Chicagoland, . . . people were buying . . . territories, so to speak [on which] that they had the first right of refusal.[156]

While Shah emphasized that for the Bank, these loans were simply good business, he also observed that, in retrospect,

> [W]e created wealth . . . [A]nd Dan [Broughton] would tell you, you open one store, or two stores, and you're buying yourself a job. Once you have five plus, or ten stores, you're creating wealth. And you're creating wealth for the next generation, and you're creating a better livelihood.[157]

One of the reasons the Dunkin' Donuts network is useful to explore here is that it provides an excellent point of comparison as a collaborative enterprise. This example suggests that franchises can function as more formalized versions of the collaborative business networks that I have described. Moreover, they are a more vertically integrated version of sharing, effectively a hybrid between, on the one hand, a business with multiple subsidiaries that together can take a product or service from creation, to development, to distribution in the market, and on the other, the "horizontal" networks that I have described in this book.

Several of my interviewees noted that not all franchises are successful in this regard, but that Dunkin' Donuts appears to have been so for several reasons. First, as Broughton described, Dunkin' Donuts has filled a well-defined niche, and it has also been careful in not overly saturating the market, for example by spacing its stores far enough apart that they are able to bring in a reasonable profit. Second, its franchise arrangements are structured in such a way as to share critical resources. As Cliff Kellogg, who worked in the business lending department for several years, noted, "Franchises have a supply network. Franchises provide advertising to support all of their stores. They have price points for what products should sell for. Franchise owners know approximately what their costs should be in every category . . . In a way, it's an instant seal of quality."[158] These are just a few examples of shared resources, and in the case of the South Shore Dunkin' Donuts franchisees (and it appears, Dunkin' Donuts franchisees more generally), it is clear that these owners also shared suppliers and manufacturing facilities. Finally, franchisees are a favorite of community banks, and also large banks having to comply with the Community Reinvestment Act, precisely because the franchisor invests so many resources into its franchisees and standardizes so many of the business operations that (especially in the start-up phase) can trip up small businesses. All of these features of franchises

156 *Id.* 157 *Id.* 158 Kellogg Interview.

teach important lessons for new business owners. They also may be an instructive model for the range of collaborative business networks I describe in this book.

**Manufacturing Businesses in the Austin Neighborhood of Chicago**

In addition to supporting franchisees, the Bank's business lending department also worked very hard to support the development of at least two other networks. One was a much more loosely defined network of local, minority-owned businesses covering a range of industries in South Shore, including a hairdresser, a bowling alley, a dry cleaner, and a seafood restaurant.[159] I will have more to say about the struggles inherent in this effort later in this chapter.

The other network was not in South Shore, but rather in the Austin neighborhood in the western part of Chicago. This was an effort to strengthen the community by creating a labor force intermediary to coordinate job preparation, together with an enterprise strategy to support local businesses. It was called the Austin Initiative. Cliff Kellogg, who opened an office of the Bank in that neighborhood in the early 1990s, led the enterprise strategy:

> [T]his was a neighborhood with a lot of small manufacturing companies in it . . . I moved an office there as the first commercial loan officer to be full-time officed outside of 71st and Jeffery [the Bank headquarters], and started making loans to those companies . . . [S]ome days, I would take a fistful of business cards and just knock on the door of one company after another, and leave a card. Austin also had some neighborhood manufacturing groups that were a little bit like community development corporations, like a small Chamber of Commerce; they might focus on just the businesses in the neighborhood. I would attend those meetings and introduce myself. The Bank sponsored neighborhood educational events, to introduce ourselves to the local businesses there. Gradually, we built a successful portfolio in the Austin neighborhood.[160]

Kellogg described the goal and approach of the Austin Initiative:

> The idea of the Austin Initiative was to try to rebuild the strength of the Austin neighborhood, not just by helping people find any job, but by helping them find jobs locally in the small manufacturing businesses that ringed the neighborhood . . . [W]e certainly weren't the only ones to observe that . . . [this] neighborhood that was probably more than 90 percent African American was not accessing jobs in the small manufacturing companies. There was a real disjunction between the employment opportunities right in their own neighborhood, and the job networks available to the African American residents. And partly that was due to historic factors. Martin Luther King marched through the town of Cicero, which is adjacent to the Austin neighborhood. I don't mean to say that the owners of the manufacturing companies shared those racial views, but . . . the business environment of the manufacturers was different than the day-to-day job seeking by residents of Austin. They just didn't

[159] *Id.* [160] *Id.*

> really overlap, or connect. We thought that ... a promising way to strengthen the neighborhood would be to bring those two different communities together ...
>
> In terms of its activities, the labor force intermediary coordinated with job training programs and the local high school so that residents had the skills that company owners were looking for. The labor force staff formed job clubs of Austin residents, as well as a job placement agency for part-time workers.
>
> On the enterprise side, we attempted several strategies to strengthen the small manufacturers. One strategy was to provide consulting services to individual companies. We had an engineer and a former plant foreman on staff ... The second intervention with small manufacturing companies was to form peer groups of the company owners themselves ... The third strategy was an African American entrepreneurship group called the Runners Club ... This is long before anybody talked about accelerators and incubators, but that's what we were doing with high-potential entrepreneurs and investors ... And the fourth intervention was a special loan fund to lend to manufacturing companies, with a special incentive kicker: we would reduce the interest rate if the business owner hired local residents.[161]

But in the end, the Austin Initiative was not sustainable. When I asked Kellogg to reflect on why, he shared several key insights:

> [I]t was very hard to keep the peer groups together, except for the African American Runners Club of entrepreneurs, which did continue for a few years. The peer groups would meet four or five times, but then the energy would dissipate ... I suppose the West Side manufacturing companies and the West Side residents – both types of self-help groups – never quite saw enough gain of staying with the initiative. In comparison, the South Side rehabbers' groups found a lot of benefit from learning from each other, and they could make a good living from learning from each other. In the rehabber groups, they had role models, examples of folks who had started in the real estate business, and over five or ten years had started to do generally pretty well. That benefit keeps people coming back, and sustains the energy. A few of the small manufacturing companies really did prosper, but not enough to build a strong employment base. The Austin Initiative did successfully place at least a hundred residents into jobs, but it simply wasn't successful enough, for the amount of effort, to get those results.[162]

## COLLABORATIVE CAPITALISM IN SOUTH SHORE

The story of the networks of businesses that developed around ShoreBank is a unique story, filled with strong personalities, distinctive context, and of course an extraordinary institution at the center. As this section will demonstrate, however, it is also possible to trace through this story the outlines of collaborative capitalism that I have delineated in Chapter 3. My purpose in describing the development of collaborative capitalism in South Shore is not to present an agenda for replicating

[161] *Id.* [162] *Id.*

it elsewhere. Rather it is to build my argument that collaborative capitalism exists in contexts such as this one, and further, as I will discuss in Part III, that by paying attention to the particular market practices in such contexts we can develop regulatory and other means to support them. This, then, is my focus in describing the particular features of collaborative capitalism as they appear in the South Shore context.

### *Coordinated Activities of Businesses*

The most unambiguous example of coordination in South Shore was in the area of financing. The Bank purposefully employed a strategy of providing loans for rehab *in* South Shore and other focused communities, imposing terms that limited incentives for flipping and speculating, and creating synergies for development of market rate units in sub-neighborhoods that had already benefited from affordable housing development. By means of this sophisticated system of lending with certain incentives, the Bank coordinated business activity *through the medium of financing*.

In addition, while the coordination among the mom-and-pop rehabbing businesses in South Shore is very different from the coordination over vocational training, wages, and work terms and conditions that has occurred in the home care example, it is nonetheless quite startling to realize the level of coordination that did in fact take place in the South Shore network. These businesses relied on each other in sharing the labor required to accomplish the multiple components of rehabilitating a multifamily building. Partly because of the special regulations involved, building rehab can be more expensive than new construction. And it takes knowledge of the many different aspects of construction to do it successfully. Despite having very few employees each, and therefore specializing in only one or two of the necessary trades for completing a rehab, these businesses managed to share labor in such a way as to complete each project efficiently. Using a horizontal structure of shared labor, the businesses developed a "peer-to-peer" system before that became a term of art. Eventually, thanks to Jim Bringley's efforts and to the ongoing interests of business owners themselves, the businesses also developed an informal training system, whereby they began to teach each other management and specialty construction skills in an effort to internalize some of the functions that they earlier had to externalize.

### *Institutional Intermediaries That Serve a Coordinating Function*

ShoreBank acted as the main institutional intermediary that served a coordinating function among the small-scale developers who rehabilitated housing as a means of earning income and building a future home for themselves. Perhaps most importantly for this particular success story, the Bank provided financing in such a way and with such a deep level of both expertise and commitment to multiple and local bottom lines and stakeholders as to create a unified trajectory for the development of businesses, individuals, housing and community. Not surprisingly, the Bank played a significant role in nearly all facets of coordinating and strengthening the network in South Shore. From lowering critical costs, to prioritizing a focus on local neighborhood development, to finding and exploiting an ideal niche market, the Bank had an important institutional role to play. In these respects, it did the work that several coordinating intermediaries typically do together in national coordinated economies.

Especially since the Bank's closing, the Community Investment Corporation has also served as a sharing intermediary. It has been a significant source of financing. And working with its affiliates, it has encouraged the further development of local trade associations and other means of communication and collaboration.

Moreover, these two financing sources were by no means the only intermediaries in this network. In this story, we have several rich examples of local trade associations that developed from a very early point in the network's existence. The earliest example is the informal group of rehabbers who met at a local McDonald's store and whom Jim Bringley invited to meet on a regular basis at the Bank as well. This group, though informal, appears to have been an amazingly powerful locus of mentoring, vocational education, and information sharing. Over time, and it appears especially at the point when the Bank closed, we also have two examples of cohesive, well-attended, and well-functioning formal trade associations. Arguably, these associations function like many others around the United States. But it is also reasonable to wonder whether the level of commitment, attendance and investment in these associations is higher than in other places partly because of the shared experience that many have had with ShoreBank. At least it is fair to say that these associations articulate multiple bottom lines and engage in a level of resource sharing that puts them on the most collaborative end of the spectrum of trade associations that operate in this country. Moreover, it is noteworthy that these associations also increased the Bank's confidence in lending to their members. As Alice Lamos described, "[T]hey mentored me, and they went to the Bank, and they spoke up for me. So that gave the Bank some type of security too."[163]

### *Coordination Lowers Costs and/or Risks*

In the German context, the coordination among businesses in certain industries appears to allow businesses to apply cost savings from coordination to greater investments in employees. In the South Shore context, by contrast, it appears that the coordination of labor and financing allowed the small mom-and-pop rehab businesses *to survive* over the relatively long term. Rather than stopping at one "three-flat" building, the ability to share labor and to obtain serial loans allowed

[163] Lamos Interview.

many of those businesses to grow and stabilize. It meant the difference between a one-off opportunity and a sustainable job.

### *Multiple (and Localized) Bottom Lines*

As Ron Grzywinski described, the mom-and-pop rehabbers participated in the market in large numbers primarily because they wanted to earn a livelihood.[164] But it was also clear from my interviews that many of the owners expected to be in the neighborhood over the long term, and they were invested in building better housing. Moreover, the African American owners who developed housing in South Shore clearly displayed an interest in developing and maintaining South Shore's middle-class roots.

The Bank capitalized on this investment by owners in their own neighborhoods. Meanwhile, the Bank layered its own priorities of development of South Shore through the investments of its own shareholders. Here again, in its role as intermediary, the Bank strengthened what had already begun to grow organically. In its institutional role, the Bank was able to look at the larger picture in a way that the individual business owners did not have the luxury to do. Given the Bank's careful lending choices, it would be a mistake to describe the private development of the real estate market in South Shore during those decades as accidental.

### *Local Stakeholders, Local Financing*

The Bank's lending strategy exemplified local financing, and more broadly, stakeholding in South Shore. From 1973 onward, the Bank had an intense interest in developing South Shore. As Michael Bennett described: "what Jim [Bringley] was doing, without putting the anti-gentrification tag on it, was funding people who already lived in the community, or worked in the community."[165] This is particularly noteworthy in the later decades of the Bank's operation, when the founders engaged extensively with initiatives aiming to replicate aspects of the Bank around the country and the world.[166] While the Bank's leadership invested many resources in these efforts, the interest in local development remained.

The Bank also was local in another important sense: its *own* shareholders and investors included both local individuals and institutions, and investors around the country, interested in local development of South Shore.[167] The Bank's

164 *Id.* 165 Bennett Interview.

166 For discussions of such efforts, see, e.g., Richard P. Taub, Doing Development in Arkansas (2004); Ian Smillie, Freedom from Want: The Remarkable Success Story of BRAC, the Global Grassroots Organization That's Winning the Fight Against Poverty 198 (2009); Jim Hightower & Susan DeMarco, Swim against the Current: Even a Dead Fish Can Go with the Flow 60 (2008).

167 Many of these investors were equally interested in the potential of bank holding companies to be self-sustaining community development vehicles.

"development deposits" are a key example. This kind of financing strategy allowed the Bank to remain mission-focused in a way that distinguished it from the vast majority of financial institutions in the United States. But as Grzywinski described, it also had a down side:

> [T]he investors not only agreed that they were investing to do development, they were agreeing that there would be very limited liquidity in their shares. And that became a hindrance to raising additional capital. It would have been easier if there were mechanisms to be able to raise capital, I mean some of what we're seeing now in crowdfunding, and maybe B Corps, and things of that sort. But there were always limits on what we could do in terms of raising capital.[168]

Finally, the local development goal exemplified by the Bank's double mission was itself a powerful form of local stakeholding that went far beyond financial investment. Throughout the Bank's life, from 1973 onward, the Bank's leaders participated in community meetings, involved themselves in the lives of the neighborhood residents, and met with public officials and private individuals and organizations focused on developing South Shore.[169] In these respects, they developed a broader network, one that was invested in the social justice mission, around the network of rehabbing businesses.

## *Niche Industry*

It should be evident that the rehabber network operated in a niche market that was uniquely fertile on both the supply and demand sides. Perhaps the best demonstration of the importance of a niche in this story is to consider the contrasting stories told by Mary Houghton and other Bank employees about the Bank's experiences in its business lending department, which made loans to a variety of local, small businesses in South Shore. In describing the work of that department, Gordon Hellwig commented:

> [I]t was very hard, because ma-and-pa retailers just weren't succeeding. They couldn't compete with the malls. Imagine the inventory you can carry if you're a ma and pa, and you got $30,000 worth of inventory in women's clothes. That's not a whole lot of inventory ... So people aren't going to shop there ... So there were huge headwinds for ma-and-pa ... retailers.[170]

George Surgeon observed:

> You can't invest that amount of money, or that amount of time putting these deals together. They all had to be hand crafted. They were all different. There was no real template for putting the deals together. And we had everything from grocery stores,

168 Grzywinski Interview.
169 *Id.*; Bennett Interview; Grzywinski, *The New Old-Fashioned Banking* at 91.
170 Hellwig Interview.

> to auto dealerships, to auto repair businesses, to insurance agents, clothing stores – it was all mixed up, it was all different, every deal was a real slog.[171]

By contrast, the size of the residential rental market was large enough to allow for specialization, both by the rehabbing businesses and the Bank. That particular industry took advantage of work skills that the local residents already had – and that they could trade. While there was a lack of spillover effect on the retail lending side, the special role of comparable market value in real estate helped to create a virtuous cycle for those involved. The mom-and-pop rehabbers experienced virtually no competition from big businesses. And, of course, there was a ready supply of consumers wanting good rental housing in South Shore. This particularly winning combination speaks volumes about the importance of developing a business network in an industry that has at least some of these features. The Dunkin' Donuts franchisees also had the benefit of a niche that shared some of these same qualities.

Reflecting on the accomplishments of the rehabber network almost 40 years after its inception, Ron Grzywinski added another insight. He commented that the network "created a sense of community self-confidence, because people in the community invested their own money, time, and energy to improve the community. They were at risk, and they proved that this kind of thing can be done."[172]

[171] Surgeon Interview. [172] Grzywinski Interview.

# 5

# Regulating against Sharing

Over the past two decades, during the expansion and bursting of the most recent economic bubble, we have seen the risks inherent in policies that promote "trickle down," "self-help," or a combination thereof. As I have argued in Chapter 3, we have seen that investment by big businesses in the urban core regularly produces gentrification at the expense of poverty alleviation and dead-end jobs in place of career ladders. We have also witnessed the cycle of risk and loss that results from developing independently operating small businesses that fail to grow or fail completely. Meanwhile, even many of those who study, support, and govern urban markets have largely missed the organic development of a different style of market behavior in urban contexts across the country. To the extent these intriguing examples of capitalist difference have garnered attention, those who notice them have failed to capture fully the breadth and uniqueness of their market behavior.

Why do well-intentioned policymakers persist in supporting such a narrow and risky range of solutions to the problem of urban underdevelopment? Why are their imaginations seemingly so constrained in devising meaningful new options for local economic development, especially when compelling examples of market alternatives already exist? Chapter 3 argued that the answer lies partly in the intuitive appeal of an individualistic and localized approach to economic failure and degradation, an intuition that is supported by our liberal market form of capitalism. As discussed in Chapter 3, given the apparent success of our national economy, policymakers appear to engage in a conceptual quarantining in which they assume that our system only fails in limited pockets where markets are idiosyncratic.

In this chapter, I elaborate on that basic answer by discussing the role of law in this picture. Exposing the role of law in shaping local urban markets can help us understand the case studies discussed in Chapters 2 and 4 at a deeper level. I have already described how the legal infrastructure supported home health care workers in New York while failing sufficiently to serve as a stabilizing foundation for the

South Shore network. In this chapter, I describe the law's more systemic role in privileging only two narrow paths to economic stability for workers in the urban core.

By exposing the web of regulations that shape and limit local urban markets, I demonstrate the dramatic extent to which such regulations constrain the options that policymakers believe are available for solving inner-city underdevelopment. For example, because policymakers assume that it would be too interventionist to require big businesses to hire local workers, they only institute local hiring preferences in the context of granting government contracts or in exchange for zoning or other concessions. These and other assumptions leave businesses very free to hire and shed workers as they please. And this, in turn, leads policymakers to create incentives for small business development because they assume they cannot expansively control the local market behavior of big businesses. This analysis of law's more systemic role in the urban core also serves as an introduction to my third case study, in Chapter 6. Because the network in Austin is newer than my other two examples, it is easier to trace the law's impact on the development of that network.

To understand how our legal infrastructure shapes and constrains local urban markets, let us start by considering the options available to a hypothetical group of workers living in a dense urban neighborhood in a large Midwestern city. This group of 25 workers has recently received vocational training, and the workers now are looking for opportunities to put their newly acquired skills to practice in return for a livable income. Imagine that the workers have received training in small-batch, specialty food manufacturing.[1] The training is a yearlong program, embodying a collaboration between a local community development corporation and a community college. The workers have been able to combine knowledge of traditional recipes and techniques that they have learned from their own families with training in food safety, production, packaging, and labeling among other things. While the training program has done admirably well in making the workers "job-ready," it does not have the resources to provide job placement services for the workers. The challenge for these 25 workers now is to convert their knowledge and skills into work opportunities.

As this section will show, there are two main income-producing paths available to the workers, with relatively limited opportunities to deviate from these paths. The first is to seek jobs with established businesses, which would likely be large enough businesses to be able to hire – and further train – workers with no prior work experience in the industry. The second path is for the workers each, or in pairs or very small groups, to start their own small businesses manufacturing specialty foods and distributing them to grocery stores or restaurants. Each of these paths is further constrained by the laws regulating employment, business formation, property rights, permitting, financing, and the numerous other regulatory regimes that govern the

[1] This hypothetical example is inspired by the work of the Pratt Center for Community Development in New York City, which is working to assess and overcome distribution challenges faced by small specialty food and beverage manufacturing businesses in that city.

participation of businesses in local markets. These various laws are the product of lawmaking at the municipal, state, and federal levels, and this chapter will describe how regulations and policies at each of these three levels of lawmaking shape the choices available to the workers following (or trying to deviate from) each path.

## GETTING HIRED

In urban America, examples in which established businesses act in coordination with local community colleges, nonprofit organizations, and local governmental agencies to train and hire workers for relatively long-term positions are rare. Seventy years ago, unions served as an important bridge between businesses and workers, but today it is more likely than not that our 25 hypothetical workers would not have the benefit of union support in finding jobs with established businesses.[2] Thus, the path for the workers to get hired would depend largely on the choices made by private businesses involved in wholesale food manufacturing.[3]

Two sets of choices would particularly impact the workers' chances of being hired. The first would be the question of whether an established food manufacturing business would be located near enough to the workers to make employment viable. For very large businesses, the chances of our 25 workers being hired by a manufacturing business would partly be driven by the tax incentives provided by their state government. As Peter Enrich has discussed, states compete with each other to provide tax breaks and credits to businesses for locating within their states. While such incentives do not seem to influence the choice of location between states, they may affect where exactly in a state or city a business might choose to locate.[4]

An even more relevant locational decision would be driven by local laws, specifically zoning laws, governing the siting of industrial businesses. Thanks to this powerful property law device, municipal governments are typically granted the authority from the state government to establish a zoning plan whereby each municipality (and county) is divided into districts, each with an authorized set of uses. Often described as Euclidian zoning, such a plan seeks to separate out incompatible uses, such as residential from industrial.[5] In doing so, it has typically been assumed to have the laudable benefit of protecting people from the environmentally harmful effects of heavy industry in residential areas. But over the course of the twentieth century, it also became apparent that Euclidian zoning has

[2] Jake Rosenfeld, What Unions No Longer Do 1 (2014) ("The country's unionization rate is lower than at any point since the early decades of the twentieth century.").

[3] *Id.* at 2.

[4] Peter D. Enrich, *Saving the States from Themselves: Commerce Clause Constraints on State Tax Incentives for Business*, 110 Harv. L. Rev. 377, 378, 382 (1996).

[5] Joseph William Singer et al., Property Law: Rules, Policies, and Practices 429–431 (6th ed. 2014); Daniel P. Selmi, *The Contract Transformation in Land Use Regulation*, 63 Stan. L. Rev. 591, 598–599 (2011).

its costs.[6] Among these costs is the sprawl that comes from locating industry and other businesses in the suburbs and beyond, a result that has made it more difficult for urban workers to find entry-level employment close to home.[7]

The ready availability of ample industrial space in the suburbs is often augmented by special zoning deals that allow large businesses effectively to create a customized community comprised of manufacturing space, office space, and residential space packaged according to the business's particular needs.[8] In turn, these zoning incentives are supported by a suite of local and state-level decisions relating to the development and financing of roads, schools, and other city services in support of the business's locational choice.[9] In short, state and local policymaking create many incentives for businesses that could hire entry-level workers trained in light manufacturing to locate their factories in places where urban workers cannot easily reach them. Thus, it is likely that our 25 workers would not find a food manufacturing business close to their urban neighborhood.

The second set of business choices that would greatly affect our workers' chances of getting hired would be grounded in state-level laws that give businesses extraordinary latitude to hire, fire, and govern the terms of employment of their workers. Because employment relationships are governed largely by private contract law, employers have the power to impose at-will employment on their employees.[10] This gives businesses the freedom to hire and shed workers with relative impunity. As Hall and Soskice have described, this freedom in turn creates a "fluid" workforce that values the ability to switch employment frequently over the course of a career.[11] However, if we consider the worth of mobility to urban workers who are tied to their geographic locations for reasons of income level, family ties, or housing, it is reasonable to conclude that workforce mobility can be a disadvantage rather than a benefit for such workers. What it may well mean for our 25 workers is that they would be commuting to a job in the suburbs in which they would have little if any job security.[12] It would also mean that their employer would have more incentive to

[6] *See* Sarah B. Schindler, *Of Backyard Chickens and Front Yard Gardens: The Conflict Between Local Governments and Locavores*, 87 TUL. L. REV. 231 (2012); Selmi, *The Contract Transformation*; Edward L. Glaeser & Joseph Gyourko, *Zoning's Steep Price*, 25 REG. 24 (2002); Francesca Ortiz, *Biodiversity, the City, and Sprawl*, 82 B. U. L. REV. 145 (2002).

[7] Jeremy R. Meredith, *Sprawl and the New Urbanist Solution*, 87 VA. L. REV. 447, 458 (2003); ANDRES DUANY ET AL., SUBURBAN NATION: THE RISE OF SPRAWL AND THE DECLINE OF THE AMERICAN DREAM (2001).

[8] Selmi, *The Contract Transformation* at 610; Carol M. Rose, *Planning and Dealing: Piecemeal Land Controls as a Problem of Local Legitimacy*, 71 CALIF. L. REV. 837, 841 (1983).

[9] Ortiz, *Biodiversity* at 146.

[10] HENRY H. PERRITT, EMPLOYEE DISMISSAL LAW AND PRACTICE 4 (5th ed. 2017) ("In no U.S. jurisdiction does the common law require private employers to demonstrate just cause for terminating an employee.").

[11] Peter Hall & David Soskice, *Introduction*, *in* VARIETIES OF CAPITALISM: THE INSTITUTIONAL FOUNDATIONS OF COMPARATIVE ADVANTAGE 40 (Peter A. Hall & David Soskice eds., 2001).

[12] David Dante Troutt, *Ghettos Made Easy: The Metamarket/Antimarket Dichotomy and the Legal Challenges of Inner-City Economic Development*, 35 HARV. CIV. RTS.-CIV. LIB. L. REV. 427, 467 (2000).

provide lower pay and benefits (and perhaps also fewer hours), impose less-favorable work conditions, and in general make their jobs less attractive to keep over the long term. Doing so would allow the employer to replace our workers more easily if and when our workers requested higher pay or better conditions.

Despite these disadvantages, however, it is reasonable to expect that most of our 25 workers would jump at the chance of even short-term employment with an established company rather than accepting the crucible of starting up their own businesses. Assuming that the workers were lucky enough to have trained for work that was available at a nearby, established manufacturing company, could we expect the company to hire at least half of our workers? Unfortunately, the answer may well be no. Again, thanks to the ground rules established by private contract law, employers have no obligations, and typically no incentives, to hire locally or to provide training to their workers. Practically speaking, this means that businesses are going to try to minimize risks in their choice of workers. If the workers have no prior work experience, as may well be the case for many of our workers, this will be a perceived risk.[13] If they are graduating from a welfare-to-work program, such as one a community nonprofit might run, this could add to the perception of risk.[14]

This disassociation between vocational training and local employment means that our workers will have had to do a great deal of guesswork to train for jobs that they think may be available in their area within the next decade.[15] They also must accept a real likelihood of poor work conditions, low pay, and job insecurity. And in the end, they may still be passed over in favor of employees that appear less risky because they appear more tested.[16]

The extent to which policymakers accept this level of business freedom as a basic reality is highlighted by the exceptions to this reality. One prominent exception is when local governments impose local hiring requirements in return for zoning and other concessions. Local hiring requirements may also be imposed when developers seek to build very large developments such as stadiums in a community and, in the course of doing so, enter into so-called community benefits agreements with non-profit organizations representing the local community.[17] Such examples are often considered dramatic wins for urban neighborhoods, and justifiably so. But they also reveal the norm in which businesses are largely unconstrained by ties to local urban

[13] Alan H. Peters & Peter S. Fisher, State Enterprise Zone Programs: Have They Worked? 40 (2002).

[14] Joel F. Handler, *Welfare Reform: Is It for Real?*, 3 Loy. Poverty L. J. 135, 145 (1997).

[15] *See* Rose, *Planning and Dealing* at 841.

[16] Andrew S. Gruber, *Promoting Long-Term Self-Sufficiency for Welfare Recipients: Post-Secondary Education and the Welfare Work Requirement*, 93 Nw. U. L. Rev. 247, 273–274 (1998).

[17] Richard C. Schragger, *Mobile Capital, Local Economic Regulation, and the Democratic City*, 123 Harv. L. Rev. 482 (2009); Scott L. Cummings, *Law in the Labor Movement's Challenge to Wal-Mart: A Case Study of the Inglewood Site Fight*, 95 Calif. L. Rev. 1927, 1981–1997 (2007); Scott L. Cummings, *Mobilization Lawyering: Community Economic Development in the Figueroa Corridor*, in Cause Lawyers and Social Movements 302 (Austin Sarat & Stuart Scheingold eds., 2006).

communities.[18] As the remainder of this chapter discusses, this is a norm grounded in our particular form of competitive capitalism in which the relationships between businesses and their employees, customers, other businesses in their industry, and local government are governed by arm's-length contracts and open bidding processes.

A second prominent exception is the "sectoral" approach taken by the Bronx home care network, in which they have attempted to change work conditions in the entire home health care industry in New York State and well beyond. This strategy has been well described both by the leadership of the Bronx network and by scholars such as Peter Pitegoff.[19] This is an example in which the combination of strong union involvement, support from state and local governmental agencies, and the leadership of businesses such as CHCA, ICS, and PHI have forced the entire industry to standardize wages and vocational education to the benefit of workers.

Meanwhile, from the company's perspective, the perceived risks of hiring untested workers with limited mobility are heightened by one other piece of the legal infrastructure that is worth noting here, namely the importance of shareholder value in internal corporate governance. By now, a robust critique has developed arguing that the primacy of shareholder value has allowed much mischief, especially in developing countries where local authorities seem powerless to limit the seemingly unconstrained priority of profitmaking combined with the limited liability inherent in the corporate form of doing business.[20] Critics have argued that shareholder value permits too many negative externalities to be imposed on local communities – ranging from environmental degradation, to natural resource stripping, to unfair labor conditions. Federal- and state-level corporate laws allow, and some argue even *require*, such conditions on the grounds that the corporate form of business prioritizes protection of shareholders' interests.[21] For my purposes, it is useful simply to observe that such a critique applies with equal force to the urban American contexts discussed in this book. Moreover, it is important to note that the primacy of shareholder value radically limits the possibilities for creating private or public incentives for employees to share in ownership or equity participation in the businesses that employ them.

I have thus far described the legal infrastructure supporting the freedom of businesses as governed by state and local governmental decisions. It is important to note, however, that federal laws have empowered state-level governance of these major aspects of business behavior. Federal laws have also reinforced this freedom.

18 Schragger, *Mobile Capital.*

19 *See, e.g.*, Inserra et al., *The Cooperative Home Care Associates*; Pitegoff, *Worker Ownership in Enron's Wake.*

20 Lynn Stout, The Shareholder Value Myth: How Putting Shareholders First Harms Investors, Corporations, and the Public (2012); Einer Elhauge, *Sacrificing Corporate Profits in the Public Interest*, 80 N.Y.U. L. Rev. 733 (2005).

21 Stephen M. Bainbridge, Corporation Law and Economics 419–429 (2002); Robert Charles Clark, Corporate Law 17–19 (1986).

One obvious example that I will only mention, but not analyze, in this book is the long history of federal legislation and federal court decisions that have weakened the ability of unions to strike, collectively bargain, and unionize.[22]

For our 25 workers, then, getting hired requires a rather extraordinary level of foresight about what kind of training to seek. It requires the sacrifice of commuting out to locations typically far from where they live, and perhaps also of accepting low pay and poor work conditions. And ultimately, it requires luck in finding businesses that choose to locate nearby and that ignore the perceived risks of hiring workers with little or no prior work experience.

## STARTING UP

It is hardly surprising, then, that many policymakers and working individuals such as our 25 workers turn instead to starting up small businesses that allow such workers to directly manage, and effectively *own*, their new skills. Indeed, this is the path that policymakers at the local, state, and federal levels have invested vast resources in making more accessible to urban workers.[23] But as this section demonstrates, it is also a path that is constrained by regulations made in the name of protecting market entry and competition for all businesses, but that in fact protect a relatively narrow range of market practices and competition.[24] The restricting influence of these regulations is best demonstrated by imagining the journey that a subset of our 25 workers might have to take if they started their own small specialty food manufacturing business.

Let us assume that three of these workers decide to open a business specializing in the production of tortillas for wholesale distribution. Assume these three entrepreneurs are very comfortable with the recipes and techniques they will have to use in making the tortillas. They also trust and are comfortable with each other as co-owners and co-workers. Finally, thanks to the training they have just received, they have a clear picture of the regulations that require them to properly manufacture, package, and label their tortillas for sale, as well as the processes for doing these things. With these pieces in place, their priorities will now be to find a location for their tortilla manufacturing facility, obtain the necessary permits to operate, and buy and install the equipment necessary to make the tortillas. These needs are related because, unlike some businesses, such as in-home day cares or even small craft-

22 Rosenfeld, What Unions No Longer Do at 17–18; Tayyab Mahmud, *Debt and Discipline: Neoliberal Political Economy and the Working Class*, 101 Ky. L.J. 1, 5 (2012–2013); Michael L. Wachter, *Labor Unions: A Corporatist Institution in a Competitive World*, 155 U. Pa. L. Rev. 581, 583 (2007); Cynthia Estlund, *Rebuilding the Law of the Workplace in an Era of Self-Regulation*, 105 Colum. L. Rev. 319, 322–323 (2005).

23 For a discussion of these investments, see Rashmi Dyal-Chand & James V. Rowan, *Developing Capabilities, Not Entrepreneurs: A New Theory for Community Economic Development*, 42 Hofstra L. Rev. 839 (2013).

24 Robert C. Bird & Elizabeth Brown, *Interactive Regulation*, 13 U. Pa. J. Bus. L. 837, 858 (2011).

making businesses, the production of tortillas and many other specialty foods requires large equipment and cannot be done at home or in residential spaces. These are manufacturing businesses in more than name, and they require the space and equipment for proper and efficient production. In the case of tortilla making, one of the most important and bulky pieces of equipment is the tortilla press. Our three tortilla makers are devoted to using a traditional tortilla press that is made from heavy cast iron and imported from Mexico.

Consequently, very early in their start-up process, our three entrepreneurs will encounter the same local zoning laws that would be encountered by a large specialty food manufacturing business – only they will not have the market power or personal flexibility to negotiate special zoning deals in the suburbs.[25] These laws will significantly constrain the tortilla business in finding a location for its factory.[26] In some cities, zoning laws and zoning boards may protect a few urban pockets from residential and commercial retail real estate development, preserving them instead for the siting of small industrial facilities.[27] Let us assume that our business is lucky enough to find such a pocket in which to locate. The scarcity of this space, however, will force the business to compete with other manufacturing businesses for limited space. This will likely drive up the rental price for any industrial space the business is lucky enough to find.

For a small business such as this, an equally imposing set of local laws will govern its ability to obtain the appropriate permits to start a manufacturing business. In Massachusetts, for example, the permitting process requires completion of an application and payment of a fee.[28] As part of the pre-permitting review process, Massachusetts requires an onsite inspection in which the inspector will review the following things:

> plant construction and design, water supply and plumbing, employee health and hygiene, maintenance of equipment and utensils, control programs for monitoring the safe handling of food, temperature controls, sanitation and cleaning operations, product labeling, and cleanliness and maintenance of the grounds and indoor area.[29]

25 *Id.* at 855–856.

26 James L. Huffman & Elizabeth Howard, *The Impact of Land Regulations on Small and Emerging Businesses*, 5 J. Small & Emerging Bus. L. 49, 50 (2001) ("State and local governments frequently fail to consider costs imposed on a small business as a result of new or expanded regulations . . . Land use regulations influence property acquisition costs, construction expenses, operating costs, employee salaries, and legal fees required to start and operate a small business.").

27 Such a discussion is under way in New York City. *See Building a Vibrant Manufacturing Sector: A Blueprint for New York City*, Pratt Center for Community Development (June 7, 2017), http://prattcenter.net/sites/default/files/industrial-policy_issue-brief_final.pdf.

28 The list of application forms required for food processing permits can be found at *Application Forms*, Massachusetts Executive Office of Health and Human Services (June 7, 2017), www.mass.gov/eohhs/gov/departments/dph/programs/environmental-health/food-safety/application-forms.html.

29 *Starting a Wholesale Food Business*, Massachusetts Executive Office of Health and Human Services (June 7, 2017), www.mass.gov/eohhs/gov/departments/dph/programs/environmental-health/food-safety/starting-a-wholesale-food-business.html.

The three entrepreneurs will have to invest a meaningful amount of time and resources to obtain their permit to operate. This permit will be one of several permits required; others include, for example, a business license and a license to distribute food wholesale.[30] It is likely that these costs will be the same as those faced by an established food manufacturing business siting a new facility in a given state. Importantly, however, our tortilla business will be facing these costs with fewer resources to absorb them.[31] In contrast to the established business, the new business will also face the challenge of learning about and negotiating the permitting system for the first time.

It is likely that the most difficult step for our business will be to obtain financing for buying equipment, leasing space, and accomplishing the other steps necessary to start operation. Many small businesses finance their start-up using the savings of their founders, loans from families and friends, and even credit cards.[32] Although these are not ideal options, because they lay a foundation that is undercapitalized, they are often the only options for new businesses. However, these options are less likely to be viable for manufacturing businesses because of the high up-front costs resulting from the purchase of heavy equipment. Thus, our tortilla business may well have to rely on the two more traditional sources of financing available to businesses: loans from banks and equity financing from one or more investors.

Considering each form in turn, in order to convince a bank to loan them money for the purchase of equipment and other costs, our three entrepreneurs will likely have to provide the bank with a business plan, security interests in their equipment, and personal guarantees to pay the loan back in the event of default by their business. Business plans are not easy to write. They contain 30 to 50 pages of material detailing the business's vision, business and management strategy, products and market, plan of operation, and financing plan and forecasts. They also typically include information about the industry in which the business operates and the business's key competitors.[33] We will have to hope either that the vocational training provided to the entrepreneurs included a crash course on writing a business plan or that the entrepreneurs will be able to find substantial technical assistance for this piece.

Business plans are also often optimistic, and the privatization of business information as an asset prevents banks from being able to verify all of the claims made by a business in its business plan. This is one reason why entrepreneurs must provide other forms of security. For the entrepreneurs to provide security interests in their

30 *Id.*

31 Dyal-Chand & Rowan, *Developing Capabilities* at 856–866; Louise A. Howells, *The Dimensions of Microenterprise: A Critical Look at Microenterprise as a Tool to Alleviate Poverty*, 9 WTR J. AFFORDABLE HOUSING AND COMMUNITY DEV. L. 161, 167 (2000).

32 Rashmi Dyal-Chand, *Exporting the Ownership Society: A Case Study on the Economic Impact of Property Rights*, 39 RUTGERS L. J. 59 (2007); Rashmi Dyal-Chand, *From Status to Contract: Evolving Paradigms for Regulating Consumer Credit*, 73 TENN. L. REV. 303 (2006).

33 THOMAS W. ZIMMERER & NORMAN M. SCARBOROUGH, ESSENTIALS OF ENTREPRENEURSHIP AND SMALL BUSINESS MANAGEMENT Chapter 11 (4th ed. 2005).

equipment, they may well have to purchase the equipment outright. This will preclude the possibility of saving up-front costs by sharing equipment. Moreover, the requirement by many banks that small business founders back up their loan requests with personal guarantees will impose substantial pressure on the three entrepreneurs and their families to put their personal assets and savings at risk in support of the business.[34]

In summary, these are difficult requirements to meet, and there are many new businesses that simply cannot meet them.[35] Meanwhile, there are very few banks that are willing to waive them. This fact of private financing is partially a result of regulation. For example, large national banks have very few motivations to deviate from their standard lending criteria unless they have extra incentives to lend to small businesses pursuant to the Community Reinvestment Act, which requires local investment in connection with bank mergers and acquisitions.[36] Smaller, local banks may well have more incentives to invest in local businesses. But like large banks, they are constrained by safety and soundness requirements imposed by federal regulators.[37] While safety and soundness regulations are obviously important for protecting the integrity of the banking system, they are geared to the standard operating procedures of large banks with national and international operations, not to local banks with local investments. One consequence is that both large and small banks lend to a relatively narrow range of small businesses that are perceived to be less risky investments, and they do so using relatively standardized criteria.[38]

Here too, the exceptions to the norm highlight the potency of the norm. One notable exception of course is ShoreBank in Chicago. By developing a deep specialty in lending to a particular subset of real estate businesses, the Bank was able to waive many of the lending requirements imposed by traditional banks, thereby making its loans readily accessible to new businesses. Simply put, ShoreBank was one of a kind. While efforts to replicate it continue, there are very few banks willing and able to invest in small businesses to the extent that ShoreBank did.

Financing from venture capitalist or angel investors will likely require many of the same things that banks would require, including a business plan, and detailed financial projections. Moreover, given recent trends in venture capital financing,

34 *Id.* at Chapter 12.

35 Keith N. Hylton, *Banks and Inner Cities: Market and Regulatory Obstacles to Development Lending*, 17 Yale J. on Reg. 197, 213 (2000) ("If the business relies, as small businesses typically do, on local consumption patterns, the labor-market skills of local residents, the reliability of local input providers, and other features of the community in which the borrower lives or intends to run the business, then it would be difficult for a loan officer to assess independently the prospective borrower's claims.").

36 *See* Barr, *Credit Where it Counts.*

37 Hylton, *Banks and Inner Cities* at 198 ("Banks that are forced to choose between satisfying the safety and fair lending requirements will choose the former, since a failure to satisfy safety demands can lead to harsh disciplinary action by regulators.").

38 Michael S. Barr, *Banking the Poor*, 21 Yale J. on Reg. 121, 183 (2004) ("Financial institutions may be reluctant to expend the resources for research, product development, training, marketing, and education, which are necessary to expand financial services to lower-income clientele.").

it is hard to imagine that a tortilla business such as this could capture the imaginations of these sources of equity capital, which often are more intrigued by businesses involving high technology and the possibility of valuable intellectual property and high growth.[39] The focus among many venture capitalists is on innovation. As is the case with banks, there are very few venture capitalists and angel investors who invest with a view toward local development or even social entrepreneurialism.[40]

The impositions on new businesses of financing, permitting, and finding an appropriate location in turn drive a range of second-level business decisions. These second-level decisions, governed largely by state laws, have the effect of standardizing the business form and operating practices of small businesses in such a way as to make them "look and act" like their larger counterparts. One key example is choice of business entity. While it might be practically very useful for a new business like our tortilla manufacturer to organize as a worker-owned cooperative, this is a form that is less well understood by traditional banks and investors. It spreads risk in a way that is less familiar to financing sources, and importantly, it appears to use profits differently also.[41] Described abstractly, the worker-owned business conflates the interests of workers and shareholders. Traditional financing sources, which may assume that workers would make different decisions about the use of profits than the shareholders, may worry (often illegitimately) about the returns on their investments or loans.

The same analysis applies to business operating practices, key among them practices relating to property ownership and business contracting. For example, traditional American businesses internalize virtually all the functions critical to their success in the marketplace, and indeed their success in the market is often linked to their ability to outcompete other businesses in their efficient use – and ownership – of information and other internalized resources and functions.[42] They own and exclusively use, rather than lease or share, many of their more valuable assets. They transact business by means of formal contracting among the market participants.[43] These practices are supported by a robust legal infrastructure dedicated to the protection of private property ownership and contractual rights. They are also supported by laws governing competition which in their more extreme forms treat the sharing of resources and especially information as antitrust violations – or at least

39 Zimmerer & Scarborough, Essentials of Entrepreneurship at Chapter 12.

40 One notable exception is Boston Community Capital in Massachusetts.

41 Scott L. Cummings, *Developing Cooperatives as a Job Creation Strategy for Low-Income Workers*, 25 N.Y.U. Rev. L. & Soc. Change, 181, 185 (1999).

42 In the area of technology development and dissemination, for example, Hall and Soskice note that "[u]ntil the National Cooperative Research Act of 1984, American firms engaging in close collaboration with other firms actually ran the risk of being sued for triple damages under antitrust law; and it is still estimated that barely 1 to 7 per cent of the funds spent on research and development in the American private sector are devoted to collaborative research." Hall & Soskice, *Introduction, in* Varieties of Capitalism at 31.

43 *Id.* at 8, 30–33.

as anticompetitive. It thus can be a legal violation for businesses within an industry to share too much market information.

In turn, the regulatory support of hierarchically managed businesses, arm's-length contracting, and competition produces a structure in which individual businesses have incentives to internalize much of the information that supports their market participation.[44] These relatively more formal business procedures permeate the different spheres of relationships that businesses must maintain in order to succeed in the market. In their discussion of varieties of capitalism, Hall and Soskice divide such relationships into five categories, namely industrial relations, vocational training, corporate governance, interfirm relationships, and employee relations; and we can observe the formality of business practices in all of these spheres.[45] Thus, for example, large and small businesses within a given industry compete with each other for employees who have a relatively general set of skills. These businesses have little incentive to coordinate the training of workers.[46] Similarly, the institutions of private contract law and shareholder value produce incentives for businesses to outbid each other for contracts that can in turn have the effect of driving down wages for their employees.

In summary, the pressure from financing and other sources to look and act like larger businesses has the domino effect of pushing small businesses to choose the traditional corporate forms over worker cooperatives, to manage their employees hierarchically, and to push for higher profits in the name of shareholder value. This pressure also motivates them to internalize information and other start-up resources in order to privatize access and ownership of them. And this internalization of resources in turn forces each small business to internalize the costs associated with the process of resource acquisition. Finally, the interplay between regulation and capitalist practice produces a very specific agenda for vocational education, in which the imperative to learn the rules of resource acquisition and management, robust competition, and profitmaking may at times take priority over the development of new skills and technologies.

Looking back at the first few steps that our three entrepreneurs must take in starting a tortilla factory, it is no doubt obvious that it would help new businesses tremendously if policymakers could eliminate some of those steps or make them easier to accomplish. And indeed, many well-intentioned policymakers have done exactly that. Specifically, they have created regulatory exceptions for small businesses that impose more limited versions of some of the laws applicable to businesses in their industries and that bypass other regulations.[47] They also have invested

44 *Id.* at 8, 33. 45 *Id.* at 6–7. 46 *Id.* at 27–33.

47 Some prominent examples are discussed in: Bird & Brown, *Interactive Regulation* at 838 (discussing the Regulatory Flexibility Act and its potential to accommodate interests unique to small businesses); Wilton Hyman, *Empowerment Zones, Enterprise Communities, Black Business, and Unemployment*, 53 Wash. U. J. Urb. & Contemp. L. 143, 144 (1998) (discussing the federal Empowerment Zones and Enterprise Communities program, designed to "encourage businesses to locate and operate in economically distressed communities by reducing taxes, regulatory burdens, labor costs, and other disincentives to operate within those areas.").

resources in small business development centers and other providers of technical assistance to help small businesses quickly understand and comply with applicable laws.

However, these exceptions are to rules that are perceived as the standard American rules of commercial behavior. This is not just a technical point. By creating exceptions, policymakers are looking for ways in which to reduce some of the costs of starting up with the expectation that at some (early) point in the process, these new businesses will be able to comply with the standard rules. In the course of creating exceptions, policymakers are not seeking or making opportunities for businesses to comply with a different set of rules that would support a different kind of commercial norm.

Looking at the big picture, there is a very real, practical difference for a small business between creating exceptions to standard rules and developing a new set of rules governing its behavior. Let me demonstrate this point by turning once more to our hypothetical tortilla makers. Imagine that thanks to exceptions created by local regulators for small businesses, our tortilla-making business is able to go through a streamlined permitting process. Imagine also that it is able to find industrial space in the founders' neighborhood because of a local zoning exception, and that it has received technical assistance in the process. The point nonetheless is that it has had to do each of these things for itself. The costs, though lower, have still been internalized by the small business, and they will be internalized by each small specialty food manufacturing business throughout the city.

Consequently, if we return to the choices made by our three entrepreneurs even earlier in their quest for sustainable income, it is clearer why such workers in American cities are limited just to two paths – employment with large businesses or the starting up of their own small businesses. There is not much infrastructure, nor are there many legal rules, for taking a middle path.[48] For example, little opportunity exists for workers to start small businesses that are networked to support each other and to receive support from institutions developed for the purpose of providing such specialized support.

Despite this, there are examples of manufacturing networks that have developed with the support of wonderful institutions. The Pratt Center for Community Development has been working with small food manufacturers in New York to collaborate especially in developing distribution strategies. In Monmouth County, New Jersey, the nonprofit Interfaith Neighbors has a business development center

[48] Michael G. Gottesman, *From Cobblestones to Pavement: The Legal Road Forward for the Creation of Hybrid Social Organizations*, 26 Yale L. & Pol'y Rev. 345, 358 (2007) (concluding, after evaluating for-profit, nonprofit, and hybrid business structures, that while there are "compelling reasons to continue exploring how the laws can foster such hybrid structures ... the best road forward is to work first within existing laws."); Keren G. Raz, *Toward an Improved Legal Form for Social Enterprise*, 36 N.Y.U. Rev. L. & Soc. Change 283, 286–287 (2012) (identifying social enterprise as a "new type of entity with needs left unmet by both traditional and emerging legal structures," and concluding that its core characteristics are a mere foundation to a "vexing structural problem.").

that supports specialty food manufacturers, including by working with a large, local food retailer who provides shelf space for products made by such businesses. In a more rural setting, the Carolina Textile District (CTD) is an intermediary serving 21 businesses involved in some facet of textile manufacturing. As described by Steven Dawson in a recent publication,

> The primary motivating factor for CTD participation is access to larger and more profitable markets – of the 21 CTD partners, 75 percent expanded their workforce within the past year. Yet these enterprises also share fundamental values, all grounded in a profound sense of place, pursuing: environmental sustainability; collaboration over competition; local ownership; and self-determination. And in North Carolina, which has the second lowest rate of unionization in the U.S., the CTD's commitment to high-quality labor practices provides crucial stability to the region's working class families – both native and non-native born.[49]

But imagine the effect for such networks if policymakers created a different set of rules allowing networks of small specialty food manufacturers in the city to colocate and to share the costs of obtaining licenses and permits. This would allow each business to externalize the costs, sharing them within a network of similarly situated businesses. It would also maximize the benefit of shared information within the network. This second possibility – the creation of a different set of rules – is what Part III explores. Indeed, as I discuss in Chapter 10, many of the rules I propose can also be useful to workers on the more traditional paths described here. Before analyzing the potential for law to support collaborative capitalism in American cities, however, let us consider one additional case of collaborative capitalism in action. The example of the Southwest Key network in Austin, Texas, is one in which many of the constraints felt by our hypothetical food manufacturers also surface.

[49] Steven Dawson, Social Enterprise: Proceed, With Caution, The Pinkerton Foundation, June 15, 2017, at 5, www.thepinkertonfoundation.org/wp-content/uploads/2017/02/Pinkerton-Papers-No4-Dawson-FINAL-WEB.pdf.

# 6

# More Than a Day's Work in Austin

[T]his community, ... it's a poor community, a lot of Latinos, and a lot of immigrants. And we have a lot of people who haven't worked in a long time, or if they worked, they've worked in very low-paying jobs, with day jobs, where you go and you work and they pay a hundred bucks and you're done. And you don't know when you're going to get hired again. And so we went after some folks that we could develop. So that we [could] say [to them:] create and build this business. And we've been fortunate that a couple of those folks that started a few years ago are still with us, and they're helping to try to bring new people in and help us manage some of these people. In the café, we always knew that we wanted to hire people from this community that could cook, but we had to train some people ... Then they got a little training, and then they got more training, and some of them are now managers and supervisors ... So it's interesting to see that some of those folks have really evolved, and they love it here, and they're committed to being here.[1]

Juan Sánchez, President, Southwest Key Programs

Founded in 1987 by Dr. Juan Sánchez, Southwest Key Programs is a nationally respected nonprofit organization that is probably best known for its work with youth and children. It has worked with hundreds of thousands of young people, providing safe shelters, alternative and culturally relevant education, and a range of programs to divert youth from prisons and other institutions.[2] It is a large organization, with an annual budget of over 200 million dollars, more than 2,000 staff nationwide, and offices in six states.[3] Its headquarters are in East Austin, Texas, where it also operates a charter school.[4]

While the organization has received well-deserved attention for its extraordinary work with youth and children,[5] one of its lesser-known initiatives is its development

[1] Interview with Juan Sánchez, President, Southwest Key Programs (June 10, 2015).

[2] *Our Mission*, SOUTHWEST KEY PROGRAMS, www.swkey.org/about/overview.

[3] Sánchez Interview.

[4] *Annual Report for FY2015*, SOUTHWEST KEY PROGRAMS, www.swkey.org/about/annual_report.

[5] *See, e.g.*, Neelum Arya, *Family-Driven Justice*, 56 ARIZ. L. REV. 623, 690 (2014); David Androff, *The Human Rights of Unaccompanied Minors in the USA from Central America*, 1 J. HUMAN RTS & SOCIAL WORK 71, 74–75 (2016); Ellen Marrus, *Best Interests Equals Zealous Advocacy: A Not So Radical View of Holistic Representation for Children Accused of Crime*, 62 MARYLAND L. REV. 288 (2003);

of several "social enterprise businesses." These include a café that operates onsite at Southwest Key's East Austin headquarters, a maintenance company, a job placement company (known in Texas as "workforce development"), a green energy and construction company, and a florist. The focus of this chapter is on this cluster of for-profit businesses, all of which are wholly owned by the nonprofit Southwest Key Programs. It is to explore how such a network emerged from an organization that focuses on youth and children, how it developed into a well-functioning group of businesses, whom it employs, and what challenges it faces.

## *Context*

As with the Bronx and South Shore case studies, the geography of Austin is a political subject. Although its exact boundaries are disputed, a number of sources identify East Austin as the set of neighborhoods that lie approximately five miles to the east of the Texas State Capitol and downtown Austin.[6] Many would say that the Colorado River is the southern boundary of this area. Interstate Highway 35 separates it from downtown Austin to the west. Martin Luther King Junior Boulevard marks its northern boundary, and it is unclear just how far east this set of neighborhoods extends. Although East Austin has been described as "inner city," it defies at least some of the stereotypes associated with that term. Rather than being built upward like the inner cities of Eastern metropolises, its housing stock consists largely of small, one- or two-story bungalows.

Like many American cities, Austin underwent a process of residential segregation by race in the first half of the twentieth century. Although the racial composition of particular neighborhoods (and especially the extent of racial intermingling among different groups of color) is the subject of some dispute, it appears a commonplace that by the 1930s, East Austin was populated by African American and Latino families.[7]

Historian Jason McDonald observed in his 2012 book that

> Today, despite the major transformations wrought by the black and Chicano protest movements of the Civil Rights era, Austin has not fully cast off the legacy of ethnoracial discrimination and inequality . . . East Austin, for example, is still the site of a large black ghetto and Latino barrio . . . At the beginning of the twenty-first century, nine-tenths of local whites had graduated from high school, compared with four-fifths of African Americans and one-half of Mexican Americans . . .

Rosa Ehrenreich, *Unaccompanied Children in I.N.S. Detention*, 5 Georgetown. J. on Fighting Poverty 279 (1998).

6 Jason McDonald, Racial Dynamics in Early Twentieth-Century Austin, Texas 102–103 (2012); Lorna A. Monti, Social Indicators for Austin, Texas: A Cluster Analysis of Census Tracts 20–21 (1975).

7 McDonald, Racial Dynamics at 102–103 (citing a study by William B. Hamilton, *A Social Survey of Austin*, University of Texas Bulletin, no. 273, Humanistic Series, No. 15 [1913], and a master's thesis by Earl Monroe Connell).

> The median family income in Austin in 1999 was $64,226 for whites, but only $36,165 for Mexican [Americans] and $35,685 for blacks. While 10.8 percent of whites lived below the poverty level in 2000, 18.3 percent of blacks and 21.7 percent of Mexican [Americans] did so.[8]

Of course, the impact of immigration across the southern border of the United States into Texas cannot be understated. As Martha Menchaca described in a recent book, Texas was not only the biggest entry point for Mexican immigrants, but also the state in which the majority of such immigrants lived in the nineteenth and early twentieth centuries. Consequently, it has been the site of a great deal of law and policymaking about naturalization and other immigration-related rights.[9] Immigration's impact on labor rights, on education and the rights of children, and on the Texas and national economy have all been the subject of much study and debate.[10]

Given this particular context, so affected by the realities, and at times brutalities, of immigration experienced by children and their families, Southwest Key chose to intervene by supporting the children. Its initial focus in the 1980s was on developing educational and other programs to help youth who might otherwise be channeled into prisons and other institutions.[11] In 1999, Southwest Key supplemented these efforts with an educational program combining both individualized education and counseling for students who had not succeeded in traditional schools. Within a few years of its founding, Southwest Key also opened shelters for immigrant children who entered the United States unaccompanied by parents or guardians. These shelters provide a comprehensive range of onsite medical, educational, and counseling services with the goal of family reunification.[12] In 2007, the organization opened a charter school in East Austin, which is part of an initiative intended to provide comprehensive "wraparound" services for children and their families.[13] East Austin is also the location of Southwest Key's headquarters.

The headquarters is just one of many Southwest Key offices located in six different states. But if its physical presence is at all representative of the organization's effect

8 McDonald, Racial Dynamics at 327–328.

9 Martha Menchaca, Naturalizing Mexican Immigrants: A Texas History (2011). Hiroshi Motomura explores a range of legal issues arising from the status of immigrating "outside the law" in his recent book. Hiroshi Motomura, Immigration Outside the Law (2014).

10 For recent examples, see John Weber, From South Texas to the Nation: The Exploitation of Mexican Labor in the Twentieth Century (2015); Marjorie Faulstich Orellana, Translating Childhoods: Immigrant Youth, Language and Culture (2009); Pablo Vila, Crossing Borders, Reinforcing Borders: Social Categories, Metaphors, and Narrative Identities on the U.S.-Mexico Frontier (2000).

11 Marguerite Moeller, Nat'l Council of La Raza, Reauthorizing the Juvenile Justice and Delinquency Prevention Act: The Impact on Latino Youth (2011), http://publications.nclr.org/handle/123456789/1382.

12 *Immigrant Children's Shelters*, Southwest Key Programs, www.swkey.org/programs/shelters. *See also* Androff, *The Human Rights of Unaccompanied Minors* at 74–75; Moeller, Reauthorizing at 4.

13 Sánchez Interview. *See also Community Connections*, Southwest Key Programs, www.swkey.org/programs/youth_justice/CommunityConnections.pdf.

on the East Austin communities it serves, then it suggests a dramatic impact. Built largely of glass and brick, the multistory building projects a sense of openness and warmth, rising out of a neighborhood of small bungalows. It is landscaped with bright, flowering trees and outdoor seating, an inviting scene even in the midday Texan heat. The day I arrived was the first day of the summer camp hosted onsite at Southwest Key's headquarters. An outdoor plaza in the center of the campus was brightly decorated and approximately 50 children were participating in ice-breaking exercises with their camp counselors. There was a sense of both joy and order. The only institutional building (other than the school) in a neighborhood that is described as "inner city" and a "ghetto," the headquarters appear to provide a place for community gatherings, both formal and informal.

### *Origins*

Both in terms of raw numbers, and by Dr. Sánchez's description, Southwest Key's nonprofit programs far eclipse its social enterprise network. The annual budget for Southwest Key's nonprofit work is over 200 million dollars, while it hopes to achieve a quarter of a million dollars of profit from its social enterprises.[14] Moreover, the first for-profit business affiliated with Southwest Key was not founded until approximately 20 years after Sánchez founded the nonprofit. As he described, the formation of the first for-profit business had everything to do with the nonprofit's physical expansion:

> [A] few years ago, when we moved to this building, we began to think "who's going to take care of our basic stuff? . . . Who's going to take care of our grounds? Who's going to clean this building?" Well, we can contract somebody to do it, or we can build our own company . . . And then once they do it here, you take the workers and you get other contracts too . . . [W]e also have a school, [so] then we had another expansion to [a] site that's bigger than this, it's 24 acres long – big. And so now we're doing all the maintenance, and all the cleaning, and all the food services.[15]

By building for-profit companies, the organization hoped not only to meet critical service needs filled by its own reliable service providers, but also eventually to channel income from those businesses to the nonprofit mission. Indeed, Sánchez described this provision of income as one of the primary goals, if not the primary goal, of the businesses today.[16]

But in answering the question who *exactly* would take care of the grounds, the buildings, and the food for the school, Southwest Key discovered a powerful way to contribute to its overall mission. Sánchez continued:

> And then we've hired the kids' parents, so a lot of the kids' parents are the ones that are providing the meals for their kids, and . . . they've got a job, and they're making some money, and they're taking care of their families. And so that's how we started.[17]

[14] Southwest Key, *Annual Report for FY2015*. [15] Sánchez Interview. [16] *Id.* [17] *Id.*

As this description reveals, Southwest Key's decision to "do it ourselves"[18] inspired new thinking about the value of adding for-profit businesses. While Dr. Sánchez's consistent references to "social enterprises" evidences a continuing desire for these businesses to fund the parent organization's nonprofit mission, it also became apparent that the businesses were themselves a means of supporting that mission. Specifically, the production of stable, well-paying jobs for local workers could be a powerful way to support their children, who were the primary population served by Southwest Key. The success of this strategy was strongly affirmed by the workers I interviewed. For example, Oralia Castro, who works as a supervisor in the café, commented, "I like serving the kids, as I am a mom … My younger girl started [at Southwest Key's charter school], and she's still there, and it really helps me because I … like being close to my daughter."[19]

Goals aside, however, Southwest Key's leadership quickly discovered that "for-profit businesses are … a different animal … [Y]ou've got to manage them differently, you've got to think about profit, you've got to think about employing people."[20] And for businesses started under Southwest Key's umbrella, it went without saying that this all had to be done *without* succumbing to the shortcuts taken by competing businesses, which hired workers one day at a time and with no strings attached.

### *Development of a Market*

How, then, did Southwest Key build several for-profit businesses that have survived for almost a decade when most start-up small businesses, including those started by social enterprise clusters, fail in half that time? As described by Dr. Sánchez,

> Well I think you've got to be very wise about what you get into, right? And … you've got to find a niche that you think you're going to be able to be good at … [T]hey're difficult to set up, and then to maintain them is also difficult, because you've got to constantly be finding business that's going to support your folks. We're lucky because we have a nonprofit that is big, that helps us with our maintenance and it helps us with our café. You know, we have our own school, they feed all our kids, 800 kids we have in our school, plus, … the construction company … We've been able to find niches where we can go in, and they're needed. But I think some folks [came in and said] "What about an ice cream company?" … and they couldn't make it.[21]

According to Dr. Sánchez, then, the essential condition for the success of these businesses was to find niches for them to fill. When he talks about "niches," Dr. Sánchez is talking about customers. More precisely, those niches had to be connected to two different customer bases. During the businesses' very early existence, they required a customer base that was immediately available and large

[18] *Id.* [19] Interview with Oralia Castro, Supervisor, Café del Sol (August 19, 2016).
[20] Sánchez Interview. [21] *Id.*

enough to sustain the businesses almost singlehandedly. For Southwest Key, the obvious place to look for such a customer base was internally. By starting a business that could feed the 800 children in its school, for example, Southwest Key ensured a stable demand for its café. But at the same time, for the café ultimately to fulfill the nonprofit organization's purpose in starting a business cluster, the café had to develop beyond that original customer base. Even feeding the 800 children in its school did not alone produce enough of a profit for the café to provide income to the nonprofit. And this was true for each of the other businesses. To understand fully the importance of developing a niche in this story, it is important to understand how each of these businesses was conceived with an eye toward the *next* critical step in its development by transitioning its customer base to include customers from outside Southwest Key as well.

As a demonstration of this powerful point, consider the growth of the café. The café was losing money for the first several years of its existence before it began to provide meals for the new charter school. Before the school was built, the café's only steady customers were the staff members of Southwest Key who worked in the new headquarters building where the café was located. By making the charter school the café's first major customer, its management radically improved the café's financial condition.[22] This then allowed for further growth of the customer base. As Dr. Sánchez described,

> I think the other thing that happened is more people started to learn about the café. The café started to expand its own advertis[ing]. They got a nice website. They are now set up to do ... really nice catering. More people began to order from the café ... from around here, ... sometimes from the capital, we take a bunch of tacos there ... And I think, especially with cafes, as you serve better food, ... you get to be known.[23]

Today, 10 years into its existence, the café is a gathering place in a neighborhood that is otherwise devoid of restaurants and other similar places of public amusement. Sánchez described its effect on the community as quite special, an effect that I witnessed during my own visit:

> People love to come in. People come to get something to eat, to eat at café, and drink at café, eat, hang out with the people in the restaurant, eat there, order there, buy there. And ... many of them are from this community, many of them, their kids are in our school. And they love it, they love people to come in, and they joke with them, and share with them, and serve them. And I think ... our maintenance company is that way as well. They're becoming places where people are beginning to get settled and established and saying, "This is where I work, this is what I do, I'm proud of it."[24]

Dr. Sánchez's description of the café's new catering service reveals a particularly nuanced approach to the development of a new customer base:

[22] *Id.* [23] *Id.* [24] *Id.*

> [The café] just developed a whole new system for catering, . . . so they've begun to expand it. . . . [T]hey found some other contractors, other nonprofits, so they're feeding other companies. So when you put all of that together, even though your profit margin is small, it's enough to sustain it.[25]

Sonia Gallegos, Southwest Key's Director of Social Enterprises, added key details about this approach. As she described it, the café sought out foundations and other nonprofit organizations that would be interested in supporting the overall mission of Southwest Key. And in doing so, the café shared information about how its work supports Southwest Key's mission:

> I introduced the ladies, and I wanted our customers and our clients to know that these ladies started off as unskilled workers, and that the work and the effort that they put to make this happen really is something that we're extremely proud of. And so, . . . that would be our focus, . . . that this is done by them, by the community and for the community . . . I think in terms of Southwest Key partners that already support Southwest Key, I think that they would be more inclined to continue to do so if they're going to receive some benefit out of it . . . And if they're going to order from somewhere else, why not order from some ladies that belong to the community and that are giving back to the community.[26]

Thus, in developing its catering service, the café's management thought carefully about how to develop a niche within the catering industry. Recognizing that it might be too difficult to break into an industry that may well take advantage of cheap "off-the-books" labor and that already has well-established big names, the café focused on developing a catering clientele that not only came for the delicious and healthy food it produced, but also to support its mission of providing good, long-term jobs to local individuals.

This same pattern of development is occurring to varying degrees in several of the other Southwest Key businesses. For example, Southwest Key's nonprofit organization and charter school are the biggest customers for both Southwest Key Maintenance and Southwest Key Green Energy & Construction. These two businesses are in the process of looking for additional stable sources of customers. In the case of the cleaning company, one outside customer is the Mexican Consulate in Austin.[27] As is evident from Southwest Key's website, the other businesses also use the café's approach of advertising their services to clients who are interested in supporting Southwest Key's broader mission. For example, on the cleaning company's website, the description of available services is followed by the following statement:

25 *Id.*

26 Interview with Sonia Gallegos, Director of Social Enterprises, Southwest Key Programs (June 10, 2015).

27 Interview with Artenio Guerrero, Supervisor of Maintenance at East Austin College Prep, Southwest Key Maintenance, LLC (August 19, 2016).

> Southwest Key Maintenance, LLC is a wholly owned subsidiary of Southwest Key Programs, the fourth largest nonprofit organization in Austin. Southwest Key Programs has provided school, shelter, and services to youth in the juvenile justice system for over two decades and is using its tested approach to the prevention of juvenile delinquency in the Johnston/Govalle neighborhood by supporting business enterprises designed to hire and train the parents of these youth as a way to generate positive family outcomes. Reasonable profits from the maintenance company go to support the work of Southwest Key Programs.[28]

Finally, while Southwest Key's workforce development company provides a standard package of services as dictated by its contract with the state, Regional Director Henry Castillo described how it translates Southwest Key's mission into a highly effective approach to providing placement services for the individuals it serves:

> We develop close relationships with our customers. We have close relationships and that helps us help them, because they're more trusting of us ... And so when they start seeing successes result from our advice and our suggestions, and the word starts getting out, more and more people come here. And again, that ties back to the ... mission and the values of Southwest Key. That's something that's always been in the forefront ever since Southwest Key has been here. And so when we're looking to hire new staff, these are things that we try to identify. We don't want just a technically savvy person, ... but is this person willing to take that technical know-how and join our family and [be] a true family member, not just another employee? ... You know, that's part of Social Enterprise as a whole ... That would probably be the biggest thing that differentiates us in Southwest Key Workforce from other workforce boards, because we're very competitive. We're high achievers. But ... what I'm most proud of is that we're able to do that while at the same time ensuring that we are helping our customers succeed.[29]

Indeed, as Castillo described, this approach of treating customers – and the state workforce board that contracts with Southwest Key Workforce Development – as family members is the key to this company's high performance, which has earned it awards from the State of Texas every year since 2011.[30] While Castillo did not use the term "niche," he described the company as developing a particular approach within the industry that targets state agencies interested in supporting that approach.

[28] *Southwest Key Maintenance, LLC, Enterprises*, SOUTHWEST KEY ENTERPRISES, www.swkey.org/enterprises/maintenance.

[29] Interview with Henry Castillo, Regional Director, Southwest Key Workforce Development, LLC (August 18, 2016).

[30] *Id.*

Just as it did in fine-tuning its development of niches, the network also worked hard to develop the employment practices and policies that would help its businesses thrive while supporting its overarching mission. For example, it looked for the right balance of experienced employees and local community members who could contribute to the enterprise after receiving training.[31] In this regard, the café benefited enormously from hiring Sonia Gallegos, who at first offered her expertise pro-bono, but later agreed to join the café as a fulltime employee with the expectation that she would eventually be replaced by those she trained.[32] The network also experimented with forms of employee compensation to enhance the motive to make profit, settling on a profit-sharing scheme by which employees receive 10 percent of the business's profit as bonuses.[33]

While it is impressive that Southwest Key developed these sophisticated approaches to starting for-profit businesses so rapidly, it also made mistakes along the way that led to important lessons. Each of these mistakes contributed to the organization's understanding of how to develop its niches. First, as Dr. Sánchez described, the organization learned that it was going to be very difficult to partner with large businesses in the area, businesses which had no regulatory or other strings requiring them to hire locally or otherwise invest in the local community:

> [O]ne of our ideas was, before we had any businesses, I noticed that every time we called [a large communications company], they gave you good service, [but] it just took them a while to answer your calls, right? And the, president, who I got to become good friends with, said, you know, "I'm having trouble training people, particularly bilingual people and keeping them employed. And I may train, you know, 50 people, and a few months later, I may have 10 of them left." And I said, "OK, why don't you let us, Southwest Key, do the recruitment, and you train our staff to train these people, and every now and then I'll give you 20, 30 people that you can keep, that I'd have already trained them around not only the technical parts that you need train[ing] in, but why it's important to keep a job, why it's important to call in, why it's important to show up, and all the customer service stuff." And we were moving, . . . we had put stuff in writing, he was looking at it, we were looking at it, and then he got promoted . . . and he had to move to New York. And it was such a blow for us, because the lady that came in, we tried to explain it to her, and she says, "I just can't get my arms around that stuff," . . . and so it all died right there.[34]

Among other things, this experience appears to have taught Southwest Key about the value of using its own nonprofit organization as a stable customer in the early years of its new business ventures. Doing so avoided many of the risks of partnering with large institutions with too few incentives to invest in the new businesses.

31 Sánchez Interview.

32 Gallegos Interview; Interview with Alma Alfaro, Manager, Café del Sol (June 10, 2015).

33 Sánchez Interview. 34 *Id.*

Second, through a process of trial and error, Southwest Key developed knowledge about which markets to avoid. These markets tended to rely on such cheap labor and other inputs that Southwest Key's businesses would never be able to outcompete other businesses in those markets. As Sánchez described,

> [Y]our profit margins too on some of these things are small. And you've got to be looking for something that's going to give you a big enough profit margin that you're able to keep people employed, pay them, give them the benefits that they need. And you're competing with some folks who don't even provide that stuff, they go out and hire people for a day, they pay them out of their pocket a hundred bucks, they don't have to worry about taxes or anything else, . . . and you're competing against them, right? And so I think that's what . . . has made it difficult for us to go and compete against other businesses . . . And it's difficult. I mean, we got into picking up trash in the highways, right? And we bid so low, we had to bid low to get it, that we got it, but we lost money . . . We had to ask the question, "Why are we doing it if we're losing money?" So we got all these contracts to go pick up all this trash in all these highways, but we're losing money every month. And there was no hope that you would . . . change that at some point.[35]

In contrast to the café, trash picking would never allow Southwest Key to make a sustainable profit. The competitors could hire labor too cheaply, and there was no natural customer base of clients who valued the mission to which Southwest Key's businesses contribute.

Finally, Sánchez identified the value of finding niches involving low start-up costs and skills that local community members already have:

> I've had people here with business degrees and master's degrees, and [they said,] "We can . . . build . . . very small containers where you could grow more lettuces and more tomatoes and more cucumbers in a small plot of land . . . And all of those things I think were wonderful. But how do we get there, . . . what's it going to cost us to do that, and how are we going to get the people to do that, and how do we produce that stuff? It just got to the point where it was major, major investment, and you didn't know if it was going to work or not.[36]

## *The Network in Mature Form*

Today, the five businesses in Southwest Key's cluster employ a total of more than 100 people.[37] The smallest of these enterprises is a florist that operates seasonally.[38] The largest business in the cluster is the workforce development business,[39] which has approximately 80 employees and a 12 million dollar

[35] *Id.* [36] *Id.* [37] *Id.* [38] The Blooming Florist, www.thebloomingflorist.com.

[39] *Southwest Key Workforce Development, LLC, Enterprises*, Southwest Key Enterprises, www.swkey.org/enterprises/workforce.

annual operating budget. In addition to the café and maintenance company, the cluster also includes a green energy construction and remodeling company.[40]

While this is a very different story from my other two case studies, all three feature highly resilient networks of businesses that survived and thrived despite the apparent odds. Obviously, Southwest Key's network is much younger and smaller than the other two, and thus it is untested in important respects. By Dr. Sánchez's own description, it remains a work in progress. Nevertheless, it has had a promising start.

Even at this relatively early stage, it is apparent that the Austin network is maturing into a form that is more of a hybrid than the other two networks. Abstractly described, the key difference among the networks is as follows. The Bronx and Philadelphia home care network has found a way for a network of businesses to collaborate in providing stable employment to workers. Referring to the two main paths for stable income that I described in Chapter 5, the home care network has followed the path of getting workers hired. But of course it has done so by starting its own worker-owned cooperative businesses and thereby redefining employment for urban core workers. In this respect, it has substantially changed the course of the getting-hired path for those workers. By contrast, the South Shore network developed a way for networks of small businesses to collaborate in the process of starting up. In doing so, it focused on the starting-up path described in Chapter 5. But it too changed the course of that path by finding ways for the businesses to survive and thrive by collaborating with each other and with ShoreBank.

The Austin network has thus far attempted to change the course of both paths for the low-income workers involved with its businesses. It has developed four small businesses that are networked with each other and with the nonprofit. In addition it has attempted twice, once successfully, to make the getting-hired path more accessible for the local, low-income workers involved in its network. The successful attempt has resulted in its largest for-profit business, Southwest Key Workforce Development, which has worked with hundreds of individuals to increase access to education, training and jobs. The unsuccessful attempt was its effort to contract with a large company to provide trained customer service employees. By networking all of these businesses together, Southwest Key appears to have increased their chances of survival and success well beyond the average start-up business's chances. But, as I will discuss in Chapter 7, it is appropriate to

[40] Sánchez Interview; *A Homeland Connection*, Café Del Sol, http://cafedelsolaustin.com; *Southwest Key Maintenance, LLC, Enterprises*, Southwest Key Enterprises, www.swkey.org/enterprises/maintenance; *Green Energy & Construction, Enterprises*, Southwest Key Enterprises, www.swkey.org/enterprises/gec.

ask whether this hybrid strategy may also be hindering the network's continued growth and expansion.

Let us begin by exploring the businesses in their current form. The café, maintenance company, and green energy company each employs approximately 10 individuals. Each of these businesses started up around 2008 as the nonprofit's new headquarters and the charter school were being built. All three initially were started up to serve the needs of the nonprofit and the school.[41]

As I have described, the café has made great strides in adding to its customer base. In addition to its own charter school, for example, the café now serves as the caterer for a local high school. Moreover, the students from a third school located near the café go there for many of their lunchtime meals.[42] The café also continues to develop its catering arm beyond its school clientele. Although this portion of its business is not yet a steady source of income, it has been at times a highly productive one that the café's management perceives as having great potential for growth and profit. The café's employees describe regularly providing catering for events involving as many as 500 meals at one time.[43] The maintenance and green energy businesses have not yet made this transition to new customer bases. Meanwhile, the florist, though it only employs one or two individuals, does seem to have a stable, local customer base outside of the Southwest Key network.[44]

Southwest Key Workforce Development is the fifth and largest business in the network. Founded in approximately 2009, this business began with the purpose of winning a contract from the Texas workforce board to provide job placement services in Cameron County, which is located approximately 320 miles away from Austin and is one of the poorest, most marginalized communities in the state. Of its 80 employees, approximately 70 percent work on the workforce development contract, providing services related to furthering education, job training, and job placement. These services are provided largely through two one-stop centers in Brownsville and Harlingen, Texas. They include support on writing and updating résumés, obtaining referrals for education, skill-building workshops, and on-the-job training, which includes wage subsidization for the trainees. The business also took over a contract for childcare services that the nonprofit had obtained from the State in 1999. The remaining 30 percent of the business's employees work on the childcare side of the business.[45] Regional Director Henry Castillo believes that roughly half of the business's employees have "benefited from our programs in the past, as youth or younger adults."[46] Moreover, the retention rate for this business

[41] Sánchez Interview. [42] Castro Interview.
[43] Alfaro Interview; Castro Interview; Gallegos Interview. [44] Sánchez Interview.
[45] Castillo Interview. [46] *Id.*

(approximately 75 percent) and the others in Southwest Key's network is very high. As one employee of the maintenance business described, "People are always in awe that I work for such a company."[47]

While Southwest Key Workforce Development's two contracts with the state are fairly standardized in the package of services offered, this business has developed what Castillo described as "profit-making" ventures that richly connect with Southwest Key's mission. One impressive example is Project Phoenix, as described by Henry Castillo:

> Basically what we did is we worked with youth in diversion programs. These were not incarcerated youth, but they were in a variety of diversion programs of the juvenile justice department. We went on sites to the juvenile justice facility, and we did job readiness and soft skills workshops. We did career awareness. We helped students start thinking about careers. For those that were old enough, sixteen and above, we helped them register for work with Work with Texas, which is the state's employment database, very similar to a Monster.com, or an Indeed, or Yahoo Jobs. . . . And then we worked with our juvenile justice partners to identify 24 of the . . . 100 kids that we served last year, . . . to put them in summer employment, so that they could put to practice the things that we had taught them in the workshops . . . I wasn't aware of anybody else in the state that was doing anything like it . . . So those are the types of things, it's these special projects that we'll . . . negotiate with the board to put in our contract . . . Again, it's above and beyond what is typically expected, and what typically happens in most workforce boards across the state.[48]

Obviously, one of the most salient aspects of the Southwest Key network is the place of the nonprofit organization in this story. As I have described, the nonprofit has provided a stable early customer base for the new businesses. But it has done much more than that. To fully understand the role of the nonprofit, it is useful to describe its formal legal relationship with the businesses. Each of the businesses is organized as a traditional for-profit corporation of which the nonprofit is the sole shareholder. As Dr. Sánchez described, this ownership interest is deeply reflected in the nested structure that Southwest Key has created for the businesses' management:

> [E]ach one of these entities has its own board of managers which is three people, and I'm in all of them . . . [A]nd then there's a social enterprise board of directors. Now I am on that board . . . [S]o there's a social enterprise board of directors, and those . . . directors are approved by our Southwest Key nonprofit entity.[49]

The end result is a management structure that could be depicted as follows.

[47] Interview with Silvia Evangelista, Southwest Key Maintenance, LLC (August 19, 2016).
[48] Castillo Interview. [49] Sánchez Interview.

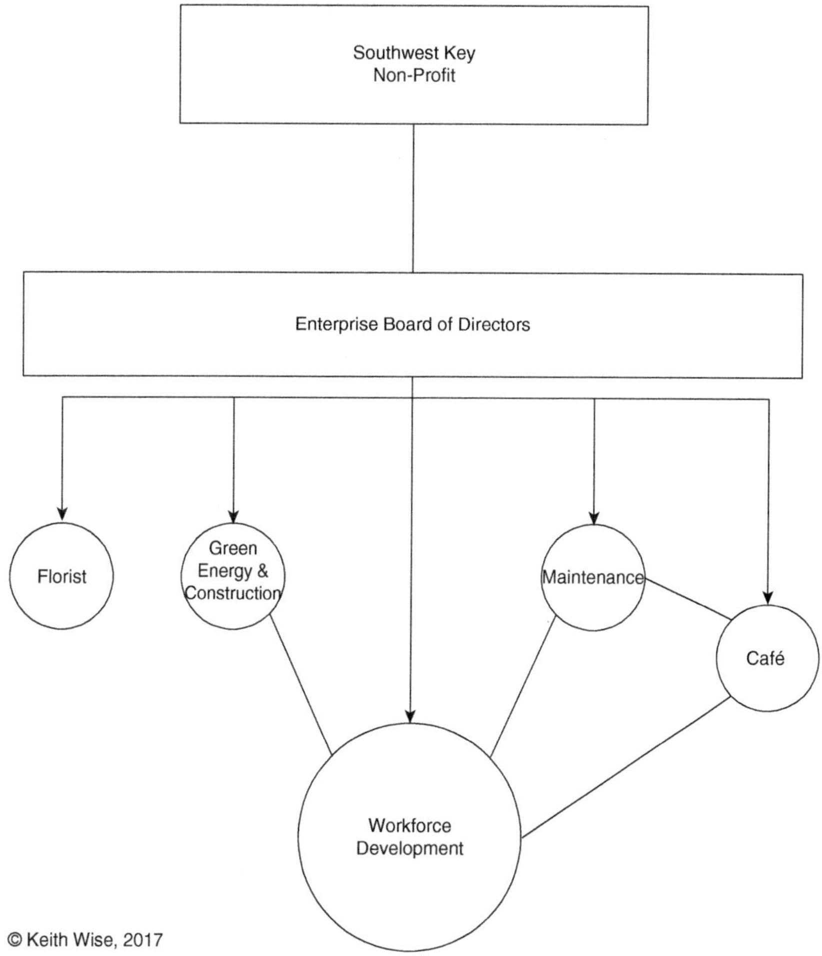


One of the most noteworthy consequences of this structure is that the presence of Dr. Sánchez on all of these boards, and the related organizational buy-in, has produced a level of patience on the part of the nonprofit board that might otherwise not have existed. Again, from Dr. Sánchez:

> [I]n our café, the first two or three years, we must have lost well over $100,000. And the board kept asking me, "How long are we going to keep these businesses going?" And I kept saying, … "Well give me a chance." … And then our school started, and more people started coming, and we've … gotten better at it, and in one year we made $100,000 profit … But you had to sustain it for three years, where you were losing 30,000, 40,000 dollars a year, and you're [saying] "Are we in the right business here?" … [S]o you've

> got to be able to find the niche, have some kind of ongoing support that's substantive.[50]

### Intermediaries in the Network

As should be clear by now, the nonprofit Southwest Key Programs has provided critical support to the for-profit businesses in this network by absorbing the early losses, the failed strategies, the missteps in hiring, and many of the other inevitable risks of starting up a business.

Financing is one of the nonprofit's essential contributions. While the nonprofit provided funds to some of the businesses in their start-up phase, it mainly used its expertise as a grant-seeker to support the development of its businesses. For example, the organization obtained a large pair of grants from the US Department of Commerce in connection with starting the maintenance company and the green energy business. These grants were essential for the purchase of equipment and seeding salaries. Dr. Sánchez still believes that grants are the most viable source of funding for businesses such as these.[51] When asked whether he ever sought financing for the businesses from traditional banks, he replied,

> I didn't go to them, and I don't think they would have given us any money … They're so protective of themselves and what they do, and … they give you money if you have money … Even though I have a long relationship with them, I never went to them for this, because I didn't think they'd give us any money … None of the traditional financial institutions that you think could help you, I didn't go to any of them.[52]

As importantly, just as Independence Care System does for the Bronx home care network, the nonprofit has served as a stable customer base for several of its businesses. As with the Bronx network, the nonprofit provided this resource to its for-profit affiliates upon discovering that price competition was a barrier for contracting with large businesses in the area that do not share Southwest Key's double-bottom-line mission. Such businesses did not have any incentive to hire the local, low-income workers for whom Southwest Key sought employment, at least not as permanent employees with health and other employment benefits. In contrast to the Bronx network, the nonprofit's strategy appears to be only to serve as a major customer during the start-up phases for these businesses rather than as a permanent source of contracts. Nevertheless, this source of contracts has been essential for the viability of three of the businesses. Without this patient investment, for example, it is hard to imagine the café being able to withstand several years of losses.

In addition, the nonprofit organization continues to provide several critical pieces of what Dr. Sánchez described as "infrastructure" to the new businesses. For

[50] *Id.* [51] *Id.* [52] *Id.*

example, each of the businesses pays the nonprofit a management fee in return for back-office services, including payroll, accounting, information technology, and legal support. The nonprofit also provides training on various topics that are common to all the businesses, such as occupational health and safety.[53] Implicit in this description is the enormous amount of staff- and board-member time and expertise contributed by the nonprofit – sometimes for a fee, but often with no formal remuneration.

It is also important to remember what the nonprofit gains from this investment. There is, of course, the hope that the businesses will one day produce enough income to channel some of it back into the nonprofit's mission. There is the provision of jobs for the parents of the children whom the nonprofit serves. And there is also the sense of community created by businesses such as the café and the maintenance company, whose employees work for and with their neighbors – and in doing contribute to a greater sense of community health and pride. In these respects, the businesses and the nonprofit work together toward a double bottom line. They work hard to increase the profits of each individual business, but they remain together in the same network as an explicit statement of the additional goals that they seek jointly to achieve.

While the nonprofit is the main intermediary of note in this collaborative business network, it is also fair to describe Southwest Key Workforce Development as an intermediary that has served as a resource to the other businesses and to the nonprofit on issues of workforce development and training. For example, Henry Castillo described support he has provided to the green energy business:

> I've had many conversations, and had the privilege of working closely with Sonia [Gallegos] on issues where we can provide some guidance, some training. And when I'm talking training, I'm not talking about anything that's funded … I remember [I] actually went up to Austin to meet with Sonia and some of the other staff. They were trying to build up the green housing construction … And they wanted to know what's the best way of identifying people, identifying the skill sets, the labor force. And because that is something that we do on a regular basis, … researching labor market information, … I was able … to help them think about some ways that they could look at identifying and building up their work force for green housing construction.[54]

More broadly, Castillo described the contributions of the workforce development business for the entire Southwest Key network:

> A lot of what we do touches a lot of the things that they can do, especially with the other businesses as they're trying to build their workforce in those businesses and they run across different employment issues. Those are areas where we can step in, … giving them some guidance on employment law and local resources. We've helped Southwest Key enterprises in Austin, but also Southwest Key Programs.

53 *Id.* 54 Castillo Interview.

> [We] helped to connect them with other workforce areas in Texas, and outside of Texas, to help them with hiring as they're opening new operations in other places ... We've always partnered with them, to help them meet those hiring needs.[55]

## *Working within the Network*

To understand fully the power of a network like Southwest Key's, it is important not only to view it as a functioning whole but also to explore it from the perspective of individual workers within it. The purpose of this section is to do exactly that by viewing the network from the perspective of Alma Alfaro, who began as a volunteer at the café and is currently the café's manager.

Alfaro joined the Southwest Key business network when she enrolled one of her children in Southwest Key's newly opened charter school. First, she was asked to serve as a parent volunteer supporting the school as part of a nascent parent-teacher organization. At that time, she earned income by selling her own burritos, tacos, and tamales in the neighborhood. Southwest Key took note of her cooking skills, and after six or eight months as a volunteer, she was asked to work part-time in the café. Another six to eight months later, Alfaro began working at the café full-time.[56] It was around that time that Sonia Gallegos, who had deep experience in providing "back of the house Spanish training" for independent restaurants,[57] joined the café. According to Alfaro,

> [W]hen Sonia came on board, and started developing systems, and organizing us, and developing some form of structure, she offered me the opportunity to become a supervisor, and so I've been on board as a supervisor for two years.[58]

Even this brief description reveals a remarkable level of professional development in a breathtakingly brief period of time. According to Alfaro, working in the café is "totally different" from her work selling food on her own: "It's still working with food, but it's not just about making it. It's about presentation, it's about customer service."[59] For Alfaro and many of her colleagues at the café, these work opportunities have come with fatigues, strains, and challenges.[60] For example, Gallegos described a recent week at the café as the employees focused on developing their catering services:

> Just recently we hosted a VIP event, and they came in at 5:30 and did their regular job, fed the kids, took care of everything, and stayed until 10 o'clock ... Today we have another catering that's for 250 people and they'll put in another 12- [or] 14-hour day. So certainly we want to be able to have enough money to hire enough people,

55 *Id.* 56 Alfaro Interview. 57 Gallegos Interview. 58 Alfaro Interview. 59 *Id.*

60 For Alfaro, the challenges included strains on friendships she has with other employees whom she now has to supervise. *Id.*

> but for now, it's all of us, you know. We'll all roll up our sleeves, and we'll all do a little bit of everything.[61]

Gallegos also described some of the many areas of training that were required to work in the café:

> [O]ne of the biggest transitions and challenges for me was – because most of them are from Mexico and so they learned the metric system there – in terms of recipes. And so I had to teach them the American pounds. And . . . a lot of them participated in basic computer skills, they didn't have any experience with that. And then recently, I think eight of the 15 . . . received their manager certifications, so they not only have their food handlers [certification], but they passed their managers. And I can't tell you how difficult that is, even for someone that's been in the food industry for such a long time. There [are] such technical questions.[62]

For some employees, the challenges included difficult personal circumstances that the team worked to address in the course of achieving professional development. Again, from Gallegos:

> I had a lot of experiences with the ladies on a personal level, that they were going through divorce, that . . . a lot of them were in a domestic violence type of situation, and you really have to reach that core . . . Help them believe in themselves, and once you create that environment, then they're going to be happy to come to work and stay as long as it takes, because it's not going to seem [like] work.[63]

This approach to professional development by means of collaboration and attention to the needs of the individual workers is common in the descriptions by both Gallegos and Alfaro. For example, Alfaro noted,

> [W]e don't have too many benefits working for the café, but . . . one of the great benefits is that we've learned not only just to work as a team, but to learn about each other's needs on an individual basis, on a personal basis. And we have a lot of young mothers that have different needs from some of [us] that have older kids, and . . . we've all worked as a team to create a schedule that benefits everyone.[64]

Indeed, all the workers I interviewed commented on the supportive, collaborative, familial environment they experienced at Southwest Key. For example, Silvia Evangelista commented, "[I]t's just a blessing to move to Austin, and be able to work for this company that treats me like family . . . [T]he priority at Southwest Key is about respect. It's about the person . . . I have come to . . . respect myself as a person."[65]

For Alfaro, this sense of collaboration translated directly to her approach as a manager:

> [A]s a leader, I would tell them to learn every aspect of your team's job, whether it be throwing trash, dishwashing, whatever, because you can't expect to train them if you

[61] Gallegos Interview. [62] *Id.* [63] *Id.* [64] Alfaro Interview. [65] Evangelista Interview.

don't know specifically what it is that they do. But most importantly, handle your team in a professional way, and always treat them with the courtesy and respect that they merit, and keep them happy, because if they're happy, they're going to do a good job for you.[66]

Meanwhile, Gallegos was clear about her ultimate goal in this process of professional development:

I've always told them that I want them to learn to the point that they take my job, and it's coming to fruition. I've just recently been promoted to interim director of enterprise. And [Alma] will take my position as café manager. And so that has always been my focus, so that I'm out of a job in five years or so, and that they are the ones that are holding the fort, because they certainly deserve it. They have put in all of the work, and all of the effort, and they just needed a facilitator, and that's simply what I've been, just a facilitator and a translator, so that they had the opportunity to grow. Just create more jobs for them, because they're so many and there's so much need.[67]

Alfaro's professional trajectory has been dramatic, but the changes in her personal circumstances have arguably been just as dramatic: "I lived in government housing for 10 years, and … it's been two years now since I've become a new homeowner, and … eight months [since I] bought myself a new car."[68] Alfaro also expressed her wish for her two sons to have opportunities to continue participating in Southwest Key's various programs.[69] Gallegos described the extra effort required for Alfaro to achieve these personal milestones:

[W]e're unseen, we handle jobs that are dirty jobs, and nobody is interested in doing, and so you know, I think that merits a lot more respect and more acknowledgement … [T]hese ladies are really good in terms of savings, and they will make stuff work. I mean, Alma for example was able to give a hefty down payment for her home, and she told me of one experience where she went to a bank, and they wouldn't even speak to her in reference to that, once they knew what she did. And so I'd like to change that, so that they wouldn't have to go through stuff like that. That makes me very sad … And she had a hefty amount to deposit in that bank.[70]

Here again, Alfaro's story is echoed by the other employees I interviewed. One talked about help with immigration. Another about support with flexible hours. Artenio Guerrero, who is the supervisor of maintenance at the charter school, stated,

[W]hen I first started, they had an interview, and they asked all the maintenance, all the landscaping people what is it that we wanted for the future? And the main thing that I wanted was a house for my family … And because of Southwest Key and their support, I was able to get that house, and I'm very grateful to them for that.[71]

66 Alfaro Interview. 67 Gallegos Interview. 68 Alfaro Interview. 69 *Id.*
70 Gallegos Interview. 71 Guerrero Interview.

Finally, it is interesting to note the ways in which Southwest Key's broader mission has affected Alfaro and her colleagues in the café. As Alfaro described,

> [We] have been lower on the totem pole, and so we never were invited to participate in other programs related to Southwest Key ... until last year, [when] we handled the emergency shelters in Ventura, California. And we were allowed to travel, and to participate, and I absolutely adored the experience ... That was my first time flying.[72]

Broadening out from her own experience, Alfaro continued:

> I can certainly relate to those that are in need, that are out there, that are in need of work, because I was one of them ... And ... [I am] happy to represent an entity that can offer those services to other people, because I used to be one of them ... [I]t's the Latin community, ... my people ... [I]t's going to afford them an opportunity to help their kids grow as well, because it provides a little bit more money for them to do so. [T]hey have a job.[73]

In these and other respects, it appears clear that the café and those who work there are connected to a broader enterprise. As Gallegos poignantly described, "And now ... the outlook has changed, the environment has changed, where they feel acknowledged, you know, and valued, and so I think that that's a huge accomplishment."[74]

### *Regulatory Context*

A consensus theme among those I interviewed at Southwest Key is that, while the social enterprise network is off to a great start, they have bigger aspirations for it. Although the law was not an explicit subject of much discussion in my interviews with participants in this network, it has shaped the network's development in multiple and overlapping ways, and it will be an important force in the network's future growth. Given the hybrid nature of this network's development along both the "getting hired" path and the "starting up" path, it may be useful to consider the effects of the legal framework in these two areas.

Consider first the relevance of law to the café, green energy company, maintenance company, and florist in their first decade of existence. One of the most obvious aids to these new businesses has been the nonprofit organization's ability to serve as their parent holding company. This is due to the Texas law of business organizations, which is among the more capacious in the United States. Briefly described, Chapter 22 of the Texas Business Organizations Code provides a great deal of flexibility for nonprofit organizations to function in most respects like for-profit businesses. This includes serving as a holding company for for-profit subsidiaries.[75] As a result of this flexibility, the nonprofit parent in the Southwest

[72] Alfaro Interview. [73] *Id.* [74] Gallegos Interview.

[75] Tex. Bus. Orgs. Code Ann. §§ 22.001–22.409 (West 2017).

Key network has been able to use grant funding to support its subsidiaries' development to the full extent allowed by federal tax law.[76] Chapter 251 of the Texas Business Organizations Code also provides a framework for the creation of cooperatives, including worker-owned cooperatives.[77] It is not clear, however, whether even the Texas Code is capacious enough to allow for the partial ownership, or at least governance, of workers cooperatives by a holding company such as the Southwest Key nonprofit.

A second critical influence of the legal framework has been in the area of wages and employment benefits. Not surprisingly, given the café's extraordinary growth in a limited time period, both Alma Alfaro and Sonia Gallegos identified the need for more employees at the café.[78] Gallegos also focused on the importance of expansive health benefits because their work involves a great deal of physical labor.[79] Other workers I interviewed share the desire for higher wages and more benefits. Alfaro and Gallegos both also emphasized the need for time and space for additional vocational education. As Alfaro described, "[T]hey need hands-on experience because … we learn as we go, but we also need extra hours, and we also need a separate room so that I can teach them."[80]

While Dr. Sánchez recognized the importance of growing the number of employees in the café, he also candidly articulated the restraints:

> [W]e're having to deal with things like competing with companies who are cleaning the highways for example, who could just go hire people for the day, pay them cash, and not worry about [it]. We were not like that, we were trying to pay people a decent wage, you know, we're trying to pay our taxes, we're paying all the benefits … and it's hard to compete against those folks.[81]

The simple fact is that Texas law creates challenges for this network as it tries to expand its employee base while ensuring good wages and benefits. Texas has neither the higher minimum-wage laws nor the wage-parity laws that support home care workers in New York. These deficits are compounded by the local economic context, in which day labor (probably provided disproportionately by undocumented workers) is prevalent. The result, as documented by numerous studies in Texas, California, and elsewhere, is the disregard for labor and employment laws by local employers, which goes uncontested by local authorities.[82]

Dr. Sánchez also described the challenges associated with obtaining more financing for these ventures:

[76] Sánchez Interview. [77] Tex. Bus. Orgs. Code Ann. §§ 251.001–251.452 (West 2017).

[78] Gallegos Interview; Alfaro Interview. [79] Gallegos Interview. [80] Alfaro Interview.

[81] Sánchez Interview.

[82] *See* Weber, From South Texas to the Nation; Scott L. Cummings, *Litigation at Work: Defending Day Labor in Los Angeles*, 58 UCLA L. Rev. 1617 (2011); Abel Valenzuela Jr., *Working on the Margins in Metropolitan Los Angeles: Immigrants in Day-Labor Work*, 2 Migraciones Internacionales 6 (2002).

> [I]t would be good if there were some folks who were willing to invest in these kind of businesses that would come and help. But . . . you almost have to get that help in grant money, rather than going out and saying, "It's going to cost me $250,000, and I've got to buy this business over the next five years."[83]

While he conceptualizes the problem as a business problem, rather than explicitly a legal problem, it is important to recognize the role law plays here. As discussed in Chapter 5, even under the federal Community Reinvestment Act, there is no legal requirement – and very little legal incentive – for banks to lend money to businesses such as these. Texas law does not add incentives, through crowdfunding legislation, securities laws, or other means. As a result, the start-ups in this network have had to rely more on grant financing than is ideal.

Finally, it is important to recognize the role that state and local governmental agencies in Texas could play in providing supportive infrastructure for businesses such as Southwest Key's. One clear example is the use of minority-owned business contracts for state construction and other needs. This possibility seems ripe for exploration, given the informal entrée that local governmental agencies have already provided these businesses, such as catering opportunities for the café.

The law's effect is apparent on the "getting hired path" too, most obviously in the framework of labor and employment laws that I have already described. But we should add to this picture the interesting position taken by the Texas Workforce Commission, the state agency charged with overseeing job development and placement services in Texas. There is much to appreciate about this agency's structure, mission and philosophy, which seem genuinely focused on providing meaningful, employment-related services for Texas residents.[84] It also is an enormous credit to the commission that it contracts with businesses like Southwest Key Workforce Development, a company that works hard to find sustainable income opportunities for low-income workers.

But it is also noteworthy that Southwest Key Workforce Development has been constrained in the services it can provide because of the standardization in services required by the state agency. While this business has developed some creative approaches to job development, it has only been able to do so as a profit-making venture above and beyond its standard package of services. This obviously limits the range of creativity in developing additional paths to long-term and sustainable employment. Worker-owned cooperatives, apprenticeships with big companies, youth training programs, and other vehicles are all contemplated by Texas law, and even to some extent available. Relatively minor changes to the commission's philosophy could allow – and ideally require – more experimentation with these vehicles, leading to more and better long-term employment opportunities for the individuals the commission serves.

[83] Sánchez Interview.

[84] The commission's website is evidence of this. *See Welcome, We're Here to Help*, TEXAS WORKFORCE COMMISSION, www.twc.state.tx.us.

This is especially true in the realm of developing relationships between networks such as Southwest Key's and large, local businesses. Imagine how Dr. Sánchez's story may have ended differently if the commission or another state agency provided an incentive for local hiring to the telecommunications company with which Southwest Key tried to partner. Imagine also the possibilities for sectoral development if a city such as Austin committed to supporting workers in the food service, landscaping, or maintenance industries. Such incentives could take the form of tax breaks, zoning, or licensing provisions, or even small grants.

These possibilities for rethinking the laws in Texas provide an interesting lens on a struggle that Dr. Sánchez perceived as a transitional problem for the Southwest Key businesses. He described these businesses' need to move from an informal start-up stage, making creative use of nonprofit strategies, to a more formal structure, taking advantage of for-profit thinking. Herein lies an interesting disjunction between Sánchez's approach as compared to a prototypical American large business. On the one hand, Sánchez and others at Southwest Key define the success of the social enterprise clusters as including several bottom lines. These include traditional for-profit goals such as business survival and growth, as well as profit for the shareholder. But of course, the shareholder is the nonprofit organization, and channeling profits to it is a way of supporting the nonprofit mission. In addition, Sánchez and the other interviewees clearly defined success to include the creation of jobs and livable incomes for local community members.[85] On the other hand, Sánchez's instincts about how to grow the cluster further to more fully meet its multiple bottom lines are to develop the businesses more along the path of traditional American businesses. This means writing and following business plans, hiring more employees with business degrees, finding new niches, and thereby acquiring greater market share in Austin to compete more aggressively with their more traditional competitors.[86] This disjunction is a creature partly of laws. One purpose of Chapter 10 is to provide leaders like Dr. Sánchez with a much greater level of support as he works to grow his network, whether using the getting-hired path, or the starting-up path, or one or more additional paths.

## COLLABORATIVE CAPITALISM IN AUSTIN

As with my other two examples, the network that has developed around Southwest Key is distinctive in context, personality, strengths, and weaknesses. It too has an exceptional set of leaders, who are consistently described by workers in the network as being the best part of their work experiences. But in addition to these unique characteristics, this network also exhibits the pattern of collaborative capitalist behavior that I have identified in the other two examples.

[85] Sánchez Interview. [86] *Id.*

### *Coordinated Activities of Businesses*

As Dr. Sánchez described, most of the businesses in this network were initially formed to provide a necessary service to the nonprofit organization, the charter school or both, with the additional expectation that the businesses would grow customer bases outside of the network. Thus, much of the coordination among the businesses is in serving the two major customers within the network.

In return, the businesses receive lower-cost, well-tailored, and more streamlined support from the nonprofit in the form of trainings, back-office support, and management expertise. In all of these areas, the support from the nonprofit is doubtless of a higher quality than the businesses each would be able to afford if they had to internalize these functions. For example, the level of back-office support is significantly more formal than in the average start-up business, which is lucky if it uses even a technological platform such as Quicken to keep its accounts.

The quality of support is particularly important in the areas of training and management expertise, because these inputs directly benefit the workers in these businesses. For example, in contrast to most cleaning businesses or start-up restaurants, the workers in the Southwest Key network benefit from regular occupational safety trainings. All of the employees I interviewed commented on the value of the training they received. Oralia Castro noted, "Sonia [Gallegos] has ... worked very hard to get training for the employees. That's a first for me because in my previous jobs, I didn't have trainings like I have here."[87] Moreover, management at the nonprofit and "enterprise" levels ensures that the "social" part of the social enterprise cluster translates into tangible benefits. They tailor working hours and other work conditions to fit employees' needs. They provide meaningful incentives in the form of bonuses. They provide support with personal finances. Most importantly, they provide health and other employment benefits that simply would not be affordable for similarly situated businesses outside of the network. More abstractly, managers at all levels work hard to maintain a sense that working in these businesses means that you are a part of the Southwest Key *familia*.

Another critical area of coordination has been in the form of grant funding that has supported the starting up of several of the businesses. Finally, thanks to the workforce development business, the other businesses in the network receive support in the form of job placement services and market data. It is also noteworthy that the businesses have shared labor among themselves during their start-up phases.

### *Institutional Intermediary That Serves a Coordinating Function*

As in the case of the South Shore network, the Austin network features an intermediary organization that plays the role of a range of intermediaries in a national coordinated economy. By providing a stable customer base, low-cost and high-

[87] Castro Interview.

quality support services, and expert management, the nonprofit organization has helped the for-profit businesses in the network to survive and in some cases thrive. The nonprofit also plays a critical role in maintaining the multiple bottom lines of the network, a function that seems uniquely effective in increasing the workers' economic and social welfare.

The workforce development business also bears mention as an important intermediary in the Austin network. Thanks to its expertise in surveying markets for job development needs and potential, this business has repeatedly provided guidance to its affiliates in the network as they have developed new customer bases and new positions.

### *Coordination Lowers Costs and/or Risks*

It is hard to imagine how the individual businesses in this network could have survived without the sharing of critical resources. As I have described, the profit margins for each of these businesses are thin because of the price competition from businesses within the same sectors (restaurants, landscaping, cleaning, and construction) that make use of day labor. If the Southwest Key businesses had been forced to internalize any of the functions provided by the nonprofit, it is reasonable to expect that this could have made the difference between survival and failure.

Indeed, if we add in the fact that coordination has allowed the managers in the Southwest Key network to provide workers with both long-term employment and a range of employment benefits, it is virtually impossible to imagine that these businesses could have survived in anything close to their current forms. In this respect, the Southwest Key network is a microcosmic example of national coordinated economies, which translate cost savings in areas such as research and development into long-term investments in employees.

### *Multiple (and Localized) Bottom Lines*

Obviously, the self-labeling of this network as a "social enterprise" network bespeaks the multiple bottom lines that are important to this group of businesses. As I have described, for the for-profit businesses, this is not just a matter of contributing financially to the nonprofit parent. It is also about using private businesses to provide stable employment for the parents of children the nonprofit serves. For the workers, this has included simply being near their children, making their lunches, or cleaning their classrooms. It has also meant being a part of the Southwest Key *familia*, an intangible benefit that was nevertheless emphasized by every one of the individuals I interviewed.

### *Local Stakeholders, Local Financing*

The local focus of the Austin network is most evident in its mission of employing the local parents of children the nonprofit serves. As with the other case studies, the

Southwest Key businesses have turned to those in their own city first in seeking support for this mission. For example, the café has sought out local foundations and nonprofit organizations to broaden its customer base, with the explicit invitation for these customers to support the local workers it employs. The same is true for the maintenance company and the green energy and construction business.

Of course, the nonprofit's important role as a source of "patient capital" for the businesses makes the financing for these businesses hyper-local. This is compounded by the nature of grants received by the nonprofit. Although these grants came from the US Commerce Department, their purpose was local economic development. It is noteworthy, though, that financing for these businesses has been thin, and has not included local banks or other traditional financing sources.

### *Niche Industry*

The Austin network provides an opportunity to evaluate the importance of a niche to the successful practice of collaborative capitalism in American cities. Just as members of management did in the other two examples I studied, Juan Sánchez emphasized the development of niches as the most important contributor to the network's success thus far. Members of the management in the businesses also discussed the value of specialization within their particular industries. Thus, in the management's own analysis of the businesses' successes (and failures), the niche is a critical factor.

Yet the Austin network also presents a significant contrast to the other two case studies, both involving businesses within a network that are all in the same industry. I will discuss this difference in greater detail in Chapter 7. For now, it may be useful to observe the potential impacts that the dispersion of businesses within several industries may have made on the Austin network's development. At the outset, it is important to note several commonalities among the niche industries in the Southwest Key network, some or all of which could have benefited the businesses and the network as a whole in its first few years. Specifically, these are all industries in which market entry was relatively easy and where entry-level skills were either not required, transferable from other settings, or already acquired by the workers that the businesses in the network sought to hire. They are also industries in which a market exists for a service or product that costs more because it supports a double mission that involves paying good wages to local workers. This is in contrast with the business of collecting trash on the highways, in which Southwest Key could find no customers interested in its double mission. It is also important that these are industries in which work can be neither outsourced nor mechanized. Moreover, for purposes of occupational health and safety trainings, back-office support, and financing, there are enough similarities among the businesses to allow for sharing of resources. Finally, by starting businesses in several industries, Southwest Key diversified its risk in a way analogous to having a diversified portfolio of investments.

On the other hand, this network does not have the same synergies in the provision of training and vocational education, for example, that the home care network has. Nor does it have the same opportunity to *exchange* labor that the South Shore network has had. Nor is it a dominant enough force in an industry to be able to negotiate specialized deals for supplies. Nor can it take advantage of the possibility of colocating with similar businesses. Instead, the managers and workers in each business have had to research a range of markets and develop specialized knowledge that cannot be shared across a range of similarly focused businesses. Perhaps most importantly, each of the industries in which this network competes involves fierce competition that the network has thus far not been able to combat by developing a niche within the entire network that allows it to take a meaningful share of the overall market for any particular product or service in Austin.

# 7

# Understanding Collaborative Capitalism

The purpose of this chapter is to provide a synthetic and cross-cutting perspective across the three case studies. My aim is to analyze the concept of collaborative capitalism that emerges from the three cases considered together. My approach in doing so is to compare and contrast these cases by examining several key questions that have animated the research underlying this book. I have organized this chapter accordingly.

The first section examines what exactly each collaborative business network shares and how the intermediaries in the networks facilitate, and hinder, the sharing of those resources. It also analyzes the corollary question of how (if at all) such sharing contributes to the economic stability of the network and its workers. The second section analyzes the work of the intermediaries in each of these networks, focusing on their particular strengths and weaknesses in facilitating sharing. It also offers some early ideas about how better to support these intermediaries. The third section engages in a more conceptual analysis that searches for lessons that may be applicable well beyond the collaborative business networks that I have discussed. Assuming that these networks do indeed represent alternative paths to sustainable income in urban cores, this third section asks whether the three cases also provide information about best practices or strategies for increasing worker stability along the two established paths for income generation in American urban cores. The final section extracts a set of early lessons that can be drawn about the concept of collaborative capitalism which I frame as design principles for those interested in supporting the many collaborative business networks that have started to develop across the United States. While these lessons also may be generalizable to the more established paths for low-income workers, my focus in the final section will return to the important question of how best to support collaborative business networks in American cities.

## MAXIMIZING SHARING

It is difficult to categorize some of the resources that have been shared in the networks described in this book. As I will discuss, I have also found that traditional

TABLE 1

| Resource Shared | Home Care | Rehabbers | Austin Network |
|---|---|---|---|
| Financing | X | X | X |
| Vocational Education | X | X | X |
| Management Expertise | X | X | X |
| Information | X | X | X |
| Risk | X | X | X |
| Customers | X | | X |
| Back-Office Support | X | | X |
| Physical Space | X | | X |
| Labor | | X | Limited |

categories do not at times do full justice to the sharing that has occurred. Nevertheless, even a conservative count reveals that the following things have been shared in at least two of the three collaborative business networks discussed: financing; vocational education; management expertise; information, including market studies, research, and development; risk; customers; back-office support; physical space; and labor. The networks have been highly creative in sharing these resources, often with the aid of key intermediaries. This section explores the sharing that has occurred in each of these major categories, starting with the categories in which all three networks have shared resources. The above table depicts the sharing categories and the networks that have shared in each category.

### *Financing*

All three case studies have involved the sharing of financing among businesses and organizations within the network. In some cases, as in the home care network, the sharing has been indirect. In others, it has been direct. The most important commonality to note here is that financing has been a critical resource for all three networks, perhaps the most critical. Managers in all three cases have discussed the risks related to finding appropriate financing and the failures associated with undercapitalization. It is therefore significant that all three networks have obtained financing partly by means of sharing.

In the home care and Austin networks, this sharing takes a similar form, and one that is quite different from the South Shore network's sharing of financing. In both the home care and Austin networks, the for-profit businesses in the networks have benefited from grant funding that was obtained, used and managed by the nonprofit intermediaries. In the home care network, Paraprofessional Healthcare Institute has obtained grant funding from governmental and private sources for the purpose of developing its extensive, cutting-edge training program for home care workers. PHI also has used grant funding for research, development and market studies, all of which have benefited Cooperative Home Care Associates and Home Care Associates. This financing has not been directly transferred to CHCA and HCA. Rather, the two cooperatives have externalized the functions of research and development, and some aspects of training, to PHI, which has both performed this work and obtained financing for it. In the Austin network, the nonprofit Southwest Key Programs obtained a grant from the US Commerce Department to start up its first several for-profit businesses. In this respect, the financing was more directly channeled from the nonprofit to these businesses.

It is important to remember that, throughout its existence, ShoreBank benefited from equity investments by several foundations, including the Ford Foundation. However, the funding for the for-profit rehabbing businesses in the network came from private sources. And typically, the main private source of that funding was ShoreBank. Thus, the sharing that occurred in this network was in the common use of the Bank as a main and consistent source of financing. Rehabbers in South Shore referred members of their networks – their mentees, partners, and friends – extensively to the Bank. Indeed, many interviewees commented that the Bank's commercial real estate portfolio was built largely by word of mouth.

This comparative perspective makes it possible to draw some tentative conclusions about these two quite distinct strategies for sharing financing. Turning first to the sharing in the home care and Austin networks, these two networks have developed an innovative way to enlarge the financing pie for for-profit businesses. By including a nonprofit organization as an intermediary in the network, externalizing certain critical business functions to that nonprofit, and relying on the nonprofit to finance those functions from sources typically unavailable to for-profit businesses, these two networks effectively financed the nonprofit pieces of their multiple missions. This then was an explicit recognition of a different way of doing business, just as adopting the benefit corporation organizational form can be.

The disadvantages, of course, are the flip side of the same coin. Nonprofit funding is resource-intensive to obtain and difficult to retain over the long term. It requires proof of an ongoing and significant nonprofit mission.[1] And under current laws, nonprofits that appear engaged in commercial or business activities must negotiate what one commentator has described as a "murky legal swamp" of tests to determine whether they have gone too far beyond their charitable missions.[2] Stated more generally, grant funding is not a traditional source of financing for for-profit businesses, and its nontraditional nature has corollary complexities and risks.

[1] A Treasury Regulation elaborating the Internal Revenue Code's requirements regarding charitable status states, "An organization may meet the requirements of section 501(c)(3) although it operates a trade or business as a substantial part of its activities, if the operation of such trade or business is in furtherance of the exempt organization's exempt purpose or purposes and if the organization is not organized or operated for the primary purpose of carrying on an unrelated trade or business." Treas. Reg. § 1.501(c)(3)-1(e) (as amended in 2014).

[2] Thomas Kelley, *Rediscovering Vulgar Charity: A Historical Analysis of America's Tangled Nonprofit Law*, 73 Fordham L. Rev. 2437, 2473 (2005).

The biggest risk is that this form of financing is only temporary, serving as a bridge for collaborative business networks as they grow. Although this can be a powerful financing strategy, it can also lead to inefficiencies if for-profit businesses externalize business functions over which they would rather retain more control. Furthermore, it is important to ask whether the availability of grant funding also lulled the businesses and intermediaries in these networks into being less aggressive in approaching – or developing – more traditional sources of financing. Was grant funding too easy an option that replaced more permanent financing possibilities?

The South Shore network avoided a number of these questions by relying on a much more traditional source of financing for for-profit businesses. But of course that source, ShoreBank, was traditional with a twist. It was an "un-bureaucratic" source of capital that made extensive use of its status as a community bank, and later a community development financial institution, to invest heavily in South Shore. Although it provided financing in the form of loans, its level of investment seems in many ways more akin to that of an equity investor. This was particularly true given the Bank's strategy of lending repeatedly to borrowers as they developed their real estate portfolios over the course of years, even decades.

Assuming that such a strategy is sustainable for the financial institution, it is highly beneficial to the for-profit businesses for many reasons. Most obviously, it is a financing source that is easy to access, trustworthy, and loyal. As Chapter 5 revealed, it is not an exaggeration to say that this combination of characteristics is non-existent for most small businesses in the United States. The networks that do include financing institutions, such as the East Los Angeles Community Union (TELACU) network of real estate businesses in East Los Angeles, appear to be some of the largest and most robust.[3] Moreover, because ShoreBank was in fact a private bank that operated in many important ways like other private banks, it was easy for borrowers to transition to using other banks that entered the market. There is evidence that this is exactly what happened from the mid-2000s onward. Those rehabbing businesses that had grown large enough were approached by other banks, offering at times more competitive rates and terms than ShoreBank was able to offer. And some of those banks became key financing sources for the businesses once ShoreBank closed.

But of course, ShoreBank's closing raises questions about how sustainable its strategy was for its own long-term health and survival. Did the Bank incur too much risk by lending so heavily to support the local real estate market? Should it have diversified its portfolio? Could its investments have been protected by support from secondary market investors? Did it overly adopt the approach of an equity investor, and in doing so, incur too much risk? And could some of its risk have been

[3] *The TELACU Family of Companies*, TELACU, telacu.com/telacu-family-of-companies/financial-services/telacu-community-capital. The most impressive example of such a network is the Mondragon network in Spain. *About Us*, MONDRAGON CORPORATION, www.mondragon-corporation.com/en/about-us.

addressed by appropriate regulation? While the Bank's story is too complex to permit me to draw causal connections (at least on the basis of my research), Chapter 10 addresses some of these questions by considering the regulation question. Obviously, too, the long-term survival of the Bank greatly affected the long-term survival of the businesses that borrowed from the Bank. There were many rehabbers that survived the crisis and remain stable in business. But there were also many that did not survive, and this was at least partly due to their heavy reliance on the Bank for financing. In this respect, the Bank's financing strategy was deeply intertwined with the financing of the network as a whole.

Finally, the financing strategies of these three networks provide further evidence about one intransigent problem in small business financing. While my sample is obviously very small, it is still noteworthy that none of these three networks has solved the problem of accessing true equity investors. The home care network is looking into this question by considering crowdfunding strategies. Meanwhile, a notable exception to my claim is that some of the rehabbing businesses, especially those built by North Siders, that have survived and thrived have turned (in some cases exclusively) to private equity investment to raise capital.[4] However, these three networks have not developed sharing mechanisms for this form of financing. As Chapter 9 reveals, this is a contrast to the mature coordinated economies, where banks often play a more hybrid role as lenders who regularly also take formal equity stakes in their borrowers' businesses.

## *Training and Vocational Education*

It is also noteworthy – and rather extraordinary – that training and vocational education play such a critical role in all three of these collaborative business networks. Their importance bespeaks the prioritization of workers in such networks. By directing considerable resources to training and vocational education, the networks have given particular precedence to the acquisition of skills that allow workers to remain employable, ideally at higher incomes than they otherwise would receive.

The home care network has the most extensive and formalized training component. Several of the organizations in that network, namely PHI, CHCA, HCA, and the local union, have worked hard to develop and deliver a highly specialized and effective curriculum to train home health aides.[5] As I have described, the curriculum is distinct from the industry standard in many respects, and most of my interviewees emphasized its importance to the overall success of the businesses in the network. It appears that the more extensive training provided to workers in this

4 Silver Interview; Feldman Interview.

5 For an excellent description of the values of providing "employer-embedded training," see Steven L. Dawson, *When the Employer is the Trainer: Lessons from Cooperative Home Care Associates*, PINKERTON PAPERS, June 2017, at 1, 1–6, www.thepinkertonfoundation.org/wp-content/uploads/2017/07/Pinkerton-Papers-No5-Dawson-FINAL-WEB-4.pdf.

network correlates directly with the businesses' ability to provide a higher quality service and thereby preserve their market niche. Repeatedly, this network has shown the value of higher levels of training and skills in an industry that had presumed that home care was unskilled labor. In this respect, training has been a core component of the business strategy. But one limitation of this strategy has been in the financing of it. One critical question for the Bronx network in particular is whether it can develop a long-term financing strategy for its training programs that is not so reliant on grant funding.

Interviewees also emphasized the value of training for several of the businesses in the Southwest Key network. As in the home care network, the nonprofit organization in the network leads the effort to develop appropriate curricula and deliver them to workers in the businesses. Given the size and age of this network, the training programs are less comprehensive than the home care network's, but they are still an important piece of what is shared. Interestingly, despite the diversification of its businesses across several industries, the network has managed to share some training components across its network. One example is occupational health and safety training. Another is job readiness. A key question for this network is whether moving toward a single niche industry would create valuable efficiencies on the vocational education side.

In the South Shore network, the vocational education component was initially delivered through an informal peer-to-peer system that eventually became more formalized in some respects. It began when Jim Bringley started inviting some of the more established rehabbers to meet monthly to share knowledge and advice about different skills within the trade. It also happened more informally through a peer mentoring process within each of the subnetworks of rehabbers. Over time, some of the rehabbers began to give formal seminars at the Bank's request and often at its offices. In addition, some rehabbers formed trade associations which, among many other things, provided opportunities for business owners to learn about new practices and initiatives in the industry. This approach to training is in marked contrast to programs in which businesses arrange to use certain projects as teaching opportunities with the expectation that doing so will increase costs beyond a reasonable market price that could be charged to a customer. In such cases, the presumption seems to be that the businesses take a loss on the construction projects. There were some early discussions in the South Shore network about employing this same strategy. But it appears that the more effective approach was peer-to-peer education, which occurred *alongside* the sharing of skilled labor. People learned from each other on the job as well as on the side at monthly meetings.

Clearly, the relative need for, development of, and delivery of training and vocational education is driven by the particular industry in which the business is operating. One very general observation to make about all three networks, but especially the home care workers and rehabbers, is that the particular approach to training has impacted the protection of the businesses' niche. In the home care network, this has to do with quality of service. The same could be said of Southwest Key's café. In South Shore, it has had to do with maintaining a competitive price for rehabbed properties. This observation leads to the further tentative conclusion that there may be a sweet spot for such networks to develop in industries with relatively low barriers to market entry, but those that still require some level of skill. In contrast to the fast-food industry or trash-picking for example, where there are no barriers to market entry, the need for *some* skills means that businesses that provide quality training can get a leg up in defining a niche and thereby recoup the costs invested in training their employees.

It is also important to note that the prioritization of training and vocational education has much broader implications for workers, beyond their participation in these collaborative business networks. While the businesses in these networks have higher retention rates than the industry standard, it is also the case that training received through these networks can be the basis for leaving the networks for better work elsewhere. Interviewees in the home care and rehabber networks shared examples with me of "career ladders" that were consciously created for workers in those networks, of employees leaving for jobs with higher wages and benefits, and about the support management gave them in pursuing better work, including by providing state-recognized credentials.[6] HCA's Angelique Montgomery and Nana Nemeiar, for example, shared their ambition of becoming nurses, or in Nemeiar's case, opening a hospital in her home country, which they developed as a result of their training and experience at HCA.[7] These were often ambitions developed after experiencing the job stability and longevity afforded by businesses such as HCA, when many of these individuals had previously only worked for short periods in jobs that required no training.

The home care network also provides vivid examples of the value of training for employees' personal development: "[T]he one part of the training that sticks out for me the most … is what they call the four Ps [paraphrasing and repeating, pulling back, presenting options, and passing it on] … I use them in my everyday life, with coping with people and decisions."[8] "I became a changed person … [T]his job keeps me positive … I never, ever wanted to buy a house in my life … [Now] I'm about to go through a first-time buyer's program … I matured … I'm saving money now."[9] "It helps you to have patience. It helps you with just how to deal with people in general."[10] "It made me more sensitive, and I teach my kids to be like that."[11]

The Manchester Bidwell network in Pittsburgh is an excellent example of a collaborative business network focused primarily on vocational education. While it includes a small cluster of social enterprises, much of its energy seems to go to a broader vocational education program in which its own businesses serve as training

6 Spence Interview; Clark Interview; Perkins Interview; Dixon Interview.

7 Montgomery Interview; Nemeiar Interview. 8 Montgomery Interview.

9 Whitehead Interview. 10 Carroll Interview. 11 Calvo Interview.

grounds.[12] In these respects, the vocational education provided by these networks adds value along all the available paths for earning income.

### *Management Expertise*

Two of the three networks have extensive sharing of management expertise which is sewn into their organizational structures. The home care network formally shares management expertise by means of cross-board relationships. These are supported by dense informal relationships across the network of formally affiliated organizations. Interviewees also recounted many, many examples in which they have worked through business challenges by means of informal consultation with management in the affiliate organizations. This has all been supported by the longevity of positions held by some of the key leaders. A similar strategy is evident in the Southwest Key network, although this network has gone a major step further by formally organizing itself in a holding company structure. Key leaders are on the boards of all the enterprises in the network. In addition, the nonprofit mission flows through to each for-profit business by means of this formal structure. Of course here, as well, the managers of different businesses provide consultations and support without formal remuneration.

In South Shore, the sharing of management only extended through the formal subsidiaries and affiliates of the ShoreBank holding company. In that respect, the Bank's holding company structure looked quite similar to Southwest Key's. The Bank did not have any kind of formal management stake in the rehabbing businesses. Informally, however, it is evident that Jim Bringley and others in his department had extensive knowledge of, and even influence over, the growth and development of some of the rehabbing businesses. To describe this influence as "management" is excessive. But it is important to recognize that it went significantly beyond the kinds of reviews conducted by most banks.

As I will discuss in more detail in the last section of this chapter, one of the things that is both unique and inestimably important in each of these networks is the extraordinary leadership. This is one of the reasons that replication is so difficult. But even if these leaders cannot be cloned, each network has successfully spread the value of their leadership by means of these formal and informal sharing mechanisms. Indeed, it is worth asking whether the South Shore network would have benefited from a more formal sharing of management expertise between the Bank and the rehabbers, especially in the lead-up to the financial crisis. But of course, the uniqueness of the leaders in these networks can be a weakness as well as a strength. Only the South Shore network is now experiencing the full absence of the original leaders of ShoreBank who contributed so much to the network's development. Meanwhile, the home care network is just experiencing the transition to new leaders

[12] Manchester Bidwell Corporation, http://manchesterbidwell.org.

in some of its core businesses and intermediaries. Thus far, the transition has been very thoughtfully executed, but it is much too early to tell what this and the Austin networks will be like when their founders are no longer involved.

### *Information*

Information is a resource for which it is difficult to describe the full value, and which includes such a range of sharing that it is difficult also to capture in one category. Yet, using this general label does help make the point that one of the great values of collaborative business networks is their extensive sharing of many kinds of information.

In the home care network, information is shared in numerous and critical ways. The network benefits from the research and development activities of PHI, which has developed mechanisms for quality control and efficient service delivery across the spectrum of services provided by CHCA, HCA, and other home care providers to whom PHI provides consulting services. Indeed, this work has been so effective that the network has developed a national reputation for advancing the so-called sectoral strategy, which involves changing the conditions of work and service delivery in an entire industry. Relatedly, PHI and the other organizations participate extensively in gathering and sharing market data. This sharing involves much broader networks that have developed on both the supply and demand sides of the market. CHCA and HCA participate in networks of worker-owned cooperatives. CHCA participates in a network of B corporations. ICS participates in patient advocacy and managed care networks. HCA participates in the Pennsylvania Home Care Association network, which negotiates reimbursement rates. CHCA participates in the networks led by the Service Employees International Union. Additionally, ICS could be described as providing a level of vertical integration on the demand side of the market. The shared knowledge between ICS and its "preferred providers" such as CHCA creates great efficiencies in supporting ICS's specialty as a managed care organization serving individuals with physical disabilities.

While entirely different in nature, the South Shore network's sharing of information has also been extensive and effective. Here, the sharing has occurred both through the Bank and via peer-to-peer contacts among the rehabbing businesses. First, the Bank effectively translated its own due diligence in the lending process into information that would support its borrowers' business activities. As Ron Grzywinski pointed out, this was more the norm in neighborhood banking in the earlier part of the last century, and indeed banks still regularly serve this function in both business and consumer transactions. But ShoreBank was particularly effective in the rehabber network, because the knowledge of Jim Bringley and his colleagues in the commercial real estate department was so thick, local, and consistently offered. Bringley worked in that department for approximately thirty years, and he met personally with most of the Bank's rehabber borrowers. This depth of knowledge has been matched by the extensive formal and informal contacts among borrowers, who often share ethnic, geographical, cultural and other ties. Indeed, the ability of the rehabbers to acquire local, skilled and unskilled inputs of labor seems to have been uniquely the product of local knowledge and neighborhood connections. Over time, and especially around the time of the Great Recession, this network's sharing of information became formalized through the formation of at least two trade associations through which borrowers still meet monthly to discuss a broad range of issues that arise in their work.

The Southwest Key network has also shared knowledge in ways that seem critical to its survival and growth. One key example is the information about job placement and market data that has been provided by its workforce development business to the other businesses in the cluster. Another obvious example is the information about occupational health and safety that flows across the network. More generally, the network has benefited from both the expertise and the thick, local knowledge of its management and board members. It is apparent that these individuals have deep knowledge about local markets and work opportunities in Austin. And they have used this knowledge to create sustainable work in several industries. But it is important to note again here that the opportunities especially for peer-to-peer sharing of information are more limited in the Southwest Key network presumably because of the diversity of its businesses.

The varieties of information shared and the forms in which it is shared raise important questions about best practices that require further research to answer. It is possible, however, to make several observations about the information sharing in these three networks. First, and perhaps most generally, both the home care and rehabber examples demonstrate that some of the most significant information sharing appears connected to developing specialization on both the supply and demand sides of the market. Regularly, such information supports the development of a market niche. Second, these networks seem to affirm theories that neighborhood insiders can sometimes exploit information about local markets more quickly and efficiently, thereby outcompeting outsiders. The rehabbers' sharing of information and labor relating to local tradespeople is a clear example here. Third, while intermediaries have facilitated sharing in each of these networks, there is some evidence that peer-to-peer information sharing is also an important factor. The less successful efforts of ShoreBank to develop manufacturing jobs in the Austin neighborhood of Chicago supports this conclusion, as does the story of Cooperative Home Care of Boston. In both of these examples, the intermediaries worked hard to develop and exploit thick, local knowledge. But for a variety of reasons, there was less peer-to-peer exchange in those two contexts. In both cases, it appears that the information flow from the intermediary to the businesses did not suffice in creating long-term stability for the workers.

These observations support an additional hypothesis that warrants more research. It is reasonable to postulate that the more active sharing within these networks takes *better* advantage of local, thick knowledge than either the incubators that have been popular in local development experiments or the industry clusters discussed by Michael Porter and others. In these latter two examples, experts argue that simply locating businesses within a single industry close together in a physical space leads to synergies. This may well be true, but there is also reason to believe that the more active coordination and use of information in collaborative business networks could be equally effective, if not more so. One important question for future research is whether the more active coordination supports the more efficient development of niches that serve to protect each business's market position as it develops.

### *Risk*

The final category in which sharing has occurred in all three networks is in the area of risk. From a lay perspective, risk might appear to be a disadvantageous thing to share or spread. But each of these networks reveals how important risk sharing has been to the start-up and growth of the businesses in those networks.

Turning first to the home care network, the very existence of ICS is the most obvious (but by no means only) example of risk spreading. By developing a managed care company that has a special interest in just the kinds of services provided by CHCA, the Bronx home care network greatly protected its market share, and indeed doubled in size. As Peggy Powell so powerfully described, it is partly a matter of "control[ling] our own fate."[13] But there are many other examples as well: the outsourcing of research, development and some aspects of training to PHI, the initial capitalization of CHCA on the basis of grant or "soft" funding from the ICA Group and other sources committed to the business's multiple missions, and the development of independent businesses with cross-board relationships. Although they may not always have been described or even thought about in such terms, all of these mechanisms helped to spread the risk beyond the individual businesses. This externalization of risk to the network seems especially wise, given the importance of worker ownership to the overall mission.

In the South Shore context, the sharing of risk occurred between the Bank and individual borrowers. By developing thick, local knowledge and a borrower base of repeat players, the Bank was able to limit its own risk. And in the process, of course, it absorbed some of the risk borne by the rehabbers. At the time the founders converted the Bank into a community development bank, no other bank was making loans in South Shore because of the perceived risk of doing so. This meant that local businesses did not have a local source of capital. By absorbing the risks associated with starting up, ShoreBank allowed a market to exist where previously there had been no such market. Another important example of risk spreading and hedging in South Shore was in the individual behavior of borrowers. Thanks to advice from the

[13] Powell Interview.

Bank, they kept their day jobs until they owned a large enough number of units to provide stable income. And as Mary Houghton described, they shared labor in order to smooth out their incomes.

Finally, the nonprofit's support of the Café del Sol exemplifies the sharing of risk in the Southwest Key network. Although nontraditional, the nonprofit was a source of patient capital and management expertise for the café. Critically, it and the charter school also served as stable customers. All of these efforts saved the café from failure in the early years. The same is true for the maintenance and green construction companies in that network.

The enormous value of risk-spreading in these networks teaches a powerful lesson for those interested in supporting small businesses and businesses with multiple bottom lines. It appears that businesses in all three networks faced many of the early challenges and avoided some of the pitfalls faced by start-ups by spreading the associated risks across the networks. Rather than weakening the entire network, this risk sharing seems to have strengthened it.

This observation in turn leads to a key lesson that may be drawn about risk-sharing within collaborative business networks. From these three examples, it appears that a nonprofit organization may be able to serve a unique function in absorbing or spreading risk. Here, it may be helpful to contrast the home care and Southwest Key networks with the South Shore network. In the former two networks, the nonprofits were able to accept risks and (in the case of Southwest Key) absorb financial losses that may not have been acceptable to shareholders of for-profit businesses. But perhaps partly because these risks and losses were consistent with the nonprofit mission, they appear to have been worth taking. By contrast, ShoreBank was a private bank, subject to safety and soundness requirements, other banking regulations, and ultimately also to its investors.

### *Customers*

Two of the three collaborative business networks in this book also used sharing strategies to acquire a stable customer base. In the Bronx network, the strategy was to establish a managed care organization within the network that could serve as a stable source of contracts for CHCA. It appears that the network contemplates a long-term customer/provider relationship between ICS and CHCA. In the Southwest Key network, the strategy was to use the large nonprofit organization and the charter school as stable customers for the café, maintenance company, and construction company. In this network, the strategy appears to be to rely on these two organizations as customers over a relatively short-term start-up period, with the expectation that the businesses will eventually expand their customer bases significantly beyond the organizations in the network.

The use of an intermediary as a customer base was both innovative and valuable for these two networks. Both have essentially benefited from a patient customer, or perhaps more aptly an engaged customer, who values the higher quality services and products as well as the multiple missions of the businesses that serve it. But it is also important to consider the limitations of this strategy. One important limitation, as Dr. Sánchez of Southwest Key discussed, is that the intermediaries are limited in the amount of demand they can create by servicing their own needs. This appears to be a more pressing concern in the Southwest Key network than in the Bronx context. The Bronx context, however, raises a second limitation, namely that CHCA would suffer significantly if ICS were to go out of business or experience some other major business disruption. While these intermediaries have thus far been the source of market stability and growth, they could also be the source of instability unless the businesses in their networks are able to maintain diverse customer bases.

These limitations suggest that one important objective in networks where intermediaries serve as customer bases should be to develop market data and strategies for moving beyond those customer bases. The Southwest Key network is exemplary in this regard, because as Dr. Sánchez described, each of the businesses was developed with a view toward serving both an immediate customer base and transitioning to new customers outside of the Southwest Key network. But it is also reasonable to question whether the intermediaries have created an artificial market of sorts that cannot be replaced by a broader market for the niche developed within the network. This is a substantial concern that requires continued attention in both networks. In the Bronx, for example, it is reasonable to ask whether the ideal of quality care through quality jobs can be fulfilled in a market still so dominated by price competition. In Austin, it will be important to continue to ask the difficult question of whether enough demand exists in the food service, maintenance, and construction industries to support businesses that prioritize good wages and work conditions for their employees.

### *Back-Office Support and Physical Space*

The Bronx and Austin networks also involve the sharing of back-office support (such as accounting and cleaning services) as well as physical space for colocated businesses. Both of these forms of sharing take advantage of the same efficiencies that are available through incubator programs. They are a simple mechanism for reducing business costs. They also appear to be a stable and long-term form of cost savings for businesses. Their simplicity should not detract from their importance, however. Often these types of costs are the difference between survival and failure. When these resources are not readily available, new businesses regularly take shortcuts that violate applicable laws and hurt their own profitability. Moreover, some real estate markets can make it very difficult to find good and affordable space. In Austin, for example, before she began working for the café, Alma Alfaro sold food from a food cart rather than a restaurant. The impermanence of her physical space signified the impermanence of her business.

### *Labor*

Finally, in both the South Shore and Southwest Key networks, there was an early sharing of labor among businesses. In the South Shore network, the sharing appears to have been initiated by the businesses themselves, and may have been a function partly of the mentoring relationships that existed in the subnetworks. In the Southwest Key context, the sharing was quite limited, and seems to have been instigated by the nonprofit as a way of providing stability in work hours for the workers involved as well as a ready supply of labor in the very early start-up phases of one or two of the businesses.

In the South Shore network, the sharing of labor seems to have been especially important for the first wave of rehabbers. These individuals were operating in a context where there was no established market for the variety of trades that they required to complete their rehabs, other than union labor. Union labor was too expensive. Consequently these rehabbers had little choice but to turn to each other until they were able to develop their own skills and hire their own employees. After this initial stage, the rehabbers also developed a network of contractors whom they trusted and shared. While the rehabbers appeared to initiate this informal network of labor inputs themselves, the Bank was an important extender of this strategy by virtue of Jim Bringley's referrals of borrowers to each other.

## UNDERSTANDING INTERMEDIARIES

Throughout this book, I have emphasized the importance of intermediary organizations and principles to the practice of collaborative capitalism. At the same time, I have noted their unfamiliarity in American markets. We all are familiar with banks, nonprofits, unions, and trade associations. But many Americans are far less familiar with community development banks and nonprofit managed care companies. And even those who are familiar may not know about or understand what these organizations do to facilitate the sharing of resources. Our knowledge is emergent in this respect. As research into the role of sharing intermediaries continues, it will be important to examine both their contributions to, and their hindering of, the development of collaborative business networks. The purpose of this brief section is to begin that conversation by providing some early impressions about the comparative strengths, weaknesses and needs of the several types of intermediaries discussed in this book.

As I have described, the home care network revolves around the principle of worker ownership, which I have described as a core institution for sharing within that network. Of course, the network also includes two nonprofit intermediary organizations, a union, and a range of business associations focused on more discrete aspects of this network's activities. As Chapter 9 will make apparent, the home care network looks more similar to the coordinated economies in other parts of the world than do the other networks discussed in this book. Perhaps for all these reasons, the great focus and strength of the intermediary institutions in this network are on the support, training, and protection of workers. In both CHCA and HCA, most of the workers interviewed described this as the best job they had ever had and expressed deep loyalty to their employers and satisfaction with their employment situations. This despite the relatively low wages they receive. This appears the case for the other collaborative business networks as well, but the point here is that the home care network has developed formal institutions to ensure (or at least increase the likelihood) that workers will have such a positive relationship with their work and their employers.

Meanwhile, the home care network continues to be challenged by the dearth of financing options available to it. It is reliant on the vagaries of Medicaid and Medicare reimbursements, and this is less than ideal. It has been innovative and tenacious in its use of grant funding, but this also comes with risks and costs. Additionally under current laws, the choice of worker ownership undermines the network's ability to use equity investments, thereby eliminating an important source of capital that is available to traditional businesses.

Taken together, these observations suggest that networks that use the institution of worker ownership, and that rely on intermediary organizations to enhance the values of worker ownership and participation, could benefit from a market and regulatory environment that recognizes these values. As Chapter 9 describes, Germany, France, and Japan have exactly that. While it is unrealistic to try to replicate such markets in the United States, the experience of the home care network in New York especially shows that some change is possible. New York has already instituted a higher minimum-wage and wage-parity laws, and it is possible to imagine the home care industry moving toward higher certification requirements in recognition that home care workers are in fact skilled workers, especially if the state creates incentives in that direction. It is also possible to imagine creating incentives in the industry for the development of more discrete niches that could reduce the aggressive price competition that currently exists in the market. Finally, it would be valuable to research the creation of market incentives for banks and venture capitalists to develop specialties in financing worker-owned cooperatives. Boston Community Capital in Massachusetts is just such a financing source, and it should be examined as a model for other urban cores.[14]

In meaningful respects, the South Shore network is a mirror image of the home care network. For decades, it solved the problem of financing extremely effectively. Moreover, the ownership of rehabbing businesses by individual mom-and-pop proprietors also effectively distributed worker ownership widely among previously marginalized, low-income, and nontraditional business owners. There is significant evidence also that these business owners provided opportunities to workers who had

[14] Boston Community Capital, www.bostoncommunitycapital.org.

otherwise been marginalized in the workforce. Finally, the Bank's nonprofit affiliate, the Neighborhood Institute, was dedicated to workforce development and worker protections, though it did not do much work with the rehabbers. Thus, the Chicago network did accomplish many of the same protections for workers that we see in the home care network, albeit using quite different mechanisms. However, focusing narrowly just on the rehabber network, it is also evident that the network did not have many formal institutions in place for ensuring the support, training, and satisfaction of workers. This raises questions about whether worker protections were merely a happy accident within this network or an integral and permanent feature.

The ultimate demise of the Bank suggests that even this exemplary financing institution had needs that, if met, could have improved both its services and its chances of survival. A number of my interviewees took the opportunity to reflect on what those needs were, and many of their comments addressed the issue of risk. Bank founders Mary Houghton and Ron Grzywinski discussed the absence of a secondary market for the loans the Bank made to rehabbers. Rehabber Len Hoyles suggested that, as deep as the Bank's knowledge was, it could have gone further by requiring new rehabbers to take a class on owning and maintaining rental properties, or it could have done more extensive screening on issues of property rental.

Given the complementary roles of worker-owned cooperatives and community development banks, it would be interesting to examine a business network in the United States that includes both of these institutions. At this time, no such network exists in American urban cores. The Mondragon Cooperatives in the Basque region of Spain, which include a cooperative bank as a central component, have been the subject of much discussion and the model for some experimentation in the United States, but none recently with lasting effect.[15]

As my research has affirmed, social enterprise clusters, and the nonprofit organizations at their center, are much more diverse and malleable institutions than worker cooperatives and community banks. My example in this category, the Southwest Key network, has a mission that emphasizes many of the same values as the home care network's. Thus, it is not surprising that the network has developed formal and informal strategies along both the small business path and the traditional employment path for protecting workers and enhancing their skills. The most pervasive example is the philosophy of *familia* articulated by so many of my interviewees. The great strengths of the nonprofit are indeed its ability to flexibly represent and protect the nonprofit-focused pieces of the multiple missions in these networks. This is a core feature, and my three case studies have provided many innovative examples of how to make the most of it.

[15] David Ellerman's case study for the Harvard Business School remains one of the most detailed sources about the Mondragon system. David P. Ellerman, Harvard Bus. School, The Mondragon Cooperative Movement 1–31 (1984), www.ellerman.org/wp-content/uploads/2012/12/Mondragon-HBS-Case.CV_.pdf.

Not surprisingly, the challenges for nonprofit intermediaries, including Southwest Key's, relate to financing and scalability. I have reviewed the financing challenges already. On the scalability question, it may suffice to say that, while nonprofits can be very large in size, their nonprofit status can be jeopardized if they invest too directly in for-profit affiliates.[16] This impacts the extent to which for-profit subsidiaries of nonprofit organizations can grow. Thus, it is reasonable to question whether and how nonprofits can serve as intermediaries for certain kinds of sharing over the long term and as the businesses in their networks grow.

We have also seen business associations acting as intermediaries in these networks, most notably in the South Shore network since around the time of the Great Recession. In South Shore, they have played a particularly intriguing role by filling some of the vacuum left by the Bank after its closure in 2010. We have also seen a union serving as an important intermediary in the Bronx network. Both of these types of intermediaries are ubiquitous in national coordinated economies in other parts of the world. Although my research provides very little information from which to draw conclusions about their unique contributions or essentiality in American collaborative business networks, they have played enough of a role in these examples to warrant additional research. At least it seems safe to conclude that these organizations have served as additional facilitators of sharing.

As I discuss in detail in Chapter 8, one question that will be particularly important to research is whether organizations such as trade associations and unions can help to preserve a balance of power between the intermediaries and the businesses in collaborative business networks. In each of my examples, it appears that some combination of deep commitment to the prioritization of workers, extraordinary and selfless leadership, transparency, and integrity has contributed to the sharing of power and control between the intermediaries and the businesses, the management and the workers. This may not always be the case, either in these networks in the future or in other collaborative business networks. But as Chapters 9 and 10 suggest, it may be essential to maintaining economic stability for both the networks and the workers. Thus, it will be important to continue to explore strategies for maintaining such a balance in collaborative business networks.

## SUPPORTING OTHER MEANS OF INCOME GENERATION

Although the primary focus of this book has been on sharing as a basis for developing alternative paths for urban-core workers, my research has also yielded important

[16] Thomas Kelley provides a detailed examination of the difficulties of financing hybrid businesses with multiple bottom lines. Thomas Kelley, *Law and Choice of Entity on the Social Enterprise Frontier*, 84 TUL. L. REV. 337, 354 (2009) ("Social entrepreneurs' difficulty raising start-up or expansion capital has driven many away from the non-profit sector ... [F]or-profit social entrepreneurs generally cut themselves off from the sources that traditionally have funded socially beneficial activities – private foundations and governments.).

information about how to create greater economic stability for workers on the more traditional paths for income generation. This brief section discusses two key lessons for supporting workers on those more traditional paths. Neither of these lessons is surprising; both have been discussed extensively in prior literature on community development and poverty alleviation. But the research underlying this book does add to the evidence supporting these lessons.

Beginning with the path of employment with a large business, the home care network adds to the many arguments about the value of democratic participation in the work place. In this respect, it is a particularly vivid contrast with sharing-economy giants such as Uber, which I will discuss in Chapter 8. Several employees commented on the rareness and value of being able to connect with the highest levels of management in their companies. As their remarks suggest, worker ownership is connected to a desire to remain employed at these businesses over the long term, which of course contributes to job stability. Ownership imbues these individuals with a sense of belonging and connection that contributes to longevity of employment.

While CHCA and HCA are two of the largest worker-owned cooperatives in the country, they are by no means the only ones. The Arizmendi Bakeries in the bay area in California – named after Father Arizmendi, who founded the venerable Mondragon Cooperatives in Spain – are among the oldest networks of worker-owned cooperatives in the United States.[17] CCA Global Partners is a fascinating example of a network of worker-owned cooperatives. It uses what amounts to a franchising system to network worker-owned cooperatives in specific industries, a number of which involve home improvement such as carpeting, flooring and lighting.[18] Newer networks of worker-owned cooperatives include the Evergreen Cooperatives in Cleveland.[19] And of course, agricultural cooperatives, such as Organic Valley, Cabot Creamery, and Equal Exchange are a staple of the rural American economy.[20]

These networks provide examples of, and strategies for, achieving both worker ownership and democratic participation. While I would hold up worker cooperatives as the ideal form of democratic participation, the many examples provided here include plenty of alternative strategies for employers to consider. As these businesses

[17] Shanta Nimbark Sacharoff, Other Avenues are Possible: Legacy of the People's Food System of the San Francisco Bay Area 133–135 (2016) ("In 1971, the first Arizmendi collective . . . was converted by its two owners from a private retail cheese business into a worker-owned collective . . . They developed a unique model fashioned after Mondragon co-ops in Spain . . . Unlike corporate franchise paradigms, where expansion is based on the sale of a business model for a substantial sum of money, plus royalties on sales, the co-op bakeries share recipes and business models to encourage increased workplace democracy.").

[18] CCA Global Partners, www.ccaglobalpartners.com.

[19] Tyler Gurss, *Coop Businesses: Ownership for the Disowned*, 20 Pub. Int. L. Rep. 140, 140–141 (2015).

[20] Organic Valley, www.organicvalley.coop/why-organic-valley/cooperative-benefits; *Our Roots*, Cabot Creamery Co-operative, www.cabotcheese.coop/our-roots; *Worker-Owned*, Equal Exchange, equalexchange.coop/worker-owned.

demonstrate, increasing democratic participation in the workplace is simply a good business strategy.

On the path of small business development, the South Shore network exemplifies the value of having a financial institution as part of the network. It is hard to imagine a more efficient funding mechanism for small businesses. As many of my interviewees who worked at ShoreBank commented, the Bank's unique community development mission also kept the Bank and its investors committed over the long term. Here, it is useful to note the connection between the Bank's mission and the particular market niche filled by the rehabber network. The two were complementary in a deeply synergistic way.

The TELACU network is another compelling example of a network with its own financing institutions. This enormous self-described "family" of businesses engaged in the real estate and construction industries includes three financial institutions. TELACU Community Capital and Community Commerce Bank are both community development financial institutions that support local small businesses. Community Commerce Bank claims to be one of the most profitable community banks in the country. New Markets Community Capital receives new markets tax credit allocations from the US Treasury Department and uses these to support investments in local commercial, retail, and industrial developments.[21] Here again, the synergy between the network's niche and the specialized focus of New Markets Community Capital is noteworthy.

Another venerable example of a network with a financial institution at its center is that of the Self Help Credit Union in North Carolina, whose first major project was to help employees of local mills that were shutting down to form worker-owned cooperatives to continue operating those mills. This institution now operates in four different states and serves over 100,000 customers.[22]

The broader lesson to draw from these examples is the value of having local banks that specialize in supporting local small businesses. As ShoreBank's experiences with manufacturing businesses in the Austin neighborhood of Chicago and with the commercial developments it supported in South Shore reveal, this is not easy to do. It is difficult to develop a deep enough level of local knowledge and an extensive enough portfolio to make such lending efficient. But some of the rehabbers whom I interviewed in South Shore gave me examples of community banks other than ShoreBank that had loan officers dedicated exclusively to supporting rehab lending in the neighborhood during the years when the network was at its largest.[23] Most of

21 *The TELACU Family of Companies*, TELACU, telacu.com/telacu-family-of-companies/financial-services/telacu-community-capital.

22 Howard E. Covington Jr., Lending Power: How Self-Help Credit Union Turned Small-Time Loans into Big-Time Change (2017); Thad Williamson, David Imbroscio & Gar Alperovitz, Making a Place for Community: Local Democracy in a Global Era 224 (2002); *Our Story*, Self-Help Credit Union, www.self-help.org/who-we-are/about-us/our-story.

23 Feldman Interview; Silver Interview. Of course the CIC in Chicago is a contemporary example of a lender with a development focus. CIC is a large CDFI. Crane Interview.

these banks have now disappeared, but my research adds support for the growing literature calling for the chartering and development of many more local banks. Reintroducing such banks into local markets may be one of the most potent ways to support small business development in urban cores.

## DESIGN PRINCIPLES FOR COLLABORATIVE CAPITALISM

In this final section, I provide a set of basic design principles for supporting collaborative capitalism in American cities. My aim here is not to give a toolkit for replicating the networks I have described. A great deal more research will be required before that is possible. Rather, my effort is to provide some general guidance for identifying the collaborative business networks that have developed organically across urban America and for supporting the growth of those networks. My intention in having provided a range of examples of collaborative business networks is to aid experts involved in local economic development in delineating the features of collaborative capitalism on the ground and in a rich variety of manifestations.

Let me begin first by listing the features of these collaborative business networks that are unique and that likely have made attempts to replicate them so difficult. The first overarching feature is the uniqueness of context in each of these examples. This includes geography (a few miles from downtown and a golf course in South Shore; the enormity of New York City, which makes it useful to hire home care workers who live near their customers). It includes infrastructure (the availability of public transportation in Philadelphia, the location of schools in Austin). It includes migration patterns (the development of the African American middle class in South Shore, the immigration of children and their families to Austin). It includes market conditions (the availability of Medicaid and Medicare reimbursements for home care, the quality of buildings in South Shore). And it certainly includes local regulatory frameworks (the regulation of day labor in Austin, the building codes in Chicago).

Second, it is impossible to account fully for the uniqueness and value of the leadership in each of these networks. Third, it is very difficult to dictate the development of a market for any given niche. Several of my interviewees commented that their discovery of a niche was a product of luck and timing rather than expertise. Finally, it is impossible to plan for catastrophic occurrences such as the Great Recession. While that crisis teaches important lessons about future protections to build into collaborative networks and the institutions that support them, it is also reasonable to conclude that no amount of preplanning can protect against such occurrences. No doubt there are more unique factors at work in each of these cases, but this list should at least sound a cautionary note about why replication is so difficult.

I turn now to the features of these networks that might be capable of generalization, at least for the purpose of identifying already existing networks. I have divided these features into two main categories. The first is a set of principles that seem particularly efficacious in supporting workers in collaborative business networks. The second is a set of principles that seem particularly useful in identifying and supporting potentially successful networks. Both sets of design principles are also intended to provide guidance about how to maintain economic stability for the networks, businesses, and workers.

### *For the Economic Stability of the Workers*

**Ensure democratic participation.** Given my earlier analysis of the importance of worker ownership and participation, it is not surprising that my first design principle in support of worker stability is to ensure democratic participation in these networks. Again, the worker-owned cooperative is a model form of participation, but these networks provide a variety of forms that are useful to consider.

**Provide vocational education with a long view for the worker.** The networks in this book demonstrate the value of vocational education in developing a sustainable market niche. But their missions also justify the development of vocational education curricula that prioritize long-term work opportunities for workers both in the networks and beyond. This requires incorporating a certain amount of generalization in curricula that otherwise may be very specially designed to support the market niche. The home care network is exemplary here. It could focus its curriculum more heavily or even exclusively on providing care for adults with physical disabilities. But it is apparent that the network has developed a curriculum focusing on the provision of quality care in a range of settings, thereby providing workers with a platform for seeking opportunities beyond the network. The same is clearly true in the Southwest Key network. These networks both provide opportunities for certifications that are also and perhaps especially portable.

**Protect and increase wages and benefits.** The virtues of providing good wages and benefits are obvious, especially given the prioritization of workers in these networks. What is important to bear in mind, however, is that the development of niches, choices of financing, and other business choices must be made to ensure that this is possible. For example, the Southwest Key network learned that it simply could not engage in the trash-picking business, because it could not pay its workers high enough wages under the contract price to which it had agreed. Another more extensive example is the home care network's multifaceted strategy of legislative development and advocacy, training and niche development with an eye toward paying better wages and benefits. Finally, we see in these networks a consistent effort to ensure full-time work. This is a critical piece of the struggle toward economic stability, and it has made an enormous difference to the workers in these networks.

### *For the Economic Stability of the Businesses*

**Find and support the "right" market niche.** The first design principle in the category of developing stability for the businesses relates to the all-important market niche. No doubt, this is one of the most difficult pieces to identify, both for network participants and those seeking to support them. Like the US Supreme Court's test for obscenity, it may also be possible that the best test is that you know it (in this case, a good market niche) when you see it. But the three networks described in this book, and the many other examples that I have cited, do provide some basic information that serves as a good starting point for identifying and further exploiting valuable market niches.

The niches developed in these three networks all share several common features. They had relatively few barriers to market entry, but they did not entirely lack barriers. This again, has allowed the networks to outcompete other businesses by providing appropriate training and vocational education. They require a level of skilled labor that can neither be outsourced nor replaced by machines. They are in markets where financing was available from sources other than private equity investors. For example, the home care network took advantage of Medicaid and Medicare reimbursements. And the rehabbers were able to rely largely on debt financing from ShoreBank. In the home care and Southwest Key networks, the niches allowed the networks to develop products or services that were competitive on the basis of quality rather than price. This in turn allows the businesses to charge high enough prices to be able to provide higher wages and benefits to their employees. Finally, and most obviously, these are all markets with a high level of local demand.

There are too few examples in my research to allow me to draw conclusions about particular industries that have these characteristics, though it is at least worth noting that two of the biggest collaborative business networks that I have cited, the South Shore network and TELACU, are in the construction industries. It is clear, however, that some industries have too many of the negative criteria cited above to be good places to start. For example, fast-food employment (as distinguished from franchise ownership) and trash-picking both appear to involve a cut-throat level of price competition.

For experts looking for networks in local contexts, of course, one important criterion to look for is a cluster, much as Michael Porter suggests doing.[24] Information about business clustering should be readily available from local and

[24] Michael E. Porter, *Location, Competition, and Economic Development: Local Clusters in a Global Economy*, 14 ECON. DEV. Q. 15, 24–25 (2000).

regional planning agencies, and it should be quite useful in providing a first level of analysis about the potential development of collaborative business networks in any given urban core.

**Consider the potential for a market catalyst.** In all three of my case studies, it is possible to identify a significant market catalyst that may have jump started the virtuous cycles experienced in these networks. In the home care context, that catalyst was the sudden availability of Medicare and Medicaid reimbursements for home care. In the South Shore context, it was the influx of investments by RESCORP, which resulted in the rapid development of hundreds of units of market rate housing that were immediately snatched up by ready renters. In the Southwest Key context, the opening of the nonprofit's new headquarters and particularly the charter school turned the café around from a money-losing enterprise to one that made a regular profit. As these examples show, the existence of a catalyst appears to provide particularly useful information about market demand. In this respect, it is also a useful indicator of a potential market niche.

**Find a local bank or other financing source interested in the market niche.** Given my earlier analysis, most of the remaining design principles in support of networks require little explanation. Because of the importance of financing, it would appear ideal for intermediaries in the network either to serve as a local financing source for the network or to be in conversation with such a source. While both the home care network and the Southwest Key group benefited from federal sources of funding, I emphasize the local because of the multiple benefits provided by ShoreBank to its borrowers. Obviously, there are very few networks that have solved the problem of financing. But given its importance to business survival, it is appropriate here to delineate a best practice to which to aspire and, as I will do in Chapter 10, around which to develop supportive regulations.

**Develop innovative ways to spread risk.** As my examples have shown, all of the networks have benefited from the sharing of risk. In particular, it appears important to spread risk in the areas of financing, as well as in developing market demand and a customer base. In the area of financing, I have emphasized the value of a local "in-network" bank. But, as I have described, reliance on such a financing source must be balanced with extra protections for the loans or investments made by such a source as well as protections for the businesses. In the area of market demand, the reliance on a market niche, especially one that can be filled by customers in the network, can be a powerful means of jumpstarting new businesses. But as it develops market demand and in-network customers for its niche, the network must continue to pursue a broader and more diverse customer base. Both of these risk-spreading strategies relate to my final design principle, which focuses on developing strategies for the network to connect back into the broader local and regional economies. The basic point is that risk spreading is important, but businesses should avoid creating artificial demand and supply in the market that is not sustainable over the long term.

**Spread management expertise.** This recommendation requires little additional explanation. The leadership in these networks is extraordinary. Just as these networks have done, it will be advantageous for other collaborative business networks to spread the value of management expertise as broadly as possible throughout the network.

**Develop strategies for hooking back into broader markets.** One of the things that makes the collaborative business networks in this book so special is that they have developed such innovative means for financing their businesses, creating and maintaining market demand, and providing sustainable jobs for workers, and they have done so over a long period of years and in two cases decades. But one critical question that networks such as this face is whether their different style of doing business ultimately limits their growth, and if it does, whether that matters. This is a question unique to the American practice of collaborative capitalism, because in countries such as Japan and Germany, the sharing that underlies their practice of coordinated capitalism occurs on a national scale.

One important source for examining this question is the growing literature on the value to businesses of staying small. For example, as Michael Haedicke has discussed in his book *Organizing Organic: Conflict and Compromise in an Emerging Market*, the organic food sector has involved a debate between social activists who favor the focus on small business in the industry because it impedes the concentration of power in big business interests, while at least some of the businesses in this sector are actively seeking market and business expansion.[25] The discussions of moral capitalism and social economies in this literature take up important questions about the relationship between size and community participation, democracy, and distribution. This is a particularly useful literature for collaborative business networks because of their prioritization of worker interests and protections.

Of course, notwithstanding its innovative business practices, CHCA is enormous, especially compared to other worker-owned cooperatives in the United States. But the use of the cooperative form, financing from community development banks and nonprofit sources, and other business practices in these networks may be more meaningful limits on the growth of other networks. This is a key question that requires more research. It is also an important question for the participants in the networks themselves to answer.

[25] Michael A. Haedicke, Organizing Organic: Conflict and Compromise in an Emerging Market 7 (2016).

For the remainder of my analysis in this book, I am going to assume that it is desirable for collaborative business networks to continue to grow in size. My main reason for doing so is to support opportunities to provide employment and economic stability to ever greater numbers of individuals in the urban core. But my interest in growth also requires me to face the very real possibility that further research will indeed determine that there is a limit to the extent to which collaborative business networks can grow in the United States. Thus in the absence of additional research, I am going to assume that the use of alternative financing, and the creation of niches responsive to local markets, ultimately limits size.

On the basis of this assumption, I propose one additional design principle. It will be important for collaborative business networks to develop techniques for hooking back into more traditional American capitalist practices. Most importantly, such networks will need to educate themselves on traditional sources of financing to which to turn after a certain stage of growth. They will also need to explore additional market niches and customers that allow for expansion. Café del Sol is exemplary in this regard, by virtue of its exploration of catering opportunities outside of its network. HCA in Philadelphia also is exemplary in having adjusted so successfully to changes in the market, including the decision by its largest customer to develop its own home care business. And the rehabbers in South Shore have expanded their niche by spreading over time into new neighborhoods in the South Side and beyond. Collaborative networks can explore opportunities to hook in through their research and development efforts as well as their training, as PHI has done for the home care network. One key example of this occurred when Cooperative Home Care of Boston provided trainings for certified nursing in the last few months before it closed. These kinds of efforts are important for all small businesses, and they are especially critical for those interested in long-term stability for their workers.

# PART III

# Collaborative Capitalism Reinvigorated

# 8

# Collaborative Capitalism Refined

## *The "Sharing Economy"*

In this final section of the book, I turn to the question of how to change laws to support collaborative capitalism in American cities. Indeed, I intend the law reforms I discuss in Chapter 10 to support workers in search of economic stability across a range of paths for income development, including those seeking jobs with large businesses and those going it alone in starting their own small businesses. In the two chapters that precede Chapter 10, I present two divergent regulatory perspectives on sharing. In Chapter 8, I analyze the so-called sharing economy as a vehicle both for refining my definition of collaborative capitalism and for exploring current American regulatory responses to business practices that are explicitly described as sharing. In Chapter 9, I discuss Germany's regulation of its own coordinated economy.

Chapter 8 has two main purposes. The first is to explore the extent to which the six features of collaborative capitalism are essential ingredients of the whole concept. In this book, I have provided three case studies of well-established collaborative business networks that exhibit each of the six features of collaborative capitalism. I have also cited many additional examples of sharing networks that appear to be engaged in collaborative capitalism. The point of this chapter, however, is to use the example of one sector of the sharing economy in the United States to build my case that each of the six features of collaborative capitalism is important. Airbnb, Uber, and other sharing economy giants claim to facilitate sharing by allowing people to share assets they own so that others can use those assets. However, these networks do not exhibit several of the features of collaborative capitalism. Specifically, the intermediaries in these networks do not facilitate democratic participation and distribution within their networks. These intermediaries do not have an ethic of multiple bottom lines that includes economic stability for their workers. And these particular examples within the sharing economy do not rely on local stakeholding or financing. In other words, not just any sharing amounts to collaborative capitalism.

The second purpose of this chapter is to demonstrate that legal regulation may deeply affect the connection between sharing and economic stability. Currently, the American regulatory framework does not explicitly recognize collaboration as a basis for capitalist behavior. Nor does it recognize the role of intermediary institutions and organizations in facilitating collaborative capitalism. As a result, in some of the most well-known American sharing economy networks, the organizations that act as intermediaries are able to exploit the workers by overburdening them with the risk of doing business and excluding them from deliberative and democratic participation in the networks. Law has facilitated this power imbalance, and law can also intervene to rebalance the power in these networks.

I have not used a qualitative methodology as the basis for my analysis of the sharing economy in this chapter. Instead, I rely on the extensive secondary literature to analyze the network of one sharing economy giant – Airbnb. My effort here is to engage in a theoretically grounded, normative analysis, examining the importance of each of the six definitional features of collaborative capitalism and the regulatory responses to Airbnb in the United States as a starting point for proposing law reforms in support of collaborative capitalism.

## THE SHARING ECONOMY AS A MATURE SHARING NETWORK

The sharing economy, in which typically urban dwellers share their homes, cars, and other assets for extra cash, has achieved a flashpoint level of attention, particularly in the search for jobs and income during the "jobless recovery" that has occurred since 2008.[1] Given Wikipedia's status as a shining example of our new, technologically enabled era of sharing,[2] it is fitting to begin an examination of the sharing economy by considering Wikipedia's definition:

> The Sharing Economy . . . is a socio-economic system built around the sharing of human and physical assets. It includes the shared creation, production, distribution, trade and consumption of goods and services by different people and organizations. These systems take a variety of forms, often leveraging information technology to empower individuals, corporations, non-profits and government with information that enables distribution, sharing and reuse of excess capacity in goods and services. A common premise is that when information about goods is shared, the value of those goods may increase, for the business, for individuals, and for the community. Collaborative consumption as a phenomenon is a class of economic arrangements in which participants share access to products or services, rather than having

1 *Peer-to-Peer Rental: The Rise of the Sharing Economy: On the Internet, Everything is For Hire*, THE ECONOMIST (March 9, 2013), www.economist.com/news/leaders/21573104-internet-everything-hire-rise-sharing-economy; Kevin Roose, *The Sharing Economy Isn't About Trust, It's About Desperation*, NEW YORK MAGAZINE (April 24, 2014), http://nymag.com/daily/intelligencer/2014/04/sharing-economy-is-about-desperation.html; Jason Tanz, *How Airbnb and Lyft Finally Got Americans to Trust Each Other*, WIRED (April 23, 2014), www.wired.com/2014/04/trust-in-the-share-economy.

2 David A. Hoffman & Salil K. Mehra, *Wikitruth Through Wikiorder*, 59 EMORY L.J. 151, 156–157 (2009).

> individual ownership. Often this model is enabled by technology and peer communities. The collaborative consumption model is used in marketplaces such as eBay, Craigslist and Krrb, emerging sectors such as social lending, peer-to-peer accommodation, peer-to-peer travel experiences, peer-to-peer task assignments or travel advising, car sharing or commute-bus sharing.[3]

While Wikipedia's definition of the sharing economy is so broad as almost to render the word "economy" meaningless, it is clear even from this definition that a significant subset of the sharing economy comprises a *market*. This subset is the subject of this chapter: the actors and activities within the sharing economy that involve sellers and buyers engaging in market transactions. Thus, this chapter does not seek to understand Wikipedia and similar examples of peer-to-peer sharing without expectation of profit.[4] Instead, the particular interest of this chapter is the phenomenon of very small businesses and individuals sharing a network of information and other critical business resources and functions, with help from large intermediaries, to develop a stable market. In this respect, they depend on coordination with others in renting or sharing goods or services that they own individually. Even more specifically, the focus of this chapter is on one discrete sector of the sharing economy – short-term home rentals – and on one particular giant in that sector: Airbnb. This narrow sector of the sharing economy signals important trends in market development and especially regulatory responses. In the latter section of the chapter, I touch on the significant diversity in the broader American sharing economy by analyzing the potential for platform technologies to engage in collaborative capitalism as defined in this book.

Like the other examples in this book, the sharing economy defies the quintessential image of entrepreneurship whereby an entrepreneur leverages her business and personal assets to take advantage of information asymmetries as a means of developing new products or services.[5] The business strategy in these markets claims to rely on sharing, rather than on the private use by individual firms or entrepreneurs of asymmetrically held information.[6]

Consider the paradigmatic examples of businesses in the sharing economy. Airbnb, Uber, and TaskRabbit are all examples of individuals "renting" their homes, cars, and expertise to others using a centralized intermediary that arranges the transactions. Airbnb is a company that operates a website through which individuals can rent rooms in others' homes. Airbnb describes itself as an online "trusted community marketplace for people to list, discover, and book unique

3 *Sharing Economy*, WIKIPEDIA, THE FREE ENCYCLOPEDIA, http://en.wikipedia.org/wiki/Sharing_economy#cite_note-Gansky-8.

4 Hoffman & Mehra, *Wikitruth Through Wikiorder* at 157 ("Wikipedia remains a site largely run and created by volunteers.").

5 *See, e.g.*, MARK CASSON, THE ENTREPRENEUR: AN ECONOMIC THEORY 39 (2d ed. 2003); ISRAEL M. KIRZNER, PERCEPTION, OPPORTUNITY, AND PROFIT 110–111 (1979).

6 Carl Alviani, *Uber Learned the Hard Way: Transparency Rules the Sharing Economy*, WIRED (May 9, 2014), www.wired.com/2014/05/uber-learned-the-hard-way-transparency-rules-the-sharing-economy.

accommodations around the world."[7] If an individual wants to rent a property through Airbnb, she begins by typing her destination and travel dates into a search bar on the website, just as she would on Expedia and numerous other online travel services. After searching available properties, the customer can send a request to book a property to a particular host. Depending on the host's preferences, the next step can involve a conversation between host and guest, which can be carried out using a private messaging service on the website, or the host can enable an instant booking feature on the website. In either case, the guest is asked to complete a profile and provide payment information. Once a host accepts a reservation, payment is typically processed through the website. After travel is completed, both the guest and host have the option to write a review of each other for the benefit of other Airbnb users.[8]

According to Airbnb, the process is largely under the host's control. Hosts can choose the people to whom they wish to rent, set the rental price, and define the parameters of advertising and other details. A host begins by listing her property on the website, making her own determination about how to describe the property and what to charge for renting it. The host has the option to allow instant booking or instead to screen potential guests.[9] Of course, one of the most unique features of Airbnb is that hosts regularly rent out just an extra room or even just a couch, with the expectation of contemporaneously sharing their homes with strangers.[10] This forcefully distinguishes many Airbnb rentals from hotels and even from the typical bed-and-breakfast, where the host is not living contemporaneously in the property with her guests.

Relying largely on smartphone applications, car-sharing services such as Uber and Lyft employ an even simpler process for those wishing to sell rides in their cars.[11] In the case of Uber, for example, customers start by creating an account through Uber's website, which also entails entering their credit card information.[12] Then, when a customer wants to hire a ride through Uber, the customer touches an app on her mobile phone, which uses a GPS device to find her location and send a nearby Uber driver. The customer's credit card is charged for her ride once she arrives at her destination.[13]

Web-based businesses such as eBay take this basic concept to a new level by providing a centralized location where individuals can auction and buy a vast array

[7] *About Us*, AIRBNB, www.airbnb.com/about/about-us.

[8] *How to Travel*, AIRBNB, www.airbnb.com/help/getting-started/how-to-travel.

[9] *How to Host*, AIRBNB, https://web.archive.org/web/20130806215755/www.airbnb.com/help/getting-started/how-to-host.

[10] Elizabeth A. Harris, *Short-Term Rentals via the Web: Lucrative But Often Illegal*, N.Y. TIMES (November 5, 2013), at A22.

[11] *The Uber App*, UBER, www.uber.com/about; Michael B. Farrell, *New Lawsuit Claims Uber Exploits Its Drivers*, BOSTON GLOBE (June 26, 2014), www.bostonglobe.com/business/2014/06/26/uber-hit-with-class-action-lawsuit/JFlTJLMuBoXuEmMU3elTAI/story.html ("Uber makes a smartphone app that riders use to hail a private car service. The company describes itself as a software platform that its 'partners' – not drivers – use to build their own small businesses.").

[12] *Sign Up to Ride with Uber Today*, UBER, https://get.uber.com/sign-up.

[13] UBER, www.uber.com.

of products.[14] In the cases of home and car sharing, and to some extent in peer markets such as eBay, individuals share the excess capacity of assets that they do not fully use or need themselves, with strangers, for a price. The start-up costs for each individual renting out rooms, or selling rides or unused items, are negligible because the individuals rely on an intermediary, typically a website or smartphone service, to advertise their products and services and connect them to potential customers.

Peer-to-peer lending networks such as Kickstarter and Indiegogo have found a way to introduce sharing into the marketplace for financing. These services also make extensive use of technology to provide "crowdfunding" in which individual businesses can seek start-up and other funding from geographically dispersed strangers.[15] In return for the service of advertising the businesses' needs and pooling a group of "backers," the lending networks typically take a portion of the proceeds. For example, Kickstarter takes 5 percent of the funds raised for any business venture.[16]

One overriding feature of many of the markets in the sharing economy is that they sell products and services at lower prices than those set by their analogs in the "non-sharing" economy. Time and again, buyers and renters of rooms through Airbnb, rides through Uber, and services through Craigslist comment that they are motivated in very large part by the price savings.[17] Professor Yochai Benkler has provided a thorough analysis of the "information collection cost" savings of peer-to-peer networks,[18] and it appears that when such networks operate in a *market* (as distinguished from non-profit-seeking networks), these savings accrue partly to the benefit of buyers in the form of lower prices.

Another oft-cited reason for the robust success of sharing markets is their Adam Smithian feature of product and service variety.[19] Many sellers provide a diverse array of products and services to meet the diverse needs and interests of buyers. As Airbnb advertises, you can rent anything from a room in a castle to a condo in an idyllic urban location through its service.[20] The market for financial investments is an even more startling example of this feature. In contrast to the quite standardized features of markets in both equity investing and debt financing, businesses and

14 *Who We Are*, EBAY INC., www.ebayinc.com/our-company/who-we-are/.

15 *Bring Creative Projects to Life*, KICKSTARTER, www.kickstarter.com/?ref=nav; *How it Works*, INDIEGOGO, www.indiegogo.com/learn-how-to-raise-money-for-a-campaign.

16 *What Is Kickstarter's Fee?*, KICKSTARTER, www.kickstarter.com/learn?ref=nav.

17 *See Peer-to-Peer Rental*, ECONOMIST, www.economist.com/news/leaders/21573104-internet-everything-hire-rise-sharing-economy; Fleura Bardhi et al., *Four Myths on How Consumers React to the Share Economy*, WALL STREET JOURNAL (May 7, 2014), http://blogs.wsj.com/accelerators/2014/05/07/myth-and-reality-in-the-share-economy; Neil Irwin, *Uber, Lyft and a Road Map for Reinventing the Ride*, N. Y. TIMES (July 11, 2014), www.nytimes.com/2014/07/12/upshot/uber-lyft-and-a-road-map-for-reinventing-the-ride.html?_r=0.

18 Yochai Benkler, *Coase's Penguin, or, Linux and the Nature of the Firm*, 112 YALE L.J. 369, 407–415 (2002).

19 HERBERT HOVENKAMP, ECONOMICS AND FEDERAL ANTITRUST LAW 2 (1985).

20 *Airbnb Picks*, AIRBNB, www.airbnb.gy/wishlists/airbnb_picks.

investors participating in crowdfunding can seek matches in a much more diverse array of financing opportunities.

Finally markets in the sharing economy often exhibit other competitive advantages. One claim about car-sharing services is that it is faster to obtain cars through Uber or Lyft than to call a taxi.[21] In the case of Airbnb, both hosts and renters claim to be able to find guests and rooms that are more suited to their comfort levels and needs.[22] These markets often claim to outperform their non-sharing counterparts by consistently providing product features that their counterparts are not able to provide.

## INTERMEDIARIES IN THE NETWORK

In a network such as Airbnb's, the technological platform and the provider of the platform are the key intermediaries. They play a role in reducing the transaction costs associated with performing such critical business functions as conducting market analyses, advertising products and services, ensuring stable supplies of customers, and streamlining contracts for sales or rentals of goods and services. Through its website, Airbnb provides a comprehensive technological platform for homeowners to rent rooms to strangers for short-term stays. The private flow of information contributes to the use of a specialized platform that streamlines hosts' ability to acquire, contract with, and serve customers.

In addition to providing a website through which owners can list their properties for rental, Airbnb provides a system whereby guests can book rooms and pay for their rentals through the website. It provides a "host guarantee" of up to $1,000,000 for damage to a host's property.[23] And it provides a "Resolution Center" for addressing disputes between hosts and guests.[24] Airbnb also makes extensive use of social media to enable hosts and guests to monitor each other and to share information with the broader community of guests and hosts.[25] The technological platform thereby facilitates monitoring in a way that previously could only be accomplished by specific contractual provisions requiring certain levels of inspection or permitting.

However, Airbnb is not the only institution that enables Airbnb hosts (and guests) to share information and resources. There are a number of additional online fora in

21 *The New UberX: Better, Faster and Cheaper Than a Taxi*, UBER NEWSROOM (June 11, 2013), https://newsroom.uber.com/us-california/uberx-cheaper-than-a-taxi; Geoffrey Fowler, *Testing UberX, Lyft and Sidecar Against a Cab in Six Cities*, THE WALL STREET JOURNAL (March 12, 2014), http://online.wsj.com/news/articles/SB10001424052702304250204579433113467536876.

22 *Airbnb Picks*, AIRBNB, www.airbnb.gy/wishlists/airbnb_picks.

23 Ron Lieber, *A Liability Risk for Airbnb Hosts*, N.Y. TIMES (December 5, 2014), www.nytimes.com/2014/12/06/your-money/airbnb-offers-homeowner-liability-coverage-but-hosts-still-have-risks.html.

24 *What Is the Resolution Center?*, AIRBNB, www.airbnb.com/help/article/767/what-is-the-resolution-center.

25 *Trust & Safety*, AIRBNB, www.airbnb.com/trust.

which Airbnb hosts can share information.[26] Topics on one such forum, airhosts forum.com, recently included information about a scam, email templates for hosts to use, and a discussion about how to meet San Francisco's permitting requirements.[27] While this kind of information sharing has not generally risen to the level of informal contracting among hosts for additional services or resources, it is certainly a nascent system for establishing basic standards of hosting conduct, as well as a forum for developing expectations about safety, quality, and other critical features of property rental.

## REGULATORY CONTEXT

Regulators have responded to the new business models proliferating in the sharing economy with a mixture of confusion, indignation, and alarm. In general, regulations have been reactive and piecemeal, rather than proactive or comprehensive. At times, regulators in different states and at the federal level have treated the same business practices quite differently. Often, in their haste to protect some market participants, they have ignored the needs of others. Current regulatory dilemmas in this arena are best captured by four examples of regulatory responses to the sharing economy.

### *Consumer Safety*

Among the most well-publicized regulations of the sharing economy are those responding to safety concerns raised by consumers, especially those who use home- and car-sharing services such as Airbnb and Uber. For example, a rash of recent reports has raised unsettling questions about the extent to which car services such as Uber and Lyft protect against sexual assault, harassment, and other forms of unsafe behavior by their drivers.[28] While renters also have raised similar concerns with respect to home-renting services, some of Airbnb's most prominent troubles have been raised by hosts whose homes were burglarized or

[26] *See, e.g., We Are Your AirBnB Hosts Forum*, AirHostsForum.com, www.airhostsforum.com; *Airbnb Hosts*, Facebook, www.facebook.com/airbnb.hosts.forum; Urban Bellhop, http://urbanbellhop.com (offering to manage guest interactions for rental hosts).

[27] *AirBnb Scam Alert*, AirHostsForum.com, www.airhostsforum.com/t/airbnb-scam-alert/29; *Overcoming Subleasing Clause in Lease with New San Francisco Regulation*, AirHostsForum.com, www.airhostsforum.com/t/overcoming-subleasing-clause-in-lease-with-new-san-francsico-regulation/267; *Share Your Welcome E-Mail Templates!*, AirHostsForum.com, www.airhostsforum.com/t/share-your-welcome-e-mail-templates/173.

[28] *See, e.g.*, Mazaheri v. Doe, No. CIV-14–225-M, 2014 WL 2155049 (W.D. Okla. May 22, 2014); Matt Hamilton, *Uber Driver Faces Charges*, L.A. Times (December 10, 2014), at AA6; Tracey Lien & Russ Mitchell, *L.A., S.F. Slap Uber with Lawsuit*, L.A. Times (December 10, 2014), at B1; Kim Lyons & Andrew Goldstein, *Hampton Native Was Hit by Driver for Uber*, Pitt. Post-Gazette (January 8, 2015), at B-1; Carlos Sadovi & Tracy Swartz, *2nd Uber Driver Is Charged in Sex Assault*, Chi. Trib. (January 15, 2015), § 1, at 8.

misused by renters.[29] Although it has not yet been the subject of litigation, selling products through sites such as eBay also raises questions about product safety and its regulation.

In general, the regulatory response to safety concerns such as these has been either to ban sharing businesses from operating or to require them to obtain the same permits required of their competitors in the non-sharing economy for rooms, rides, and other services. Often these actions are taken on consumer protection grounds. For example, in early 2014, the Virginia Department of Motor Vehicles issued cease-and-desist letters to both Uber and Lyft, ordering them to stop operating in that state.[30] Various states have also made repeated efforts to require some level of permitting for these and other car-sharing services.[31] Meanwhile, Airbnb is embroiled in a series of disputes about the legality of its business operations in cities such as New York City and Paris, again because of concerns about the safety and needs of both participants and neighbors.[32]

The intermediary institutions typically fight these regulatory measures by arguing that they are not hotels, rental agencies, or taxicab companies.[33] Rather, some argue that they are only the providers of software that facilitates markets for these services, to help them develop and thrive.[34] They pair these responses to external regulation with their own internal regulations to assure market participants about the safety and viability of the services. For example, Uber claims to screen criminal and driving records and to provide a transparent system for reviewing driver profiles and the anonymous ratings of other drivers.[35] Uber also collects a $1 "Safe Rides Fee" in the "UberX" category of its vehicles to

29 *See* Tom Heyden, *Airbnb Battles: Would You Stay with Strangers?*, BBC NEWS (February 6, 2013), www.bbc.com/news/magazine-21339891; James Temple, *Airbnb Victim Describes Crime and Aftermath*, S.F. CHRON. (July 30, 2011), at D1.

30 Rachel Weiner, *Virginia Trying To Put Brakes on Taxi-Like Services*, WASH. POST (June 27, 2014), at B1.

31 *See* Rasier, LLC, No. 2014–372-T (Pub. Serv. Comm'n of S.C. Jan. 15, 2015) (Order No. 2015–46), http://dms.psc.sc.gov/pdf/orders/5A23B2F8-155D-141F-23C07EAA18BA1E64.pdf (ordering Uber to cease and desist operations in South Carolina until a regulatory determination has been made); Lori Aratani, *A 'Balancing Act' for Ride-Sharing Services*, WASH. POST (May 12, 2014), at B1; Katherine Driessen, *Ride-Share Operators Gain Access to Houston Airports*, HOUS. CHRON. (November 13, 2014), at A1; Paul Nussbaum, *PUC Approves UberX for State, Not Philadelphia*, PHILA. INQUIRER (November 14, 2014) at A15; Andy Vuong, *Likely Ride-Sharing Nod Would Be a First*, DENV. POST (April 30, 2014), at 10A.

32 Harris, *Short-Term Rentals via the Web*; John Lichfield, *Beware Airbnb if You're a Tenant Looking for a Quick Euro*, INDEPENDENT (London) (May 23, 2014), at 32; David Streitfeld, *Airbnb Listings Mostly Illegal, State Contends*, N.Y. TIMES (Oct. 16, 2014), at A1.

33 Harris, *Short-Term Rentals via the Web*; Streitfeld, *Airbnb Listings Mostly Illegal*; Aratani, *A 'Balancing Act' for Ride-Sharing Services.*

34 Aratani, *A 'Balancing Act' for Ride-Sharing Services* (reporting claims by Uber and Lyft that they are "go-betweens" that link car-owning drivers with customers looking for a ride, rather than transportation companies).

35 Joe Sullivan, *Details on Safety*, UBER NEWS (July 15, 2015), http://newsroom.uber.com/2015/07/details-on-safety.

finance the company's ability to ensure safety for Uber passengers in cars Uber does not own.[36] Airbnb has gone considerably further by providing hosts with its million-dollar host guarantee. The company also purports to protect both hosts and renters by allowing them to complete much more detailed profiles that enable each to take their own steps to verify the other's trustworthiness.[37]

### *Regulating Anticompetitive Behavior*

A second well-known set of regulatory interventions has attempted to prevent perceived anticompetitive behavior by sharing economy businesses. Traditional businesses, such as hotel or taxicab companies that compete with sharing networks, raise these claims. They argue that by avoiding the costs associated with obtaining permits and complying with other regulations, sharing businesses operate at lower costs.[38] This, they contend, is nothing short of cheating. Taxicab companies in Maryland have claimed antitrust violations on the grounds that Uber engages in price-fixing.[39] This claim seems ripe for further exploitation if regulators come to view the sharing economy in a way that more closely matches the perspectives of many participants, namely that the providers of products and services are individual businesses. To the extent that is true, it is arguably also true that these individual businesses engage in price-fixing through their use of intermediaries such as Uber.

The regulatory responses to these claims of anticompetitive behavior have generally involved revising state or local anticompetition and permitting laws to apply to sharing networks. For example, Chicago and Houston have considered ordinances banning or imposing permitting requirements on car-sharing services.[40] The major intermediaries in the sharing economy have poured tremendous lobbying and other resources into disputing the claim that they are engaging in anticompetitive

36 *I Was Charged a Safe Rides Fee (US + Canada Only)*, UBER, https://web.archive.org/web/20151209012513/https://help.uber.com/h/4fa83c50-ab30-434c-b911-f63ad11cd4d9.

37 *Why Do I Need To Have an Airbnb Profile or Profile Photo?*, AIRBNB, www.airbnb.com/help/article/67/why-do-i-need-to-have-an-airbnb-profile-or-profile-photo.

38 Kelly Goff & Kate Larsen, *Taxicab Drivers Protest Uber, Other Ride-Share Apps*, NBC LOS ANGELES (June 11, 2014), www.nbclosangeles.com/news/local/Taxicab-Drivers-Protest-Uber-Other-Rideshare-Apps-262564181.html; *Maryland Taxi Companies and Drivers Sue Uber*, WHO'S DRIVING YOU.ORG (July 7, 2014), www.whosdrivingyou.org/blog/maryland-taxi-companies-and-drivers-sue-uber; Joshua Brustein, *While Uber Thrives in New York, Its Competitors Lobby Legislators*, BLOOMBERG BUSINESS WEEK (June 2, 2014), www.bloomberg.com/news/articles/2014–06-02/while-uber-thrives-in-new-york-its-competitors-lobby-regulators.

39 *Maryland Taxi Companies and Drivers Sue Uber*, WHO'S DRIVING YOU.ORG, www.whosdrivingyou.org/blog/maryland-taxi-companies-and-drivers-sue-uber.

40 Andy Gavil & Chris Grengs, *Getting Around Town in the Share Economy*, FEDERAL TRADE COMMISSION BLOGS (APRIL 21, 2014) www.ftc.gov/news-events/blogs/competition-matters/2014/04/getting-around-town-share-economy; Molly Ryan, *Houston Cab Companies File Suit Against Uber, Lyft*, HOUSTON BUS. J. (April 10, 2014), www.bizjournals.com/houston/morning_call/2014/04/houston-cab-companies-file-suit-against-uber-lyft.html?page=all.

behavior,[41] and it appears that their arguments have some traction. In a recent letter to a Chicago alderman, Federal Trade Commission staff members opined that car services such as Uber and Lyft are contributing to healthy competition rather than inhibiting it, and that any permitting or other regulations imposed on them ought to protect their ability to contribute to a competitive market.[42] Despite this and other votes of confidence in the sharing economy,[43] claims of anticompetition are proliferating.

### *Protecting Workers*

Critics of sharing giants such as Uber have also started to take aim at their treatment of the individuals who provide products or services through their networks. Specifically, several lawsuits have raised the argument that these individuals are not really independent businesses that contract with companies such as Uber; rather, they are employees.[44] This distinction has significant consequences, because some states (such as the Commonwealth of Massachusetts) provide extensive protections to employees, including requiring employers to provide unemployment and health benefits.[45] Lawsuits in Massachusetts and California also have implied that Uber's restrictions on the ability of drivers to request and retain tips contributes to the company's de facto status as an employer of hundreds of drivers rather than merely an intermediary providing a technological platform for a network of small businesses. Of course, Uber disputed the claims, arguing instead that it has a much more limited role.[46] At the same time, Uber has recently changed its tipping policy, now allowing riders to use the Uber app to add tips for drivers.[47]

### *Monitoring Financing*

Regulatory dilemmas have also arisen concerning crowdfunding, in which small businesses have used web-based portals to seek collaborative funding from large numbers of private individuals. This sharing approach to financing has caught the

41 Tarun Wadhwa, *The Sharing Economy Fights Back Against Regulators*, Forbes (September 16, 2014), www.forbes.com/sites/tarunwadhwa/2013/09/16/the-sharing-economy-fights-back-against-regulators-with-an-advocacy-group; Brustein, *While Uber Thrives in New York*.

42 Gavil & Grengs, *Getting Around Town in the Share Economy*.

43 *See, e.g.*, Michael B. Farrell, *Uber Gets Some Support from New Mayor*, Boston Globe (March 1, 2014), www.bostonglobe.com/business/2014/03/01/car-service-uber-not-yet-boston-regulators-sights/vQjDKrnbpT6NPg0CAQCs3O/story.html.

44 Farrell, *New Lawsuit Claims Uber Exploits*.

45 *Id.* These protections are buttressed by a very strict statute recently enacted to classify many of the people working as "independent contractors" instead as employees. *See* Mass. Gen. Laws ch. 149, § 148B (2017).

46 Farrell, *New Lawsuit Claims Uber Exploits*; *Uber Drivers: Don't Sign Away Your Rights*, Uber Lawsuit, http://uberlawsuit.com.

47 *In-App Tips on Uber*, Uber, www.uber.com/ride/how-it-works/tips.

attention of the US Securities and Exchange Commission (SEC) because it seeks to reach ordinary investors, as distinguished from so-called accredited investors, who are typically wealthy and savvy enough not to need the extensive disclosures required by the SEC when "public" companies seek funding from ordinary investors. The SEC has developed specific rules tailored to allowing some forms of crowdfunding, but only with certain conditions and for limited amounts of funding.[48] Such rules also extend to intermediaries such as Kickstarter, because as the SEC reasons, by "curating" the websites in which they decide which financing campaigns to support, these intermediaries are providing "investment advice."[49] In a refrain consistent with their responses to other regulations, both the intermediaries and many small businesses and individuals in the networks are looking for ways to avoid and limit these regulations, citing overburdening costs associated with compliance.[50]

## COLLABORATIVE CAPITALISM IN THE SHARING ECONOMY?

This section analyzes the extent to which Airbnb's network manifests the six features of collaborative capitalism. It concludes that, although there is significant coordination via the platform technology and other more informal associations, this network lacks several of the features of collaborative capitalist behavior.

### *Coordinated Activities of Businesses*

While it is hard to view Uber drivers as anything other than employees, there is a stronger argument that Airbnb hosts are the owners of tiny businesses in which they leverage a major asset – their homes – to earn an income. These businesses share a technological platform to find guests who wish to rent rooms in their homes. On the supply side, what makes these markets revolutionary is the outsourced sharing of key business functions by the individuals involved in networks for peer-to-peer rentals. For example, in the Airbnb network, individual hosts have outsourced to Airbnb the tasks of determining market demand, advertising their homes for rental, maintaining a stable supply of customers, and providing the platform through which deals are made. Information is clearly part of what is shared, but it is by no means all. Without this shared technological platform, each of the individuals would have to find means of performing each of these tasks on their own, by for example advertising and inquiring at local tourist offices and writing and entering into individualized rental

48 Andrew Ackerman, *SEC Urged to Scale Back 'Crowdfunding' Rules*, WALL STREET J. (February 27, 2014), http://online.wsj.com/news/articles/SB10001424052702304071004579409323759964120.

49 Crowdfunding, File No. S7-09-13 (proposed Oct. 13, 2013) (to be codified at 17 C.F.R. pts. 200, 227, 232, 239, 240, 249).

50 Ackerman, *SEC Urged to Scale Back 'Crowdfunding' Rules*. For a discussion of the crowdfunding provisions in the Jumpstart Our Business Startups Act which called for the promulgation of rules, see Lisa T. Alexander, *Cyberfinancing for Economic Justice*, 4 WILLIAM & MARY BUS. L. REV. 309 (2013).

agreements with customers. For many people involved in these networks, the costs of performing such tasks on their own would be unacceptably prohibitive.

The stability of demand and supply is maintained for the entire network through the technological platform. Access to the platform regularly equates with access to a national or international market of customers.[51] As a result, the hosts do not have to conduct their own research about specific markets. The platform does that work for them. The collaboration that occurs here is in sharing a common source of customers and the technology to access those customers efficiently and cheaply.

### *Coordination Lowers Costs and/or Risks*

As is the case for the collaborative business networks I have described, the coordination provided by the platform serves needs and functions that are critical to the success of the individual hosts. The business activities that are externalized to the network as a whole are often necessary to the very survival of these tiny businesses.[52] Services such as Expedia blur the lines between Airbnb and traditional hotels and rental agencies, because such services also allow potential renters to search among a variety of rental options on the basis of price and other requirements. However, it is important that Airbnb's website is the predominant (often the only) means by which hosts renting rooms can engage in rental transactions, whereas most of the hotels renting rooms through Expedia have their own websites and toll-free numbers.

### *Niche Industry*

As with my rehabber and home care examples, the Airbnb network operates within a niche industry. Airbnb hosts all have the benefit of sharing information and resources within a single market, that of short-term property rentals. Moreover, within that sector, they have a further specialty of providing a lower cost *and* distinctive alternative to hotel rooms, inns, and even bed-and-breakfasts. They are competitors with these different categories of room-renting businesses. But as competitors, they have developed a subniche that has very effectively captured a large market share within a market that appears to have a high level of demand. Because the platform technology provides the work of market analysis, advertising, and a template for rental contracts, the hosts do not require any special skills for market entry. Plus their ownership of the homes they rent means that they already have the asset they need to start operating. Like the other examples, this too is an industry where work can be neither outsourced nor mechanized. It also may be the case that

[51] *See, e.g.*, *Hosts Love Using Airbnb*, AIRBNB, https://web.archive.org/web/20101114122933/www.airbnb.com:80/info/why_host ("Rent out extra space effortlessly. It's free to sign up and with a built in community, your listing will be seen by a worldwide audience.").

[52] Harris, *Short-Term Rentals via the Web* (quoting Airbnb representative who stated that "almost 90 percent of our hosts have only one listing and it's the home they live in.").

some of the values of real estate markets that are observable in the South Shore example support the Airbnb network. With respect to niche, the Airbnb network is operating within an industry that has many of the advantages of the home care and rehabber industries.

### *Institutional Intermediary Serves a Coordinating Function, But Does Not Share Power*

The principal difference between networks such as Airbnb's and the collaborative business networks I have described in this book lies in the role of the platform provider as an intermediary within the network. Although the platform provider facilitates coordination, the coordination leads to unequal distribution within the network in important respects. Relatedly, the intermediary does not support multiple bottom lines – or, if it does, none of these prioritizes economic stability for the hosts within the network. Nor does the intermediary, or the network as a whole, rely on local stakeholding or financing. Indeed, the absence of these three features of collaborative capitalism from the Airbnb network teaches important lessons about their *combined* significance in collaborative business networks.

Airbnb is an excellent vehicle for exploring the absence of these three features of collaborative capitalism, because unlike Uber, Airbnb is not a clear-cut case. Uber decides how much to charge for a ride, including by means of its controversial surge-pricing system.[53] It controls the terms and form of payment.[54] It has a system by which passengers can rate drivers—with a consequence of "deactivation" for drivers whose ratings fall below a certain level.[55] In short, Uber appears to be the employer of hundreds of drivers, and it has thus far largely avoided the costs associated with being an employer. By contrast, according to Airbnb, individual hosts can choose the people to whom they wish to rent, set the rental price, and define the parameters of advertising and other details.[56] The platform provider in the Airbnb network offers a range of opportunities for hosts to make use of the platform without wholly controlling all of the hosts' business choices.

But the glue that allows sellers to find buyers in the Airbnb network and other sharing economy markets is technology, namely technological platforms through which businesses in the networks sell or rent their products and services. This

53 *See* Annie Lowrey, *Is Uber's Surge-Pricing an Example of High-Tech Gouging?*, N.Y. TIMES MAG. (January 10, 2014), www.nytimes.com/2014/01/12/magazine/is-ubers-surge-pricing-an-example-of-high-tech-gouging.html.

54 *See Sign Up To Ride with Uber*, UBER, www.uber.com/info/signup-ftc.

55 Ellen Huet, *How Uber's Shady Firing Policy Could Backfire on the Company*, FORBES (October 19, 2015), www.forbes.com/sites/ellenhuet/2014/10/30/uber-driver-firing-policy/; *Warned or Deactivated for Low Rating*, UBERPEOPLE.NET, http://uberpeople.net/threads/warned-or-deactivated-for-low-rating.943.

56 *How Do I Host on Airbnb?*, AIRBNB, https://web.archive.org/web/20140709104643/www.airbnb.com/help/article/103.

contrasts sharply with the intermediaries in my three case studies. This difference comes with a number of collateral attributes. Perhaps most importantly, platforms such as Airbnb's are not the result of an initial collaboration among product or service-providers. Rather they are the work (and intellectual property) of high-tech start-ups that have made many millions of dollars from developing the platforms. The hosts and other workers in these networks do not share in the profits from the development and use of the platform, nor do they have the right to change the technology.

Second, there is no benefit to these platform providers from connecting workers to *each other*. The relationship is in one direction: the workers benefit from the technology in return for paying a fee for its use. And in the case of Uber, TaskRabbit, and other platform providers on the controlling end of the sharing economy spectrum, the consideration flowing from the workers is not just in the form of a fee, but it also includes surrender of a great deal of control over wages and work conditions. The platform providers do not work like Jim Bringley did in the South Shore system to connect businesses to each other for mutual support and resource sharing. Nor do they cultivate opportunities like Southwest Key does for sharing of market information and management expertise among businesses in its network. Nor, in most overt contrast to CHCA and HCA, do they appear to have any interest in worker ownership of the resources that are shared. It is true that individual hosts own their own homes. But they do not own any part of the platform that turns their homes into money-making ventures. The platform provider owns that, and it can withdraw this critical resource from the network, or from individual hosts, at its will.

Third, risk within these networks flows in one direction. The responsibility for carrying liability insurance in the Airbnb network is exemplary of this point. Early in the growth of this network, the platform provider was the target of negative publicity when its hosts suffered a rash of thefts and other property losses at the hands of guests who stayed in their homes. Airbnb responded with two measures that are more protective of hosts than is evident in many other sharing economy networks. It began to provide hosts with a free million-dollar host guarantee, which it advertised widely as evidence of its excellent treatment of workers in its network.[57] This liability insurance, however, is a secondary policy, which only is available after the hosts obtain payouts under their own primary insurance policies. Part of the problem with this system is that it appears the vast majority of the homeowner's policies that cover hosts do not in fact cover their rental activities. This leaves hosts badly exposed for injuries and deaths of their guests. The platform provider also purports to protect both hosts and renters by allowing them to complete much more detailed profiles that enable each to take their own steps to verify the trustworthiness of the other. As is evident from both of these responses, although it claims to be at the forefront of

[57] Lieber, A *Liability Risk for Airbnb Hosts*.

sharing risk with its hosts (and it may well be, compared to other sharing economy giants), Airbnb still offloads a tremendous amount of risk onto the workers in its network.

Fourth, and more broadly, as this analysis demonstrates, the platform provider does not give workers opportunities for democratic participation in the overall management of the network. Again, it does not share access to its technology for purposes of further improvement or development. It does not provide for shared ownership of resources. It does not provide cross-management opportunities. It does not even appear to include hosts in an advisory council or other mechanism for simply airing questions and concerns.

Importantly, the platform provider may not be the only intermediary in Airbnb and similar networks. In a number of these networks, additional, informal associations of Uber drivers, Airbnb hosts, and TaskRabbit taskers can exchange information about safety, quality, and other critical features of their work using Facebook pages and alternative websites.[58] But it is important to note that these alternative platforms are still at a very early stage of use and development, and they do not yet serve in the place of the deeply connected and committed intermediaries that we see in the three case studies.

At this point, it is fair to say that the platform providers in these networks are the dominant intermediaries, both in terms of coordinating resources and in their power within the networks. It is also fair to say that while these intermediaries provide a basis for coordinated market activity, coordination is not the same as sharing – at least as defined by my other three examples. The critical differences appear to be that the risk only flows in one direction (away from the intermediaries) and that the intermediaries do not promote or facilitate workers' democratic participation in these networks.

### *Multiple Bottom Lines That Do Not Include Worker Stability*

As this description of platform providers in the sharing economy makes clear, the workers in these networks are not a priority. To the extent that these networks claim to have multiple bottom lines, they do not include the workers' economic or social advancement. Many networks do not even provide basic protections for workers.

This is somewhat ironic, given both the label of sharing that advocates of the sharing economy have adopted and the claims made by some of its most vocal proponents that the sharing economy represents important values that challenge capitalist beliefs. For example, Wikipedia (in defining the sharing economy), Lisa Gansky, and others have commented poignantly that the sharing economy is not

[58] *See, e.g.*, Sarah Jaffe, *Silicon Valley's Gig Economy Is Not the Future of Work—It's Driving Down Wages*, GUARDIAN (July 23, 2014), www.theguardian.com/commentisfree/2014/jul/23/gig-economy-silicon-valley-taskrabbit-workers; *We Are Your AirBnb Hosts Forum*, AIRHOSTSFORUM.COM, www.airhostsforum.com/; *Uber Drivers Forum*, UBERPEOPLE.NET, http://uberpeople.net.

about ownership but rather is about access.[59] Philosophers of the sharing economy claim that increasing access to property can best capture the surplus value of property, not collateralizing it or excluding others from it.[60] A related value to this romantic image of access over exclusion is that of trust in the broader "community of strangers" participating in the sharing economy.[61] A third related value is that of urbanism: proponents emphasize the efficiency and sustainability of sharing assets.[62]

These consumer-focused claims may be true, but they also may be obtained at the expense of workers in the sharing economy. Proponents of the sharing economy claim that these workers are motivated by the promise of social and psychological rewards. Such claims of social connection and reward imbue the marketing of services and products in the sharing economy. Airbnb, for example, claims that hosts who rent out rooms in their homes can meet interesting people from around the world.[63] Meanwhile, the regulatory landscape reveals that, in some of these networks, workers do not receive even the basic protections due to employees because they are deemed independent contractors who are responsible for ensuring or maintaining work conditions, benefits, and other employment protections for themselves.

### *Communities That Are Not Local*

Given the seeming connection between investment in workers and local stakeholding in my three case studies, it may be possible that the de-prioritization of workers in major sharing economy networks is related to the apparent absence of investment in local place and space in these networks. Whereas my other examples exhibit strong ties to the people and places in the urban cores where the networks are located, networks such as Airbnb, Uber, and TaskRabbit appear to capitalize on arguably the opposite framework. They claim to have created a community that is dispersed, via technology, and able to provide the same basic kinds of services regardless of location. As Jason Jackson and others have shown, this horizontal monopolization

59 *See, e.g.*, *Sharing Economy*, WIKIPEDIA; LISA GANSKY, THE MESH: WHY THE FUTURE OF BUSINESS IS SHARING (2010); Arun Sundararajan, *From Zipcar to the Sharing Economy*, HARVARD BUSINESS REVIEW BLOG NETWORK (January 3, 2013), http://blogs.hbr.org/2013/01/from-zipcar-to-the-sharing-eco.

60 GANSKY, THE MESH; Rebecca Grant, *Disownership is the New Normal: The Rise of the Shared Economy*, VENTURE BEAT (April 2013), http://venturebeat.com/2013/04/03/disownership-is-the-new-normal-the-rise-of-the-shared-economy-infographic/.

61 *See Sharing Economy*, WIKIPEDIA; Keld Jensen, *Trust: A Fragile, but Wealth-Building Commodity*, FORBES (June 22, 2014), www.forbes.com/sites/keldjensen/2014/06/22/trust-a-fragile-but-wealth-building-commodity.

62 *See Sharing Economy*, WIKIPEDIA; April Rinne, *Sharing Economy in Cities: Moving Towards a More Inclusive Urban Future*, GUARDIAN (June 26, 2014), www.theguardian.com/sustainable-business/circular-economy-policy-cities-inclusive-urban ("From Chicago to Seoul, the sharing economy can transform business and cities, boosting urban resilience and sustainability.").

63 *Host Testimonials*, AIRBNB, https://web.archive.org/web/20101114122933/www.airbnb.com/info/why_host ("People who come in contact with us become forever friends that will return again. They will feel 'at home' more than they do at home.").

*across* urban areas appears to be replacing localized and traditional businesses and business networks.[64] An obvious example is Uber's displacement of local taxi networks across entire metropolitan areas. Relatedly, while the networks do draw workers from urban cores, they also appear to draw a relatively broad cross-section of workers overall, including those who "moonlight" for these networks to supplement more stable sources of income.

Nor is the financing in these sharing economy networks local. One noteworthy source of financing for such networks is a subcategory of venture capital financiers with an apparent specialty and interest in investing in sharing intermediaries despite the legal and other known and unknown risks associated with doing so. While these sources are specialized, they are not particularly local. And again, they do not appear to be particularly focused on worker protections. More broadly, neither the financing sources nor the management of these networks appear to be much engaged in the urban communities from which they draw many of their workers.

## REGULATION CAN MAKE A DIFFERENCE

If my six features of collaborative capitalism are important pieces of the whole concept, then Airbnb is not engaging in collaborative capitalist behavior. It should also be apparent that other sharing economy giants are not doing so either. But could they eventually develop into collaborative capitalist networks? The sharing economy is at a crossroads in its development. As the example of Uber demonstrates, the sharing economy can be a vehicle for a technology-based attenuation of the firm to the point where employees are essentially eliminated from the firm's structure. But this section begins to explore the possibility that law can affect future development of the sharing economy by promoting platform technologies as the basis for redistributing resources, market participation, and ultimately economic stability for lower-income, urban individuals. It concludes that there is potential for at least some sharing economy networks to engage in collaborative capitalism, and that law can play a major role in steering them in that direction.

In Chapter 5, I analyzed the American regulatory framework, which at the local, state, and national levels, limits the paths available for urban workers in finding sustainable means of income generation. In this section, I continue that analysis, by discussing the ways in which this same regulatory framework views the sharing economy. In short, this framework does not recognize the potential for collaboration in the sharing economy. Nor does it recognize the platform providers as intermediary institutions that ought to have different rights and responsibilities to ensure fair play and stability within sharing economy networks. In these respects, current

64 Jason Jackson, "Taxis versus Uber": Planning vs. Markets, or Markets as Planning? (February 1, 2017) (unpublished manuscript on file with author).

regulations do little to open the sharing economy as an alternative path to economic stability in urban cores.

As my description of the regulatory context surrounding the sharing economy revealed, the disjointed nature of early attempts to regulate the sharing economy evinces a profound confusion about fair play in these markets. The most conspicuous message that flows through these regulations is that sharing economy networks fail to meet the standards required by traditional American capitalist rules and practices. For example, policymakers work hard to fit the new models of sharing into the liberal market framework. They have great difficulty with the task of categorizing or defining the roles of the intermediaries in sharing networks and also of the individual businesses. Is Airbnb a hotel, a rental agency, or a provider of a software product? Is Uber an employer, a taxicab company, or a software developer? Are those who rent homes through Airbnb or drive cars through Uber employees or independent businesses making use of a common resource? Is Kickstarter an investment advisor or a portal for small businesses to connect with individuals who want to invest in their success? The answers are not apparent to regulators because in their vision of capitalism, there simply are no intermediary institutions of the type that exist in coordinated market economies such as Germany's.

These attempts to fit sharing economy participants into ill-fitting categories bring out regulatory suspicions that the participants are avoiding some of the costs and constraints associated with those categories. The regulatory reasoning appears to be that Airbnb would have no reason not to accept the label of employer if it was willing to accept the costs of providing benefits for its hosts. Or that Airbnb is obviously a hotel company, but for the fact that it is avoiding the costs of registering and obtaining permits to operate as one.

The result of the current regulatory framework's failure to recognize the potential for collaboration could be twofold. At best, it has the potential to force some sharing economy giants such as Uber to bear the full costs of doing business. There is a growing refrain among commentators that the sharing economy is just a new chapter of a continuing story in which workers lose job protections, benefits, and stability by engaging in piecemeal and temporary forms of underpaid labor.[65] Because Uber controls virtually all aspects of the means and manner of work its drivers perform, traditional legal tests argue strongly in favor of regulating the company as a large business employing thousands of workers.[66] Thus, it is possible that forcing Uber to play by the traditional rules of American capitalism will actually benefit Uber drivers.

[65] Robert Reich, *The Sharing Economy Is Hurtling Us Backwards*, SALON (February 4, 2015), www.salon.com/2015/02/04/robert_reich_the_sharing_economy_is_hurtling_us_backwards_partner/; Juliet Schor, *Debating the Sharing Economy*, GREAT TRANSITION INITIATIVE (October 2014), http://greattransition.org/publication/debating-the-sharing-economy.

[66] The test for determining when an individual is an employee, rather than an independent contractor, is well described in C.C. Eastern, Inc. v. NLRB, 60 F.3d 855, 858 (D.C. Cir. 1995).

At worst, however, the failure to recognize the potential for collaboration in these networks will increase the power of platform providers without making them pay those costs or protect their workers. While it is true that policymakers have failed effectively to regulate intermediaries largely because of their own narrow perspective on fair play, the intermediaries likely share that limited view. As a result, companies such as Airbnb and Uber have been able to develop a new model for doing business that takes advantage of coordination without accepting all the associated costs. One such cost is that these companies have to share more power and responsibility with the workers involved in their networks. Their failure to do so produces negative externalities (especially for the workers) that regulators have thus far largely failed to recognize.

Policymakers responding to the sharing economy could address these failures on the part of platform providers. They could start by evaluating individual platform providers to determine whether they are so controlling of the business operations in their networks that they should be regulated as employers of their product and service providers, or whether instead they are acting more like sharing intermediaries. By engaging in such an evaluation, policymakers could force the platform providers to share the risks that they currently offload onto their workers. Moreover, if policymakers determine that the platform providers are indeed acting as bona fide sharing intermediaries, they could further regulate the providers and the networks as a whole to induce them to facilitate a greater level democratic participation within their networks. These same regulatory initiatives also could be expected to create incentives for the networks to prioritize worker stability as well as local investment. Chapter 10 provides a range of law reforms, many of which would accomplish these functions for sharing economy markets. Let me conclude this chapter by describing two regulatory measures that should suggest the many possibilities.

I have described the development of alternative fora and associations of Airbnb hosts, Uber drivers, and Taskrabbit taskers who consult with each other on business matters. Thus far, it appears that fora such as these have been invisible to regulators. One regulatory possibility is for policymakers to establish advisory boards or other mechanisms that develop the potential of such fora to provide a richer range of sharing opportunities *among* workers within a network. Could such fora propose alternative permitting standards for hosts or drivers? Could they develop their own mechanisms for monitoring and sanctioning bad hosts or drivers? These are questions that regulators ought to be exploring alongside the question of whether Airbnb ought to comply with hotel licensing requirements. Thus, if regulators notice a discussion underway about whether Airbnb hosts could develop an alternative permitting system, they ought to consider inviting representatives of such fora to join with policymakers to discuss the subject.

Such regulatory choices could be made with a view toward enhancing democratic participation in sharing networks by encouraging the formation of worker-controlled business associations within such networks. This could have the effect of redistributing power between the platform providers and the network of workers, which may well be a welcome trade-off for workers facing the additional costs of obtaining permits. For example, in the case of Airbnb, such a business association could provide a voice for hosts negotiating with Airbnb on insurance coverage for their rental activities. More broadly, it could address the question of how to ensure an appropriate level of property protection, which is one of the most frequent concerns raised by hosts. It could negotiate with local authorities to develop a streamlined permitting process. It could pool resources for obtaining health benefits. Over the longer term, it could even pool resources to obtain financing for hosts independent of Airbnb's financing endeavors.

One of the reasons business associations such as these could be so beneficial in the sharing economy is that they could support workers in switching to other, more established paths to economic stability. For example, by developing training programs in the hospitality industry, such associations could provide support for workers who might ultimately prefer to become employees at traditional hotels. Or they may provide support for Airbnb hosts to develop properties into more traditional bed-and-breakfasts. These are things that the platform provider currently has no incentive to do. Yet they are paths well worth exploring. These are just a few ways in which law reform can make an enormous difference.

While much of the attention on the sharing economy is on giants such as Airbnb and Uber, many observers have noted that not all platform-based networks are so unequal in their power distribution. One noteworthy counterexample in the ride-sharing context is the nonprofit RideAustin, which entered the market in Austin after Uber and Lyft withdrew services from the city in reaction to the fingerprinting and other regulations imposed on those businesses. In its website and marketing descriptions, RideAustin explicitly prioritizes workers' rights, claiming for example that its nonprofit status helps it direct more income to workers. It also advertises prioritization of charitable donations by inviting passengers to round up their fares with the expectation that the business will donate the difference between the actual fare and the rounded up amount to local charities.[67] Indeed, in its multiple bottom lines, its focus on workers, and its local connections, RideAustin seems to fit comfortably within my definition of collaborative capitalism. One noteworthy detail here is that Uber and Lyft recently reentered the Austin market, and RideAustin has reportedly been struggling to keep a decent market share as a result.[68] This is precisely the kind of circumstance in which supportive regulations could make a world of difference for sharing networks like RideAustin. Veena Dubal and Sushil Jacob have been actively exploring such possibilities in their research on ride-sharing cooperatives. Many of my proposals in Chapter 10 could also be useful in such efforts.

[67] *RideAustin: A Nonprofit TNC Built for Austin*, Ride Austin, www.rideaustin.com/#introducing-ride-austin.

[68] Gary Dinges, *Ride Austin Lowers Fares to Better Compete with Uber, Lyft*, Austin American-Statesman (June 13, 2017).

# 9

# Regulating for Sharing

The regulations in any given context support a highly specific manner of doing business. In the US urban cores, this can mean that urban workers are limited to just two clear paths for generating income, namely employment with an established business or starting their own businesses. The collaborative business networks that I have described show us that there are alternative paths in American urban cores. Unfortunately, however, such alternatives are not well supported by the current regulatory framework. The purpose of this chapter is to provide a detailed description of one regulatory system that does support a more collaborative form of capitalism. I provide this description by continuing the analysis begun in Chapter 5 of the 25 workers who have recently completed a vocational education program in specialty food manufacturing. This time, however, I assume our 25 workers are living in a city in Germany rather than in the United States. Germany is by no means the only example of a national collaborative or coordinated economy. But I have chosen Germany in part because Germany's status as an industrial juggernaut highlights two broad claims about collaborative or coordinated capitalist behavior. First, it is possible for coordinated capitalist systems to achieve enormous success and amass significant wealth for the businesses and workers involved. Second, a key ingredient in the success of these systems is a regulatory framework that supports coordination *and* the welfare of workers in the system.

I should be clear from the start, however, that my purpose in describing the mature coordinated economy of Germany is not to advocate for creating the full range of paths and possibilities available to German workers. There are many details and much context within that system that are simply not replicable in American cities. Moreover, there are significant aspects of it that may not be desirable to many Americans. And of course, the coordinated economy of Germany has its own share of risks and disadvantages. One prominent example is the appalling level of fraud that occurred in the recent Volkswagen controversy over emissions standards, where it has been argued that the close institutional connections between Volkswagen executives and the German government prevented officials from discovering and halting such flagrant behavior.[1]

Instead, my purpose in this chapter is to open a conceptual space for developing one or more intermediate paths for urban American workers between being hired by large businesses that are minimally invested in such workers and starting up their own independent businesses. In doing so, I hope also to promote the development of a framework that better supports workers on those two traditional paths. As my case studies show, the forms of collaboration and the institutions that support sharing networks in American cities are different from those in mature coordinated economies such as Germany's. Rather than adapting institutions that exist in places like Germany, the task for US policymakers is to develop an infrastructure to support the unique institutions of collaborative capitalism in the United States. In doing so, policymakers should use mature coordinated economies such as Germany's as a rough model rather than seeking to replicate their institutions exactly.

## DIFFERENT PATHS

Imagine, now, that our 25 workers are located in a large German city rather than in a large city in the Midwestern United States. The introductory facts of our hypothetical example are much the same. The workers have recently completed a yearlong vocational training program in specialty food manufacturing. The training has covered many of the same topics: food safety, production, packaging and labeling. However, even at this early point of the description, there would likely be a fundamental difference between the two examples. As I have described, in the case of the American workers, the development of a training program in specialty food manufacturing would likely have been the product of both unusual foresight and luck, a result of the research and community relationships forged by the community development corporation and the community college that provided the training. These providers would likely not have had a commitment from one or more local businesses to hire their trainees. Nor might they even have had the benefit of knowing what kinds of skills or training would make entry-level workers most hirable by local businesses.

By contrast, the 25 German workers would likely be in a training program resulting from active coordination between the training providers and local food manufacturing businesses. This coordination is exemplary of a style of capitalism that Hall and Soskice call a "coordinated market economy." Although Hall and Soskice characterize it somewhat differently, emphasizing different aspects of market behavior, such a coordinated economy can be defined using the same basic characteristics that I have used to define "collaborative capitalism." The observations that have led Hall and

[1] Geoffrey Smith & Roger Parloff, *Hoaxwagen*, FORTUNE (March 7, 2016), http://fortune.com/inside-volkswagen-emissions-scandal.

Soskice to label certain economies coordinated are certainly the inspiration for my claim that we are seeing a uniquely collaborative form of capitalism developing in some urban pockets in the United States. Most basically, Hall and Soskice emphasize the "strategic interaction" among businesses, a mode of interaction in which businesses share what might be described in the United States as private or "insider" information, often about employment terms, sources of financing, dissemination of technology and business governance.[2] Let me demonstrate the similarity between Hall and Soskice's coordinated economies and the collaborative capitalism that I claim exists in some US cities by using the features of collaborative capitalism to describe the workers' experience in a hypothetical German city.

**Coordinated activities of businesses.** If our 25 workers lived in a German city, the decision to run a vocational training program focused on specialty food manufacturing would likely have been the result of an understanding between the program providers and local businesses that these were the skills the businesses sought. This understanding would very possibly also encompass a commitment by one or more of the businesses to hire the graduates of the training program. As Hall and Soskice describe, German workers within a given industry can expect to participate in publicly subsidized training programs that regularly take the form of apprenticeships. The training provided is a product of negotiated skills categories and training protocols for the industry.[3] Both the apprenticeships and the negotiated training protocols increase the likelihood that workers will be hired by the firms where they apprenticed or at least that they will have marketable skills that increase the likelihood of employment at another local business in the industry.

This coordination over the training of workers would likely extend into other aspects of the workers' futures. For example, the workers could expect that businesses in the specialty food manufacturing sector would coordinate with each other and with unions representing the workers to set wages at each given skill level within their industry. They could also expect "works councils" and supervisory boards within each business to provide some security from the arbitrary shedding of workers.[4] Even smaller businesses within the industry could be expected to participate in wage coordination efforts, though a number of scholars have noted that such participation has produced more firm-specific agreements with unions and less

[2] Peter Hall & David Soskice, *Introduction, in* VARIETIES OF CAPITALISM: THE INSTITUTIONAL FOUNDATIONS OF COMPARATIVE ADVANTAGE 8–9 (Peter A. Hall & David Soskice eds., 2001).

[3] *Id.* at 25–26; Pepper D. Culpepper, *Employers, Public Policy, and the Politics of Decentralized Cooperation in Germany and France, in* VARIETIES OF CAPITALISM: THE INSTITUTIONAL FOUNDATIONS OF COMPARATIVE ADVANTAGE 275 (Peter A. Hall & David Soskice eds., 2001).

[4] Hall & Soskice, *Introduction,* VARIETIES OF CAPITALISM at 24–25; Kathleen Thelen, *Varieties of Labor Politics in the Developed Democracies, in* VARIETIES OF CAPITALISM: THE INSTITUTIONAL FOUNDATIONS OF COMPARATIVE ADVANTAGE 71, 82–85 (Peter A. Hall & David Soskice eds., 2001); Stewart Wood, *Business, Government, and Patterns of Labor Market Policy in Britain and the Federal Republic of Germany, in* VARIETIES OF CAPITALISM: THE INSTITUTIONAL FOUNDATIONS OF COMPARATIVE ADVANTAGE 248, 270–272 (Peter A. Hall & David Soskice eds., 2001).

overall uniformity within the sector.[5] The point nevertheless would be that both large and small businesses in the food manufacturing industries would participate in a negotiated process of coordination concerning the wages, terms of employment, and working conditions.

Meanwhile, we could expect that the incentives for food manufacturing businesses to coordinate their approaches to workers and work conditions would be complemented by the systems for financing, internal governance, and asset development supporting such businesses. Recall that in our hypothetical American city, both large and small food manufacturing businesses would face much the same lending criteria from banks. These criteria would require the businesses to provide information about how they performed within the broader industry of food manufacturers. Because the information provided in business plans and other reports would not all be verifiable by American banks, such banks would also likely require personal guarantees and other forms of security. By contrast, in Germany and other coordinated economies, Hall and Soskice describe a system of "patient capital," in which "insider" business information is made available to banks by virtue of the businesses' participation as shareholders in the management of other businesses in their sector as well as by their participation in industry associations.[6] The availability of "patient capital" and other factors reduce the pressures that managers might feel to achieve profits in the near term.[7] And this in turn frees businesses to provide more stable employment terms for their workers.

Finally, the common interest among food manufacturing firms to share the costs of industry-specific training in return for workers with more relevant and specific skills would be expected to complement the sharing of other types of resources. One critical example is the sharing of technology, which would be accomplished not by the poaching of innovative and productive workers from other businesses in the industry, but rather from the shared financing of research and development and ultimately the dissemination of new technologies among businesses participating in an industry association.[8] Said another way, there is a complementarity between the availability of stable financing, the sharing of research and development costs and benefits, and the stabilization of employment terms across the industry. Businesses in such a market may well compete for customers, but they do not have as much incentive to compete with each other for employees, intellectual property, and financing.

[5] Peter A. Hall, *The Evolution of Varieties of Capitalism in Europe, in* BEYOND VARIETIES OF CAPITALISM: CONFLICT, CONTRADICTIONS, AND COMPLEMENTARITIES IN THE EUROPEAN ECONOMY 39, 69 (Bob Hancke et al. eds., 2007).

[6] Hall & Soskice, *Introduction*, VARIETIES OF CAPITALISM at 22–23.

[7] Other factors include financing out of retained earnings and managerial incentives to reach consensus with workers. *Id.* at 23–24.

[8] *Id.* at 26–27; Orfeo Fioretos, *The Domestic Sources of Multilateral Preferences: Varieties of Capitalism in the European Community, in* VARIETIES OF CAPITALISM: THE INSTITUTIONAL FOUNDATIONS OF COMPARATIVE ADVANTAGE 213, 220–221 (Peter A. Hall & David Soskice eds., 2001).

In summary, one hallmark characteristic of coordinated market economies such as Germany's is the much more extensive level of coordination among businesses within a market, which coordination relies on institutions and organizations other than hierarchies, formal contracts, or what Hall and Soskice term "market" relations.[9] Another way to describe this kind of "non-market" coordination is that, rather than being outside the market, it involves sharing information and resources *within* a market. In any given market or industry in a coordinated economy, businesses share resources such as research and technology competencies, vocational education, market data and financing sources, information and functions that would be privately managed and leveraged in the United States.[10]

**Institutional intermediaries that serve a coordinating function.** From this brief description of coordinated market behavior, it may already be apparent that well-developed institutions facilitate the coordination among individual businesses in any given sector. Understanding this different form of capitalism requires policymakers to understand its institutions because such institutions do the work of achieving the level of collaboration, monitoring, and even sanctioning that so defines coordinated economies such as Germany's. In Germany, these institutions include strong labor unions, powerful business associations and a relational form of contracting.[11] This type of coordination could be more aptly described as maintaining a horizontal set of relationships. By contrast, a liberal market system such as the United States relies on a hierarchical structure for accomplishing many of these same functions *within* a business.[12]

Consider the institutions that would likely affect our 25 German workers' ability to find stable employment in the food manufacturing industry. First, their vocational training program would likely have been sponsored and supervised by industry-specific employer associations and trade unions. These two intermediaries could be expected to negotiate the skills categories and training protocols the program should cover. They might also work with (and pressure) local businesses to develop appropriate apprenticing programs. Once the workers were hired, these intermediaries would have the important duty of negotiating wages for skill levels across the industry. Second, within each business, the efforts of these two intermediaries in establishing employment terms and conditions would be supplemented by works councils, comprised of worker representatives, and supervisory boards, comprised of worker representatives and shareholders. By virtue of their representation of a variety

9 Hall & Soskice, *Introduction*, VARIETIES OF CAPITALISM at 22–24.

10 *Id.* at 21–33; Orfeo Fioretos, *The Domestic Sources of Multilateral Preferences* at 220–223.

11 Hall & Soskice, *Introduction*, VARIETIES OF CAPITALISM at 21–27.

12 For discussions of a range of relationships on the spectrum from vertical to horizontal, see Ronald J. Gilson, Charles F. Sabel & Robert E. Scott, *Contracting for Innovation: Vertical Disintegration and Interfirm Collaboration*, 109 COLUM. L. REV. 431 (2009); OLIVER E. WILLIAMSON, THE ECONOMIC INSTITUTIONS OF CAPITALISM (1985); Benjamin Klein et al., *Vertical Integration, Appropriable Rents, and the Competitive Contracting Process*, 21 J.L. & ECON. 297 (1978).

of interests, these additional organizations exhibit the capacity and leverage to make binding decisions about layoffs and other significant changes in work conditions.[13] Thus, we could expect the workers to have better chances overall of being hired by local businesses and being employed on a longer-term basis. Given the more democratic representation on works councils and other intermediaries, we could also expect the terms of their employment to reflect at least some of the perspectives of the workers themselves.

Finally, the relatively high level of consensus on employment terms and conditions would in turn be supported by institutions that have developed to ensure the availability of stable capital, asset development, and corporate governance. The stability of financing in the face of economic highs and lows requires specialized institutions for monitoring the performance of businesses – and sanctioning businesses that do not comply with financing terms. Thus, the organizations and institutions that Hall and Soskice describe specialize in particular forms of monitoring. Key among these are business associations, which include representatives from most or all of the businesses in a given industry.[14] Because of the extensive sharing – of research and development projects, standard-setting, and vocational education – that occurs through the work of these intermediary organizations, member businesses know a great deal about each other. This knowledge is supplemented by a system of cross-shareholding, and even of close and shared relationships between businesses and their customers and suppliers.[15] As Hall and Soskice describe, the sharing in these spheres of business activities complements the sharing of information and resources in the area of employment relations.[16] Thus, the work of business associations and other institutions that set the terms of corporate governance and asset development are critical to the institutions that directly manage employment relations in a coordinated economy such as Germany's.

**Coordination lowers costs and/or risks.** Especially when we consider the complementarities produced by the interaction of multiple institutions, it becomes evident that the sharing among businesses reduces important costs, risks, or both costs and risks for each individual business in the network. This may not seem obvious upon a first look, nor may it be true in all spheres of business behavior. For example, the food manufacturing businesses in our hypothetical example may pay higher wages than their American counterparts, and they may bear higher costs for employment terms that are more favorable to employees. However, the efficiencies gained from

[13] Hall & Soskice, *Introduction*, VARIETIES OF CAPITALISM at 25; Culpepper, *Employers, Public Policy, and the Politics of Decentralized Cooperation*; Thelen, *Varieties of Labor Politics*; Wood, *Business, Government, and Patterns of Labor Market Policy*.

[14] Hall & Soskice, *Introduction*, VARIETIES OF CAPITALISM at 23. Fioretos, *The Domestic Sources of Multilateral Preferences* at 220 ("95 per cent of German firms belong to the Federation of German Industry [a business association]").

[15] Fioretos, *The Domestic Sources of Multilateral Preferences* at 220–221.

[16] Hall & Soskice, *Introduction*, VARIETIES OF CAPITALISM at 27.

sharing the costs of monitoring associated with financing, joint research and development, and shared technology transfer may well offset the higher investments in employees. Moreover, my point here is not that either German or American businesses have lower costs or risks vis-à-vis each other. Rather, my point is that the sharing within German networks reduces some critical costs for each individual firm. It appears that by externalizing some functions (such as research and development or satisfying the monitoring requirements of lenders) to the industry as a whole, each firm reduces those costs. In turn, the cost reduction in these critical areas offsets higher costs in the employment sphere. But such cost reduction also is beneficial in other respects. For example, it appears to stabilize the finances of participating businesses, thereby increasing their chances of survival in economic downturns and other difficult moments.[17] This reduction of costs thus seems to be one of the tangible benefits of sharing in cooperative economies such as Germany's.

The critical point for my purposes is that the collaboration within this industrial network provides a means for workers employed by these businesses to achieve more favorable employment terms. For policymakers exploring alternative models for economic development, a prototypical German industrial network thus provides an interesting example. It demonstrates a means of sharing costs and resources with the result of producing higher wages and better working conditions. This is certainly not the result in all German networks. Moreover, Hall and other scholars have acknowledged that this set of complementarities is becoming more fragmented in Germany as a result of the influx of small businesses, temporary employment, less patient capital, and different standards for "service workers," among other changes.[18] Nevertheless, it is a system that is well worth studying. As Hall has argued recently, even in its less archetypal form, it presents a markedly different approach to doing business than what we are used to seeing in the United States.[19]

**Multiple (and localized) bottom lines.** The scholarship on varieties of capitalism does not appear to dwell directly on the question of whether the different styles of capitalism can be associated with distinctive values or priorities. This is one obvious difference between the varieties of capitalism literature, which focuses on institutional arrangements supporting national economic outcomes, and my discussion of collaborative capitalism in local contexts. Hall and Soskice do claim that the informal rules and understandings underlying the formal institutions and organizations in a given capitalist scheme are central to their investigations. These informal

[17] *Id.* at 22–24; Sigurt Vitols, *Varieties of Corporate Governance: Comparing Germany and the UK, in* Varieties of Capitalism: The Institutional Foundations of Comparative Advantage 337, 353–355 (Peter A. Hall & David Soskice eds., 2001).

[18] Hall, *The Evolution of Varieties of Capitalism in Europe*; Thelen, *Varieties of Labor Politics* at 83–84; Margarita Estevez-Abe, et al., *Social Protection and the Formation of Skills: A Reinterpretation of the Welfare State, in* Varieties of Capitalism: The Institutional Foundations of Comparative Advantage 145, 160–163 (Peter A. Hall & David Soskice eds., 2001).

[19] Hall, *The Evolution of Varieties of Capitalism in Europe*.

rules, they argue, are a product of culture and history.[20] An obvious example is the very different development of labor unions in countries such as Germany and France, as distinguished from their recent lack of development in the United States.[21] Another example from the United States is the confluence of political and social movements that propelled this country into the Cold War and beyond the fall of Soviet Communism, which surely are relevant to the development and reinforcement of a unique American understanding of competition.[22] These contribute to a set of values that valorize certain forms of capitalist behavior such as individualized ownership and contractual freedom.[23]

For this book's purposes, it is useful to examine local culture and history as aids in cataloging and understanding the values and priorities embodied by the collaborative business networks studied here. As Chapter 3 discussed, one overarching value these networks embody is a deep connection with local needs, values, stakeholders, and even financing. Because varieties of capitalism theory focuses so heavily on institutional arrangements, it is possible to extract a sense of the overarching values and priorities expressed in mature coordinated economies. Two overarching values are particularly relevant here.

First, in coordinated economies, institutions such as unions, works councils, supervisory boards, and business associations appear to ensure a broader spectrum of democratic participation than the corporate structure of the typical American firm allows. Because shareholders are at the top of the American firm's vertical structure, their interests are paramount. In coordinated economies, many important resources are shared horizontally within the industrial network. Consequently, these networks require key members of each business to participate in the coordinating institutions. This broader level of democratic participation makes it less likely for shareholder profit to be prioritized above other interests and needs, including those of the managers, workers and financing sources. Instead, it appears more possible for such networks to have a range of priorities that protect a range of values representing the interests of different constituents of the institutions.[24]

Second, in mature coordinated market economies, the democratic representation within these institutions produces a network conducive to processes of joint

20 Hall & Soskice, *Introduction*, VARIETIES OF CAPITALISM at 12–14.

21 *See* Thelen, *Varieties of Labor Politics* at 71–103.

22 The particular package of legal institutions that were exported by the law and development movement is again a useful indicator of this relationship. *See* Kenneth L. Karst, *Law in Developing Countries*, 60 L. LIBR. J. 13, 16–19 (1967); Maria Dakolias, *A Strategy for Judicial Reform: The Experience in Latin America*, 36 VA. J. INT. L. 167 (1995–1996); Bryant G. Garth, *Building Strong and Independent Judiciaries Through the New Law and Development: Behind the Paradox of Consensus Programs and Perpetually Disappointing Results*, 52 DEPAUL L. REV. 383 (2002).

23 *See* Alvaro Santos, *The World Bank's Uses of the 'Rule of Law' Promise in Economic Development, in* THE NEW LAW AND ECONOMIC DEVELOPMENT: A CRITICAL APPROACH 29 (David M. Trubek & Alvaro Santos eds., 2006).

24 Vitols, *Varieties of Corporate Governance*; Culpepper, *Employers, Public Policy, and the Politics of Decentralized Cooperation* at 679–692.

deliberation among its members.[25] Hall and Soskice define deliberation as a capacity to "engage in collective discussion and to reach agreements with each other."[26] Their claims about the effects deliberation can have for a network are quite bold:

> Deliberation provides the actors with an opportunity to establish the risks and gains attendant on cooperation and to resolve the distributive issues associated with them. In some cases, the actors may simply be negotiating from positions of relative power, but extensive deliberation over time may build up specific conceptions of distributive justice that can be used to facilitate agreement in subsequent exchanges.[27]

While Hall and Soskice are careful to note that all varieties of capitalist economies develop institutions that provide complementary advantages for those economies, they claim that coordinated economies are uniquely adept at developing institutions capable of deliberation.[28] Thus, where deliberation is possible, the democratic participation within a network can encompass the most basic priorities involving critical issues of distribution, rights and access. In short, deliberation is a mechanism for educing and protecting multiple priorities as they develop over time. It also seems likely that these priorities are more localized to the particular contexts and needs of the ever-evolving network.

**Local stakeholders, local financing.** It should be obvious too that although Hall and Soskice do not delineate participation by local stakeholders as a feature of coordinated economies, the institutionalized practice of collaboration within these networks ensures that this occurs. This includes participation by management, shareholders and workers from each participant business. Importantly, local stakeholding also involves local *share*holding as a result of the cross-shareholding that regularly exists between local businesses in these networks.

Finally, one vital form of local stakeholding in such economies is the participation of financing institutions providing stable access to capital within these networks. The extraordinarily thick knowledge among financing sources of the particular businesses within the network reduces risks that appear prohibitive to American banks and equity investors. In this respect, the networked economies of Germany, France, and Japan have found a way to overcome the information asymmetries that profoundly impact American small business financing.[29]

## DIFFERENT BENEFITS

It should be apparent by now that our 25 workers could well be operating in a markedly different style of market in a German city than in an American one. The discussion so far should also have revealed some of the benefits for our 25

[25] Hall & Soskice, *Introduction*, VARIETIES OF CAPITALISM at 9–12. [26] *Id.* at 11. [27] *Id.* at 11–12.
[28] *Id.* at 11. [29] Sigurt Vitols, *Are German Banks Different?*, 10 SMALL BUS. ECON. 79 (1998).

workers if they were living and working in a German city. First, in contrast to the United States, the coordinated styles of capitalism provide a better-developed path to achieving good employment prospects and terms for workers. In the United States, much of the focus in protecting the interests of urban workers has been to create incentives for drawing large businesses into underdeveloped urban areas in the hope that solving the locational issue will catalyze local investment by those businesses. When that has failed, policymakers have attempted to teach low-income workers how to emulate the practices of large businesses. These, again, are the two main paths available to our 25 American workers. The strategies employed in developing these two paths assume that certain gaps will be filled. For example, Michael Porter's strategy for inner-city investment assumes that if big businesses hire inner-city workers for temporary employment and low pay, these workers will be on a path that will eventually lead to permanent employment and higher pay. But his strategy does not include clear steps for the workers to achieve these things. Similarly, those who invest in small businesses assume, without a clear strategy to support this assumption, that a satisfactory number of those businesses will achieve high growth and eventually lift a meaningful number of workers out of poverty.

The coordination within coordinated economies provides concrete measures for filling these gaps. If our 25 workers were in Germany, they could expect a range of institutions and organizations to protect their interests in full-time, permanent employment at reasonable pay and under reasonable terms. Representatives from unions, works councils and supervisory boards would negotiate employment issues on the workers' behalf.[30] This would likely be the case whether the workers were hired by the large businesses of Porter's vision or by small businesses. In either case, coordination within the industry would explicitly address questions left unaddressed in the United States.

Second, in contrast to many US contexts, the workers could expect their employers to be more engaged on questions of distributive justice *among* the various participants in the network. As Chapter 3 discussed, recent policymaking especially at the state and local level in the United States has acknowledged the problematic increase in inequality in US cities. When it comes to developing regulations that require US businesses to address the problem, however, concrete ideas are lacking. By contrast, in Germany, the regulatory framework supports many institutions that manage coordination within business networks. The high level of participation by repeat players representing a range of interests ensures robust democratic participation. At its best, such participation can lead to explicit negotiations on questions of distributive justice. In this respect, the coordinating institutions in these economies provide a mechanism for directly addressing questions of distribution and inequality.

Third, our 25 German workers could expect higher average incomes and job security than their US counterparts. Several scholars have used cross-cutting

[30] Vitols, *Varieties of Corporate Governance* at 355.

comparisons of coordinated market economies against liberal market economies to establish that workers in coordinated economies have higher income and more favorable employment terms and conditions on average than those in liberal economies.[31] The case studies in this book provide qualitative evidence to support the conclusion that a more direct institutional and regulatory focus on workers' needs results in better protections for workers. My case studies also suggest that such a focus translates into a generally higher level of neighborhood development and prosperity.

Finally, mature coordinated economies demonstrate that coordinated capitalism is still *competitive* capitalism. On the world stage, Germany has rightly earned the reputation of being an industrial superpower. It is evident that German businesses can outcompete businesses housed in the full range of alternative economies while still protecting the rights and needs of workers. This is not to say that Germany has the best form of capitalism. But it is to say that coordinated capitalism is not a second-best form. For my purposes, this is an important advantage over current development strategies in the United States. For example, it is well documented that inner-city small business development programs can have the effect of creating alternative markets in the inner city that are smaller, less well capitalized, more impoverished, and marginal to the broader local and regional economies.[32] Once created, these alternative markets are difficult to integrate into the broader economies surrounding them. By contrast, the business networks in this book are examples of robust, competitive systems that regularly challenge their more traditional counterparts for customers and wealth. One of my claims is that their success should also facilitate their integration into the broader economies surrounding them. Indeed, policymakers can and should develop regulatory means for integrating these networks into the surrounding economies once these networks become independently successful.

## DIFFERENT REGULATIONS

Just as the legal structure extensively shapes the options available to our 25 hypothetical workers in the United States, so too does the legal infrastructure in coordinated economies significantly shape those markets. This section is the counterpart to my

[31] Cynthia Estlund, *Individual Employee Rights at Work*, *in* COMPARATIVE EMPLOYMENT RELATIONS IN THE GLOBAL ECONOMY (Carola Frege & John Kelly eds., 2013); Evelyne Huber & John D. Stephens, *Continuity and Change in Welfare State and Production Regimes in Advanced Industrial Societies*, *in* NEOLIBERALISM AND INSTITUTIONAL REFORM IN EAST ASIA: A COMPARATIVE STUDY 180 (Meredith Jung-En Woo ed., 2007); JONAS PONTUSSON, INEQUALITY AND PROSPERITY: SOCIAL EUROPE VS. LIBERAL AMERICA 32–66 (2005).

[32] David Dante Troutt, *Ghettos Made Easy: The Metamarket/Antimarket Dichotomy and the Legal Challenges of Inner-City Economic Development*, 35 HARV. CIV. RTS.-CIV. LIB. L. REV. 427 (2000); David Dante Troutt, *Ghettoes Revisited: Antimarkets, Consumption, and Empowerment*, 66 BROOK. L. REV. 1 (2000); Rashmi Dyal-Chand & James V. Rowan, *Developing Capabilities, Not Entrepreneurs: A New Theory for Community Economic Development*, 42 HOFSTRA L. REV. 839 (2014).

earlier analysis of US laws and regulations. It highlights ways in which laws and institutions contribute to the production of a collaborative market, with particular options and limitations for the workers operating in it. Briefly stated, the laws of Germany and other coordinated economies have created a robust infrastructure for promoting collaboration and so-called strategic interaction among private businesses within a market.

It follows, then, that the most fundamental difference between US and German regulation of our 25 urban workers is that the regulations of a coordinated economy such as Germany's are tailored to developing and supporting a range of institutions and organizations that facilitate collaboration. Hall and Soskice organize the forms of collaboration into three broad functions: the sharing of critical business resources, the monitoring of network participants, and the sanctioning of such participants.[33] For example, the varieties-of-capitalism literature is replete with examples of business associations and trade unions that set employment terms within a given sector. Indeed, it should be apparent by now that many more of the laws relevant to our 25 German workers are employment-related as contrasted with the suite of laws affecting our 25 American workers. This highlights the vastly different level of coordination between large firms and both governmental and nongovernmental representatives of workers in Germany. One of the challenges for policymakers seeking to support collaborative capitalism in the United States will be to develop an infrastructure that does not depend on such a deep level of coordination with large American businesses.

Outside of the employee relations sphere, German businesses collaborate on the development of technologies and products critical to the advancement of the industry as a whole.[34] They develop standard forms of contracts and share market information.[35] They work in association with chambers of commerce and governmental officials to develop industry-specific standards of safety.[36] The development of such sector-specific standards, technology, contracts and codes is aided by the private information that flows within the network, allowing the intermediary to tailor these things for the particular purposes of the sector.

An observer steeped in the American legal tradition might describe such an arrangement as self-regulation. But Hall and Soskice note that intermediaries such as these "enter into 'implicit contracts' with the government to administer

33 Hall & Soskice, *Introduction*, VARIETIES OF CAPITALISM at 10.

34 *See* J. NICHOLAS ZIEGLER, GOVERNING IDEAS: STRATEGIES FOR INNOVATION IN FRANCE AND GERMANY (1997); David Soskice, *German Technology Policy, Innovation, and National Institutional Frameworks*, 4 INDUSTRY & INNOVATION 75 (1997).

35 *See* Gunther Teubner, *Legal Irritants: How Unifying Law Ends up in New Divergences*, *in* VARIETIES OF CAPITALISM: THE INSTITUTIONAL FOUNDATIONS OF COMPARATIVE ADVANTAGE 417 (Peter A. Hall & David Soskice eds., 2001); Steven Casper, RECONFIGURING INSTITUTIONS: THE POLITICAL ECONOMY OF LEGAL DEVELOPMENT IN GERMANY AND THE UNITED STATES (Ph.D. dissertation, Cornell University 1997).

36 Hall & Soskice, *Introduction*, VARIETIES OF CAPITALISM at 26–27.

polic[ies]."[37] If we strip away the different labels drawn from different political and economic viewpoints, what we see in coordinated economies is regulation that maintains a relationship between government and the private intermediaries that support business networks. In the case of employee relations, this may well entail more regulatory intervention than is typical in the United States. Although such regulation could take the softer forms of pressure, subsidies and nudging, it would allow for more government involvement in setting employment terms than the private contract scheme of US law contemplates. Meanwhile in a sphere such as consumer protection, as the Volkswagen controversy suggests, German regulations may well be less interventionist than those in the United States, relying on the business association to lead a process of standard setting for consumer safety within a given industry. Abstractly, the difference in regulatory focus for a coordinated economy is the greater attention to intermediaries rather than just to individual businesses. Given the greater level of democratic participation in the typical German intermediary, this different attention also engenders a commitment to a range of priorities rather than primarily to the priorities of the business's shareholders.

A second overarching regulatory difference noted by Hall and Soskice is the reliance on so-called relational contracting to complement and support the work of intermediaries. As Hall and Soskice describe,

> Because of the many contingencies that can arise in close inter-firm relationships involving joint research or product development, tightly written, formal contracts are often inadequate to sustain such relationships. However, the German courts permit unusually open-ended clauses in inter-firm contracts on the explicit condition that these be grounded in the prevailing standards of the relevant industry association.[38]

Interestingly, one of the best examples of relational contracting in the United States is the contracting governed by Article 2 of the Uniform Commercial Code, which provides a basis for court enforcement of what amount to industry practices among (typically) large businesses which regularly transact with each other.[39] Meanwhile, courts require more formal contracts between firms that courts perceive to have unequal bargaining power. For this same reason, courts require formal contracts in many consumer contexts. In the consumer context, this requirement has resulted in extensive enforcement of contracts of adhesion, which, while formal,

[37] *Id.* at 47. [38] *Id.*

[39] There is a large body of literature on this subject. *See, e.g.*, L.L Fuller & William R. Perdue, *The Reliance Interest in Contract Damages* 1, 46 YALE L. J. 52 (1936); L.L Fuller & William R. Perdue, *The Reliance Interest in Contract Damages*: 2, 46 YALE L. J. 373 (1937); Allan Farnsworth, *On Trying to Keep One's Promises: The Duty of Best Efforts in Contract Law*, 46 U. PITT. L. REV. 1 (1984); Melvin Eisenberg, *The Responsive Model of Contract Law*, 36 STAN. L. REV. 1107 (1984); Ian R. MacNeil, *Relational Contract: What We Do and Do Not Know*, 1985 WIS. L. REV. 483.

do little to protect consumers because consumers have no power to negotiate them.[40]

In Germany, these power differentials are addressed not through formal contract law, but rather through the work of intermediary associations which rely on democratic participation and institutional strength to set industrywide standards. The negotiation of such standards appears to be captured in less formal contractual relationships. Open-ended contracts also govern interfirm transactions that refer to industry standards as a basis for establishing the terms of contract performance. When courts enforce such contracts, they also are enforcing the industry standards that were originally developed through a process of "self-regulation."[41]

The legal norm of relational contracting would likely affect our 25 workers in myriad direct and indirect ways. It would underlie the negotiations between trade unions and business associations in setting the terms of their vocational education. It would facilitate the effort of works councils and supervisory boards in negotiating limitations on layoffs and other employment terms.[42] It would contribute to the thick network of knowledge necessary to maintain relationships with financing sources providing patient capital. And it would provide a mechanism for building trust among businesses sharing the costs and rewards of joint research and development.

A third broad area in which the regulatory infrastructure supports collaboration is social policy regulation, particularly as it affects the rights and benefits of workers. I have already described the many incentives built into collaborative economies for businesses to retain employees over long employment terms. Standardized wages, high incentives for managers to achieve consensus, more limited focus on short-term profitability, and less frequent use of stock options as a form of compensation all contribute to long employment terms. Thus, in coordinated economies, we see a use of private contract law to support long-term employment, as distinguished from the more fluid, at-will employment relations that prevail in the United States.

Social policy laws in coordinated economies explicitly support such a structure. For example, in countries such as Japan and Germany, these laws provide unemployment benefits with high replacement rates. As Hall and Soskice discuss, these benefits are not just the product of union negotiations. They are also supported by private businesses, which are able to point to the replacement rates as a basis for persuading employees to invest in firm-specific skills.[43] Meanwhile, the availability

40 *See* Cheryl B. Preston & Eli McCann, *Llewellyn Slept Here: A Short History of Sticky Contracts and Feudalism*, 91 Or. L. Rev. 129 (2012).

41 Steven Casper, *The Legal Framework for Corporate Governance: The Influence of Contract Law on Company Strategies in Germany and the United States*, *in* Varieties of Capitalism: The Institutional Foundations of Comparative Advantage 387 (Peter A. Hall & David Soskice eds., 2001).

42 Vitols, *Varieties of Corporate Governance* at 355; Culpepper, *Employers, Public Policy, and the Politics of Decentralized Cooperation*; Thelen, *Varieties of Labor Politics*.

43 Hall & Soskice, *Introduction*, Varieties of Capitalism at 50–51.

of generous disability and early retirement benefits provide a basis for firms to shed employees without violating the norm of long-term employment.[44]

Of course, the collaboration of unions and private business associations in developing these types of welfare policies is set within a thick infrastructure supporting the development and strength of unions and other intermediaries that represent workers' interests. This infrastructure demands, rather than inhibits, wage standardization and other forms of worker representation. In these respects, it presents a marked contrast to the much more limited support provided to unions and worker representation in American federal law and policy.

A fourth set of legal mechanisms that encourages collaboration in coordinated economies is the range of laws falling under the umbrella of corporate governance laws. These laws play a crucial role in creating a structure for monitoring corporate behavior for the purpose of providing long-term and stable capital. Obviously, the securities laws in coordinated economies create space for "insider" information to be used for the purpose of long-term monitoring. Securities laws also support a dense system of cross-shareholding. In addition to protecting the system of patient capital, some of these mechanisms also support the more consistent use of retained earnings to fund business operations than what is typical among US businesses.[45]

Securities regulations, tax laws, and other mechanisms also constrain outsiders from engaging in hostile takeovers of businesses within a network. In doing so, they limit the pressure on businesses to resort to a short-term focus on profitability as a means of avoiding hostile acquisitions.[46] Again, the availability of patient capital from outside investors and the more regular use of retained earnings within firms create space for balancing a range of priorities. This allows businesses to prioritize the interests of workers alongside that of shareholders and management.

Finally, there is the broader subject of public investment, as distinguished from the public function of law or policymaking. It is noteworthy that coordinated economies direct substantial public subsidies to investments in collaborative efforts. One key example that I have already discussed is the use of public funding to support industry-specific vocational education that is explicitly tied to the needs of businesses within industrial networks. Another important example is public investment in the joint research, development and diffusion of new technologies within industrial networks. By working in close association with industry associations, government officials in coordinated economies take advantage of the thick knowledge within networks about the technological competencies and needs of the networks. This close working relationship contributes to targeted and effective technological development.[47]

[44] *Id.* at 50; Isabela Mares, *Enterprise Reorganization and Social Insurance Reform: The Development of Early Retirement in France and Germany*, 14 GOVERNANCE 295 (2001).

[45] Hall & Soskice, *Introduction*, VARIETIES OF CAPITALISM at 23; Vitols, *Varieties of Corporate Governance*.

[46] Hall & Soskice, *Introduction*, VARIETIES OF CAPITALISM at 23.

[47] *Id.* at 26.

In these arenas of collaboration, coordinated economies use a significantly different strategy than liberal economies like the United States. In the area of research and development, for example, businesses in the US compete for employees who can develop new technologies, and this system operates on the expectation that businesses will also lure such employees away from each other in the race for technological advancement. This creates a more competitive structure to which intellectual property laws concerning asset acquisition and protection contribute meaningfully.[48] Assuming our 25 workers are not among the relatively few high-skilled employees for which businesses are competing, it could mean that their wages are depressed as those businesses seek to offer more attractive wage and benefits packages to their high-skilled counterparts. Public investment in joint research and development is one of a number of devices within cooperative economies for avoiding this type of disinvestment in lower-wage workers.[49] Another example is the collaboration over vocational education that is valuable enough to businesses to motivate them to hire new workers who have completed the offered trainings.

## REGULATING TO SUPPORT COOPERATIVE ECONOMIES IN AMERICAN CITIES

A policymaker seeking to support urban workers in a US city might reflect on the very different paths available to our 25 German workers and conclude that it would simply be impossible to replicate the kind of coordinated economy that exists in Germany at a local level in the United States. And indeed, policymakers and advocates have tried – at times with only limited success – to adopt, adapt, or rehabilitate some of the institutions such as labor unions that we see flourishing in coordinated economies.[50] Such an endeavor would no doubt seem even more daunting to a policymaker conscious of the advantages produced by the complementary work of a range of institutions with influence both on private businesses and governmental actors. A regulator ruminating on the difficulty just of supporting labor unions in the United States would reasonably express skepticism about the likelihood of replicating the power of labor unions *combined* with strong works councils, supervisory boards, and other intermediaries all working in concert. How could we possibly reproduce the interlocking strengths of these intermediaries?

But the existence of powerful examples of home-grown coordination belies the impossibility of such a prospect. As I have demonstrated, businesses in certain local

48 Jay Tate, *National Varieties of Standardization*, *in* VARIETIES OF CAPITALISM: THE INSTITUTIONAL FOUNDATIONS OF COMPARATIVE ADVANTAGE 443, 463–468 (Peter A. Hall & David Soskice eds., 2001). *Cf.* Estevez-Abe, et al., *Social Protection and the Formation of Skills* at 175–176.

49 Again, a caution here that this system is becoming more fragmented in places like Germany.

50 *See* Michael L. Wachter, *Labor Unions: A Corporatist Institution in a Competitive World*, 155 U. PA. L. REV. 581 (2007).

pockets use the same basic market mechanisms as businesses within powerful German industrial sectors. These businesses share information and other resources critical to their market participation rather than proprietarily leveraging these against each other in a competition for market dominance. As a regulatory matter, it is this critical difference in business operation that distinguishes these business networks from many of their competitors.

Moreover, the work of the intermediaries within these local networks is a rejoinder to the skepticism that American policymakers might feel about replicating the institutions of mature coordinated economies. The difference in scale between national industrial networks in Germany and the local business networks discussed here could well make all the difference. Industrial networks in national coordinated economies require a range of coordinating institutions to provide the glue keeping such networks together. Concomitantly, national laws must support such institutions in their coordinating work. By contrast, what the intermediaries operating in American cities largely need is regulatory support at the local and state levels. The coordination within these networks is important, and strong intermediaries are critical to success. But it is still local. Given the rich history of support within our federalist system for local experiments, an important response to a skeptical policymaker is that the small, local scale of collaborative networks in American cities provides an ideal opportunity to develop mostly local regulations aimed at supporting collaboration.

Recent critiques and revisions of varieties of capitalism theory offer support for just the sort of local applications that I propose here.[51] For my purposes, two critiques are particularly relevant. Both have been made by Colin Crouch, who has considered the varieties of capitalism approach in a range of local economic development contexts. The first critique questions the assumption that varieties-of-capitalism theory is most viable if applied to national economies.[52] Although Hall and Soskice have emphasized the importance of nation-specific complementarities, histories, and legal frameworks in maintaining the forms of capitalist success,[53] Crouch has argued that distinct varieties of capitalism can be maintained successfully at more local levels.[54]

The second critique is related to the first. While it is not surprising that the progenitors of varieties-of-capitalism theory emphasize the differences between coordinated and liberal economies in their eagerness to prove that different forms

51 *See, e.g.* Colin Crouch, Capitalist Diversity and Change: Recombinant Governance and Institutional Entrepreneurs (2005); Peter Hall & Kathleen Thelen, *Institutional Change in Varieties of Capitalism*, 7 Socio-Econ. Rev. 7 (2009); Ian Bruff, *What about the Elephant in the Room? Varieties of Capitalism, Varieties in Capitalism*, 16 New Polit. Economy 481 (2011); Michele Mastroeni, *Engaging the Evolution of Varieties of Capitalism: A Two-Tier Approach to Examining Institutional Change*, 14, 4 Bus. & Pol., at 1 (2012).

52 Crouch, Capitalist Diversity and Change at 23.

53 Hall & Soskice, *Introduction*, Varieties of Capitalism at 16.

54 Crouch, Capitalist Diversity and Change at 129–150.

of capitalism can coexist,[55] Crouch and others have provided ample examples demonstrating that capitalist forms fall along a spectrum of difference rather than at two opposite poles.[56] Together, these two critiques suggest that businesses and institutions within one form of national economy can adopt features of the other, and indeed develop toward that form at a more local or regional level. Thus, while the original varieties of capitalism approach may appear to be extraneous to understanding the puzzle of the local urban economies, the modifications of that theory by Crouch and others make it much more relevant to this book.

Finally, it may be useful to pause over the question of why it is beneficial to examine the local, collaborative networks described in this book as a different system of capitalism, at times clashing with the liberal market form that prevails in the United States and also with the legal and institutional framework that supports it. Is it more accurate instead to describe these networks as one of a number of examples of collaboration embedded in – and indeed essential to – the hierarchical and competitive form of capitalism as we know it? The answer to this question is that it is entirely reasonable to describe them in this way. However, the benefit of analyzing these networks as a different form of capitalism, one that falls within a definable category with both theoretical and empirical claims about what characteristics help this form flourish, is that we can in fact refer to the other successful examples in this category as guides for designing regulations that support such collaboration across a range of regulatory needs and issues. While sharing may well be a hidden necessity within our liberal market economy, it is also clear that our liberal economy constrains collaboration beyond a certain point. By considering economies in which collaboration is given more space and institutional support, it may well be possible to develop fresh ideas for removing the current constraints on sharing in the name of (our competitive form of) capitalism.

55 Hall and Soskice acknowledge this focus on the extremes as a way to establish their basic theoretical points. Hall & Soskice, *Introduction*, Varieties of Capitalism at 15–17.

56 Crouch, Capitalist Diversity and Change at 129–150.

## 10

# Reforming Laws to Support Collaborative Capitalism

Returning for a moment to Michael Porter's vision of inner-city economic renewal, one of his basic underlying assumptions is that investing in the private sector will be the most potent means of correcting failing markets in the urban core.[1] More specifically, he argues that such private sector investment should largely take the form of investment in large, well-established businesses that will participate in inner-city markets out of their own economic self-interest once they realize the hidden potential of those markets to supply both customers and workers.[2] By channeling resources for the purpose of developing industry clusters, for example, policymakers can lay a fertile foundation for large businesses to reach out to individual low-income workers and also to businesses started by low-income individuals to create a virtuous cycle of production and consumption that includes inner-city residents.[3] Porter's assumption is talismanic in this regard. This same assumption bubbles up in the analyses of agglomeration economists such as Edward Glaeser.[4] It also is integral to the analyses of scholars of entrepreneurship – and to the programmatic efforts of those policymakers and practitioners who try to implement entrepreneurship theory on the ground.[5]

It is not obvious to many of these experts that this assumption is fundamentally legal: it requires a legal structure that will support this cycle of market relationships. As I have described, from a regulatory perspective, the assumption is also fundamentally flawed. Most obviously, there is no regulatory requirement – nor even incentive – for large businesses to hire inner-city workers. Quite the opposite.[6] Nor, as Porter and

[1] Michael E. Porter, *New Strategies for Inner-City Economic Development*, 11 ECON. DEV. Q. 11, 17–18 (1997) ("The best (and only) way to develop the economies of inner cities is to make them attractive and welcoming places in which to invest and do business, both for residents and nonresidents.")

[2] *Id.* at 14–17. [3] *Id.* at 16–18.

[4] *See, e.g.*, EDWARD L. GLAESER, CITIES, AGGLOMERATION, AND SPATIAL EQUILIBRIUM (2008).

[5] Rashmi Dyal-Chand & James V. Rowan, *Developing Capabilities, Not Entrepreneurs: A New Theory for Community Economic Development*, 42 HOFSTRA L. REV. 851–852 (2013).

[6] E. Douglass Williams & Richard H. Sanders, *The Prospects for "Putting America to Work" in the Inner City*, 81 GEO. L. J. 2003, 2028–2035, 2044 (1993) (discussing this same conundrum in the context of "Enterprise Zones").

others have assumed would be the case, have we seen large businesses reaching out to small businesses owned and operated by inner-city individuals for components, supplies, or other products or services related to the production needs of those large businesses.[7] Indeed, in Cleveland, an inner-city context claimed by Porter and others to exemplify success, even the large "anchor" institutions that invested in the development of a cluster of worker-owned cooperatives did not initially do much business with those cooperatives. There were no market or legal incentives for them to do so, even though these institutions appeared to have assumed there would be![8] There is a gap in the virtuous cycle that has not been filled, despite the sincere efforts of experts in a range of disciplines.

While regulation cannot fully fill this gap, supportive laws, policies, and investment especially at the state and local levels can make an enormous difference. Indeed – and this is key to my argument – such regulation can do much more than address the gap in Porter's assumptions about the market connections between large businesses and inner-city individuals. As importantly, such regulation can reduce the *reliance* of those individuals on investment from large businesses. A supportive regulatory framework can create more space for the proliferation of a broader spectrum of business activity involving residents in the urban core. Such activity can certainly include long-term employment by, and coordination with, large businesses. And it can include the development of small, independent businesses. But it can also include the kinds of collaborative business networking that we have seen in the examples discussed in this book.

The purpose of this chapter is to offer a very specific set of suggestions for creating a more supportive regulatory framework for urban-core workers. My effort here is to make it as easy as possible for lawmakers at all levels of government in the United States to reform laws in support of collaborative capitalism. As a result, the chapter begins by considering key areas of law reform at the state and local (or municipal) levels. Often laws at these two levels of government are passed in coordinated fashion, or at least in the case of local laws, within the scope of state grants of authority. The chapter then moves in the final section to consideration of law reforms at the national level. In effect, this chapter is a toolkit for lawmakers. While it would of course be ideal to use all of the tools described here in a coordinated manner, local and state lawmakers can and should evaluate the particular political, economic, social, and historical contexts in their cities and regions to choose those tools that they judge to have the most potential for success in their particular contexts.

Within each of the two sections on law reform, I have clustered my proposed reforms to respond to the greatest needs identified in Chapter 7. Specifically, I have

[7] *See* Scott L. Cummings, *Between Markets and Politics: A Response to Porter's Competitive Advantage Thesis*, 82 Or. L. Rev. 901, 912–913 (2003).

[8] *See* Keith Epstein, *The Spy Who Saved Cleveland*, The Democracy Collaborative (February 19, 2015), http://democracycollaborative.org/content/spy-who-saved-cleveland.

identified the following priorities for law reform: promoting the work of sharing intermediaries, protecting a niche market, obtaining financing, providing adequate wages and benefits, and developing infrastructure. Notably, these are not all the same priorities as one might see in a national coordinated economy such as Germany's. While the legal structure in Germany has extensively developed to protect employees within (typically large) firms, my law reform proposals focus on protecting and growing networks of small or worker-owned businesses in niche markets. This is an acknowledgement that the path for business collaboration in American cities is likely not one that involves large businesses with many employees. Thus, the more prototypical intermediaries in coordinated economies – trade unions, works councils, and supervisory boards – have less of a role in my proposals. Instead, I propose measures that prioritize *both* worker control *and* the survival and growth of the (typically small) businesses employing or owned by such workers. Moreover, I focus on forms of worker control that can flourish in contexts other than large businesses. Finally, it is important to state again here that the law reforms I propose serve the same goal as the design principles discussed in Chapter 7. As much as I would like to see the proliferation of more collaborative networks, my goal is not to reform laws to develop more collaborative networks, but rather to identify the networks that have developed organically across urban America and to support the growth of those networks.

## TWO OVERARCHING PRINCIPLES FOR US LAW REFORM IN SUPPORT OF SHARING

While the pragmatic focus of this chapter requires me to narrow my analysis down to specific types of regulations for lawmakers to consider at each level of government, it is appropriate to begin by defining two overarching principles that ought to guide lawmakers in their efforts. Not surprisingly, I have derived these principles from the six features of collaborative capitalism that run through the examples in this book.

The first general principle is that lawmakers should look for the potential for equitable distribution and democratic participation within sharing networks. By reforming laws to support only those collaborative networks that have at least a meaningful potential for equitable distribution and democratic participation, lawmakers can avoid difficult pragmatic and political questions. Politically, the narrower focus on business networks that explicitly pursue a "double bottom line" intended to alleviate poverty and urban degradation allows lawmakers to avoid claims that they are inappropriately privileging collaborative capitalism over more competitive forms. Pragmatically, the focus on equitable distribution and democracy will be a more specific basis on which to fashion regulations. It will be easier to develop regulations that support networks like Southwest Key's while avoiding questions about how such regulations could help the National Football League, General Motors, Best Western hotels, and other business models that arguably have some or even many of the features of collaborative capitalism without necessarily alleviating poverty or contributing to urban renewal.

The second overarching principle concerns the choice of law reform measures that support collaboration. One observation about these measures is that they generally fall into two categories. Some of the proposed measures are enabling in that they ease the work of intermediaries in achieving sharing. Such regulations may do so by reducing the costs of such things as permitting, taxes, or zoning. They may reduce the amount of red tape. They may take the form of subsidies or infrastructure development. In all these cases, their purpose would be to support the sharing that has developed organically in these networks. The other major category of regulations is protective. These regulations serve the purpose of protecting sharing business networks from competitors following a noncollaborative (or more traditional American) business model. An example would be a zoning provision that, by means of incentives or outright bans, prohibited nonsharing businesses from locating in a business district designated for sharing businesses. Another example would be the development of standards of conduct allowing for some level of self-regulation for sharing businesses, while imposing government-monitored standards of conduct for nonsharing businesses. Ideally, lawmakers will adopt a mix of both types of regulations because each type contributes differently to the success of collaborative networks.

With regard to protective regulations, one critical inquiry for lawmakers will be to determine when such protective measures will no longer apply to a sharing business network. In other words, policymakers will face the challenge of maintaining a peaceful coexistence between such protective regulations and those that support the liberal market economy that predominates in the United States. Much of their work in this regard will be accomplished by attention to two concerns. First, sharing intermediaries should be able to take advantage of sharing-specific regulations for only as long as they serve the critical functions of an intermediary. In developing an alternative set of rules for sharing intermediaries, regulators should aspire to embed in such rules incentives for the intermediaries to choose to switch to the rules governing their traditional counterparts if and when the costs of compliance with the traditional rules make it worthwhile to do so.

The second area of attention should be to ensure that regulations supporting sharing networks do not leave the kinds of regulatory gaps that we currently see in the self-described sharing platform economy. It should not be a choice for such networks to opt out of important consumer protection and other regimes. In developing regulations for intermediaries, regulators should seek to ensure a seamless web of regulation between these sharing-specific regulations and the broader regime of regulations that govern small businesses, consumer rights, and other relevant issues. Even where small businesses within sharing networks share some critical resources through intermediaries, these businesses will retain other important resources and functions. These latter, internalized functions ought to be governed by the traditional rules that govern all businesses in a given industry.

## REFORMING LOCAL AND STATE LAWS

Lawmakers at the local and state levels can make an enormous difference for urban workers by means of law reform. While I have organized my proposed reforms to respond to the broad categories of need identified in Chapter 7, it should be apparent that many of these reforms can contribute more broadly to economic stability by enhancing a range of paths to economic stability in the urban core.

### *Promoting Sharing by Supporting the Intermediaries*

The first priority is to operationalize the abstract notion of supporting the intermediaries in sharing networks. I have described the broad imperative for doing so. The purpose of this section is to provide detailed ideas for law reform that can accomplish this broad purpose. My specific proposals for reform fall into several categories, namely reform of state laws of business organizations, zoning reforms, and participation in regulatory development and self-regulation.

#### Forms of Business Organization

Most American business lawyers will tell you that the organizational form of a business should follow function.[9] The original and most critical function of the corporate form was to protect the individuals operating the business from bearing all the risk of that enterprise.[10] Over time, of course, lawmakers recognized that giving the business its own legal status as a corporation required collateral considerations, perhaps most notably that this distinct legal entity ought to pay taxes.[11] Also over time, this balance between risk and responsibility was refined and developed, including by the creation of additional business forms, such as the limited liability company (LLC) and most recently such "hybrid" entities as benefit corporations.[12] This latter development in the law of business organizations is an explicit recognition that there is a growing category of businesses today that operate with double or multiple bottom lines, and that these businesses have unique business plans, bear unique risks, and have unique financing strategies. And this led to the further recognition that such businesses ought not to be taxed in the same way as businesses with a single bottom line.[13]

However, even this new and favorable development in the law of business organizations has yet to incorporate the distinctive values and needs of the collaborative networks described in this book. This, then, is my reason for including proposals for reforming the law of business organizations. The legal requirements concerning business organizations should not be a barrier to business operation or to

9 Charles R.T. O'Kelley & Robert B. Thompson, Corporations and Other Business Associations 3 (7th ed. 2014).

10 *Id.* at 38. 11 *Id.* at 8.

12 Dana Brakman Reiser, *Governing and Financing Blended Enterprise*, 85 Chi.-Kent L. Rev. 619 (2010).

13 *Id.*

major business decisions. But as currently structured, they are a barrier to some of the networks I have described. As Rick Surpin of Independence Care System (ICS) described, the constraints imposed by the laws governing business organization have made it unwieldy for ICS, Paraprofessional Healthcare Institute (PHI), and Cooperative Home Care Associates (CHCA) to work together. If a holding company form had been available, at least some leaders in that network may well have chosen such a form. Surpin ruminated that doing so would have allowed the businesses within that network to maintain their own independent missions and cultures while still lowering costs and spreading the value of key leaders' involvement across the entire network. Such a structure could also be helpful to a network like the Evergreen Cooperatives in Cleveland, Ohio. That particular network does have a holding company structure, but certain elements of Ohio law appear to constrain it from maximizing the utility of that structure both for governance and financing. Finally, such a structure might have been useful for ShoreBank's relationship with its rehabber borrowers, both to allow more flexible investing in those businesses and for purposes of restructuring its loans as the financial crisis of 2008 threatened the Bank's stability and that of the network as a whole. Meanwhile, there are rich examples of networks with nonprofit holding companies and for-profit subsidiaries in a range of sectors. One such network is the Maryland-based Enterprise Community Partners, which is involved in affordable housing development. Another network that seems similar in structure to ShoreBank is City First Bank in Washington, DC, which has a number of nonprofit affiliates.

With these and many other examples in mind, I make two main proposals for reforming state-level laws governing business organization. The first proposal is for state lawmakers to develop one or more forms of business organization that recognize the relationship between sharing intermediaries and for-profit businesses operating within collaborative networks. The holding company model seems most relevant for this purpose. It either has been used or could have been useful in each of the three case studies discussed in this book. Indeed, the Southwest Key network in Austin, where a nonprofit parent wholly owns several for-profit businesses, is an excellent example with which to start.

Such a model should have several basic components. First, it should provide for, and perhaps separate, board level management of the multiple missions or bottom lines of the network from the profit-making management of each individual business. This could be accomplished by, for example, allowing for a board of directors for the network as a whole (or for the holding company) whose job it would be to protect the strategic direction and the non-profit-making missions of the network. It could also be accomplished by creation of a supervisory board or council more similar to that existing in German or French industrial networks. Such a board could be required to include representatives – both workers and management – from each of the businesses as well as from the holding company. This would make room for efficiencies of the kind desired by Surpin in the Bronx network by allowing a committed group of individuals to focus just on the network's unique missions and needs, while individual boards for each business could focus on the profit-making and other unique needs of each business. Such a structure is possible under most current state-level laws. However, as is the case with formation of worker-owned cooperatives, explicit legal recognition of such a structure will create both greater durability and more efficiencies for collaborative businesses.

A second component of the holding company model should be that the structure allows for financing from a variety of sources, including those traditionally available to for-profit *as well as* nonprofit enterprises. In the home care and Austin examples, this was accomplished by using a separate nonprofit organization to which either certain business functions were externalized and financed, or which directed financing to the for-profit businesses in their very early start-up phase. This worked for the networks described here because of the close connections among the top leaders in the network. But it also imposed additional costs. Moreover, the structure was dependent on the maintenance of close ties. Such a structure can be highly fragile and not easily conducive to growth and change over time.

Instead, the ability to obtain a range of financing should be incorporated into the legal structure itself. The ideal legal structure for financing purposes may be one whereby the holding company is able to receive foundation and other nonprofit funding, while the for-profit businesses remain free to receive funding (such as equity investments) that is traditionally available to for-profit businesses.[14] As is evident from my examples, some states do better than others in allowing such a structure to exist and thrive. For example, Texas law permits such a model,[15] and Southwest Key has used it to develop and support its social enterprise businesses. By contrast, the New York cooperative corporation law, which is quite advanced in some respects, does not contemplate the possibility of a nonprofit holding company for one or more for-profit worker-owned cooperatives.[16] (It probably would be hard to develop such a structure involving cooperatives in Texas too.) Meanwhile, the cooperative law in Ohio *requires* that worker-owned cooperatives be nonprofits,[17] thereby limiting the ability of the Evergreen Cooperatives to bid for public contracts because Cleveland's bidding process is only open to for-profit businesses. At bottom, none of these states' laws provides much space for the combination of business collaboration, worker control and financing flexibilities that would be ideal for the networks described in this book. The state that comes closest to the ideal is California, which has recently amended its cooperative law to allow for equity

14 Of course, federal tax laws constrain the extent to which the nonprofit could share foundation and government funding with its for-profit subsidiaries, an issue that I will address later in this chapter.

15 Tex. Bus. Orgs. Code Ann. § 1.002 (West 2017).

16 N.Y. Coop. Corp. Law § 88 (West 2017) ("Associations [cooperatives] shall be corporations that are deemed nonprofit because they are not organized for the purpose of making a profit for themselves as such, or for the purpose of making a profit for their members as such, but for their members as patrons.").

17 Ohio Rev. Code Ann. § 1729.02(B) (West 2017).

investments for ordinary citizens, so-called community investors.[18] Although this statute does not appear to contemplate the type of holding company structure I propose, its spirit is consistent with my proposal and it ought to be easy to layer such a reform on California's new law.

Moreover, I would push even the more progressive states' laws further by defining brighter lines concerning the extent to which the nonprofit parent can share foundation funding with its for-profit subsidiaries. Such laws should allow nonprofit financing until the subsidiaries are stably capitalized and remain so for five to seven years, a time period that would move them beyond the start-up phase.

Such a structure would also provide unique advantages over either a solely nonprofit form of organization or a benefit corporation. I have touched on the advantages vis-à-vis nonprofit formation already, but let me be explicit about them here. Organizing the individual businesses in the network as nonprofits would prevent them from obtaining certain kinds of financing, including in many states choosing worker ownership. It would also preclude them from making profits over a certain level.[19] Further, including them within a network but without formal legal ties, as the Bronx network has done, increases both fragility and management inefficiencies. If the individual businesses in the network were to organize as benefit corporations, they would at least partially avoid the first two of these disadvantages. However, they would still only be eligible for a subset of available foundation funding. Some scholars have concluded that this subset of foundation grants is relatively small compared to the overall pie of foundation funding, that for this reason benefit corporation status tends to benefit larger social enterprise businesses rather than smaller businesses (especially start-ups), and that foundations are still relatively cautious about making grants to benefit corporations.[20] This would make benefit-corporation status relatively less useful to networks such as those in East Austin and South Shore.

Finally, it is useful also to pause over the question of whether the franchise law of most states would obviate the need for or utility of a holding company law of the type I am proposing. The short answer is that it would not, because franchise law contemplates a close connection between the franchisor and the franchisees by and through the business model, including trademarks, promotional materials, marketing plans, operations manuals, and similar mechanisms.[21] This kind of connection closely controls the profit-making strategies of the franchisees while ignoring the possibility of additional nonprofit missions or bottom lines.[22] The model I am

[18] A.B. 816, Leg., Reg. Sess. (Cal. 2015).

[19] Emily Cohen, *Benefit Expenses: How the Benefit Corporation's Social Purpose Changes the Ordinary and Necessary*, 4 WM. & MARY BUS. L. REV. 269, 289 (2013); Robert A. Katz & Antony Page, *The Role of Social Enterprise*, 35 VT. L. REV. 59, 60, 67–68 (2010).

[20] *See, e.g.*, Reiser, *Governing and Financing Blended Enterprise* at 619.

[21] Richard E. Caves & William F. Murphy II, *Franchising: Firms, Markets, and Intangible Assets*, 42 S. ECON. J. 572 (1976).

[22] *Id.* at 573–574.

advocating effectively flips the focus by arguing for more control of the nonprofit missions of the network and providing efficiencies concerning profit-making only to the extent desired and dictated by the individual businesses within the network.

A third component of a holding company model is that it should explicitly allow the network as a whole to receive beneficial tax treatment and to receive favorable rates and packages for health and other benefits for its workers. I will discuss both tax issues and health benefits in later sections of this chapter. But my point here is that state laws concerning business organization should accommodate whatever favorable tax and other benefits are made available through federal law for collaborative networks.

In making this proposal, I am offering a form of organization that is distinct from what we might see in countries like Germany or Japan. In those contexts, we would expect to see legally independent businesses connected only by cross shareholding and/or cross-board relationships, much like what we see in the Bronx home care cluster. However, I am proposing a closer legal connection for such networks in American cities. I do so partly in reaction to the broader economic context, which requires a greater level of cohesion as a protective measure. By organizing themselves using a holding company structure, collaborative networks in American cities should be able to take advantage of financing that is not available to their competitors outside of the network. They should be able to better protect their niche. And it should be easier to treat them as distinct for purposes of antitrust and other laws. I will discuss each of these advantages at greater length, but my point here is that greater legal cohesion and demarcation will support distinct and special legal protections for these networks especially in the formation and early development stages.

My second main proposal in the area of business organizations law is for states that don't have them to adopt laws governing the creation of worker-owned cooperatives. Much excellent scholarship has been written about the value of such an organizational form.[23] The cross-cutting analysis and design principles in Chapter 7 affirm many of the conclusions in that scholarship about the numerous gains to workers in terms of income, control, job stability, business survival and stability, and worker education both about the trade and about business management. While my case studies show that it is not the only means of achieving worker control and democracy within the workplace, it does appear to be a particularly robust means of doing so.

As for the specific components of such laws, California, New York, and Massachusetts all have laws that can serve as useful models for this effort.[24] Not

[23] Two of the mainstays are Scott L. Cummings, *Developing Cooperatives as a Job Creation Strategy for Low-Income Workers*, 25 N.Y.U. Rev. L. & Soc. Change 181 (1999); Peter Pitegoff, *Worker Ownership In Enron's Wake–Revisiting A Community Development Tactic*, 8 J. Small & Emerging Bus. L. 239 (2004).

[24] Cal. Corp. Code §§ 12200–956 (West 2017); N.Y. Coop. Corp. Law § 11 (McKinney 2017); Mass. Gen. Laws ch. 157A §§ 1–11 (2017).

surprisingly, my primary recommendation to states building on these models would be to write laws that allow flexibility for the creation of such cooperatives within a holding company structure. These laws should specifically contemplate board level management of some aspects of the cooperatives by a parent holding company or works council. I have proposed that such management include questions about the missions and strategic directions of the network as a whole. Importantly, the involvement of a parent holding company should not preclude control by the workers of the individual cooperative, and it should especially preserve the cooperative's ability to direct profits from earnings to the workers. This can easily be accomplished by obtaining nonprofit status for the parent holding company. As Rick Surpin noted,

> [A]ccumulating capital is certainly one of the major things related to being a big and successful company. Worker cooperatives are not about accumulating capital ... We didn't set out to accumulate capital. We set out to have enough capital that we could be an operating business, and maximize wages and benefits for our workers who were also our owners.[25]

Moreover, such laws should be written to accommodate flexibility of financing, and more broadly of business planning and operation. For example, Ohio's well-intentioned law requiring that worker-owned cooperatives be nonprofits has had the effect of constraining the Evergreen Cooperatives from bidding for public contracts. Requirements such as this should be eliminated from laws creating and governing cooperatives. While it may make much sense to *allow* cooperatives to be organized as nonprofits, it does not seem appropriate to *require* nonprofit status.

### Zoning

Zoning is a second domain of laws that can and should be reformed to support the work of intermediaries within local business networks. In my analysis of the legal structure supporting the American liberal market economy, I commented on the enormous power of zoning laws to lay a welcoming foundation for business development. Currently these laws privilege large, established businesses by effectively creating suburban blank slates in which such businesses can cut special zoning deals to build infrastructure to their tastes. I propose instead zoning reforms that privilege collaborative business networks and the niches they have developed.

Zoning laws involve state and local legislative action. Municipalities draw their power to zone from the state's so-called police power, its obligation to protect the health, safety, and welfare of its citizens. States can (and most do) delegate pieces of this power to municipalities. In the case of zoning, they do so by means of zoning enabling acts, which establish the parameters within which municipalities may determine land uses within their boundaries by passing zoning ordinances (often

[25] Interview with Rick Surpin, President, Independence Care System (May 5, 2016).

known as bylaws).[26] These parameters are typically quite broad, and thus in most states, it would probably not be necessary to amend zoning enabling acts in order to enact the local reforms I am about to propose. It would nevertheless be a worthwhile first step for a state legislature to amend its zoning enabling law to explicitly encourage municipalities to use their zoning power to support collaboration. This alone would send a powerful message to municipalities about the desirability of supporting collaborative business networks.

While it is a more aggressive approach, I also propose a *state-level* law that would allow intermediaries in collaborative business networks to override local zoning laws in order to obtain zoning permits and other preferential zoning treatment so long as they and the networks they serve meet certain criteria. Such a law could be loosely modeled on incentive zoning laws intended to increase the development of affordable housing, such as Massachusetts' Chapter 40B.[27] Chapter 40B is so powerful because it provides a streamlined mechanism for cutting through a broad range of local zoning requirements that are routinely used as bases for rejecting permits for affordable housing developments. I have in mind a similar strategy for "inclusionary" zoning in favor of sharing.

The most important qualifying criterion for preferential treatment under my proposed law would be evidence of significant business ownership by, and/or employment of, low-income or inner-city workers. To qualify for preferential zoning, collaborative networks should also be required to provide detailed evidence of sharing by and between the intermediaries and the businesses in the networks. While additional criteria would be appropriate, it is also appropriate for these to be tailored to particular industries and locations.

Substantively, my proposed inclusionary zoning law would have two main functions. The first would be simply to make it easier for participants within a sharing network to do business in the locations that would be most efficacious for the businesses and the network as a whole. The most impactful measures for accomplishing this function would likely be those that override use-based zoning laws. For example, if in Chicago a particular neighborhood was subject to use zoning laws that prohibited development beyond a certain density, my proposed inclusionary zoning law would allow the South Shore network to override the lower density requirement so long as it met the qualifying criteria. Similarly, if one or more of the businesses in Southwest Key's network wish to locate in a residential neighborhood, my proposed law would override the residential zoning limitation, thereby allowing the businesses to colocate and achieve greater efficiencies. Returning to my hypothetical tortilla manufacturers, my proposed law could provide them with a powerful tool for conducting a light manufacturing business in an area not zoned for industrial uses.

26 Joseph William Singer et al., Property Law: Rules, Policies, and Practices 429–431 (6th ed. 2014); Daniel P. Selmi, *The Contract Transformation in Land Use Regulation*, 63 Stan. L. Rev. 591, 599 (2011).

27 Mass. Gen. Laws ch. 40B (2017).

As I have discussed, current use-based zoning measures regularly separate industrial uses far from residential areas, making it difficult for inner-city residents to travel to manufacturing jobs. My proposed measure would alleviate that problem substantially.

Such a measure could also alleviate area zoning and other permitting requirements, allowing businesses to utilize space in ways that would maximize efficiency, minimize costs, and mitigate concerns about requirements relating to setbacks, plantings, or even height.[28] Finally, as is the case with Massachusetts' inclusionary zoning law, my proposed regulation would streamline applications for water, sewer, parking and other necessary permits, forcing flexibility in local bureaucracies that can be inflexible in the absence of such laws.

The second major function of my inclusionary zoning law would be, of course, to provide space for sharing. This could be accomplished partly by the overriding function of the law. In the case of the tortilla manufacturers, for example, the law could be used to allow this small business to colocate with other specialty food manufacturers in a shared space. Ideally, the law would be written in such a way as to allow businesses to apply jointly to local zoning boards for zoning permits for shared spaces. Indeed, this could be one of the qualifying criteria that would permit businesses to qualify for inclusionary zoning relief. In addition, I propose adding incentives in the law for larger businesses to share space with smaller businesses in collaborative networks. This would fill just the kind of gap left by Michael Porter's analysis by providing large and small businesses additional incentives to cluster together.

For lawmakers considering such an inclusionary zoning measure, it is important to recognize and accommodate the legitimate differences between this kind of inclusionary zoning versus zoning for affordable housing. In most examples of inclusionary zoning for affordable housing, there is significantly less risk of siting incompatible uses near each other. A developer may seek to site multifamily housing in a single-family district, but both types of uses are residential. The inclusionary zoning measure that I propose could indeed result in the placement of commercial or industrial facilities in a residential area, raising legitimate concerns about noise, pollution, increased traffic, and other inconveniences or hazards. Lawmakers considering such a measure should certainly use procedural and other protections to respond to these kinds of concerns and ideally avoid them in the first place. In addition, such protections should plan ahead for eventualities such as business failure. For example, by assuring neighbors that the city is committed to returning a site to residential use if the businesses housed there fail, local officials can do much to assuage concerns and support sharing efforts among local businesses.

Of course, some of these same zoning privileges could be achieved at the local or municipal level, and that is exactly what I would propose either in conjunction with

[28] Julian Conrad Juergensmeyer & Thomas E. Roberts, Land Use Planning and Development Regulation Law §§ 5.14 – 5.15 (3d ed. 2013); Singer et al., Property Law at 430.

state level zoning reform or despite the lack of such reform. For example, within the broad scope of the typical state zoning enabling act, municipalities could create special exceptions allowing businesses meeting the same kinds of qualifying criteria described above to override local zoning laws.[29] Additionally, cities could create special zoning permits to provide incentives for small and large businesses to actively cluster and share space.

### Participation in Regulatory Development, Self-Regulation and Relational Contracting

A third domain in which state and local lawmakers can reform laws to support the intermediaries in collaborative business networks can be loosely described as involving the participants in these networks in regulatory development. My three general proposals in this domain cover a range of possibilities. The first is the possibility of participatory regulation. Consider the effect of a regulatory intervention in which a local authority invited participants in a collaborative business network to join an advisory council. This has already happened both formally and informally in the three examples I have described. In Chicago, business owner Eiran Feldman described a fascinating collaboration between the city's building, planning and development, and legal departments and local stakeholders:

> [U]nder those three departments, there [have] been all kinds of initiatives that have allowed the siloes to break and have all three departments sitting at the table together with community partners, or delegate agencies, and be able to focus on certain spots. [F]or example, [the] Micro-Market Recovery Program ... targeted concentrations of vacant properties and helped the city go after those properties, get them, and turn them over to responsible owners, and get them back online.[30]

In the Bronx, it was enormously productive for Rick Surpin and others to join with state and local agencies to consider issues of wage parity, reimbursement rates, and other aspects of the health care industry in New York. Surpin participated in these efforts both as a representative of CHCA and later ICS and as a representative of various advocacy organizations that were involved on certain issues.

I would propose that governmental agencies create councils that seek representation specifically from participants in such networks *on behalf of those networks*. Such a council could address the question of how to ensure an appropriate level of consumer protection. It could negotiate with local authorities to develop a streamlined permitting process. It could pool resources for obtaining insurance protection and health benefits. Over the longer term, such a council might also be able to contribute to deliberation within the network, a benefit that Hall and Soskice repeatedly emphasize as epitomizing the strengths of a coordinated

29 *See* Singer et al., Property Law at 459–460.

30 Interview with Eiran Feldman, First InSite Realty LLC (May 4, 2017).

economy.[31] Such a participatory effort could develop a feedback loop through which network participants could communicate the unique needs and challenges of collaborative businesses which lawmakers could then balance with the needs of, and costs to, other constituencies affected by the network, such as consumers, neighbors, and competitors. Councils such as this could be efficacious at both state and local levels of governance.

This type of participatory regulation could also support development of my second proposal in this area, which is for lawmakers to enable and encourage a certain amount of self-regulation by collaborative business networks. This would require lawmakers to reach out to intermediaries within the network that are positioned to support self-regulatory efforts. In some cases, it might also require lawmakers to support the creation or enhancement of such intermediaries. In the case of the Bronx network, both PHI and the Service Employees International Union (SEIU) are examples of intermediaries well positioned to engage with government on the subject of self-regulation of certain aspects of the network's business. In the South Shore case, it would likely have been ShoreBank, and currently Community Investment Corporation (CIC) does seem to play exactly this role. As in mature coordinated economies, the business associations of developer-owners in South Shore are also engaging with local authorities to such an extent that they are laying a foundation for exactly the kind of self-governance I propose.[32] Finally, in the Southwest Key case, the nonprofit parent holding company would be well positioned to play this role.

Coordinated economies in other countries can be useful in providing a model by which regulators can work with networks to target key areas for self-regulation. For example, business associations in Germany, France, and elsewhere have developed industry standards to assure customer safety and to sanction businesses that fail to comply with such standards.[33] These industry-led certificates of trust are a means of developing acceptable minimum safety and quality standards to protect consumers in such markets. They serve as an alternative to established permitting and licensing requirements.[34] The purpose of such an industry-led process would be partly to allow businesses within the network to collaborate on standards that would be specifically tailored to their operational needs and structures. It would also help to reduce costs. Consider, for example, the possibilities inherent in allowing the rehabber network to participate more fully in setting appropriate standards for rehabilitation of residential housing in Chicago. Note also that the process I am

31 Peter Hall & David Soskice, *Introduction*, *in* Varieties of Capitalism: The Institutional Foundations of Comparative Advantage 9–12 (Peter A. Hall & David Soskice eds., 2001).

32 Interview with Jack Crane, Senior Vice President and Director of Lending, Community Investment Corporation (July 6, 2017).

33 Hall & Soskice, *Introduction*, Varieties of Capitalism at 24–25.

34 Rashmi Dyal-Chand, *Regulating Sharing: The Sharing Economy as an Alternative Capitalist System*, 90 Tul. L. Rev. 241, 287 (2015).

proposing explicitly reserves a role for government to facilitate the development of standards, thereby ensuring sufficient protections for consumers.

By means of tailored regulations such as these, regulators can take advantage of the role of intermediaries *for the purpose of regulation*. This regulatory choice recognizes the uniqueness of creating a market in which an intermediary institution does for an entire network some of the things that individual businesses typically must do. The US regulatory framework currently constrains this kind of regulatory solution by means of antitrust and anticompetition laws. This is one area in which regulators will have to develop a new set of standards applicable to sharing businesses.

The notion of self-regulation is also linked to my third proposal in this domain, which is for both legislators and courts at the state and local levels to recognize the value of informal or relational contracting within collaborative business networks. Thus, for example, one rich regulatory possibility could be to require intermediaries within such networks to provide evidence that they had contracted with the individual businesses to meet certain safety standards. While this may not be a substitute for certain kinds of governmental permitting (such as food safety), it may well be a useful requirement for others (such as building permits or the acquisition of insurance). Here too, Germany's example of relational contracting within a network could be a useful guide.[35] If governmental standards could encourage the development of a more robust (if relatively less formal) set of contract terms establishing and maintaining an industry standard concerning some safety issues, then customers should be able to participate in a market with fewer unknowns and less variability on critical consumer protection issues. Such a solution in turn could drive the development of a broader regulatory framework supporting it.

The second and third proposals I have described in this section rely on a combination of enabling legislation, regulatory collaboration, and perhaps also confirming legislation. As in the zoning context, it will be important for lawmakers especially at the state level to promote the value of collaborative business networking by signaling the establishment of advisory councils, industry-led regulation, and other means of regulatory participation. It will also be valuable for lawmakers eventually to capture some of the rules that originated in self-regulation in a more permanent framework of statutes.

However, support of self-regulation and relational contracting need not and should not come just from state and local legislators. Courts also play an important role here. As they have done in other contexts such as health care, courts should recognize and monitor these additional forms of rule-making. For example, in the medical context, courts have recognized a tort of negligent credentialing, which can be enforced by individual consumers or state attorneys

[35] Hall & Soskice, *Introduction*, VARIETIES OF CAPITALISM at 26–27.

general.[36] This tort provides a remedy for individuals harmed by a provider that has inappropriately obtained an industry-determined credential. It requires courts to recognize the credential in the first place, but also to ensure that it meets a certain standard of reasonableness that is established by authorities outside of the industry. Similar torts should be available to consumers and others who do business with sharing networks that employ self-regulation and informal contracting. Courts play an important role in policing the boundaries between the local norms within such networks and the broader legal norms surrounding them.

In addition, in interpreting relational contracts, courts can serve an important function by recognizing the different norms of contract interpretation that exist in these contexts. A rich literature has examined the details and sustainability of relational contracting norms.[37] Courts also can and should develop a presumption of at times telling parties who are *both* participants in a given sharing network to "go work it out on your own." Rather than presuming that the "four corners" of the written contract govern in a given case, courts should consider affirming the self-regulatory norm among parties who have willingly chosen it by at times refusing to resolve issues of contract interpretation, thereby promoting further deliberation between the parties.

## *Protecting a Niche*

Each of the case studies in this book has revealed the importance of a niche market to the success of these collaborative business networks. Yet we have also seen that it is one of the trickiest pieces in the successful development of such networks. Many of the managers I interviewed chalked up the discovery and development of a niche to "luck," "timing," and similarly uncontrollable factors. While it may be true that the discovery of a niche is a matter of luck, there are a number of regulatory possibilities for enhancing and protecting market niches for sharing networks once they are discovered. Moreover, local and state lawmakers should take notice that these measures are largely within their purview. I will focus on three sets of measures that are particularly promising. For each of these to succeed, the first step for lawmakers is to pay attention to the patterns of small business development in urban cores. This should be easily accomplished by tracking data that are likely

36 The field of health law might provide a good set of examples in this regard. *See, e.g.*, Andrew R. deHoll, *Vital Surgery or Unnecessary Procedure? Rethinking the Propriety of Hospital Liability for Negligent Credentialing*, 60 S.C. L. Rev. 1127 (2009); Casey L. Moore, *"In the Wake of the Rose" and "Life After Romero": The Viability of a Cause of Action for Negligent Credentialing in Texas in Light of Recent Texas Supreme Court Decisions*, 58 Baylor L. Rev. 549, 566–567 (2006).

37 Stewart Macaulay is a key figure in this literature, and he discusses its development in a recent coauthored article. Stewart Macaulay & William C. Whitford, *The Development of Contracts: Law in Action*, 87 Temp. L. Rev. 793, 800–801 (2015).

already kept by local and regional development agencies. In Boston, one of the best resources for such data is the Metropolitan Area Planning Council.[38]

## Zoning

The first reform is for cities to amend their zoning ordinances in order to create space explicitly for such niches. One bold proposal for doing this would be to establish a special business district for particular niches upon application from collaborative business networks. These could be for a broad range of products and services, including specialty foods, green manufacturing or construction, residential building rehabilitation, and health services. Some excellent examples already exist that can guide lawmakers in this effort, though not all of these are the result of zoning laws. Perhaps the most splendid is in Northern Italy, where villages are known for particular crafts and the businesses in those villages are supported by a semipublic organization (CNA).[39] In the United States, a recent and promising example is the advertising done by municipalities to promote the purchase and use of local products.[40] These "buy local" campaigns could go further and be more impactful if backed by the power of zoning. A third example is New York City's discussion about rezoning certain urban areas to allow small-scale or light manufacturing.[41]

[38] *See* METROPOLITAN AREA PLANNING COUNCIL, www.mapc.org.

[39] *See* Bennett Harrison, *Industrial Districts: Old Wine in New Bottles?*, 26 REGIONAL STUD. 469, 469–483 (1992) ("In the recent literature, the paradigmatic industrial districts are those located in that region of north-central, and north-eastern Italy known as the 'Third Italy' … In the ideal-typical industrial district, each small firm specializes in one or a few phases of a complete production process … On any particular project, the small flexible firms will often cooperate with one another, sharing tools, information, and even skilled personnel, only to compete fiercely for a share of the next new contract or market opportunity."); MICHAEL J. PIORE & CHARLES F. SABEL, THE SECOND INDUSTRIAL DIVIDE: POSSIBILITIES FOR PROSPERITY (1984). Ron Grzywinski recounted a conversation he had with Charles Sabel about CNA in which Sabel described the defining characteristics of that network as being their knowledge of machinery, their ability to husband small amounts of capital, and their ability to simultaneously cooperate and compete with each other. Grzywinski recalled thinking that if one substituted knowledge of machinery with knowledge of real estate, the same three characteristics would define the mom-and-pop rehabbers who borrowed from ShoreBank. Telephone call with Ron Grzywinski (Aug. 7, 2017).

[40] *See* MICHAEL H. SHUMAN, THE SMALL-MART REVOLUTION: HOW LOCAL BUSINESSES ARE BEATING THE GLOBAL COMPETITION (2008). Buy local campaigns are probably best known in the area of food growth and purchase. *See, e.g.*, BRIAN K. OBACH, ORGANIC STRUGGLE: THE MOVEMENT FOR SUSTAINABLE AGRICULTURE IN THE UNITED STATES 181–210 (2015). MICHAEL POLLAN, THE OMNIVORE'S DILEMMA: A NATURAL HISTORY OF FOUR MEALS (2006); ANNA LAPPÉ & BRYANT TERRY, GRUB: IDEAS FOR AN URBAN ORGANIC KITCHEN 118–128 (2006). While the local food movement has many adherents, it also has its critics. *See, e.g.*, Julian Agyeman & Benjamin L. Simons, *Re-imagining the Local: Scale, Race, Culture and the Production of Food Vulnerabilities*, *in* CITIES, NATURE AND DEVELOPMENT: THE POLITICS AND PRODUCTION OF URBAN VULNERABILITIES 85 (Sarah Dooling & Gregory Simon eds., 2012).

[41] *Building a Vibrant Manufacturing Sector: A Blueprint for New York City*, PRATT CENTER FOR COMMUNITY DEVELOPMENT (June 7, 2017), http://prattcenter.net/sites/default/files/industrial-policy_issue-brief_final.pdf.

One way to zone in support of niches would amount essentially to a heavy promotional or advertising campaign, in the vein of the "buy local" campaigns. Local governments could support such a campaign by means of signs, fliers, posters, and other materials designating a certain geographical area for the niche. They could direct their own contracts to businesses participating in the network. And they could use zoning and permitting measures to allow for the demarcation of the niche zone by means of lampposts, benches, and parking areas. Such a zone could be modeled on the use of certain parking lots in cities for farmers' markets or for service by food trucks. While it is hard to be specific, given the range of possible niches, one promising application would be a zone designated for specialty foods such as that made by Southwest Key's café. Such a zone could protect businesses like this from larger food retailers and also encourage similarly situated small businesses to develop in the area.

I would advocate for a more aggressive version of the special business district by zoning such an area also to *exclude* larger businesses that did not actively participate in the collaborative sharing network. This is obviously a much more controversial proposal, given the norms of equal access and competition in our society. Courts have policed these norms using, among other rules, the so-called dormant commerce clause doctrine, which has been described as "a judge-made doctrine rooted in the belief that power over interstate commerce was assigned to Congress by the Constitution largely to restrain states from discriminating against or burdening their neighbors' commerce as happened during the Confederation era."[42] Though controversial, it is important to point out that my proposed measure would likely be found to be constitutional. In this case, there is a strong argument that it is also appropriate. Such a measure would counteract years of zoning and other laws that have favored large businesses. In this regard, recent court cases upholding restrictions on the siting of "big-box" stores such as Wal-Mart, sometimes explicitly to protect local businesses from outside competition, are instructive.[43] Lawmakers considering such a measure should use these cases in outlining their rationale for adopting zoning protections for local businesses.

Aside from creating a special business district for niches, zoning could also be used to much more actively support colocation and other forms of collaboration. I have already discussed the example of creating zones for light industry or specialty manufacturing. I have also discussed the idea of creating zoning incentives for collaboration between small and large businesses involved in a production cycle. These examples reveal the power of zoning to shape the development of markets.

[42] Brannon P. Denning & Rachel M. Lary, *Retail Store Size-Capping Ordinances and the Dormant Commerce Clause Doctrine*, 37 Urb. Law. 907, 916 (2005). *See also* Richard C. Schragger, *Cities, Economic Development, and the Free Trade Constitution*, 94 Va. L. Rev. 1091 (2008).

[43] Wal-Mart Stores v. Turlock, 483 F.Supp.2d 987, 1020 (E.D. Cal. 2006); Coronadans Organized for Retail Enhancement v. City of Coronado, No. D040293, 2003 WL 21363665 (Cal. Ct. App. June 13, 2003). *But see* Island Silver & Spice, Inc. v. Islamorada, Village of Islands, 475 F.Supp.2d 1281 (S.D. Fla. 2007).

Some of these same advantages have been achieved without the benefit of zoning law, for example by creating incubation space for clusters.[44] However, such space is often very limited and is only available in areas already zoned for the type of business activity to be incubated. Reform of zoning laws can help by providing a means for businesses with fewer resources to take advantage of the claim that a business's success is influenced greatly by its location. By responding to the businesses' *own* judgment about where best to locate, zoning authorities can follow and support the organic development of networks, thereby increasing the likelihood of success.

**Permitting**

Another distinct area for law reform is at the local – and very specific – level of business licensing and permitting. Because of the level of specificity required in considering reforms in this area, it is hard to say a great deal here. A few examples, however, ought to suggest the importance of such reforms. Recall again the example of the tortilla manufacturers. It would save costs enormously for this small business if it had the benefit of streamlined permitting for a food manufacturing facility where it could colocate with other specialty food manufacturers. This would be especially true if an intermediary had obtained the necessary permits, thereby saving each food manufacturing business from incurring the costs of doing so. Similarly, imagine the efficiencies that could result from allowing permits for residential rehab to be obtained at and even through the real estate lending department of ShoreBank. In this regard, it is also useful to consider the value to home health aides in the Bronx network that PHI has worked with state regulators to define the standards for credentialing of home health aides and to customize its vocational education courses to streamline the acquisition of those credentials.[45]

While an inclusionary zoning law such as the one I have proposed can help a great deal in reducing the burdens of licensing and permitting, it cannot do everything. Permitting has literally enabled the existence of industries, such as food trucks, that have infused some urban economies with both jobs for low-income individuals and highly welcome products and services.[46] This is an area of law reform where city-level officials could make a world of difference for the types of networks described in this book.

**Eminent Domain**

A third legal strategy for state and local lawmakers to consider is the use of eminent domain to create a concentrated space within which a collaborative business

44 *See* Ilan Bijaoui, The Open Incubator Model: Entrepreneurship, Open Innovation, and Economic Development in the Periphery (2015); Dinah Adkins, A Brief History of Business Incubation in the United States (2003); Colin Barrow, Incubators: A Realist's Guide to the World's New Business Accelerators (2001).

45 Interview with Peggy Powell, National Director, Workforce and Curriculum Development, PHI (May 12, 2016).

46 Lenore Lauri Newman & Katherine Burnett, *Street Food and Vibrant Urban Spaces: Lessons from Portland, Oregon*, 18 Loc. Env't 234, 234–235 (2013).

network could develop its niche. Due in part to the US Supreme Court's decision in *Kelo* v. *City of New London*,[47] and the so-called slum clearance cases of a few decades before that decision,[48] the use of eminent domain power in aid of local development is highly controversial. As I propose using it, however, it need not be. Here, an utterly unique use of eminent domain might serve as a powerful illustration. In 1988, four years after its formation, the Dudley Square Neighborhood Initiative in Boston became the first and only community organization in the United States to be delegated the power of eminent domain.[49] It used this power to acquire almost entirely vacant land in a concentrated urban area. After acquiring the land, DSNI assembled the parcels and established a land trust to own and develop the land into affordable housing. Eminent domain served as a powerful foundation for the community to take control of its neighborhood, which had been the site of degradation from environmental dumping, crime, arson, and public disinvestment for decades before that.

Although it would be untenable to use eminent domain in a wide array of contexts, local lawmakers ought to consider Dudley Square as a model in an urban area that is degraded, that has a concentration of largely abandoned property, and that has a collaborative network the local community trusts. Although DSNI used this power to create affordable housing, there is no reason why it could not also serve as the basis for supporting the growth of a niche industry, particularly where a nonprofit holding company could actively protect multiple missions including local workforce development.

## *Obtaining Financing*

In addition to the challenge of developing a niche, our three case studies have revealed the enormous challenges imposed by inaccessible financing. As Chapter 7 discussed, in the area of financing, the South Shore network underscores the remarkable value of involving a financial institution as an intermediary in a collaborative network. Another example of this strategy successfully employed is the TELACU network in East Los Angeles, which has two financial institutions that provide financing for its family of businesses. In these cases, the financial institutions have provided easy, un-bureaucratic access to loans, which appears to have been essential to the early development of the businesses in the network.

In general, both debt and equity financing, the two main sources of financing available to for-profit businesses, impose barriers for the types of networks I have

47 Kelo v. City of New London, 545 U.S. 469 (2005).

48 *See* Olga V. Kotlyarevskaya, *"Public Use" Requirement in Eminent Domain Cases Based on Slum Clearance, Elimination of Urban Blight, and Economic Development*, 5 CONN. PUB. INT. L. J. 197, 203–205 (2006).

49 PETER MEDOFF & HOLLY SKLAR, STREETS OF HOPE: THE FALL AND RISE OF AN URBAN NEIGHBORHOOD 142, 144, 145 (1994).

examined. In my discussion of the law of business organizations, I proposed a holding company model designed partly to maximize the ability of collaborative business networks to use hybrid financing strategies that include foundation and government grants. However, law reforms should ideally also address the continuing barriers to accessing private sources of debt and equity financing. Reform is needed because foundation and governmental grants cannot alone suffice in financing these networks. Nor are they a viable long-term source of financing, especially as the businesses in the network grow. Financing is one area in which federal laws will have to be changed, and thus some of my proposals concerning financing will appear in the section on federal law reform. In this section, I propose two reforms that can be implemented at the state and local levels to make a meaningful difference for the three networks discussed in this book, and likely for many others as well.

### Crowdfunding Support

My first proposal concerns crowdfunding, a contemporary financing strategy that seems to have significant potential to infuse equity capital into small businesses and nonprofits.[50] This strategy calls for a large number of ordinary (as distinguished from rich and sophisticated) individuals (i.e. a "crowd") to invest small amounts in both for-profit and nonprofit enterprises, typically by means of platform technology. Previously, the main methods for obtaining investments from the public were either by going public or by accepting donations.[51] Companies such as Kickstarter and Indiegogo are pioneers in this arena, and both originated this investment genre by focusing on nonprofit, typically artistic, ventures.[52]

In 2012, Congress made the strategy more useful for small businesses by passing the Jumpstart Our Business Startups (JOBS) Act.[53] This law created exceptions to federal securities and other laws that had constrained members of the public from investing in companies that had not gone public. The JOBS Act imposes caps on investment by any one individual in the course of a year, and also annual caps on the amount a small business can raise using crowdfunding.[54] However, the JOBS Act

[50] Darian M. Ibrahim, *Equity Crowdfunding: A Market for Lemons?*, 100 MINN. L. REV. 561, 562–564 (2015); C. Steven Bradford, *Crowdfunding and the Federal Securities Laws*, 2012 COLUM. BUS. L. REV. 1, 5, 10 (2012).

[51] Kurtis Urien & David Groshoff, *An Essay Inquiry: Will the JOBS Act's Transformative Regulatory Regime for Equity Offerings Cost Investment Bankers' Jobs?*, 1 TEX. A&M L. REV. 559, 560–561 (2014).

[52] Bradford, *Crowdfunding and the Federal Securities Laws* at 5.

[53] Jumpstart Our Business Startups Act, Pub. L. No. 112–206, 126 Stat. 306 (2012) (codified in scattered sections of 15 U.S.C.).

[54] Urien & Groshoff, *Will the JOBS Act's Transformative Regulatory Regime for Equity Offerings Cost Investment Bankers' Jobs?* at 573 ("Title III of the JOBS Act exempts transactions involving the offer or sale of securities by an issuer provided that: (A) the aggregate amount sold to all investors does not exceed $1,000,000 in a twelve-month period; (B) the aggregate amount sold to an investor with a net worth less than $100,000 is $2,000, and to an investor with a net worth equal to or more than $100,000 is $10,000; (C) the transaction is conducted through a broker or funding portal; and (D) the issuer complies with § 4A(b).").

has been the subject of criticism on a number of fronts. Perhaps the most relevant here is the criticism that it is too easy for larger businesses to take advantage of the JOBS act and harder than expected for small businesses to do so, partly because of limitations imposed on the platform-providing intermediaries.[55] This is one reason why some states have passed their own laws supplementing the JOBS Act.

In 2015, California passed the California Worker Cooperative Act, a statute that is exemplary both in its support of worker-owned cooperatives and in its support for a higher level of investment in such businesses by members of the public.[56] For example, it allows cooperatives (including both worker and consumer coops) to sell memberships up to a cap of $1,000 per purchaser while still being exempt from certain securities laws. In addition, the statute creates a special class of investor called a "community investor." According to an educational document prepared by the Tuttle Law Group and the Sustainable Economies Law Center, a community investor is "a person who is not a worker-member and who holds a share or other proprietary interest in a worker cooperative."[57] In addition to facilitating access by worker-owned cooperatives to financing from "ordinary" individuals, this statute also contemplates the sale of equity stakes without affecting the control by workers of their cooperatives. It is no accident that the California statute is so thoughtful in its regulation of worker-owned cooperatives. Both the Sustainable Economies Law Center and the Tuttle Law Group championed this law and both are at the forefront of legal groups that are developing innovative approaches to sharing economies and markets. Indeed, Janelle Orsi, a cofounder of the Sustainable Economies Law Center, provides many pragmatic ideas for lawyering in support of sharing in her book, *Practicing Law in the Sharing Economy: Helping People Build Cooperatives, Social Enterprise, and Local Sustainable Economies.*[58]

California legislators have also been considering a statute that would authorize a significantly higher level of intrastate financing of small businesses through crowdfunding. In early 2017, a version of this bill proposed authorizing the sale of securities by means of crowdfunding up to an annual limit of two million dollars for a business, and an individual investment cap of $5,000 or 10 percent of the individual's net worth, in a 12-month period.[59]

I propose that state lawmakers build on laws such as those passed and proposed in California by developing crowdfunding statutes with provisions specifically targeting worker-owned cooperatives and collaborative business networks. Such laws

55 *See* Ibrahim, *Equity Crowdfunding* at 587–606. 56 A.B. 816, Leg., Reg. Sess. (Cal. 2015).

57 Tuttle Law Group & Sustainable Economies Law Center, Capital-Raising for Worker Cooperatives: Using the AB 816 Community Investor Provision, https://d3n8a8pro7vhmx.cloudfront.net/theselc/pages/21/attachments/original/1455749077/AB_816_Community_Investor_Memo.FINAL.pdf?1455749077.

58 Janelle Orsi, Practicing Law in the Sharing Economy: Helping People Build Cooperatives, Social Enterprise, and Local Sustainable Economies (2012).

59 AB-1517, California Assembly (2017), http://leginfo.legislature.ca.gov/faces/billNavClient.xhtml?bill_id=201720180AB1517

should allow for higher investment caps and more flexibility for sharing intermediaries. This again may be one context in which such provisions should be available only for networks using the nonprofit holding company model.

**Incentives for Venture Capital**

Despite its potential, crowdfunding is still a relatively new and untested form of financing.[60] It would still be very desirable for the networks discussed here to have access to traditional sources of equity capital such as angel and venture capital investors. For a variety of reasons, however, the businesses in these networks do not attract such investments.[61] These reasons likely boil down to the perceived risks of investing in businesses without high rates of return, where much of the profit is channeled directly to the workers and where other missions appear to cloud the profit-making effort. My second proposal addresses some of these concerns by proposing additional incentives to attract equity investors.

Recall PHI's Jodi Sturgeon's comments about the infusion of tens of millions of dollars' worth of capital for "platform economy home care agencies":

> [I]t's interesting, you know, we were having a senior management meeting last week, and someone said, "It's not like they're smarter than us in this industry... But the reality is, they have money and time to actually think, to be creative."[62]

The question for state and local lawmakers to ponder is how to reduce the risk perceived by private equity investors. One answer is to lower the start-up costs even more than the network can do on its own to reduce the risk of failure in the start-up phase. It is a common assumption within the venture capital world that a VC will only receive return on its investment in one out of every four businesses in which it invests.[63] If supportive regulation can increase the likelihood that collaborative business networks can survive past the start-up phase, it ought to increase the infusion of private capital in those networks. Happily, some of the law reforms already discussed can be useful for this purpose too. For example, by streamlining zoning and licensing for collaborative businesses, state, and local lawmakers can signal to private equity sources that they are helping to reduce the risk of business failure. They can even reserve some of the benefits they provide for networks that receive private equity as a means of encouraging them to seek this form of financing.

A second measure that lawmakers can consider in an effort to make investment in collaborative networks more attractive to private equity is to help develop these networks using business models that are particularly attractive to such sources. For example, it appears that the platform economy is currently a source of fascination for

60 Ibrahim, *Equity Crowdfunding* at 562–564. 61 *Id.* at 562–563, 574–576.

62 Interview with Jodi Sturgeon, President, PHI (May 12, 2016).

63 Jeff Schwartz, *Should Mutual Funds Invest in Startups? A Case Study of Fidelity Magellan's Fund's Investments in Unicorns (and Other Startups) and the Regulatory Implications*, 95 N.C. L. Rev. 1341, 1389 (2017).

venture capital.[64] In the Bronx context, it would probably be quite effective for New York policymakers to leverage private equity by providing financing for research and development of platform technology for use by the Bronx network. Given New York's clear investment in this industry, it should just be a matter of educating both state and local policymakers and potential equity investors about the benefits of state funding for research and development in this area.

A third, and likely more controversial, measure that could reduce equity investors' perception of risk would be for the state to invest in collaborative networks not only by means of grants, but also by providing a financial guaranty of a certain rate of return for equity investment in collaborative networks. Such a guaranty could and should be made up to a cap, and it should certainly be made with strings attached, such as requirements concerning local hiring and multiple bottom lines. This could be viewed as an alternative means of investing in a supportive infrastructure for collaborative business practices.

### *Providing Adequate Wages and Benefits*

While sharing takes different forms in our American examples than it does in coordinated economies in other parts of the world, one commonality is the prioritization of workers' needs and rights. Although Chapter 7's cross-cutting analysis reveals some key areas for regulatory development that would likely not be priorities in mature coordinated economies, it also reveals that (as in mature sharing economies) regulatory support for workers remains paramount in the American context. In this domain, New York, a state that serves as the setting for one of our case studies, provides a wonderful model for other states to examine in developing regulations.[65] New York is exemplary in two respects, both of which are the basis for my first two proposals in this section.

#### **Minimum Wage**

The first is the minimum wage law, which mandates a floor for the minimum wage to be paid New York's workers that is higher than the federally mandated minimum wage.[66] Of course, unions and many other organizations have advocated for years for a higher minimum wage, and they have done so for a variety of excellent reasons.[67] The experience of the collaborative business networks I have described supplements the already robust case for a higher minimum wage by focusing on the issue of competition. As we see in the case of the Bronx network, before New York passed its

64 Orly Lobel, *The Law of the Platform*, 101 MINN. L. REV. 87, 90 (2016).

65 Elizabeth J. Kennedy, *Wage Theft as Public Larceny*. 81 BROOK. L. REV. 517, 537 (2016) ("New York passed a Domestic Worker Bill of Rights in 2010, which … expanded minimum wage coverage … and mandated a higher rate of overtime pay for live-in domestic workers and live-out companions. New York also passed a Home Care Worker Wage Parity Law, which established minimum 'total compensation' requirements for home care workers.").

66 N.Y. Lab. Law. § 652(1) (McKinney 2016); Kate Andrias, *The New Labor Law*. 126 YALE L.J. 2, 7 (2016).

67 Andrias, *The New Labor Law* at 51–57.

minimum wage law, CHCA already paid its workers meaningfully more than the industry average and also more than the federal minimum wage. This meant that those service providers who paid their home health aides less were able to undercut CHCA in obtaining contracts. Once the minimum wage law was passed, CHCA's ability to be profitable and compete with these providers was enhanced.

The process by which the minimum wage law was passed in New York also is worth discussing, because it reveals both the similarities and the differences between the systems for protecting workers in our local contexts as compared to mature coordinated economies. For example, in Germany and France, as well as in New York, unions and other institutions representing workers have been deeply involved in wage setting campaigns. In New York, the SEIU was at the forefront of the Fight for $15 campaign to set the minimum wage in New York City at $15.[68] However, until very recently, in Germany there was no national minimum wage.[69] Instead, businesses negotiated directly with trade unions to set industry-specific minimum wages. In effect, until recently Germany had a system of self-regulation in wage setting, while wage setting has been accomplished by formal law at the federal and state levels in the United States. This difference suggests a possible lesson for lawmakers in the United States, namely that formal law may be more necessary in developing workers' rights – and more broadly, a collaborative framework – in the United States than it has been in at least some national coordinated economies. Certainly this is a question that ought to be the subject of future research.

### Wage Parity

New York also serves as a model for my second proposal for state-level law reform, namely the enactment of wage standardizing legislation for at least those industries where collaborative networks are developing niches. The New York example is useful here because its recently passed home care wage parity law is an important component of the overall legal framework for protecting New York health care workers. This wage standardizing law requires that individuals performing the work of home health aides are to receive wages standardized by region.[70] While the wage floor for home health aides seems generally to be a bit higher than the minimum wage in New York, the wage parity law complements the minimum wage law by requiring that aides are entitled to the greater base wage rate as between the current rate set by the wage parity law and the current rate set by the minimum wage law.[71]

68 *Id.* at 48.

69 *Germany Approves First-Ever National Minimum Wage*, BBC.com (July 3, 2014), http://www.bbc.com/news/business-28140594.

70 N.Y. Pub. Health Law § 3614(c)(1)(d), (c)(2) (West 2017).

71 N.Y. Pub. Health Law § 3614(c)(3)(a)(iv) provides, "the cash portion of the minimum rate of home care aide total compensation shall be ten dollars or the minimum wage as laid out in paragraph (a) of subdivision one of section six hundred fifty-two of the labor law, whichever is higher." *And* (b)(iv): "compensation shall be ten dollars or the minimum wage as laid out in paragraph (b) of subdivision one of section six hundred fifty-two of the labor law, whichever is higher."

In effect, New York's legislative efforts have allowed CHCA to prioritize workers' wages and benefits while also competing so effectively in the industry that it has quadrupled in size over the last several years. There are too many pieces of its sophisticated strategy (including the creation of ICS) to assert a direct causal connection to the New York wage laws. It might nevertheless be useful to imagine the effect on a network like Southwest Key's of wage laws such as these. Imagine, specifically, how it might affect the café's ability to compete for catering contracts if its competitors were required to pay a higher and more standardized minimum wage for food sector workers in Texas. In Texas, such a legislative move could also have the powerful effect of forcing employers to overcome appropriately imposed hurdles to hiring day laborers at unfairly depressed wages. Rick Surpin of ICS commented that one reason why wage parity legislation was passed in the home health care industry in New York is that it is already such a heavily regulated industry, in which reimbursement rates (which drive wage rates) are directly regulated by the federal and state governments.[72] He may well be right, but the Texas example suggests that better state laws regulating wages would be beneficial in many other, less regulated industries also.

**Incentives for Local Hiring at a Living Wage**

My remaining proposals in this section build on and complement my proposals in other domains, such as zoning, licensing, and infrastructure development, which I have raised as means of increasing support for intermediaries, protecting niches, and increasing access to financing. Although I will touch on them only briefly, my main point in discussing them here is to point out that such strategies can also be very useful in producing better wages, benefits, and work conditions for workers in the urban core. Moreover, they complement the strategies I have discussed above by layering incentives on top of mandates. In raising these incentive-based strategies, however, I do not mean to suggest that they substitute for mandatory minimum wage laws and other legislation. Again, I do not claim a causal connection, but it is noteworthy in this regard that New York and California, two states at the vanguard of supporting worker-owned cooperatives, both have higher minimum wage laws and deploy various incentive-based structures for supporting workers.[73] The efforts of these two states share important commonalities with the "social policy" laws in mature coordinated economies, which create a committed regulatory structure for livable and long-term employment.

To examine the potential of such incentives, imagine the benefits to the Southwest Key network if the City of Austin were to offer this network

[72] Surpin Interview.

[73] Andrias, *The New Labor Law* at 7. ("California and New York have enacted increases to $15 an hour–nearly $8 an hour more than the federal minimum ... The wage laws have been accompanied by new regulations providing scheduling protection, sick time, and other benefits.").

streamlined zoning and permitting for a light manufacturing facility near its headquarters in Austin in return for a commitment to pay certain wages to its workers. Southwest Key is already deeply committed to providing livable wages to its workers, but its leaders have also commented on the burden of start-up costs. If these costs were at least partially alleviated by the city, it is reasonable to conclude that the network could commit more fully to sustaining its businesses and channeling more profits to its workers. The City of Austin already provides a range of incentives for local, small businesses.[74] But currently, none of these appears directed toward local hiring. Given the City of Austin's apparent interest in supporting small businesses, it and other cities ought to consider local hiring incentives as well.

### *Developing Infrastructure*

There is one additional domain in which state, and particularly local, policy-making could produce enormous benefits for collaborative business networks in American cities. This domain is best described as investment in a supportive infrastructure rather than law reform per se. It is not about writing new laws or regulations that impose mandates or create incentives for collaboration. Rather, it is about direct investment in support of these networks by local governments in particular. I focus on three forms of investment that are promising.

#### Vocational Education

As in the realm of wage legislation, New York is exemplary in this domain too, in particular in its investment in vocational education and workforce development, which is the first form of investment I propose. Here I would point to the sophisticated, long-term, and ongoing collaboration between the State and City of New York, PHI, CHCA, and Chapter 1199 of the SEIU about training for home health aides. This conversation has included state and local government grants, the joint development of credentialing standards, the involvement of local universities and community colleges, and deep interaction with service providers who will ultimately employ the workers. It has included failed and successful experiments. And it has deeply shaped the development of the Bronx network and its individual businesses. It is, in short, a tremendously successful story about the place of training and vocational education in developing an inner-city workforce within an industry. The success of the Manchester Bidwell network in Pennsylvania is another encouraging example. Both of these have clear applications in our other case studies and ought to serve as models for local policymakers to follow in other cities.

74 Small Bus. Dev. Program, City of Austin, Small Business Incentives Guide 6–12 (2014), www.austintexas.gov/sites/default/files/files/EGRSO/Small_Business_Incentive_Guide.pdf.

### Public Contracts

A second important form of investment is for city and state agencies to facilitate the ability of collaborative business networks to do business with those agencies. We have seen that state and local regulations hindered both the Bronx network and the Evergreen Cooperatives in Cleveland from bidding for public contracts as minority-owned businesses. These barriers should, of course, be eliminated. But governmental agencies should also develop their public bidding processes to invite more participation by collaborative business networks. For example, like the City of San Francisco, such agencies can embed a "hire local" requirement in their bidding processes, thereby advantaging such networks.[75] They can require evidence that successful bidders pay a living wage. Such requirements could have made all the difference for the Southwest Key network when it successfully bid for the highway trash picking contracts, but then could not earn profits because it refused to pay the depressed wages paid by other businesses.

Indeed, in their ideal form, contracts with public agencies could actually develop into a niche for some types of collaborative business networks. Or at least public agencies could serve as the initial catalyst or stable customer for such networks. This appears to be the strategy of the celebrated Dudley Square network in Boston, which has achieved national fame for its cooperative housing development strategy.[76] Recently, that network has started to develop a business focused on obtaining public construction contracts.[77] This seems an excellent strategy, since the business is no doubt extremely competitive on metrics such as minority ownership and the provision of good work at good wages.

### Financing Schools and Transportation

Finally, cities should reverse the disinvestment in urban-core infrastructure in favor of suburban business parks by investing more heavily in schools, transportation, and other infrastructure in urban neighborhoods. Here, too, a great deal of excellent advocacy has begun to turn the tide back to inner-city investment. My purpose in mentioning this strategy is to point out its utility for urban collaborative business networks. Indeed, by developing infrastructure where these networks are located, cities can take proper consideration of the needs of those who are harmed by the gentrification that sometimes results from well-intentioned investments in urban neighborhoods.

## REFORMING FEDERAL LAWS

While state and local lawmakers can do a great deal to create a local regulatory environment that nurtures and supports collaborative business networks, there are

75 San Francisco, California, Administrative Code ch. 6, § 6.22.
76 *See* Medoff & Sklar, Streets of Hope.
77 Dudley Street Neighborhood Initiative, *Sustainable Economic Development, Dudley Workforce Collaborative*, DSNI.org, www.dsni.org/sustainable-economic-development/#DudleyWorkforce.

three domains in particular where federal law reform would make an enormous difference. First, it will be important to reform antitrust laws to create a well-defined space in which such networks can share information and other resources without risking antitrust violations. Second, in the domain of financing, such networks would benefit greatly from enhancements to the laws governing community development financial institutions and also from tax incentives targeting this business form. Finally, reform is necessary to create pathways for collaborative business networks to share the costs of health benefits for workers across the networks as a whole.

## *Promoting Sharing by Supporting the Intermediaries*

### Antitrust

Arguably the most critical area at the federal level is in the domain of antitrust and anticompetition laws, specifically the Sherman Antitrust Act, the Clayton Antitrust Act and the Federal Trade Commission Act.[78] Ironically, this is not necessarily because substantial reform is required, but rather because the potential fear of antitrust liability may well be limiting collaborative business networks more than it should.[79] If nothing else, the examples in this book demonstrate the clear value of sharing for the businesses and workers in collaborative business networks. Antitrust and anticompetition laws are the most direct inhibitors of sharing activity. Thus, the purpose of my analysis is to clarify for participants in such networks what current laws allow and how to maximize opportunities to share under such laws. I will also propose law reforms that can support more expansive sharing within collaborative business networks.

Chapter 7 outlined the broad range of things that the networks described in this book have shared. These include financing, vocational education, management expertise, information, risk, customers, back-office support, physical space, and labor. First, it is important to note that many of these things, including financing, education, back-office support, space, and labor, clearly fall outside the scope of antitrust laws and should not be of concern to collaborative business networks. But there are some kinds of information and risk sharing that antitrust laws police, and the sharing of access to customers and the perceived manipulation of market demand may also fall within the scope of such laws. The paradigmatic example of sharing that violates such laws is sharing about prices, and especially the standardization of pricing among competitors in a market, which such laws prohibit as price-fixing.[80]

78 Sherman Antitrust Act, 15 U.S.C. §§ 1–7 (2017); Clayton Antitrust Act, 15 U.S.C. §§ 12–27 (2017); Federal Trade Commission Act, 15 U.S.C. §§ 41–58 (2017).

79 Inara Scott, *Antitrust and Socially Responsible Collaboration: A Chilling Combination?*, 53 Am. Bus. L. J. 97, 126–128 (2016).

80 *See* Mark A. Lemley & Christopher R. Leslie, *A Categorical Analysis in Antitrust Jurisprudence*, 93 Iowa L. Rev. 1207, 1225 (2008).

Yet it is easy to envision situations where it would be useful for businesses and intermediaries in collaborative business networks to be able to share information about pricing. It would also be ideal for such networks to be able to share information related to joint research and development, marketing, and potential customers. Given the importance of market niches for such networks, it would no doubt be helpful if participating businesses could share information in order to develop subniches. Finally, it could be very helpful to workers if such businesses could standardize licensing and certification, partly in order to streamline the process of hiring or training skilled workers.

The US Supreme Court has developed complex rules to determine whether these kinds of sharing violate antitrust and anticompetition laws. These rules include two levels of analysis of agreements to share.[81] The first, as described by the Federal Trade Commission in its "Antitrust Guidelines for Collaborations Among Competitors," is a determination of "per se" illegality:

> Certain types of agreements are so likely to harm competition and to have no significant procompetitive benefit that they do not warrant the time and expense required for particularized inquiry into their effects ... Types of agreements that have been held per se illegal include agreements among competitors to fix prices or output, rig bids, or share or divide markets by allocating customers, suppliers, territories, or lines of commerce.[82]

It seems possible that something like an agreement among businesses in a collaborative business network to develop subniches could thus be deemed per se illegal. The second level of analysis, the so-called rule-of-reason analysis, is more flexible:

> The central question is whether the relevant agreement likely harms competition by increasing the ability or incentive profitably to raise price above or reduce output, quality, service, or innovation below what likely would prevail in the absence of the relevant agreement.[83]

Obviously, if a collaborative business network is scrutinized by the Federal Trade Commission or a court for antitrust violations, it will want to be scrutinized by a rule-of-reason analysis. But just as obviously, such a network will want to do what it can to avoid such scrutiny in the first instance.

Current antitrust law appears to provide two avenues for collaborative business networks to share more expansively without being deemed to engage in

[81] *See* Alan J. Meese, *In Praise of All or Nothing Dichotomous Categories: Why Antitrust Law Should Reject the Quick Look*, 104 GEO. L. J. 835, 842–852 (2016).

[82] FED. TRADE COMM'N & US DEP'T OF JUSTICE, ANTITRUST GUIDELINES FOR COLLABORATIONS AMONG COMPETITORS 3 (2000), www.ftc.gov/sites/default/files/documents/public_events/joint-venture-hearings-antitrust-guidelines-collaboration-among-competitors/ftcdojguidelines-2.pdf [hereinafter COLLABORATION GUIDELINES]. *See also* WILLIAM C. HOLMES & MELISSA MANGIARACINA, ANTITRUST LAW HANDBOOK § 2:22 (2016).

[83] COLLABORATION GUIDELINES at 4.

anticompetitive behavior. The first is for the networks to enter formally into a joint venture. As the Collaboration Guidelines describe, joint ventures may be formed for the purpose of "production, distribution, marketing, purchasing or R&D, and thereby benefit, or potentially benefit, consumers by expanding output, reducing price, or enhancing quality, service, or innovation."[84] A joint venture involves an "efficiency-enhancing" collaboration that combines "significant capital, technology, or other complementary assets to achieve procompetitive benefits that the participants could not achieve separately."[85] This is exactly what collaborative business networks do when they use intermediaries to share critical information and resources. And as the Collaboration Guidelines describe, joint venture arrangements for this purpose can be judged under the rule of reason for activities that would otherwise be held to be per se illegal.[86]

The second avenue for protecting sharing under current antitrust law is based on the maxim that a "single entity" cannot conspire to engage in anticompetitive behavior.[87] It takes at least two to conspire. One paradigmatic example of a single entity whose component parts can share a much broader range of information is a holding company that controls its subsidiaries.[88] The key question is the extent to which control rights are concentrated in the parent and, on the other hand, the extent to which the subsidiary companies compete with each other.[89]

These two avenues provide concrete steps that collaborative business networks can take to make evident that their sharing is indeed "procompetitive" sharing that deserves to be insulated from antitrust liability, and even scrutiny. One step is for intermediaries such as trade associations to enter into joint venture agreements with businesses in their networks to formally describe the forms of sharing that occur

84 *Id.* at 8. 85 *Id.* at 7. 86 *Id.* at 8.

87 *See* Copperweld Corp. v. Indep. Tube Corp., 467 U.S. 752, 792 n.25 (1984) (Stevens, J., dissenting) ("And a single firm cannot compete with itself," quoting L. Sullivan, Law of Antitrust § 114, 326–27 (1977)). *But see* Am. Needle, Inc. v. NFL, 560 US 183, 195 (2010) ("This inquiry is sometimes described as asking whether the alleged conspirators are a single entity. That is perhaps a misdescription ... The key is whether the alleged 'contract, combination ... or conspiracy' is concerted action."). *See also* Michael A. McCann, *American Needle v. NFL: An Opportunity to Reshape Sports Law*, 119 Yale L. J. 726, 728 (2010) ("[B]ecause a single entity cannot conspire with itself, it cannot violate section 1 of the Sherman Act.").

88 Herbert Hovenkamp & Christopher R. Leslie, *The Firm as Cartel Manager*, 64 Vand. L. Rev. 813, 853 (2011). ("The decisions in Copperweld and American Needle also indicate that the nature and direction of control matters. Where does control reside? Who exercises control over whom? Most importantly, are persons with separate ownership or business interests placed under control? For example, Copperweld held that the parent corporation completely controlled its wholly owned subsidiary, which had no separate business ... [T]heir agreements are generally immune from Section One liability.")

89 Dean V. Williamson, Econ. Analysis Grp., US Dep't of Justice, Organization, Control, and the Single Entity Defense in Antitrust 4 (2006), www.justice.gov/atr/organization-control-and-single-entity-defense-antitrust.

within the network.[90] The other step, which dovetails nicely with my proposals about business organizations, is for intermediaries such as nonprofit organizations and even banks to reorganize into a holding company structure to the extent permitted by law so that they act as a single entity for purposes of antitrust law. These two steps are useful for different types of intermediaries and networks.

Taking a step back, regardless of which of these steps intermediaries choose, it will be an important contribution for them to analyze with and for the participants in their networks why and how their sharing is procompetitive rather than anticompetitive. Antitrust laws and guidelines repeatedly warn that function is more important than form and that joint venture arrangements cannot be used as shams to shield anticompetitive behavior.[91] But it is evident that collaborative business networks engage in just the types of activities that court cases, especially about joint ventures, have permitted as both procompetitive and valuable because they open markets and bring products into them that would otherwise not be available.[92] Each of the networks described in this book does just that.

At the same time, it would of course be very valuable for collaborative business networks to be able to rely on guidelines that specifically recognize the kinds of activities in which these networks engage. Not surprisingly, the court cases about joint ventures involve such entities as the National Football League and the National Collegiate Athletic Association.[93] It is important also to educate policymakers involved in developing antitrust policy about the kinds of markets in which collaborative business networks with multiple bottom lines operate, and specifically about the value of bringing new products and services into those markets. Moreover, although courts have been very reluctant to create exceptions on grounds of consumer safety and similar policy arguments,[94] there are very strong arguments for creating safe harbors for collaborative business networks so that they can actively coordinate on standardizing wages and developing subniches, especially for the benefit of their typically low-income workers. These, then, are important areas for antitrust law reform. Much of the required reform is about issuing tailored guidelines rather than changing laws. But the more aggressive reform would involve

[90] Hebert Hovenkamp, The Antitrust Enterprise: Principle and Execution 137 (2005) (stating that trade associations "also engage in rule making and standard setting for their industries" and that "the great majority of trade associations' activities are procompetitive"). *See also* Joseph F. Brodley, *Joint Ventures and Antitrust Policy*, 95 Harv. L. Rev. 1521, 1527–1530 (1982).

[91] Hovenkamp & Leslie, *The Firm as Cartel Manager* at 849–852.

[92] Collaboration Guidelines at 6 ("The Agencies recognize that consumers may benefit from competitor collaborations in a variety of ways. For example, a competitor collaboration may enable participants to offer goods or services that are cheaper, more valuable to consumers, or brought to market faster than would be possible absent the collaboration.").

[93] *See* Nat'l Collegiate Athletic Ass'n v. Bd. of Regents of the Univ. of Oklahoma, 468 U.S. 85 (1984); Am. Needle, Inc. v. NFL, 560 U.S. 183 (2010). *See generally* Herbert Hovenkamp, *Exclusive Joint Ventures and Antitrust Policy*, 1995 Colum. Bus. L. Rev. 1, 52–61 (1995).

[94] *See, e.g.*, Julie Y. Park, *PHOS and the 1996 Federal Antitrust Enforcement Guidelines: Ensuring the Formation of Procompetitive Multiprovider Networks*, 91 Nw. U. L. Rev. 1684, 1726 (1997).

creating a broader space for sharing in such networks while insulating their participants from liability.

## *Obtaining Financing*

Turning now to the domain of financing, I have discussed the ongoing challenges for collaborative networks in obtaining private debt and equity financing, and their corresponding turn to funding sources typically reserved for nonprofits. I have also provided some new ideas for obtaining equity capital from both traditional and nontraditional sources. However, if we are to judge by our three case studies, then in terms of raw impact the best way to generate something more akin to "patient capital" for such networks is to promote the development of financing sources *within* those networks. In addition, judging from the South Shore example, the most robust form for such an in-network institution may well be a bank. Thus, I begin this section by discussing reform of banking law that would enable such development. I then discuss two other areas of reform that would support a broader range and mix of financing choices for collaborative business networks.

### Reforming CDFI Law

As I discussed in Chapter 7, one of the broad lessons to be learned from the South Shore network is the unique ability of a community bank to support the early development *as well as* the ongoing stability of a collaborative business network. Because of its own multiple bottom lines, ShoreBank worked as a collaborative partner alongside the rehabbing businesses in the network. It provided a steady stream of capital that was readily accessible without some of the usual constraints imposed by private banks. It grew clients over the course of decades. It tailored repayment terms to the rehabbing and residential rental industry, thereby making debt financing less risky overall. In the United States, a community bank of this sort may well be the ideal financing source for an urban collaborative business network. Of course, this story is also important in providing another lesson, because the Bank ultimately went out of business. In the end, it could have made an enormous difference for the Bank to have had the benefit of a more supportive regulatory framework.

I focus on six particular regulatory changes that could spur the development of community banks within collaborative business networks. None of these proposals is by any means new. As many others have noted, the banking system is deeply flawed by virtue of its failure to support inner-city and other low-income communities. It is thus not surprising that there are very few institutions like ShoreBank today, nor is it surprising that ShoreBank (world-renowned though it was) was forced to close. The proposals in this section are really just a reprise of the important calls that continue to this day in favor of banking reform to support more community-based banking.

The first proposal is for the Federal Deposit Insurance Corporation (FDIC) in particular to radically facilitate the ability to obtain charters for new community development banks. It is well known that the FDIC has been extremely tight-fisted in granting charters for de novo banks since the financial crisis.[95] This practice has been devastating for community banks, partly because of the simultaneous tightening of safety-and-soundness and other banking standards that have forced such banks to close or consolidate with larger banks.[96] While it may seem naïve to include this proposal in a section on pragmatic reforms, it is too important to leave off the table. It should be an imperative for the FDIC and other banking agencies to facilitate the development and ongoing health of small community banks, an imperative that Bob Solomon and others have recently and cogently discussed. Given the devastation of such banks over the last decade, this imperative includes the granting of new charters, and the removal of barriers from the process of granting such charters.[97]

My second proposal could go hand-in-hand with the first, but it could also be implemented independently: the FDIC and other bank regulators should tailor safety and soundness requirements for community banks in order to enable them to lend more expansively in urban-core neighborhoods. Moreover, regulators ought to allow such banks to use alternative measures to the traditional "5-Cs" that are used to determine the riskiness of a loan. The 5-Cs measure the borrower's ability and willingness to pay, availability of collateral, and the borrower's overall assets and circumstances.[98] While these measures may be appropriate to compensate for information asymmetries in traditional lending relationships, it is important for regulators to accept other measures that could serve as substitutes in a more collaborative context. Such measures at least should include consideration of the health of a collaborative network as a whole, investment by nonprofit and for-profit institutions, and cross-guaranties within the network.

Third, regulators (and in particular, the Federal Reserve Board) should revise the rules by which bank holding companies may make equity investments in community development projects. It is interesting that such equity investments are among

95 Arthur E. Wilmarth Jr., *A Two-Tiered System of Regulation is Needed to Preserve the Viability of Community Banks and Reduce the Risks of Megabanks*, 2015 Mich. St. L. Rev. 249, 341–342 (2015) ("Another pressing need is for the FDIC to liberalize its current policy governing approvals of applications by de novo community banks for deposit insurance. The FDIC has approved deposit insurance for only one de novo community bank since the end of 2010. In contrast, the FDIC approved an average of 159 de novo bank applications each year between 1984 and 2008.").

96 Bob Solomon, *The Fall (And Rise?) of Community Banking: The Continued Importance of Local Institutions*, 2 U.C. Irvine L. Rev. 945, 947 (2012) ("Not surprisingly, consolidation has a dramatic effect on the number of smaller banks. In 2009, a study by Celent, a research and consulting firm, reported that from 1992 to 2008, the number of US commercial banks with assets under $100 million went from over 8,000 to under 3,000. By 2010, the number of banks with assets under $100 million dropped to 2,625, a reduction of almost 75 percent.").

97 *Id.* at 946.

98 Fed. Reserve, *Banking Supervision*, www.federalreserveeducation.org/about-the-fed/structure-and-functions/banking-supervision.

the few exceptions to the limitations on banks in providing equity financing to businesses.[99] In this respect, banking regulators have already taken a step toward a different capitalist vision than the prevailing norm in the United States. Community development is one area in which US banks are permitted to behave more like their German and Japanese counterparts, which typically have long-term and large shareholdings in businesses.[100] The Federal Reserve Board has provided detailed guidance about the scope and nature of both equity and debt investments in community development that are permissible for banks and bank holding companies under its regulatory authority. Such investments may include the following:

> Bank [community development corporations (CDCs)] or investment programs may provide debt financing along with equity investments for community development projects … Examples of debt financing include direct loans to the CDC (in which the bank or bank holding company also has invested equity), the purchase of debt securities issued by the CDC or entity, issuance of lines of credit to the CDC, or participation in loans made by the CDC.[101]

While the guidance makes clear that bank holding companies have a great deal of flexibility in the forms of equity financing they can use, it appears that bank holding companies and their bank subsidiaries are still quite limited in their ability to provide direct debt financing of small businesses that also benefit from equity investments from the holding companies or their affiliates.

I would propose amending the Federal Reserve Board rules to allow community banks and bank holding companies to make direct equity *and* debt investments in collaborative business networks. Such investments could still be made through subsidiaries of a bank holding company as a means of protecting the bank from risk. Their primary purposes should be to allow banks to provide a mix of debt and equity financing in return for participation in corporate governance.[102] This would be another means of alleviating information asymmetries that currently concern banking regulators. It could, of course, be paired with alternative safety and soundness requirements. I would also propose allowing it only for certain qualifying business networks. In many respects, this was what ShoreBank ultimately was able to do by means just of debt financing. My hope in opening the door to a combination of direct debt and equity investments is to provide a more flexible strategy that could be applied in a range of other networks.

99 12 C.F.R. § 362.3(a)(2)(ii) (2017).

100 Peter O. Mülbert, *Banks' Equity Holdings in Non-Financial Firms and Corporate Governance: The Case of German Universal Banks, in* Comparative Corporate Governance–The State of the Art and Emerging Research 445 (Klaus J. Hopt et al. eds., 1997).

101 Federal Reserve Board, *Community Development Investments—A Guide to State Member Banks and Bank Holding Companies* (1996).

102 *See* Mark J. Roe, *Some Differences in Corporate Structure in Germany, Japan, and the United States,* 102 Yale L. J. 1927, 1928–1929 (1993).

Fourth, I wholeheartedly agree with Solomon's call for a federal tax exemption for community development banks. As he points out, credit unions already have such an exemption, and there is really no reason to treat community development banks any differently. They have a double bottom line that is mandated by federal rules. The charitable nature of their mission deserves recognition by means of tax rules as well.[103]

Fifth, Ron Grzywinski has suggested that high-performing community banks should be eligible to receive higher levels of deposit insurance coverage from the FDIC.[104] Such additional coverage would be a competitive advantage to attract depositors who wish to support local community development. This is just the kind of straightforward support that such development focused banks could receive from regulatory authorities such as the FDIC without incurring additional public costs.

Finally, as Chris Horsch conceptualized when he proposed the National Community Investment Fund,[105] I would urge the Federal Reserve Board and other regulatory authorities to create more space for large-scale, passive investments in community development banks by large banks and other institutional investors.

I should acknowledge here my faith in community development banks. These financial institutions are already creatures of a particular, community-focused regulatory framework. They must meet certain criteria to be chartered as community development banks (CDBs) and to have access to the Community Development Financial Institutions Loan Fund.[106] The basic notion of developing a regulatory framework that is tailored to community banks is a sound one. It is, in my opinion, more productive at this point than continuing to rely on the Community Reinvestment Act (CRA) to motivate investment by large banks in urban cores. Despite its potential when it was first enacted in 1977 and even when it was substantially amended in 1995, the CRA has not succeeded in generating enough investment by large banks in urban cores. Its enforcement mechanisms are still ineffective. At the same time, the framework supporting CDBs and community development financial institutions (CDFIs) more generally is far too constraining to actually facilitate the proliferation and long-term stability of CDFI banks in particular. By making even some of the changes discussed here, federal lawmakers could contribute significantly to the development of collaborative business networks and to financial investment in urban cores more generally. As rehabber Alice Lamos eloquently stated, "If these banks are not willing to ... invest in the community, these communities will never turn around."[107]

103 Solomon, *The Fall (and Rise?) of Community Banking* at 960, 983.
104 Telephone conversation with Ron Grzywinski (August 7, 2017).
105 Interview with Chris Horsch, ShoreBank Corporation (October 29, 2015).
106 12 U.S.C. § 4706 (2017). *See also* Solomon, *The Fall (And Rise?) of Community Banking* at 982.
107 Interview with Alice Lamos (May 19, 2017).

**Providing Tax Incentives**

I have discussed tax incentives throughout this chapter as a means of providing additional motivation for certain private entities to invest in sharing networks and urban cores more generally. The tax exemption for community development banks is one key example. In this section, I discuss two others.

In addition to providing an exemption for community banks, tax laws should also provide more protection directly to collaborative business networks. One strategy for doing so would be for the IRS to protect the particular form of holding company that I have proposed with a nonprofit parent of a number of for-profit subsidiaries. Currently, tax rules constrain such a model.[108] The most efficacious form of protection might be for the IRS to make clear in its definition of "unrelated business income" that business income earned by the for-profit subsidiaries in such networks is "substantially related" to the nonprofit parent's mission.[109] This would protect the parent from losing its nonprofit status while exerting mission-focused control of its subsidiaries.

A second form of tax incentive that would be useful to collaborative networks would be a direct incentive for sharing. Just as there are tax credits for green energy, small business health care, and other desirable social outcomes,[110] I propose a credit also for sharing ownership of business assets. Such a credit should only be available to qualified businesses, and many of the criteria that I have discussed in connection with zoning and permitting requirements could also be shaped for this purpose. An example would be to grant a tax credit to Southwest Key's café for sharing (by way of below-market leases) some of its heavy equipment or vehicles used for its catering business with other similarly situated small businesses. This type of tax benefit could also be useful for light manufacturing businesses that were colocated in the same facility. In such contexts, it would greatly benefit sharing networks by increasing their efficient use and management of business resources.

**Reforming Securities Laws**

A number of the reforms I have proposed would likely require some corresponding reform of federal and state securities laws. None of these would be significant, and I do not pretend to provide a comprehensive or detailed analysis of the required reforms here. But it may be useful to mention the two most obvious changes briefly. One clear

108 Lloyd Hitoshi Mayer & Joseph R. Ganahl, *Taxing Social Enterprise*, 66 Stan. L. Rev. 387, 427 (2014) ("Entrepreneurs and investors who accept the constraints imposed by hybrid statutes in order to ensure the continuity of their enterprises mission . . . are giving up legitimate profits by limiting the means they will use to pursue them to those that confer a public benefit."). *See also* Peter Molk, *Reforming Nonprofit Exemption Requirements*, 17 Fordham J. Corp. & Fin. L. 475–504, 513–531 (2012).

109 Internal Revenue Code §§ 511–513.

110 Internal Revenue Code §§ 25D, 30B, 30C, 30D, 40A, 45, 54 (2017) (green energy credits); Internal Revenue Code § 45R (2017) (small business health care credit). *See generally* Internal Revenue Code §§ 21–54 (2017) (containing tax credit sections of Internal Revenue Code).

area of reform would concern the effect of new crowdfunding regulations on pre-existing securities laws. In California, for example, it may be necessary to conform state securities laws with any new crowdfunding law that is passed. If crowdfunding laws are developed or amended at the federal level, similar changes may be necessary to federal securities laws. A second obvious area for securities reform may arise if regulators do indeed allow a greater level of equity investment by community development banks in the businesses within collaborative business networks.

More broadly, it would be useful over time to consider ways in which securities laws could support the development of patient capital in the way that they have in national coordinated economies. The idea here would be to create a clear space for the sharing of "insider" information, but only within – and for the purpose of supporting – qualified collaborative business networks that operate, for example, in underserved urban cores.[111] The ultimate purpose again would be to redirect greater resources for supporting the long-term employment and economic stability of workers within the network.

### *Providing Adequate Wages and Benefits*

Federal law also is enormously relevant to the critical domain of employment protections for workers. There are a number of categories of employment-related federal laws that are beyond the scope of this chapter, but that I want to acknowledge as highly relevant. One prominent example is the regulation of unions.[112] We have seen the value that the local chapter of the SEIU provided for the Bronx home care network. It would, of course, be very beneficial for unions to operate within a more supportive regulatory framework that would allow them to leverage more economic and political power on behalf of collaborative business networks. I should note, however, that such a claim is not universally shared by those I interviewed. The owners in the rehabbers network regularly commented on how much more difficult it would have been to complete their buildings if they had been forced to use unionized workers.

The two areas of employment-related law that I do wish to focus on relate to the minimum wage and to the challenge of providing health benefits. These are both issues that were consistently (indeed virtually universally) raised by interviewees in all three cases, especially those in the "worker" category of interviewees. Here again, the home care network is exemplary. We have seen the enormous difference it has made for workers in that network to have had health benefits. In addition, in the Bronx, both managers and employees commented on the benefits of the higher wages (and reimbursement rates) negotiated by the broader network of organizations advocating for the rights of home care workers.

[111] Hall & Soskice, *Introduction*, VARIETIES OF CAPITALISM at 23–24.

[112] *See, e.g.*, Benjamin I. Sachs, *Despite Preemption: Making Labor Law in Cities and States*, 124 HARV. L. REV. 1153 (2011).

**Minimum Wage**

On the topic of wages, my proposal is both obvious and thus far painfully unattainable. As I have done at the state level, I provide additional evidence from my research in support of a call for a higher federal minimum wage. I have detailed the benefits for the workers, which of course have been articulated by advocates in many other settings. But I have also provided evidence about the meaningful advantage for collaborative business networks competing in markets where price competition regularly results in unfair and unfavorable treatment of workers. The most obvious correction is to raise the minimum wage across the country.

**Health Benefits**

While the workers I interviewed universally commented on the importance of higher wages, they also commented almost universally on the value of health benefits. In the area of employment, these benefits are what truly distinguish the businesses I have studied from their competitors. Yet, even with their employee-focused missions and their best intentions, it is an immense struggle for these businesses to provide health benefits.[113] At the same time, especially after the recent Presidential election, it is very difficult to propose meaningful reforms in this area. There is simply too much uncertainty and confusion to be able to predict whether and to what extent federal law will continue to require employers to provide health benefits to their employees.

In the face of this uncertainty, however, there is at least one mechanism that has been consistently available under federal law and that is well worth exploring for use by collaborative business networks. It is the so-called Multiple Employers Welfare Arrangement (MEWA), whereby a group of employers collectively offers health insurance coverage to the employees in that group. At the federal level, MEWAs are governed by the Employee Retirement Income Security Act (ERISA).[114] MEWAs also appear to be governed to some extent by state-level laws, although I will focus here on the federal regulation.[115]

MEWAs have been described as one of the best (sometimes the only) options for small businesses to provide health insurance for their employees.[116] It should be

[113] This is another area in which unionization is useful, because the benefits provided to CHCA's employees are provided through 1199. Interview with Lamont Spence, Director of Workforce Development, Cooperative Home Care Associates (July 3, 2017).

[114] 29 U.S.C. § 1001 et seq. (2017).

[115] Emp. Benefits Sec. Admin., US Dep't of Labor, MEWAs Multiple Employer Welfare Arrangements under the Employee Retirement Income Security Act (ERISA): A Guide to Federal and State Regulation 17–27 (2013), www.dol.gov/sites/default/files/ebsa/about-ebsa/our-activities/enforcement/healthcare-fraud/mewa-under-erisa-a-guide-to-federal-and-state-regulation.pdf [hereinafter "MEWA Guide"]. Compare MDPhysicians & Assoc. v. Texas Bd. of Ins., 957 F.2d 178, 181 (5th Cir. 1992) *with* Atlantic HealthCare Benefits Trust v. Googins, 2 F.3d 1, 5 (2d Cir. 1993). *See also* Steven Stadtmauer, *Self-Insured MEWAs: Are the Risks Worth the Reward?*, 7 Quinnipiac Health L.J. 263, 266 (2004).

[116] MEWA Guide at 3.

noted that even the federal Patient Affordable Care Act has applied only to businesses with more than 50 employees,[117] and thus only the businesses in the home care network would be required to provide health coverage under that statute. But as I have described, the management in all three networks have discussed the desirability of providing health care coverage to their employees and that is my reason for exploring the MEWA option here.

One of the classic ways to form a MEWA, and the one that is probably most useful for collaborative business networks, is for a trade association to provide coverage to employees of member businesses through a group health plan.[118] An important threshold requirement in such circumstances is that the association not be formed solely for the purpose of providing health coverage. This requirement appears to be policed in part by checking the length of the association's existence prior to the point when it begins to provide health coverage.[119] This is something for collaborative business networks to have in mind. However, it is also apparent that trade associations can and do serve multiple purposes for such networks, and thus this should typically be an easy requirement to meet.

The provision of health coverage will subject such associations and/or their member businesses to regulation under ERISA and possibly also state laws.[120] This is an important area in which intermediaries in collaborative business networks can be helpful. By educating member businesses about the disclosure and other requirements imposed by ERISA, such intermediaries can not only bear (and share) the costs of providing health benefits, but they can also bear the costs of developing the knowledge necessary to comply with applicable laws.

While it is virtually impossible to propose law reforms that would make it easier for collaborative business networks to use the device of a MEWA, it should also be apparent what such reforms could eventually address. For example, it would be ideal for ERISA to be amended to reduce costs of disclosure and other compliance for qualifying collaborative business networks (again, those that operate in underserved urban cores). It would also be ideal to ease the requirements for forming a legitimate MEWA, including the threshold requirement that associations be formed for purposes other than the provision of health coverage.

In theorizing the concept of "real utopias," Erik Olin Wright states that such communities should be

> grounded in the real potentials of humanity, utopian destinations that have pragmatically accessible way stations, utopian designs of institutions that can inform our

[117] 42 U.S.C. § 18024 (2017). [118] MEWA Guide at 7-9. [119] *Id.* [120] MEWA Guide at 17.

> practical tasks of muddling through in a world of imperfect conditions for social change.[121]

In providing law reforms and design principles that support collaborative business networks in American cities, my goal is to support the flourishing of these real utopias, institutions that have the potential to produce economic stability and growth for those involved.

[121] Eric Olin Wright, *Preface, in* Deepening Democracy: Institutional Innovations in Empowered Participatory Governance (Archon Fung & Eric Olin Wright eds., 2003).

# Appendix

## RESEARCH METHODS AND DATA ANALYSIS

This book was inspired by the many conversations I had with students in my course on community economic development at Northeastern University School of Law. Year after year, I shared the students' dismay at the apparent difficulty of solving the puzzle of urban-core development. Why is poverty and underdevelopment in the urban core such an intransigent problem? Are there examples of efforts that have really worked, over the course of decades, in providing sustainable livelihoods for urban-core residents? And what can the law do about any of this? These were the perennial questions that my students and I pondered. While I could point to diagnoses of the problem and examples of success, I felt that the available literature did not provide fully satisfactory answers, especially on the law question.

At the same time, I began to develop a hypothesis that one answer to the question about what has worked involved the extent of collaboration among businesses in some urban cores. In my many conversations with individuals in the private and public sectors who have worked in urban cores, I kept hearing about business being done differently and about networks developing in ways that seemed somehow different from the norm outside those pockets of urban activity.

My hypothesis was partly grounded in theory. As a student of international and comparative law and economic development, I had long been familiar with the theory of "varieties of capitalism" propounded by Hall and Soskice. In my work as an American business lawyer and teacher, I had experienced many examples of the "liberal market economy" norms and rules that Hall and Soskice describe as prevailing in the United States. But when I looked at how business was done in certain urban cores, I felt that I was witnessing networking and business behavior that looked more like the "coordinated economies" that Hall and Soskice describe as prevailing in other parts of the world. Somehow, it seemed more apt to describe some of the urban business networks that my students and I studied as practicing a coordinated form of capitalism rather than fitting the liberal market form that US norms and rules support.

This, then, was my beginning hypothesis. I developed some of the theoretical framework for the hypothesis in two articles. In "Developing Capabilities, Not Entrepreneurs: A New Theory for Community Economic Development," a 2013 article I coauthored with James Rowan, I delved into the question of how successful urban core development ought to be defined and measured.[1] In a 2015 article titled "Regulating Sharing: The Sharing Economy as an Alternative Capitalist System," I explored "sharing economy" networks as examples of coordinated capitalism.[2]

But I required a great deal more information than was available in the literature about whether this hypothesis contained a grain of truth. And I certainly required more information about how, if at all, coordinated capitalism works in the urban core. I concluded that obtaining this information required me to talk directly to those engaged in this different style of doing business. This was the basis for my choosing a qualitative research methodology for my book. What I learned is that some businesses do engage in more coordination and collaboration than the liberal market norm. But I also learned that such collaboration is distinct from the coordinated economies described in the varieties of capitalism literature. I coin this distinct style "collaborative capitalism."

## RESEARCH DESIGN

The purpose of this study is to explore the emergent concept of collaborative capitalism as it is practiced by networks of private businesses in American urban cores. My research focuses particularly on the mechanisms, strategies, and motivations for sharing in this specific context, as well as on the ways in which sharing contributes to business success and economic stability for both the businesses and their employees. In addition, this research examines whether and how the legal framework has hindered or helped sharing in each of these cases.

Because collaborative capitalism is an emergent concept in the literature on American cities, I found a case study methodology, relying on semistructured interviews as a primary data source, to be the most efficacious approach for exploring this concept. While there is an extensive literature on American urban studies, and also on American urban economic development, much of that literature relies on a rigid set of assumptions about the nature of American capitalist behavior. These assumptions appear even more deeply embedded when they are about the connection between capitalist behavior and law. For example, poverty alleviation efforts attempt to make use of, rather than question or disrupt, property ownership regimes and employment laws. Small business development programs dutifully follow and emulate anticompetition and corporations laws and values. The examples are endless. Neither the scholarship on American urban cores nor the policy initiatives in

[1] Rashmi Dyal-Chand & James V. Rowan, *Developing Capabilities, Not Entrepreneurs: A New Theory for Community Economic Development*, 42 Hofstra L. Rev. 839 (2013). A portion of my discussion in Chapter 3 was originally published in this article.

[2] Rashmi Dyal-Chand, *Regulating Sharing: The Sharing Economy as an Alternative Capitalist System*, 90 Tul. L. Rev. 241 (2015). Portions of my discussion in Chapter 8 were originally published in 90 Tul. L. Rev. 241 (2015).

this area provide a vocabulary for defining different capitalist practices in the urban cores. Thus, to understand the defining features of collaborative capitalism, it has been necessary to hear directly from its practitioners – those who are doing business in the urban cores. Moreover, while an ethnographic or phenomenological approach could well have yielded some of the information critical to this examination, I concluded that a comparison of several ideal or "pioneer" cases could best yield information about the features of this alternative form of capitalist behavior as it is actually practiced in a range of contexts. I also found the semistructured interview particularly efficacious because it imposes fewer preconceptions than a survey or more formally structured interview guide may impose.[3] In short, mine is truly an exploratory methodology that develops a basic and empirically grounded definition of collaborative capitalism from deep examination of three case studies. My chief aim is to identify the core features of collaborative capitalism. I hope that future researchers will build on this exploration by using quantitative methods to address critical questions of scale, generalizability, origins, and impact.

Because my focus from the start has been on the role of intermediary institutions and organizations in collaborative business networks, I sought ideal or pioneer cases which 1) involved a range of different kinds of intermediaries, and 2) were successful in producing economic stability over a long period of time. I also sought cases in which the legal frameworks appeared to impact the networks' success differently or for different reasons.

However, I initially began with the idea of examining five to six cases. I sought this number because I originally intended to examine two examples in each main category of intermediary institution that I selected, namely worker-owned cooperatives, community financial institutions, and social enterprise networks. After conducting interviews at four different sites, however, I concluded that there are too many differences among networks within each of these major categories to allow literal replication at this early stage of exploration.

In addition, by the end of my first round of interviews, I discovered that the intermediaries in each of these categories serve quite distinctive functions. They all facilitate the sharing of training and vocational education, for example, but they do so in very different ways and they also hinder network function and success in different ways. The interplay between specific strategies for sharing and the overall resilience, growth, stability, and values of a particular network are deeply connected. The distinctive roles of the intermediaries in each of these categories appears to relate much more specifically to my core theory about business collaboration than I had anticipated. As a result of these discoveries, I added a subset of research questions about the intermediaries. While my overarching inquiry remained focused on identifying the core features of collaborative capitalism, this new subset

[3] *See* Svend Brinkmann & Steinar Kvale, InterViews: Learning the Craft of Qualitative Research Interviewing (3d ed. 2015); Michael Patton, Qualitative Research (2005).

of research questions delves into the differences among intermediaries in supporting or hindering sharing.

Within each case, I sought interviews in several categories. I selected interviewees in each of the major intermediary organizations. In addition, in the home care and Austin networks, I selected interviewees in the largest businesses involved in the networks (defined by number of employees). In the case of the South Shore network, given the large number of businesses that had participated in the network and the failure of many of those businesses after the Bank closed, I used a snowball sampling technique to find business owners whose businesses still existed.

Within each intermediary, I selected interviewees who were members of the management or leadership teams, both for the entire organization and for the key departments involved in facilitating sharing within the network. My purpose in interviewing these individuals was primarily to learn about the network as a whole, the sharing that occurs within it, and the effect of the intermediary in supporting or hindering such sharing. Within each individual business, I selected interviewees who were members of the management or leadership teams, and I also selected interviewees who were in the category of "workers." I defined these categories using job titles. In the ShoreBank case, I interviewed the owners of individual businesses, who were also typically the top managers of the businesses. I used both referrals from managers who had worked for the main intermediary (ShoreBank) as well as the literature on the Bank to find some of these owners. I then used a snowball sampling technique, namely referrals from that initial group of owners, to find and interview other owners. In the management category, I interviewed the top leaders (CEOs or presidents) of each of the businesses I selected. My purpose in interviewing managers and owners of these businesses was to learn about the business and its relationship to the whole network, to understand how (if at all) it engages in collaborative behavior and with whom, and to learn how it defines its own success and that of its employees. My purpose in interviewing individuals in the worker category was primarily to learn about their individual trajectories, including as employees of the chosen businesses, and secondarily to learn about their perspectives on sharing within the network. In the worker category, I relied on members of the management to identify workers.[4]

[4] In some categories of interviewees, I did not interview comprehensively. I interviewed only a small subset of the total number of "workers" in businesses within each network, and in the case of the South Shore network I only interviewed a small subset of business owners. Particularly because I used a snowball sampling technique to select workers to interview, my findings about the workers' changes in economic and social status may not be generalizable. This remains true even though I sought to confirm these findings using both interviews with management and secondary sources. On questions of business and network structure, management, and overall function, however, I was able to obtain more comprehensive coverage. When interviewing members of the management in intermediary organizations, I extensively interviewed those who worked in the departments responsible for the particular forms of resource sharing within the collaborative business networks I studied. I did the same for members of the management teams in individual businesses heavily involved in sharing resources.

In the home care and Austin cases (with one exception), everyone that I asked agreed to be interviewed. In the South Shore case, the rate of positive responses was also very high. But a number of managers of ShoreBank and its parent holding company declined to be interviewed, as did a number of the rehabber-owners. From the literature about the Bank and my conversations with those involved in the network, I have concluded that at least some of the individuals who declined interviews were reluctant to share their experiences around the time of the Great Recession in 2008 and the Bank's closing in 2010. This gap in the data may have biased my findings because these interviewees may have been able to provide more information about how ShoreBank's work as an intermediary hindered the success of their businesses and the network as a whole. Given the unique nature of the Great Recession and the circumstances of the Bank's closing, however, I believe that this is a minor limitation. In addition, I sought interviews with several Dunkin' Donuts franchisee owners who had borrowed from the Bank, who either declined to be interviewed or did not respond to my requests. In these cases, I believe that the individuals declined because they were bound by a confidentiality agreement with the franchisor. Because this network is not my primary focus, I do not believe my findings are weakened by the absence of interviews in this category.

Between the spring of 2015 and the summer of 2017, I completed a total of 55 interviews, each lasting between 30 and 120 minutes. For the home care case, I interviewed 23 individuals and for the South Shore case, I interviewed 25 individuals. For the Austin case, I interviewed seven individuals. The following table provides more details about the numbers of individuals I interviewed in each category of intermediary and business, and of management, worker and owner. The interviews were audiotaped, transcribed, and not confidential. In all but four instances (when I made use of a translator), I conducted the interviews entirely in English. In all but two instances, I interviewed each person individually. In two instances, I interviewed two people together. I conducted the majority of the interviews in person, typically at the offices of the business where they were employed. I conducted the remaining interviews by telephone. Prior to beginning the interviewing process, I received approval to conduct "human subject" research from my university's Institutional Review Board, which required each interviewee to sign a two-page consent form. Although (with a few exceptions) I did not offer confidentiality to interviewees, I did offer them the opportunity to review and correct the written transcripts of their interviews. In the few situations in which I offered confidentiality, my offer was declined.

I used interview guides that I developed in advance for the purpose of covering the same issues across all three cases while also stimulating open-ended and detailed conversations about those issues. In addition, I conducted my interviews in several rounds. After each round, I revised my interview guides to include questions that were inspired by answers and information I obtained in the previous rounds of interviews. While the interview guides covered the same basic issues, I used two

TABLE 2 *Personal Interviews*

| Interviewee Type | Number |
|---|---|
| Home Care Case | |
| Intermediaries | 4 |
| Individual Business Managers | 10 |
| Individual Business Workers | 9 |
| Total | 23 |
| South Shore Case | |
| Intermediaries | 14 |
| Individual Business Owners/Managers | 10 |
| Individual Business Workers | 1 |
| Total | 25 |
| Austin Case | |
| Intermediaries | 3 |
| Individual Business Managers | 2 |
| Individual Business Workers | 2 |
| Total | 7 |

guides, one for management and one for workers. The guide for management included detailed questions about the structure, management, finances, and business strategies of the particular intermediaries and businesses under discussion. The interview guide for workers included questions about those same topics, though in less detail. It also included more detailed questions about the interviewees' individual economic and social "status" or development, and the effect on their lives of working for the particular businesses. While the interviews generally covered the topics in the guides, I regularly used the flow of the conversation to ask follow-up questions to particular statements.

The interviews of members of management had five main segments:

- Questions about how the interviewee came to the business and what positions she or he held.
- Questions about the business's origin and about the role of any intermediaries in supporting the start-up of the business, including:
  - What were the initial business goals and did those goals change along the way?
  - What if any factors were critical in the start-up process?
- Questions about the business's current operations, including:
  - How did the business find a market for its product or services?
  - How did the business develop a niche?

  - Who are the business's major market competitors?
  - What is the business's form of legal organization?
  - What are the business's sources of financing?
  - What are the demographics of the workforce? Where do they live, and what are their backgrounds?
- Questions about interactions, including sharing, among businesses and intermediaries in the network:
  - In what ways does the business collaborate with other businesses?
  - What does the business share?
  - In what "spheres" of business behavior does the business share resources?
- Questions about laws or rules that the interviewee perceives as impacting her work or the business more generally.

Finally, in a number of my interviews for the South Shore case as well as my interviews relating to the closure of Cooperative Home Care of Boston, I asked interviewees to reflect on the reasons why the businesses ultimately closed.

The interviews of individuals in the worker category had five main segments:

- Questions about the interviewee's connection with the business that employed her or him, including:
  - How did the individual first learn of the business?
  - When did she or he become an employee of the business?
  - What positions did she or he hold in the business?
  - What training did the individual receive before starting in the position?
  - What did the interviewee like and dislike about the job?
  - Did she or he feel that she did the job well, and what did she need to do the job better?
- Questions about the interviewee's economic and social status and trajectory before and since becoming employed by the business, including:
  - What was the individual's background and what work had she or he done before joining the business?
  - How had this job helped or hurt the individual, in terms of income, job stability, education, health, and any other factors that the interviewee felt were relevant?
- Questions about the business's mission, current operations, and employees, including:
  - What are the demographics of the workforce? Where do they live, and what are their backgrounds?
  - How is this business similar to or different from other businesses like it in the city?
  - Did the interviewee perceive this business to be successful and what did she or he think the business needed to be more successful?

- What did the interviewee believe to be the business's priorities?
- Questions about interactions, including sharing, among businesses and intermediaries in the network:
  - What other businesses or organizations did the interviewee perceive to be part of the network?
  - Did the interviewee have experience or contact with other businesses in the network?
  - What were the interviewee's perceptions of how the interaction among the businesses in the network helps or hurts the interviewee's business?
- Questions about laws or rules that the interviewee perceives as impacting her work or the business more generally.

When I conducted interviews of management in intermediary organizations, I also asked a special set of questions about the intermediary's particular role or expertise in supporting the businesses in the network. These questions were the most tailored to particular cases, and they became more so in later rounds of interviews.

In addition to semistructured interviews, I used several other sources of data. First, especially for my home care and South Shore cases, I relied heavily on secondary sources, including reports by nonprofit organizations and governmental agencies, academic articles, and news reports and articles. The leadership within the home care network has been passionate in ensuring transparency of information about its development, partly by producing many publications and case histories of CHCA and the other worker-owned cooperatives in the network. I found those reports to be very helpful. For the South Shore and home care cases, I also reviewed internal documents, especially about the finances and governance structures of the intermediaries and some of the businesses within the networks, which the management in both networks was very generous in sharing. Wherever possible, I turned to the secondary literature and internal documents to verify information provided in interviews, but it was not always possible to do so.

Second, for all three cases, I engaged in very limited participant observation. In the case of the home care networks, I visited the offices of CHCA, HCA, and ICS, and I sat in on a brief portion of a training for home care workers at HCA. In the case of the South Shore network, I attended a monthly meeting of the South Side Builders' Association, which includes a number of rehabbers who borrowed from ShoreBank and remain in business still today. Finally, in the Austin case, I visited the headquarters of Southwest Key, and I spent several hours in the Café del Sol. My time spent observing in these locations was very limited, as was my purpose. In the home care case, my purpose was to verify descriptions of the training program. In the Austin case, my purpose was to observe the connection between the café and Southwest Key's headquarters. In the South Shore case, my observation served to verify the descriptions in interviews of one of the major trade associations that continue to operate in South Shore. In addition to the interviews I did of individuals involved in the three collaborative business networks featured in this book, I did five semi-structured interviews that informed the analysis in this book. These interviews provided me with very helpful background information that informs my theory of collaborative capitalism.

Finally, as I have described, one of my key variables for analysis is the legal context for each of my three cases. Thus, I did original legal research about the applicable and relevant law in each of the jurisdictions where my three cases are located. I conducted much of this research using electronic databases, primarily Westlaw. I also used treatises and other specialized materials to explore the relevant law.

## DATA ANALYSIS

I analyzed each interview transcript using the techniques both of coding by hand on a line-by-line basis (on hard copies of transcripts) and by means of qualitative software. I began by generating a list of codes using a combination of the literature on coordinated market economies, a close reading of several transcripts from each case, my research questions, and my hypotheses about collaborative capitalism in American urban cores. I added to my code list after each of my first two rounds of interviews and recoded transcripts after doing so. Especially after my first round of interviews, my coding changed significantly because of the addition of a second subset of research questions about the differing roles of intermediaries in each network. Finally, I asked a graduate student research assistant to code several interviews for each case, adding any codes that she or he thought were important.

Both my coding and my writing process were iterative. After initially coding all the interviews for a particular case, I developed a much more detailed analytical framework for the forms, strategies and mechanisms for sharing in each of my three cases. This picture clarified gaps in my selection of interviewees, in my code list, and of course in my reporting. I used subsequent rounds of interviews followed by recoding and supplemental writing, as opportunities to fill those gaps.

The iterative nature of this process was particularly important in several respects. First, it significantly changed my theoretical conceptualization of collaborative capitalism by revealing the importance to each of these networks of a market niche. This became one of my six core features of collaborative capitalism. Second, it led to the development of a subset of research questions about how the differences among intermediaries support and hinder the networks in which they operate. And third, in each case the initial round of interviews led me to develop rival hypotheses for the successes and failures within the network. This, in turn, led me to develop and explore counterfactuals within each case.

Every one of the individuals that I interviewed spoke richly and perceptively about the topic of this book. In the chapters featuring my three cases, I quote extensively from the interviews, and I do so with very little editing of the quotations. At the same time, it is only appropriate for me to note that the stories that I tell in these chapters are coproduced. With my choice and organization of topics covered, my follow-up questions, and even my non-verbal expressions of interest and other cues, I undoubtedly affected the way stories were told. Through my process of sorting and prioritizing, and my subsequent choices of interviews, I added more layers of interpretation. And it may be the case that my position as a law professor affected the answers interviewees gave.

## LIMITATIONS OF THIS STUDY

My purpose in this study has been to use qualitative data to understand the emergent concept of collaborative capitalism in the context of American urban cores. By means of a close study of several ideal cases, my effort has been to develop a theoretical understanding of this concept and of its core features. Consequently, my findings will not provide answers to questions about the scope or scale of the practice of collaborative capitalism in American cities. I hope and expect that future qualitative and quantitative research will build on the framing I have done in this study.

There are many collaborative networks that appear to exist in a broad range of sectors from the industrial to the service professions, from skilled labor to unskilled, and covering a great deal of variation in each of these categories. In order to analyze the extent to which certain features of collaborative capitalism were core to the concept, I chose cases in a range of quite different industrial sectors. This was particularly important for my examination of the importance of a niche. The range of sectors covered in this study suggests that collaborative capitalism can indeed be practiced in a broad range of markets. But it will be critical for future researchers to consider whether my observations about niches remain valid in sectors where work has been outsourced to other countries or heavily mechanized. More generally, it will be important to research whether it is more or less possible to engage in collaborative capitalism in certain business sectors.

Relatedly, collaborative business networks appear to exist in a broad range of urban and rural settings. The geographical diversity of my cases suggests this, though the cases do not account for the full geographic diversity of the United States. While my research focuses on collaborative networks in urban cores, I have encountered many examples of collaborative networks that appear to be flourishing in rural areas. For example, when researching the South Shore network, I learned of a network that ShoreBank supported in Arkansas that involved egg production and appeared to have many of the features of collaborative capitalism. At the same time, I would expect some of the core features of rural collaborative capitalism to be different. It seems quite possible, for example, that rural networks would have very different missions from those I identified in my three cases; indeed, multiple bottom lines may not be a core feature of rural collaborative capitalism. I hope rural networks will be the subject of future empirical research.

Finally, because the Austin network is so much smaller than the other two networks I studied, I was able to interview significantly fewer individuals involved in the network. On the one hand, this sample represented a greater overall percentage of individuals in the network compared to the other two cases, and I did conclude that I achieved saturation in the Austin interviews. On the other, I did not have the same raw numbers in this case study. In the worker category, four of my Austin interviews had the additional limitation of being simultaneously translated, because four of the workers I interviewed spoke Spanish (which I do not speak). While the translators I used clearly worked hard to translate as exactly as possible, it is quite possible that they added their own layer of interpretation to the discussion. Moreover, it was more difficult to achieve a seamless conversational flow in the translated interviews.

# Index


5-Cs alternatives, 258

achievement, 52
African American borrowers, 84, 88, 96–97, 99, 108, 111–112
Airbnb
  overview, 189–190
  consumer safety, 194–195
  intermediaries, 192–193
  participation, 201
  regulations, 206
  relationships, 200
  risk, 200–201
Albany, New York, poverty rates, 2
Alfaro, Alma, 148, 149–150, 151, 152
antitrust and anti-competition laws, 253–257
"Antitrust Guidelines for Collaborations Among Competitors," 254
antitrust violations, 128, 195–196
Austin Initiative, 111–112

B Corporation certification, 30, 46
back-office support, collaborative capitalism, 171
Bank Holding Company Act amendments, 79, 102
Banks, Keith, 93–94, 96
Barth, James, 55
benefits, 40–41, 179–180, 248–251, 262–264
Benkler, Yochai, 191
Bennett, Michael, 80–81
bidding process, 45, 231, 252. *See also* competition
bottom lines
  ShoreBank, 106, 115
  Southwest Key Programs, 156
  urban core development, 66–67
  "varieties of capitalism" theory, 213–215
  and worker protections, 201–202
Bringley, Jim, 88–89, 96–97
Bronx, context, 18–19
Broughton, Dan, 104, 108–109
building codes, 106–107
business activities, coordination of, 61–66, 113, 155, 197–198. *See also* sharing and sharing economy
business entities, 128, 229–230
business incubators, 60
business organizations law, 229–234
business plans, 126–127
businesses, freedom of, 123
"buy local" campaigns, 241–242

California Worker Cooperative Act, 246
Calvo, Clara, 28, 42
Camden, New Jersey, unemployment rates, 2
Cannon, Terrell, 42
capitalism. *See also* collaborative capitalism
  collaborative, 60–61
  coordinated, 61
  defined, 5–6
  liberal, 61, 70
  mature economies, 69–71
  "varieties of capitalism" theory, 8, 11–13, 70, 129, 215, 223
careers. *See jobs*
Carolina Textile District (CTD), 131
Carroll, Recanell, 41–42
Castillo, Henry, 139, 144, 147–148
Castro, Oralia, 136, 155
Chicago, Illinois, poverty rates, 2
City First Bank, 230
City Lands Corporation, 90
Clayton Antitrust Act, 253
Clinton, Bill, 76
Coase, Ronald, 63
Colaizzi, Maryann, 47–49

collaboration
  forms of, 160, 218
  long-term benefits, 60–61
  regulations to support, 222–224
collaborative capitalism. *See also* capitalism
  in Austin, 154
  back-office support, 171
  customer base, 170–171
  design principles, 178–183
  economic stability for workers, 175–180
  financing, 160–163
  information sharing, 167–169
  intermediaries, 172–175
  labor sharing, 172
  management expertise, 166–167
  market niches, 68–69
  physical space, 171
  risk, 169–170
  sharing, 159–160
  in South Shore, 112–113
  training programs, 163–166
  vocational education, 163–166
communities, dispersed, 202–203
community benefits agreements, 122
Community Development Banking and Financial Institutions Act, 76, 103
community development corporations (CDCs), 259
community development financial institutions (CDFIs), 75, 257–260. *See also* ShoreBank
Community Development Financial Institutions Loan Fund, 260
Community Initiatives, Inc., 95
Community Investment Corporation (CIC), 95, 99, 114
community investors, 246
Community Reinvestment Act (CRA), 103, 110, 127, 260
Community Service Society, 20
competition, 60, 192, 217, 222. *See also* bidding process; market niches
connections, personal, 89
consumer advocacy, 33, 193–195
contracting, business, 128–129, 219–220, 252
Cooperative Home Care Associates (CHCA)
  overview, 7, 17
  current status, 27–34
  market development, 21–25
  origins of, 20
  unionization of, 32–33
Cooperative Home Care of Boston (CHCB), 47–49
cooperative law, 231–234
coordinated economies, 208–222
corporate governance law, 221
costs, lowering, 66, 114–115, 156, 198, 212–213
Crane, Jack, 99
credentials, 239–240
Crouch, Colin, 223–224
crowdsourcing, 45, 245–247. *See also* sharing and sharing economy
customer base, collaborative capitalism, 170–171
Cutler, Irving, 77

Davis, Milton, 75, 81
Dawson, Steven, 30–31, 45, 131
decision-making, participation in, 37–39
deliberation, 215
design principles, collaborative capitalism, 178–179
Detroit, Michigan, unemployment rates, 2
"Developing Capabilities, Not Entrepreneurs: A New Theory for Community Economic Development," 266–267
double bottom lines. *See bottom lines*
Dressler, Jerilyn, 27, 39, 41
Dubal, Veena, 206
Dudley Square Neighborhood Initiative (DNSI), 244, 252
Dunkin' Donuts franchises, 69, 108–111

eBay, 190–191
economic stability, 58, 175–178, 179–183, 202
economies, coordinated, 214–215, 222–224
Elsas, Michael, 31
eminent domain, 243–244
Employee Retirement Income Security Act (ERISA), 263, 264
employment, 2, 48, 202–203. *See also* jobs
employment law, 121–122, 196, 262–264. *See also* minimum wage
Enrich, Peter, 120
Enterprise Community Partners, 230
entrepreneurship, 52, 68, 112, 124–131. *See also* small businesses
equality, 58, 216
equity capital, 45, 127–128, 245
Estela, Regina, 31
Euclidian zoning, 120–121. *See also* zoning laws
European Union, rise of, 70
Evangelista, Silvia, 149
Evergreen Cooperatives, 230, 231
Extended Care Career Ladder Initiative, 49

Fannie Mae, 105
Federal Deposit Insurance Corporation (FDIC), 258, 260
Federal Housing Finance Agency, 105

federal laws, 252–264. *See also* regulations
Federal Reserve Board, 258–259
Federal Trade Commission, 253
Feldman, Eiran, 94, 97–98, 237
"Fight for 15" campaign, 249
financing
  5-Cs alternatives, 258
  collaborative capitalism, 160–163
  community investors, 246
  crowdsourcing, 45, 245–247
  equity capital, 45, 127–128, 245
  grants, 146, 155, 160–161
  ideal legal structures, 231–232
  for infrastructure, 252
  intermediaries, 92–95, 146–148, 160–163
  local, 67–68, 115–116, 156–157, 181, 215
  obtaining, 244–248, 257–262
  peer-to-peer lending networks, 191
  private capital, 247
  sharing economy, 196–197
  small businesses, 126
  venture capital financing, 127–128, 247–248
firms, theory of, 63
Fletcher, Jim, 75, 80–81
franchises
  Dunkin' Donuts franchises, 69, 108–111
  McDonald's franchises, 108
  regulations, 232–233
  and sharing, 64
  ShoreBank, 108–111
Frazier, George, 93, 98, 99, 102
Freddie Mac, 105

Gallegos, Sonia
  on achievement, 150
  employment of, 140, 148
  support of, 155
  on training programs, 148–149, 150
gentrification, overview, 3
Germany
  patient capital, 210
Glaeser, Edward, 225
globalization, and industry, 4
grants, 146, 155, 160–161
growth, continuing, 182–183
Grzywinski, Ronald
  on achievement, 87, 117
  on financing, 116
  on market development, 81–82
  on market failure, 101
  origins of ShoreBank, 75, 77, 79–80
  on urban core development, 83–84
  on vocational education, 88–89
Guerrero, Artenio, 150–151

Haedicke, Michael, 182
Hall, Peter. *See also* "varieties of capitalism" theory
  on capitalism, 70
  on deliberation, 215
  on employment law, 121
  on Germany, 213
  on regulations, 218–219
  on relational contracting, 219
health benefits, 263–264
Hellwig, Gordon, 83, 116
hiring. *See jobs*
holding company model, 230–231
Home Care Associates (HCA), 7, 17, 25–27, 33–34
Home Care Worker Parity Act (NY), 29, 43
home health care, business of, 35
horizontal networks of resources, 63
Horsch, Chris, 105, 106, 260
Houghton, Mary, 75, 85, 86, 87
Hoyles, Len, 89, 96, 98, 100, 102

Independence Care System (ICS)
  overview, 17
  and Cooperative Home Care Associates (CHCA), 7
  effect of, 24–25, 64
  nonprofit status, 30–31, 234
Indiegogo, 191. *See also* crowdsourcing
industry, and globalization, 4
industry clusters, 60
inequality, 58, 216
information sharing, collaborative capitalism, 167–169
infrastructure, 251, 252
Initiative for a Competitive Inner City (ICIC), 53
"Inner City 100" program, 53
inner-city, market failure, 51–55
intermediaries
  collaborative capitalism, 172–175
  contributions made by, 35–37
  financing function, 92–95, 146–148
  institutional, 64–66, 113–114, 155–156, 199–201
  sharing, 192–193
investors, community, 246

Jackson, Jason, 202
Jacob, Sushil, 206
job creation, goal of, 21
jobs. *See also* employment
  benefits, 40–41, 179–180, 215–217, 248, 262
  finding, 120–124, 153
  opportunities, 40
  previously held, 40
  quality jobs, 37–38

joint deliberation, 215
joint ventures, 255
Jones-Cooper, Tatia, 25–26, 34, 46
Jonnes, Jill, 18–19
Jumpstart Our Business Startups (JOBS) Act, 245–246

Kellogg, Cliff, 103, 111–112
*Kelo* v. *City of New London*, 244
Kickstarter, 191. *See also* crowdsourcing
Kulp, Karen, 25, 26–27

labor sharing, collaborative capitalism, 172
labor unions
  committees, 39
  differences among, 214
  power of, 3
  role of, 64
  support in finding jobs, 120
  and wages, 248–249
Lamos, Alice, 86, 96, 98, 100, 260
landlord-tenant regulations, 107
laws. *See regulations*
law reform. *See also* regulations
  antitrust and anti-competition laws, 253–257
  business organizations law, 229–234
  CDFI law, 257–260
  cooperatives, 233–234
  crowdfunding, 245–247
  eminent domain, 243–244
  employment law, 262–264
  Federal Deposit Insurance Corporation (FDIC), 258
  federal laws, 252–253
  Federal Reserve Board, 258–259
  participatory regulation, 237–240
  permitting, 243
  regulatory gaps, 228
  relational contracting, 239–240
  securities laws, 261–262
  self-regulation, 238–240
  tax incentives, 261
  torts, 239–240
  use of coordinated economies model, 238–239
  wages and benefits, 248–251, 263–264
  zoning laws, 234–237, 241–243
licensing requirements, 243. *See also* permitting requirements
Lindholm, Sara, 78, 87
loans. *See financing*
long-term relationships, value of, 21

management expertise, 166–167, 182
Manchester Bidwell, 251
market catalyst, 181
market entry, disincentives for, 52
market failure, inner-city, 51–55
market niches. *See also* competition
  Airbnb, 198–199
  Austin Initiative, 157–158
  Cooperative Home Care Associates (CHCA), 21, 68–69
  protecting, 240–244
  ShoreBank, 116–117
  Southwest Key Programs, 141, 157–158
McDonald, Jason, 133–134
McDonald's franchises, 108
Medicaid / Medicare
  policy changes, 35
  profit margins, 21–22
  recipients of, 24
  reimbursements, 42–43
Menchaca, Martha, 134
mentorships, 88–89
middle class, 53–54
minimum wage, 41, 43, 107, 248–249, 263
Molotch, Harvey, 77
mom-and-pop businesses, 116
Montgomery, Angelique, 40
Multiple Employers Welfare Arrangement (MEWA), 263–264
municipal laws. *See regulations*

Neighborhood Institute, The, 90
neoclassical economics, 63
niche markets. *See market niches*
nonprofit status
  and the holding company model, 231–232
  and tax, 261
  Independence Care System (ICS), 30–31, 234
  Southwest Key Programs, 144, 146

O'Bryant, Deborah, 38, 39, 42
Occupy Wall Street Movement, 1
*Organizing Organic: Conflict and Compromise in an Emerging Market* (Haedicke), 182
Orsi, Janelle, 246

Paraprofessional Healthcare Institute (PHI)
  overview, 7, 17
  function of, 28–29
  mission, 22–23
  origins of, 22–23
  policy changes, 35
participation, 37–39, 179, 216
participatory regulation, 237–239
Patient Affordable Care Act, 263–264
patient capital, 210, 220

peer-to-peer lending networks, 191
Peoria, Illinois, poverty rates, 2
Perkins, Ronnette, 38
permitting requirements, 125–126, 236, 243
Philadelphia, home health care market, 25–27
physical space, collaborative capitalism, 171
Piketty, Thomas, 51
Pillot, Margarita, 39
Pitegoff, Peter, 123
policy changes, 29, 35
Porter, Michael
  perspective of, 60
  regulations to support, 225
  work on competition, 51
  work on urban core development, 52–53, 216
poverty, 2–3, 56–58
Powell, Adria, 31
Powell, Peggy
  experience of, 19
  on regulations, 36
  on the role of managed care, 23–24
*Practicing Law in the Sharing Economy: Helping People Build Cooperatives, Social Enterprise, and Local Sustainable Economies* (Orsi), 246
Pratt Center for Community Development, 130
Preservation Compact, The, 95
price competition, 44
price-fixing, 195–196
private capital, 247
professions. *See jobs*
profit margins, challenges, 21–22
Project Phoenix, 144
public bidding process, 45, 231, 252. *See also* competition
public investment, 221–222

quality jobs. *See jobs*

"Regulating Sharing: The Sharing Economy as an Alternative Capitalist System," 267
regulations. *See also* law reform
  overview, 4
  Airbnb, 206
  anticompetitive behavior, 195–196
  antitrust and anti-competition laws, 253–257
  Bank Holding Company Act amendments, 102
  business organizations law, 229–234
  California Worker Cooperative Act, 246
  Community Development Banking and Financial Institutions Act, 103
  Community Reinvestment Act (CRA), 103, 110
  cooperative law, 231–234
  coordinated economies, 217–222
  corporate governance law, 221
  employment law, 121–122, 196, 248–251, 262–264
  federal laws, 252–264
  franchise law, 232–233
  franchises, 232–233
  Home Care Worker Parity Act (NY), 43
  Jumpstart Our Business Startups (JOBS) Act, 245–246
  limitations, 103–104
  minimum wage, 41, 43, 107, 248–249, 263
  participatory regulation, 237–239
  Patient Affordable Care Act, 263–264
  policy changes, 29, 35
  regulatory gaps, 228
  role of, 42–47, 102–107, 151–154
  securities laws, 261–262
  self-regulation, 218, 237–239
  sharing economy, 193–197, 203–206
  Sherman Antitrust Act, 253
  "social policy" regulation, 220–221
  state laws, 229–252
  Sturgeon, Jodi on, 45
  to support cooperative economies, 222–224
  zoning laws, 71, 120–121, 125, 234–237, 241–243
rehabber network. *See ShoreBank*
relational contracting, 219–220, 239–240
relationships, 89
rental market, 82–83, 102
RESCORP, 82–83
RideAustin, 206
risk
  collaborative capitalism, 169–170
  lowering, 66, 114–115, 156, 198, 212–213
  spreading, 181–182
Rowan, James, 267
"rule of reason" analysis, 254
Runners Club, 112

Sánchez, Juan
  on competition, 140, 152
  on financing, 146, 152–153
  on market development, 136–138
  on nonprofit status, 145–146
  origins of Southwest Key Programs, 132, 135
Schcolnik, Andy, 82, 94
schools, 252
sectoral approach, 123
securities laws, 261–262
segregation, overview, 3
self-regulation, 218, 220, 238–239. *See also* regulations
Service Employees International Union, 29, 32, 37, 64, 249, 251
Shah, Kaushik, 109–110
Shane, Scott, 54

shareholder value, 123
sharing. *See also* business activities
  overview, 64–66
  collaborative capitalism, 159–160
  crowdfunding, 45, 245–247
  supporting intermediaries, 229–240
Sherman Antitrust Act, 253
ShoreBank
  overview, 9, 75–76
  Austin Initiative, 111–112
  closing of, 100–102
  context, 77–79
  franchises, 108–111
  lending requirements, 127
  market development, 81–86
  mature status, 87–91
  origins of, 79–81
  regulatory context, 102–107
  rehabber network perspective, 95–100
  subsidiaries and affiliates, 90–91
ShoreBank Advisory Services, 90
ShoreBank Capital Corporation, 90
ShoreBank Development Corporation, 90
small businesses
  development programs, 52–53
  financing, 126–127
  starting, 124–131
  start-up process, 124–131
  and zoning laws, 242
Smigel, Margie, 82–83
Smith, Michelle, 17, 27–28, 39
social entrepreneurship, 68. *See also* entrepreneurship
"social policy" regulation, 220–221
Solomon, Bob, 258
Soskice, David. *See also* "varieties of capitalism" theory
  on capitalism, 70
  on deliberation, 215
  on employment law, 121
  on regulations, 218–219
  on relational contracting, 219
*South Bronx Rising*, 18
South Side Builders' Association, 94
South Side Community Investors' Association, 94
Southwest Key Green Energy & Construction, 138
Southwest Key Maintenance, LLC, 138
Southwest Key Programs
  overview, 10, 132–133
  context, 133–135
  current status, 141–146
  infrastructure, 146–147
  market development, 136–141
  market niche, 141
  mission, 139
  nonprofit status, 144, 146
  origins of, 135–136
  other businesses, 138–140
  regulatory context, 151–154
  worker perspective, 148–151
Southwest Key Workforce Development, 139, 141–142, 143–144, 147, 153
stakeholders, local, 67–68, 115–116, 156–157, 215
start-up process, 124–131
state laws. *See also* regulations
Sturgeon, Jodi
  on financing, 247
  on long-term relationships, 31
  on market development, 35
  on personal connections, 31
  on regulations, 45
  on training programs, 29
  on the worker-owned cooperative structure, 43–44
success, definition of, 56–58
Surgeon, George, 90–91, 116–117
Surpin, Rick
  on the effect of ICS, 24–25
  experience of, 20
  on the function of PHI, 28, 35
  on leadership, 31, 32
  on market development, 21, 30, 33, 68
  on Medicaid, 42–43
  on nonprofit status, 234
  participation in regulatory development, 237
  on policy, 35
  on regulations, 30, 36, 42–44, 46, 230
  on wage parity, 250
Sustainable Economies Law Center, 246
Sutherland, Mark, 94, 98–99

Taub, Richard, 78
tax incentives, 120, 261
TELACU, 244
Temporary Assistance for Needy Families program, 27
torts, 239–240
training programs. *See also* vocational education
  informal, 97
  investment in, 22, 28–29, 148–149, 163–166
transparency, 39
transportation, 252
Troubled Asset Relief Program (TARP), 101
Trump, Donald, 1
Tuttle Law Group, 246

Uber, 190, 194–195
unemployment rates. *See employment*

unions. *See labor unions*
Urban Partnership Bank, 100

"varieties of capitalism" theory
  overview, 8
  application of, 11–13
  critique of, 223–224
venture capital financing, 127–128, 247–248
Visiting Nurse Service of New York (VNS), 23–24
vocational education, 88–89, 163–166, 179, 251

wages, 41, 43, 107, 179–180, 248–251, 262–263
Whitehead, Stephanie, 42
Windham, Ocie, 96–97, 98, 99–100
worker-owned cooperative structure, 37–39, 43–44
workforce mobility, 4
Wright, Erik Olin, 264–265

Yago, Glenn, 55

Zeidman, Betsy, 55
zoning laws, 71, 120–121, 125, 234–237, 241–243